INSIGHT GUIDES

Created and Directed by Hans Höfer

EGYPT

Edited by Hisham Youssef and John Rodenbeck

Editorial Director: Brian Bell

Houghton Mifflin

APA PUBLICATIONS

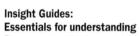

The book you are holding is part of the world's largest range of guidebooks. Its purpose is to help you have the most valuable travel experience possible, and we try to achieve this by providing not only information about countries, regions and cities but also genuine insight into their history, culture, institutions and people.

In 1970, when I created the first Insight Guide – to Bali – it was already becoming clear that mass tourism could inflict great damage on a destination. I believed then that, with insight into a country's people and culture, visitors would both enhance their own experience and be accepted more easily by their hosts. Now, in a world where ethnic hostilities and nationalist conflicts are all too common, such attempts to increase understanding between peoples are more important than ever.

Insight Guides:
Essentials for understanding

Because a nation's past holds the key to its present, each Insight Guide kicks off with lively history chapters. These are followed by magazine-style essays on the people's culture. This essential background information gives readers the necessary context for using the Places section, with its comprehensive run-down on things worth seeing and doing. Finally, a listings section contains all the information you'll need on travel, hotels, restaurants and opening times. The pictures, for which Insight Guides have become so celebrated, are just as important. Our photojournalistic approach aims not only to illustrate a destination but to also communicate visually and directly to readers life as it is lived by the locals.

No single writer can capture the essence of a destination after a short visit. So we rely heavily on locally based writers and journalists, who provide both lively prose and frank, authoritative assessments. This local input, filtered through our worldwide network of editors, ensures that the books are truly international, free of an outsider's prejudices. For this reason, the destination dictates the version of English used, British or American spelling. So our guide to New York has all the authority of an American guidebook, our book on Paris is as dependable as a French guidebook and our book on Hong Kong is as trustworthy as an Asian guidebook.

From edition to edition, our team of correspondents works hard to keep the 190 titles in the series up-to-date. As new museums open and old attractions close, as volcanoes erupt and presidents fall, as travel patterns change and new frontiers open, we bring the information to you. We take this job very seriously and, because we operate our own printing plant in Singapore, we are able to update and reprint best-selling books as often as needed.

Compact Guides
The "great little guides"

As invaluable as such background information is, it isn't always fun to carry an Insight Guide through a crowded souk or up a church tower. Could we, readers asked, distil the key reference material into a slim volume that would answer their on-the-spot questions? Our response was to design Compact Guides as an entirely new product, with original text carefully cross-referenced to detailed maps and more than 200 photographs. In essence, they're miniature encyclopedias, concise and comprehensive, displaying reliable and up-to-date information in an accessible way.

Pocket Guides:
A local host in book form

However wide-ranging the information in a book, human beings still value the personal touch. Having complimented our editors on the quality and comprehensiveness of a book, our readers would often bombard them with questions. Where do *you* go to eat? What do *you* think is the best beach? What would you recommend if I have only three days? This gave us the idea of asking our local correspondents to act as "substitute hosts" by telling us about their preferred walks and trips, listing the restaurants they go to and structuring a visit into a series of carefully timed itineraries. The result was our Pocket Guides, complete with full-size fold-out maps. The 100-plus titles in this companion series help readers plan a trip precisely, particularly if their time is short.

Exploring with Insight:
A valuable travel experience

In conjunction with co-publishers all over the world, we print in up to 10 languages, from German to Chinese, from Danish to Russian. But our aim remains simple: to enhance your travel experience by combining our expertise in guidebook publishing with the on-the-spot knowledge of our correspondents.

We also rely on readers who tell us of their travel discoveries. So please get in touch: our contact numbers are listed below.

See you soon.

Hans Höfer, Publisher
APA Publications

CONTACTING THE EDITORS

As we make every effort to update Insight Guides as often as possible, we would appreciate it if readers would call to our attention any errors or out-of-date information by contacting:

Apa Publications, P.O. Box 7910, London SE1 8ZB, England.
Tel: (44) 171 620 0008.
Fax: (44) 171 620 1074.
e-mail: insight@apaguide.demon.co.uk.

The great 19th-century explorer of Africa, H. M. Stanley, offered this opinion: "To those who wish to be wise, to be healthful, to borrow one month of pleasure from a serious life, I would say, come and see the Nile." His advice is still taken by countless visitors each year, and this book, one of 190 titles in the award-winning Insight Guides series, is designed to help them maximise their enjoyment.

Two project editors shared the task of assembling a team of writers and photgraphers who would capture the essence of this ancient land. **Hisham Youssef**, a Harvard graduate, is a native Egyptian who has travelled all over his country. His many credits include serving as photographic editor for the *Harvard Crimson* and as photographer for a *Lampoon* parody of *Newsweek* magazine. Youssef was also a contributing photographer to *Insight Guide: New England*. **John Rodenbeck** co-ordinated and edited the work of all the writing staff in Cairo.

Youssef

Rodenbeck, also a Harvard graduate, has lived in the city since 1964 and brings to the book a lengthy and close acquaintance with Egyptian society. In 1978 he founded SPARE (the Society for the Preservation of the Architectural Resources of Egypt). For two years he served on the executive committee under Mrs Sadat in the Egyptian Society of Amateurs of Archaeology (ESAA). Rodenbeck's other activities include acting in three Egyptian feature films, writing, editing, and publishing. He is the co-founder of the Hoopoe Press, a small publishing house which is based in Cairo and

J. Rodenbeck

Washington DC, and is professor in the Department of English and Comparative Literature at the American University in Cairo.

The principal photographer for this book is **Albano Guatti**. A native Italian, Guatti is based in New York City where he specialises in travel and commercial photography. The wealth of his work shown throughout the pages of this book reveals a unique vision of Egypt, the land and its people. His photographs have been published in many travel books, calendars, and magazines and he is co-founder of a publishing house in New York City.

Ayman Taher, whose photography is also among the best in this book, is a native Cairene who has lived in Egypt all his life. His main hobby, which has grown into a professional interest, is scuba diving. He has an international reputation as one of the world's top underwater photographers.

Richard Nowitz, a photographer who worked in Jerusalem for many years, also contributes to this volume. Nowitz has travelled many times in the Sinai peninsula and elsewhere in Egypt, and is also a regular contributor to Apa's other titles. Now based in America, he photographs regularly for *National Geographic*.

Guatti

Nowitz

Many writers brought their own personal insights to this book and provide it with unusual and exciting views of Egypt's rich culture and contemporary society.

Jill Kamil, a contributor to the history section, is an Egyptologist and author of many popular books including the best-selling Longman series of guidebooks to Egypt's ancient sites: *Sakkara and Memphis*, *Upper Egypt*, which covers places visited on a Nile cruise, and *Luxor*. Her *Coptic Egypt* has been published by the American University in Cairo Press. Born in Kenya,

Kamil

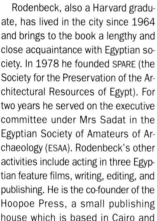

and educated in South Africa, Kamil has spent most of her life in Egypt.

Another contributor, **Elizabeth Maynard** writes: "if it hadn't been for the fact that my Virginian grandmother fell off a donkey in front of old Shepheard's hotel in 1897, she might never have met my English grandfather who happened to be smoking on the terrace at the time. He picked her up and proceeded to fall in love with her. Most of their married life was spent plying back and forth between India, England and America."

Elizabeth's father remembered going through the Suez Canal in a P&O liner sometime before World War I. Many intervening happenings and coincidences in England and Virginia finally brought the writer back to Cairo, where she has spent more than 20 eventful years.

Maynard

William Lyster, who wrote the section on Medieval Egypt, was born in Texas. It was while living in London that he began travelling through the Middle East during his holidays, making his first visit to Egypt in 1968. He later moved to Cairo, where he began the serious study of Islamic art and history at The American University. He is currently engaged in lecturing on the Islamic art of Egypt and lives in Heliopolis, a suburb of Cairo.

Lyster

Max Rodenbeck, born in Virginia, is a freelance journalist who has lived in Cairo most of his life. He not only speaks fluent Arabic – his conversational skills were perfected in the same coffeehouses that he describes in these pages – but also reads and writes it. His knowledge of the city has brought him commissions to lead tours and oversee cartographical projects, but he has also travelled extensively and intensively throughout Egypt and the rest of the Middle East. His colourful coverage of Arab politics is highly esteemed among specialists in

M. Rodenbeck

the region; and his contributions to this guide are a good sample of the style and sensitivity that have made him well known.

Carina Campobasso, a Harvard graduate in Middle Eastern and Arabic history, has lived in Egypt.

Alice Brinton, who writes about Alexandria, belongs to an American family that has been identified with the city for three generations. Alice herself lived mainly in Beirut as a child, but returned to Egypt in 1975 to work as a journalist, becoming Cairo correspondent for ABC, the American network. Though she now lives and writes in Paris, she continues to spend a few weeks in Egypt every year.

Cassandra Vivian is responsible for much of the Travel Tips section. Born in Monessen, Pennsylvania, a small steel-town south of Pittsburgh, Vivian lived in Cairo from 1976 until 1990.

Vivian

Among the other photographers who contributed to *Insight Guide: Egypt* are: **Joseph Hunwick**, **Lyle Lawson**, **John Barthwick**, **Joseph Yogerst**, **Barbara Gundle** and **Gregory Lawler** – all of them frequent contributors over the years to Apa's *Insight Guide* series.

People who contributed in other ways include: Fouad Sultan, Egyptian Minister of Tourism; Muhammad Nessim, Director of the Egyptian Agency for the Promotion of Tourism; Adel Taher, former Minister of Tourism; Ahmad al-Saeed of *al-Ahram* Newspaper and his staff, and Gloria Karuouk, Curator at the CAS Library of the American University in Cairo.

CONTENTS

CONTENTS

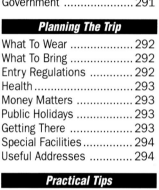

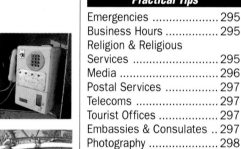

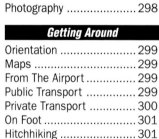

WELCOME

It isn't only archaeologists, peering into tombs or poring over pottery fragments, who have been intrigued by Egypt. The Land of the Nile has often exercised a potent spell over quite ordinary people. With such a variety of allurements, in fact, Egypt – or someone's idea of it – has inspired styles in everything from decorative iron casings for heavy 19th-century German machines to paper packaging for 20th-century American condoms and cigarettes. It's no exaggeration to say that Egypt has even influenced Western fashion in matters of life and death, often grotesquely so.

Mummies, Egyptian and otherwise: Western interest in mummified flesh, for example, arose when word spread in medieval times about the therapeutic value of powdered *mumia* in the treatment of a wide variety of ailments. By the 16th century, mummies so fascinated visitors to Egypt that an active trade in their dessicated flesh began. Ancient burial grounds were dug up, mummies were stripped of their coverings and sent piecemeal to the apothecaries of Europe. When word of this highly-prized medication reached Francis I, the king of France, he made haste to acquire a small quantity, mixed with powdered rhubarb, which he reputedly carried in a little packet everywhere he went.

Although embalming in the ancient Egyptian manner never became a fashion, two rich and influential men, Louis XIV of France (1638–1715) and Alexander Douglas, 10th Duke of Hamilton (1767–1852), ordered their bodies to be mummified. The body of King Louis survived for only about 15 years, but the Duke of Hamilton's may have lasted a little longer. It was embalmed in 1852 in a ceremony carried out after the Egyptian fashion, with T.J. Pettigrew, First Professor of Anatomy at Charing Cross Hospital and author of a *History of Egyptian Mummies*, as "embalmer and chief ritualist".

Bonaparte's inspiration: Descriptive accounts and sketches made by travellers during the 18th century joined with a trickle of small objects – scarabs, amulets, and a multitude of fakes – to excite interest in Egypt as a source of the "primitive", a search for which was one of the century's cultural preoccupations. An "Egyptian" fashion thus followed hard upon an "Etruscan" fashion, which had grown in turn directly out of the classical heritage from Greece and Rome. Napoleon's expedition to Egypt, with assorted *savants*, took place largely in response to this new fashion.

Meanwhile, during the late 18th and early 19th centuries, buildings began to be built to resemble ancient temples. Interior decorations were Egyptianised, too, and included chimney-places with Egyptian deities carved in bold relief. Furniture was also Egyptian-inspired: wooden chairs were carved in the shape of the hind legs of a lion or an ox, cabinets had such decorative motifs as the lotus and papyrus plants; and book-ends, ink-stands, vases and wine-coolers were decorated with Egyptian motifs, symbols, or texts.

Grave-robbers galore: An event that captured popular English interest in 1812 was the opening of the Egyptian Hall in Piccadilly as a museum of "natural curiosities". Later used as a theatre, the building itself was designed as an amalgam of Egyptian motifs. In 1821 it displayed the latest finds, casts and sketches by the British-naturalised Italian strongman-turned-excavator, Giovanni Belzoni, who had cleared the Temple of Abu Simbel and shipped tons of treasures back to England. There was no restriction on grave-robbing and ancient burial grounds were pillaged for anything movable.

With a new era of scholars and explorers in the later 19th century, Egyptian inspiration in architecture and furniture design subsided and the great collections were built up in the museums of the world. This meant that the general public could enjoy the material remains of ancient Egypt without having to travel all the way to the Nile Valley. Obelisks situated in public places had already become fashionable at the end of the 16th century, when Pope Sixtus V put back on public view four of Rome's 13 ancient souvenirs. Now they became interesting once again. The Paris obelisk was erected in the Place de la Concorde as early as 1833. In 1878 London put its obelisk, acquired as booty in 1801, in place on the Thames embankment; and the obelisk which stands in Central Park, New York, was erected in 1881.

The United States had first been offered an obelisk by the Khedive Ismail on the occasion of the opening of the Suez Canal in 1869, another landmark in the history of fashion. Ismail's celebrations extended archaeological knowledge to the sphere of theatrical entertainment, anticipating films such as *Cleopatra* and *Raiders of the Lost Ark*. The French scholar Mariette was commissioned to do the libretto for an opera aimed at evoking the splendour of ancient Egypt. Verdi's *Aida* was not commissioned for the opening performance – *Rigoletto* was staged instead – but *Aida* premiered in Cairo two years later.

Tut fever: The event that would capture world attention to a degree unrivalled by anything archaeological before was, of course, the discovery of the Tomb of Tutankhamen in 1922. Its 5,000 dazzling works of art were widely publicised through new techniques of communications, including the first film footage in the history of archaeology. Thousands of sightseers made their way to the Valley of the Kings. They wanted to be in on the discovery, and they also wanted to have a relic from the tomb. Local antique dealers, ready to fulfill the demand, ordered their collections from Cairo to be returned to Thebes and local craftsmen turned out instant *antikas* wholesale, bearing the royal cartouche. Even bottled sand said to have come from the tomb chamber was sold to tourists.

It was Tutankhamen, again, who brought ancient Egypt to a wider Western audience than ever before, during the exhibitions in Paris in 1967, London in 1972, Russia in 1973, and the United States in 1975. These dazzling works of art from the richest discovery in the history of archaeology resulted in a burst of modern imitations.

Egypt produced one of the earliest and most magnificent civilisations the world has ever witnessed. Five thousand years ago, when Mesopotamia was still the scene of petty squabbling between city states and while Europe, America, and most of western Asia were inhabited by Stone-Age hunters, the ancient Egyptians had learned how to make bread, brew beer and mix paint. They could smelt and cast copper, drill beads, mix mineral compounds for cosmetics, and glaze stone and pottery surfaces. They had invented the hoe, the most ancient of agricultural implements, and had carried out experiments in plant and animal breeding.

Egypt is a land of unusual geographic isolation, with well-defined boundaries. To the east and west are vast deserts. To the north is the Mediterranean Sea. To the south there was, before the construction of the High Dam at Aswan, a formidable barrier of igneous rock, beyond which lay the barren land of Nubia. Within these recognisable boundaries, however, was a land divided; Upper Egypt extended from Aswan to a point just south of modern Cairo and was largely barren, apart from a narrow strip of land flanking the river; the Delta, or Lower Egypt, spread from the point where the Nile fanned into a fertile triangle some 125 miles (200 km) before reaching the Mediterranean Sea. Linking Upper and Lower Egypt was the vital artery, the river Nile.

Before water from the Nile was harnessed by modern technology, the annual flood, a direct result of the monsoon rains on the Ethiopian tableland, spilled into the floodplain every year, depositing a thick layer of alluvial soil. Since rainfall in Egypt is almost non-existent, the people were dependent on the river for their crops; and it was ultimately on the fertility of the soil that ancient Egyptian civilisation was based.

The earliest inhabitants of the Nile Valley were hunters who tracked game across northern Africa and the eastern Sudan, later joined by nomadic tribes of Asiatic origin who filtered into Egypt in sporadic migrations across the Sinai peninsula and the Red Sea. Late Paleolithic settlements (c. 12000 BC–8000 BC) reveal that both these newcomers and the indigenous inhabitants had a hunting and food-gathering economy. Gradually, however, their lives became bound to the ebb and flow of the annual flood.

As the water rose each year in July, the inhabitants were obliged to draw back from the banks. By August, when the river waters swept across the lowlands, they took to the highland plateaux and pursued hunting activities, tracking antelope, hartebeest, wild ass and gazelle, with lances, bows and arrows. During the first half of October the river attained its highest level, and thereafter began to subside, leaving lagoons and streams which became natural reservoirs for fish.

A variety of plants grew from the fertile, uniform deposit of silt. During this season of plenty, hunting was at a minimum. From January to March seasonal pools dried out and fishing was limited, but in the swampy areas near the river there were turtles, rodents and Nile clams. At low Nile, during April, May and June, game scattered, food became scarce, and hunting was actively pursued once more.

Despite their diverse origins, therefore, there was a natural tendency for the people to group themselves together during the "season of abundance" and to split up into smaller groups during the low-flood season or during periods of drought.

Religion and agriculture: As a certain rhythm formed in their lives, they observed that the gifts of their naturally irrigated valley depended on a dual force: the sun and the river, both of which had creative and destructive powers. The life-giving rays of the sun that caused a crop to grow could also cause it to shrivel and die. And the river that invigorated the soil with its mineral-rich deposits could destroy whatever lay in its path or, if it failed to rise sufficiently, bring famine.

These two phenomena, moreover, shared in the pattern of death and rebirth that left a profound impression on the people: the sun that "died" in the western horizon each evening was "reborn" in the eastern sky the following morning; and the river was di-

Preceding pages: inside the temple at Abu Simbel. **Left**, sign language.

rectly and unfailingly responsible for the germination or "rebirth" of the crop after the "death" of the land each year. This natural sequence of rebirth after death undoubtedly lay at the root of the ancient Egyptian belief in the afterlife. As inevitably as the sun rose each morning and the flood arrived each year, man, it was believed, would rise again.

Agriculture was introduced into the Nile Valley about 5000 BC. Once grain (a variety of domesticated barley from Asia) could be cultivated and stored, the people could be assured of a regular food supply, which was an important factor in the movement away from primitive society towards civilisation. Agriculture made possible a surplus of time

occurred in both Upper and Lower Egypt. In Upper Egypt, the chief settlement was Nekhen, where the leader wore a conical White Crown and took the sedge plant as his emblem. In the Delta or Lower Egypt, the capital was Buto, and the leader wore the characteristic Red Crown and adopted the bee as his symbol.

The Old Kingdom: Unification of Upper and Lower Egypts has been ascribed to Narmer (Menes), 3100 BC, who set up his capital at Memphis, at the apex of the Delta. He was the first king to be portrayed wearing both the White Crown and the Red Crown. He stands at the beginning of Egypt's ancient history, which was divided by an Egyptian

and economic resources, which resulted in population increase and craft specialisation. Polished stone axes, well-made knives, and pottery vessels were produced, as well as ivory combs and slate palettes, on which paint for body decoration was prepared.

Slowly, assimilation took place. Some villages may have merged as their boundaries expanded; or small groups of people may have gravitated towards larger ones and started to trade and barter with them. The affairs of the various communities became tied to major settlements, which undoubtedly represented the richest and most powerful. This tendency towards political unity

historian called Manetho – who lived c. 280 BC – into 30 royal dynasties from Menes to Alexander the Great. The dynasties were subsequently combined and grouped into three main periods: the Old Kingdom or Pyramid Age, the Middle Kingdom, and the New Kingdom. Although further divided by modern historians, these periods remain the basis of ancient Egyptian chronology.

The Old Kingdom, from the 3rd to 6th Dynasties, (2686 BC–2181 BC), is considered by many historians as the high-water mark of achievement. A series of vigorous and able monarchs established a highly organised, centralised government. The great

Pyramids of Giza, on the western bank of the Nile southwest of Cairo, have secured undying fame for Khufu (Cheops), Khafre (Chephren) and Menkaure (Mycerinus).

These kings ruled during a period of great refinement, an aristocratic era, which saw rising productivity in all fields. Cattle and raw materials, including gold and copper, were transported in donkey caravans from the Sudan and Nubia. Sinai was exploited for mineral wealth and a fleet of ships sailed to Byblos (on the coast of Lebanon) to import cedar wood. The "Great House", *peraha*, from which the word *pharaoh* is derived, controlled all trade routes throughout the land, as well as all the markets.

leisure activities, as well as scenes from their personal lives.

The Old Kingdom tombs at Saqqarah, south of Giza, are adorned with painted relics of the deceased, his wife and children, overseers of his estates, supervisors of his factories, scribes, artisans and peasants. The graphic portrayals of everyday life are clear evidence that the ancient Egyptians took pride in beautiful possessions: chairs and beds (which often had leather or rope-weave seats or mattresses fastened to the frame with leather thongs) had legs carved in the form of the powerful hindlimbs of an ox or lion; the handle of a spoon was fashioned to resemble a lotus blossom.

Most of the buildings of ancient Egypt, including the royal palaces, were built of perishable materials such as brick, wood and bundles of reeds, while tombs were built of stone, to last for eternity. This distinction gives the erroneous impression that the ancient Egyptians were preoccupied with thoughts of death. Evidence to the contrary is abundant. Wishing to ensure bounty in the afterlife similar to that enjoyed on earth, they decorated their tombs with a wide variety of farming scenes, manufacturing processes and

Left, temple of Hatshepsut, Deir al Bahari, Luxor.
Above, the Ramesseum, Luxor.

The end of the Old Kingdom: In the Old Kingdom the power of the pharaoh was supreme and he took an active part in all affairs of state, ranging from determining the height of the Nile during the annual inundation to recruiting a labour force from the various provinces or to lead mining and exploratory expeditions.

Naturally, such responsibility was too much for a single pair of hands and he therefore delegated power to the provincial lords, who were often members of the royal family. The provincial nobility became increasingly more wealthy, began to exert power, and the result was an inevitable weakening of centralised authority. At the end of the 6th Dynasty some of the provinces managed to shake themselves free from the central government and establish independence. The monarchy collapsed. The Old Kingdom came to an end.

The period known as the First Intermediate Period, between the 7th and the early 11th Dynasties, saw anarchy, bloodshed and a restructuring of society in Egypt. The provincial lords who had gained power and prestige under the great monarchs began to reflect on the traditional beliefs of their forefathers. It was a time of soul-searching; and great contempt was voiced for the law and order of the past.

heralded a revival in architecture and the arts, as well as a breakthrough in literature, established the 12th Dynasty, one of the most peaceful and prosperous eras known to Egypt. Political stability was soon reflected in material prosperity. Building operations were undertaken throughout the country. Amenemhet III constructed his tomb at Hawarah (Fayyum) with a funerary monument later described by classical writers as "The Labyrinth" and declared by Herodotus to be more wonderful than the pyramids of Giza. Goldsmiths, jewellers and sculptors perfected their skills, as Egyptian political and cultural influence extended to Nubia and Kush in the south, around the Eastern Medi-

A powerful family of provincial lords from Herakleopolis Magna (near Beni Suef in Middle Egypt) achieved prominence in the 9th and 10th Dynasties and restored some degree of order. In Upper Egypt, meanwhile, in the Theban area (near Luxor), a confederation had gathered around a strong family, the Intef and Mentuhotep family, who slowly extended their authority northwards until there was a clash with the family from Herakleopolis. A civil war resulted in triumph for the Thebans.

The Middle Kingdom: The Middle Kingdom covers the 11th and 12th Dynasties (c. 2133 BC–1786 BC). Amenemhet I, whose rule

terranean to Libya, Palestine, Syria and even to Crete, the Aegean Islands, and the mainland to Greece.

In the Middle Kingdom an increasingly wealthy middle class led the ordinary man to aspire to have what only members of the aristocracy had had before: elaborate funerary equipment to ensure a comfortable afterlife. To pay homage to their legendary ancestor, Osiris, at the holy city of Abydos, thousands of pilgrims from all walks of life made their way there each year, leaving so many offerings in pottery vessels that the site acquired the name of Umm al-Gaab, which means "Mother of Potsherds".

According to legend, Osiris was a just and much-loved ruler who taught his people the arts of making agricultural implements, rotating crops and controlling the waters of the Nile. He also taught them how to adapt to a wheat diet and how to produce bread, wine and beer. Isis, his devoted wife, was equally loved. She taught the people how to grind wheat and weave linen with a loom.

Osiris had a brother, Seth, who was secretly jealous of his popularity and conspired against him. Seth tricked Osiris into climbing into a chest, had it sealed, then cast it into the Nile. Broken-hearted, Isis went in search of the body of her husband, eventually found it, and hid it. But Seth was out boar-hunting

forth an heir, Horus, whom she raised in the marshes of the Delta until he was strong enough to avenge his father's death by slaying Seth. Horus took over the throne on earth and the resurrected Osiris became king of the underworld.

Spread of the Osiris cult: The story became a classic. The traditions of the loyalty and devotion of Isis to her husband, of the piety of Horus, who avenged his father's death in a triumph of good over evil, and of the benevolence of Osiris, who was killed but rose to rule again, survived for centuries.

The cult of Osiris thoroughly captured the popular imagination in the Middle Kingdom; and it became desirable to have a stele

and discovered the body. He tore it into 14 pieces, which he scattered all over the land. Isis again went in search of Osiris, this time in the company of her sister Nephthys. The two sisters collected the pieces and, according to one version of the myth, bound them together with bandages. They lamented over the body of Osiris, fanning it with their wings in order to bring life back to it. Isis then descended on her husband in the form of a winged bird, received his seed, and brought

Left, inscription on a stele in the Nubian desert south of Aswan. **Above**, tomb paintings in the Valley of the Kings, Luxor.

or tombstone erected at or near Abydos, in order for the spirit of the deceased to join in the annual dramatisation of his resurrection enacted by the priests. Later, during the New Kingdom, when Thebes became capital, deceased noblemen were often embalmed, then borne to Abydos and placed temporarily in the precinct of the temple there, before being interred at Thebes. If for some reason they could not make this pilgrimage after death, it was made symbolically: their tombs were decorated with reliefs of boats bearing their mummified bodies to Abydos.

The end of the Middle Kingdom: At the end of the 13th Dynasty the provincial rulers once again rose against the crown. During this period of national instability the Hyksos (a Manethonian term corrupted from *Heka-khasut* meaning "rulers of foreign countries"), who are believed to have come from the direction of Syria, challenged Egyptian authority. With horses and chariots (hitherto unknown in Egypt), they swept across the northern Sinai, fortified a stronghold at Tel ad-Deba, south of Tanis in the northeastern Delta, moved towards the apex of the Delta, and swept southwards. The damage done to Egypt's great cities can only be guessed at. Pharaohs of later times inscribed declarations that they "restored what was ruined" and "raised what had gone to pieces", but the

spirit of military expansion characteristic of the New Kingdom.

The New Kingdom: The New Kingdom (1567 BC–1080 BC) was the empire period. The military conquests of Thutmos III, in no fewer than 17 campaigns, resulted in the establishment of Egyptian power throughout Syria and northern Mesopotamia, as well as in Nubia and Libya. Wealth from conquered nations and vassal states poured into Thebes (Luxor). The caravans were laden with gold, silver, ivory, spices, and rare flora and fauna. The greater part of the wealth was bestowed upon Amon who, with the aid of an influential priesthood, was established as Amon-Ra, "King of Gods". Thebes flour-

almost total absence of contemporary documents during the Hyksos occupation leaves scant evidence of what actually took place.

The humiliation of foreign occupation came to an end when Ahmose, father of the New Kingdom (18th–20th Dynasties, 1567 BC–1320 BC) started a war of liberation and finally expelled the hated invaders from the land. This first unhappy exposure to foreign domination left a lasting mark on the Egyptian character. The seemingly inviolable land of Egypt had to be protected and to do so meant not only to rid the land of enemies, but to pursue them into western Asia. Out of the desire for national security was born the

ished, and some of Egypt's most extravagant monuments were built.

The 18th Dynasty was a period of transition. Old values were passing and new ones were emerging. The spirit of the age was based on wealth and power. But grave discontent, especially among the upper classes, was apparent in criticism of the national god Amon and the materialism of the priests who promoted his cult.

Akhenaten's Revolution: It was in this atmosphere that Amenhotep IV (Akhenaten) grew up, the pharaoh who would revolt against the priests and order reliefs to be defaced, shrines to be destroyed, and the image of Amon erased. Akhenaten founded a new city at Tell el-Amarna, in Middle Egypt, and promoted worship of one god, the Aten, the life-giving sun.

Certain innovations had already begun to transform the character of Egyptian art in the early years of Akhenaten's reign. By the move to Tell el-Amarna, these had become radical reforms. For centuries portrayals of the pharaoh had been stylised; he was always depicted as being strong and powerful, and artists were not empowered to improvise. Now, with the consent, it seems, of Akhenaten, figures in varied movements were sculptured in exquisite low relief. Akhenaten himself wished to exaggerate his physical

Empire-builders: Horemheb, the general who seized the throne at the end of the 18th Dynasty, was an excellent administrator. He reestablished a strong government and started a program of restoration, which continued into the 19th Dynasty, when the pharaohs channelled their boundless energies into re-organising Akhenaten's rule. Seti I, builder of a famous mortuary temple at Abydos, fought battles against the Libyans, Syrians and Hittites; Ramses II, hero of a war against the Hittites, with whom he signed a famous peace treaty, was also celebrated as a builder of great monuments, including the famous temples at Abu Simbel; and Ramses III not only conquered the Libyans, but success-

imperfections in order to emphasise a pharaoh who was mortal; representations of earlier pharaohs had portrayed them as physically perfect god-kings.

Unfortunately, the ideal needs of a religious community and the practical requirements of governing an empire were not compatible. After the deaths of Akhenaten and his half-brother Smenkare, Tutankhamen came to the throne and the priests of Amon made a spectacular return to power.

Left, grand Portico of the Temple of Philae near Aswan. **Above**, frieze showing captives, Abu Simbel.

fully protected his country from the "People of the Sea".

All these warrior kings of the 19th Dynasty raised magnificent temples in honour of Amon. It was both a duty and privilege to serve the state god, who granted them military success; and successive pharaohs systematically tried to outdo their predecessors in the magnificence of their architectural and artistic endeavours, especially in the great Temple of Amon at Karnak. It became a temple within a temple, shrine within shrine, where almost all the pharaohs wished to record their names and deeds for posterity. As new pylons, colonnades and shrines were built, valuable blocks of inscribed stone from earlier periods were often used. The Sun Temples of Akhenaten suffered this fate: thousands of their distinctly uniform, decorated sandstone blocks, known as *talatat*, were buried in various places in Karnak, such as beneath the flagstones of the great Hypostyle Hall.

The Hypostyle Hall at Karnak is the largest single chamber of any temple in the world. Seti I was responsible for the northern half of the hall and Ramses II built the southern portion, but many other 19th-Dynasty pharaohs recorded their names there, honouring Amon.

Ramses III (1182 BC–1151 BC) was the last of the great pharaohs. His ever-weakening successors fell more and more under the yoke of the priests of Amon who controlled enormous wealth. According to a text known as the Harris Papyrus, written in the reign of Ramses III, Amon possessed over 5,000 divine statues, more than 81,000 slaves, vassals and servants, well over 421,000 head of cattle, 433 gardens and orchards, 691,334 acres of land, 83 ships, 46 building yards and 65 cities and town. Naturally such a priesthood wielded enormous power. Gradually they came to regard themselves as the ruling power of the state and, at the end of the 20th Dynasty, in 1080 BC, the high priests of Amon seized the throne and overthrew the dynasty. Theoretically, the country was still united. In fact, the government became synonymous with corruption. Anarchy blighted the land and occupation by successive foreign military powers was the result.

Centuries of foreign rule: In 950 BC, Sheshonk, from a family of Libyan descent, but completely Egyptianised, took over leadership. His Libyan followers were probably descendants of mercenary troops who had earlier been granted land in return for military service. The Libyan monarchs conducted themselves as pharaohs and their rule lasted for two centuries.

In 720 BC a military leader, Piankhi, from the region of Kush (northern Sudan), marched northward. Because his people had absorbed Egyptian culture during a long period of Egyptian rule he did not view himself as a conqueror, but as a champion freeing Egypt from the forces of barbarism that he felt had engulfed it. The Egyptians, however, did not regard the Kushites as liberators and it was only after a military clash at Memphis, when the foreigners surged over the ramparts of the ancient city, that the Egyptians surrendered. Like the Libyans before them, the Kushites established themselves as genuine pharaohs, restored ancient temples, and were sympathetic to local customs.

The Assyrians, who bear the reputation of being the most ruthless of ancient people, conquered Egypt in 671 BC, putting an end to Kushite rule. With a well-trained army they moved south from province to province, assuring the local population of a speedy liberation from oppression.

After these long centuries of foreign rule Egypt knew but one short respite: a brilliant revival, called the Saite Period, ensuing after an Egyptian named Psamtik liberated the country from Assyrian occupation in 664 BC. He turned his attention to reuniting Egypt, establishing order and promoting Egyptian tradition.

The unflagging efforts of this great leader and the Saite rulers that followed him to restore order and former greatness led them to pattern their government, religion and society on the Old Kingdom, a model already 2,000 years old. Instead of channeling their energies into creating new forms, they fell back on the traditions of the past. This conservative policy helped to earn the reputation that Egypt has long borne of being a civilisation which is largely devoid of creativity and individuality.

Egypt's revival came to an end when the Persian King Cambyses occupied the land in 525 BC and turned the country into a Persian province. The new rulers, like the Libyans and the Kushites before them, showed respect at first for the religion and customs of the country in an effort to gain support. But the Egyptians were not deceived and as soon as an opportunity arose, they routed their invaders. Unfortunately, they were able to maintain independence for only about 60 years before another Persian army invaded. This time, unfortunately, there was less tolerance of local customs.

When Alexander the Great marched on Egypt in 332 BC, he and his army were welcomed by the Egyptians as liberators.

Right, a 19th-century engraving of the Temple of Philae. Unfortunately the colour has since faded considerably.

When Alexander the Great marched on Egypt, the Egyptians had no reason to fear that this would mark the end of their status as an independent nation. He first made his way to thickly-populated Memphis, the ancient capital, where he made an offering at the Temple of Ptah, then lost no time in travelling to Siwah Oasis to consult the famous oracle of Amon-Ra. When he emerged from the sanctuary he announced that the sacred statue had recognised him, and the priests of Amon greeted him as the son of the god.

Before he left Egypt again, Alexander laid down the basic plans for its government. In the important provinces (*nomes* in Greek), he appointed local governors from among Egyptian nobles; he made provision for the collection of taxes, leaving to local officials (*nomarchs*) the task they had been trained to do for thousands of years; and he laid out the plans for his great city and seaport, Alexandria, so situated as to facilitate the flow of Egypt's surplus resources to Greece and to intercept all trade with Africa and Asia.

When Alexander died from a fever at Babylon, his conquests fell to lesser heirs. Egypt was held by a general named Ptolemy, who took over leadership as King Ptolemy I. During the three centuries of Ptolemaic rule that followed, Egypt became the seat of a brilliant empire once more.

The first of the Ptolemies: Ptolemy reputedly transported Alexander's body from Babylon to Egypt, where it was laid in a marble sarcophagus filled with white honey. He did not continue Alexander's practice of founding independent cities. In fact, with the exception of Ptolemais, on the western bank of the Nile in Middle Egypt and the old Greek city of Naucratis in the Delta, only Alexandria represented a traditional Greek city-state. Ptolemy chose instead to settle his mercenary troops (Greeks, Macedonians, Persians and Hellenised Asiatics) among the Egyptian population in towns near the capitals of the provinces into which Egypt was

divided. Although these were towns of some considerable size, they had no self-government and were probably regarded by the Greeks as not much more than villages, despite the designation *polis*: Hermopolis, "city of Hermes" (modern Ashmounein), for example, and Herakleopolis, "the city of Heracles" (modern Ihnasiya), to the south of the Fayyum. In this fertile depression in the western desert, many of Ptolemy's troops were pensioned, with large tracts of newly reclaimed land. Many of the settlers married Egyptians and by the second and third generations their children bore both Greek and Egyptian names.

In Alexandria Greeks formed the bulk of the population, followed in number by the Jews. But there was also a large Egyptian population, which lived west of the city, in the old quarter of Rhacotis. Alexandria occupied the strip of sandy soil between Lake Mareotis and the sea, where the island of Pharos stood, surmounted by its famous lighthouse, one of the Seven Wonders of the World. The island was artificially connected with the mainland, which resulted in a spacious harbour being formed on the east; and a few miles farther east was Canopus, which became a popular Greek tourist city.

The Serapis cult: Ptolemy I introduced a cult designed to provide a line between his subjects, Greek and Egyptian. He observed that the Apis bull was worshipped at Memphis, which was even then a thriving religious centre, and assumed, wrongly, that the cult was popular and widespread. The deceased Apis was known as Osiris-Apis or "Oserapis", from which *Serapis* was derived. Ptolemy himself supplied Serapis with anthropomorphic features and declared him to be a national god. To launch the new deity on his career, Ptolemy announced that he had had a dream in which a colossal statue was revealed to him. No sooner did he communicate his revelation to the people than a statue of Serapis was put on view, closely resembling his vision: a man with curly hair, a benign expression and a long beard.

The cult of Serapis was to have some success throughout Greece and Asia Minor, in Sicily, and especially in Rome where, as

Preceding pages: the Sphinx and Pyramids of Giza as seen by a painter of the Orientalist school. <u>Left</u>, statue of Herhor in the Greco-Roman Museum in Alexandria.

the patron god of the Ptolemaic empire, its presence enhanced the empire's prestige. In Egypt Serapis was worshipped in every major town, but especially in Alexandria and Memphis, where the Serapeum, the temple of Serapis in the necropolis of Saqqarah, became a famous site.

Alexandria: Alexandria became capital in place of Memphis and was soon to become the major seat of learning in the Mediterranean world, replacing Athens as the centre of culture. Ptolemy II commissioned Egyptians to translate their literature into Greek; and a priest, Manetho, wrote the history of his country. Ptolemy III issued a decree that all travellers disembarking at Alexandria should have

Archimedes, the greatest mathematician and mechanist of antiquity, inventor among other things of the Archimedian Screw. Alexandrian astronomers revised the Egyptian calendar, then, some two centuries later, the Roman one, creating the Julian calendar that was used throughout Europe until the end of the Renaissance. Literary critics and scholars edited classical texts, giving them the forms we now know. Living poets such as Theocritus, Callimachus, and Appollonius Rhodius received generous support.

The Ptolemies regarded Egypt as their land and they played a dual role in it, conducting themselves both as bearers of Greek culture and as guardians of Egyptian culture.

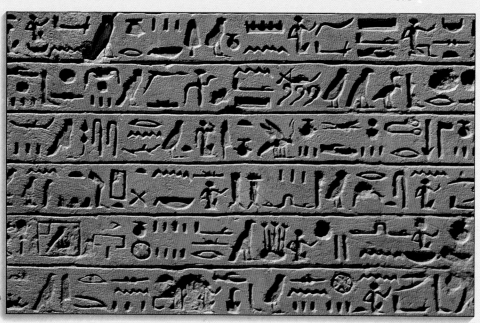

taken from them, in exchange for an official certified copy, any literature in their baggage. Research, especially with practical aims, was also fostered; and distinguished astronomers, mathematicians, geographers, historians, poets and philosophers gravitated to the Mouseion or Museum attached to the Library in Alexandria, which was a research institution.

Among the famed scientists who worked in Alexandria were Eratosthenes, the greatest geographer of antiquity, who measured the circumference of the earth to within 50 miles; Euclid, author of the *Elements,* the most famous textbook ever written, standard until the beginning of this century; and

The roles were separate, yet interrelated. They resided in Alexandria, the great intellectual centre; yet as pharaohs they lavished revenues on local priesthoods for the upkeep of temples or at least exempted them from taxes. One aspect of the power of the pharaoh was his capacity to uphold religious order; and the Ptolemies thus continued an ancient tradition. Ptolemaic temples were built on traditional lines, often on the sites of more ancient temples. The walls were adorned with scenes depicting Ptolemaic kings in the manner of the ancient pharaohs, duly equipped with names and titles in hieroglyphics. Like the ancient pharaohs, they fulfilled religious duties and made ceremonial journeys up the Nile, enjoying the public worship of political leadership that was a long-standing feature of life in Egypt.

Influence of the Greek language: Bilingual Egyptians realised long before the conquest by Alexander that if they transcribed their own language into the Greek alphabet, which was well known among the middle classes and was simpler to read, communication would be easier. Scribes started the transliteration, adding seven extra letters from the Egyptian alphabet to accommodate sounds for which there were no Greek letters. The emergence of this new script, now known as Coptic, cannot be dated precisely. The earli-

Persians had established a Jewish garrison as far south as the island of Elephantine (opposite Aswan). When Palestine fell under the control of Ptolemy I in 301 BC, he brought back Jewish mercenaries, who joined the already-established communities. Unable to speak Hebrew, which had disappeared as a living language, Egyptian Jews soon felt a need to translate their sacred books into Greek. According to legend, 72 translators were chosen from among the most learned Jewish scholars and the resulting version of the Old Testament, written in Alexandria, is known as the *Septuagint*.

The striking resemblances in Biblical and Egyptian expression and imagery are not all

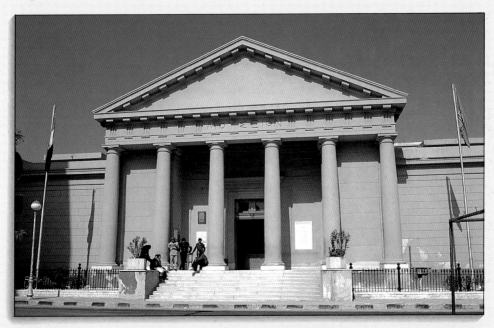

est attempt to write the Egyptian language alphabetically in Greek, feeble and faulty but nevertheless important, appears in an inscription dating to the Kushite Dynasty (750 BC–656 BC) at Abydos.

Greek also became the mother-tongue of the Jews in Egypt, who constituted the second largest foreign community. Many had been imported as soldiers, even before the arrival of the Ptolemies. For example, the

Left, elegant hieroglyphs show the skill of the ancient scribes. **Above**, the Greco-Roman Museum in Alexandria has a superb collection of Ptolemaic artifacts.

that surprising in view of the centuries of contact between Egyptians and Jews in Egypt. For example, an Egyptian sage called Amenemope (c. 1320 BC–1080 BC), whose works were widely distributed, admonished "Set thyself in the arms of God", while Moses declaimed, "The eternal God is a dwelling place, and underneath are the everlasting arms." "Yahweh weigheth the hearts" says Proverbs 2:12; and it has not passed unobserved that the only other doctrine in which a god weighs the human heart is the myth of the court of Osiris in the underworld, where it is weighed against the feather of truth. The Biblical description of men being fashioned out of clay by Yahweh is likewise similar to the ancient Egyptian image of men being fashioned on a potter's wheel out of clay from the river Nile by the god Khnum. The analogies between the Book of Proverbs and the words of Amenemope are beyond doubt, in fact, and indicate direct borrowing in thought and expression.

Racial and cultural conflicts: The Ptolemies encouraged other foreigners to come and live in Egypt. These immigrants included Syrians and Persians, as well as Greeks, who took up residence in the Delta, in certain quarters of Memphis, and the Fayyum, where an enormous settlement grew up. Egypt in Ptolemaic times was inhabited by an extremely diversified foreign population, as well as an already highly stratified European society. There was a strong anti-Egyptian feeling among the sophisticated Greeks, who did not encourage Egyptians to become citizens of Alexandria and the Greek cities. Further, although they held the Egyptian culture in reverence in many ways, they did not learn the Egyptian language or writing. Even the Greek masses, fascinated by the "sacred mysteries" and "divine oracles" of the Land of Wonders, nevertheless held the Egyptians in contempt.

There was also anti-Greek feeling among the Egyptians, who had a strong sense of cultural superiority to anyone who did not speak their language. Herodotus had remarked on this attitude even in Persian times. Although there is evidence that Egyptian priests and officials collaborated with the Ptolemies, there is also evidence that they rebelled frequently, resentful of the fact that they were treated as a conquered race. Prophetic writings were widely circulated among the Egyptians, promising the expulsion of the foreigners. One Upper Egyptian province in particular, the Thebaid (Luxor), remained the most ardently nationalistic.

The last of the Ptolemies: Towards the end of the 2nd century BC there were economic problems and political unrest in Egypt, along with a decline in foreign trade. Territories outside Egypt were lost, since the last of the Ptolemies were weak leaders, and the prosperity of the kingdom waned. The court, rich in material wealth and lax in morals, became the scene of decadence and anarchy. By the last century of Ptolemaic rule the Egyptians had acquired a position that was somewhat nearer in equality with the Greeks than they had enjoyed under the earlier Ptolemies; in fact Egyptian veterans received allotments of land like the Greeks, which may have been made possible as a result of rival claimants to the throne rallying the native population for popular support. This era saw the emergence of a landed, wealthy Egyptian population, who were ardently nationalistic and had little respect for the settlers. It was from their ranks that Coptic Christianity's great spiritual leaders were to arise.

Cleopatra VI, the most famous of the Ptolemies, came to the throne at the age of about 18, as co-regent with her even younger brother Ptolemy XII. They were at that time under the guardianship of the Roman Senate and Romans interfered in the rivalry between them, which led Ptolemy to banish his 21-year-old sister from Egypt. Cleopatra sought refuge in Syria, with a view to raising an army and recovering the throne by force of arms. When the ageing Julius Caesar came to Alexandria in 47 BC, he took the side of the banished queen and set her on the throne. Soon afterwards Cleopatra bore his only son, Caesarion.

A little over five years later, she met Mark Anthony at Tarsus. Their legendary love brought her three more children, but alienated Antony from supporters in Rome. Anthony's purported will, stating his wishes to be buried at Alexandria, angered many Romans, and gave Octavian the excuse he was looking for to declare war on Antony. Octavian marched against him, defeating him at Actium and capturing Alexandria. Anthony committed suicide; and Cleopatra, the last monarch to bear the title "Lord of the Two Lands" and to wear the crown bearing the sacred uraeus, the snake of Upper Egypt symbolising kingship, is recorded to have caused her own death by the bite of an asp. Caesarion, who had been co-regent since 43 BC, was murdered; and Octavianus became sole ruler in 30 BC.

Egypt thenceforth was a province of the Roman empire, subject only to the emperor, who lived in Rome, and to viceroys or prefects nominated by the emperor, who followed the example of the Ptolemies and represented themselves to the Egyptians as successors of the ancient pharaohs.

Roman funeral mask, Greco-Roman Museum.

21995

THE ROMAN PERIOD AND EARLY CHRISTIANITY

The Roman occupation of Egypt, ostensibly a mere extension of Ptolemaic rule, was actually markedly different. While a mutual hostility towards the Persians and a long history of commercial relations bound Egyptians and Greeks together, no such affinity existed between Egyptians and Romans. Alexander the Great had entered Egypt without striking a blow; Roman troops fought battles with Egyptians almost immediately. The Ptolemaic kings had lived in Egypt; the Roman emperors governed from Rome and their prefects took over the position formerly held in the scheme of government by the kings. To the Egyptians the prefect, not the emperor, was therefore the royal personage. And the prefect did not perform the ceremonial functions of divine kingship, which was by tradition highly personal. There was thus a drastic change in the climate of leadership.

The emperor Augustus made the mistake of arousing the ire of the Greeks when he abolished the Greek Senate in Alexandria and took administrative powers from Greek officials. Further, in response to an appeal by Herod, king of Judea, he not only agreed to restore to him the land that had been bestowed on Cleopatra during her short refuge in Syria, but also agreed to grant self-government to the Hellenised Jews of Alexandria. This caused great consternation among the Greeks. Fighting soon broke out, first between Greeks and Jews, then with the Romans' participation when they tried to separate the two. The unrest that marks the beginning of the Christian era in Alexandria had already begun. Ships in the harbour were set on fire, the flames spread and the Mouseion Library was burned. An estimated 490,000 rolls of papyrus perished in the process.

The Romans thenceforth stationed garrisons at Alexandria, which remained the capital; at Babylon (Old Cairo), which was the key to communications with Asia and with Lower Egypt; and at Syene (Aswan), which was Egypt's southern boundary. They controlled Egypt by force, and regarded the land

as no more than a granary supplying wheat to Rome. Consequently, an enormous burden of taxation was placed on the people of the Nile Valley. A census was imposed on villages throughout the land and house-to-house registration of the number of residents was made, which might have been considered normal procedure in Rome, but was regarded as an infringement of their privacy by Egyptians. Calculation of the wheat quota was based not on the productivity of the land, but on the number of men in a village.

Egyptians who had enjoyed certain privileges under the later Ptolemies and acquired considerable wealth received no special consideration by the Romans, but had their problems compounded when the Emperor Trajan declared that peasant farmers should be recruited for the Roman army. Hadrian reduced rentals on imperial lands and exempted citizens of Greek cities and Greek settlers in the Fayyum from taxation, but the Egyptian rural population was assessed at a flat rate, without regard for income, age or capacity for work. Hardship followed. There are records of men having "fled leaving no property", 43 in number, then 60, then 100 from a single village. Some took refuge in remote areas of the desert, while others hid in caves and ancient tombs flanking the Nile Valley. When men fled or hid, their families suffered the penalties.

Strategic planning: The Romans made an overt show of respect for Egyptian priesthoods by constructing new temples or completing older ones built by the Ptolemies. The temple to the goddess Hathor at Dendera, for example, which was started under the later Ptolemies, was completed some 185 years later under the emperor Tiberius; and temples in the traditional style were completed at Esna, Kom Ombo and Philae. It is worthy of note, however, that the sites for these temples were chosen for their strategic position as well as for the sake of ancient tradition. Esna had been a centre for local commerce from earliest times; Kom Ombo, situated on a hill, commanded the trade routes to Nubia in the south; and Philae was situated on Egypt's southern border.

Temple lands elsewhere, however, were

annexed and placed under the control of the Roman government. Local priests were allotted only a small part of sacred property and their own material wealth was curbed. The produce of vineyards, palm groves and fig plantations owned by temples was collected by Roman officials and taxes were levied on sheep, oxen, horses and donkeys. A Roman official held the title of "High Priest of Alexandria and all Egypt". Egypt was treated as a private estate of the emperor and a pleasure-ground for the Roman upper classes, who visited Egypt in vast numbers, coming to see the Pyramids of Giza, the Apis bull at Memphis, the ancient city of Abydos, the Colossus of Memnon, or the healing

gious learning in Christian antiquity. It was founded in 190 by Pantanaeus, a Christian scholar who is believed to have come to Alexandria approximately 10 years earlier. Its scope was not limited to theological subjects, because science, mathematics and the humanities were also taught there. Significantly, the emergence of the school coincides with the first direct attacks by the Romans on the Christians of Alexandria.

Clement (160–215), a convert from paganism who succeeded Pantanaeus, is regarded as an early apostle of Christian liberalism and taught in Alexandria for more than 20 years. He was succeeded by Origen (185–253), the theologian and writer who is re-

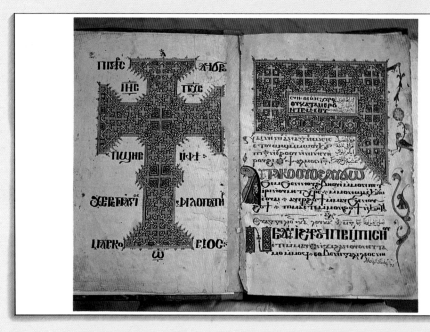

centres at Deir el Bahari and Philae.

Early Christianity: Such were the conditions in Egypt during the 1st century of the Christian era, when the apostle Mark preached in Alexandria. Remains from the period of the diffusion of Christianity in Egypt are scant, but New Testament writings found in Bahnasa in Middle Egypt date from around the year 200, and a fragment of the gospel of St John, written in Coptic and found in Upper Egypt, can be dated even earlier. They testify to the spread of Christianity throughout Egypt within a century of St Mark's arrival.

The Catechetical School of Alexandria was the first important institution of reli-

garded as the greatest of the early Christian apologists. Like Clement, he was highly critical of the Gnostic movement (from the Greek *gnosis* or "knowledge").

Gnosticism: The origin of the Gnostic communities is obscure and until recently not much was known about them: the Gnostics were hounded into silence, in the name of orthodox Christianity, from the 4th century onward and their writings were burned.

Fortunately, however, a collection of manuscripts was discovered in Nag Hammadi in Upper Egypt in 1945. These texts, which have raised important questions about the progress of development of Christianity in

Egypt, are copied from original writings that may date from as early as the second half of the 1st century.

The 12 Nag Hammadi codices were collected by Egyptians and translated into Coptic, the Egyptian language of the time. They vary widely in content, presenting a spectrum of heritages that range from Egyptian folklore, Hermeticism, Greek philosophy and Persian mysticism to the Old and New Testaments. The codices include a "a gospel of Thomas", a compilation of saying attributed to Jesus; extracts from Plato's *Republic*; and apocrypha ("secret books") related to Zoroastrianism and Manichaeism. Little wonder that the Gnostics, with such

a hierarchy rising from matter to soul, soul to reason, and reason to God, conceived as pure being without matter or form. Neoplatonists understood reality as the spiritual world contemplated by reason and allowed the material world only a formal existence. Ascetic disciplines were part of their ethical code, which urged them to ascend from the bonds of matter to the spiritual world, to become ecstatically united with the divine.

The first Neoplatonist, Ammonius Saccas, had been the teacher of Origen and was a lapsed Christian, while his famous successors – Plotinus, Porphyry, Iamblichus, Hypatia, and Proclus – were all pagans. Plotinus, born in Asyut, was the most influ-

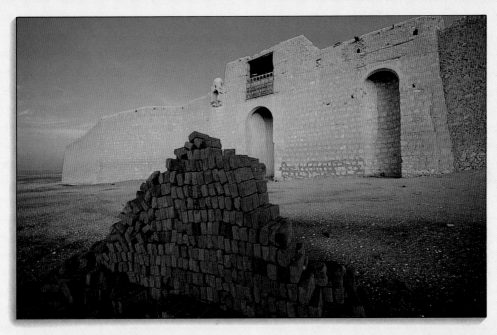

diversity, came under violent attack by orthodox Christians. The codices reveal, nevertheless, that the Gnostic movement was of greater historical consequence than hitherto supposed.

Neoplatonism: A more formidable rival to Christianity in the long run came directly from pagan thought: Neoplatonism. Coalescing in Alexandria during the 3rd century, this philosophical school revived and developed the metaphysical and mystical side of Platonic doctrine, explaining the universe as

ential, making many converts at the imperial court in Rome. Porphyry, his student, came to be regarded by the Christian bishops as their greatest enemy – they burned his books in public – and the last important work of the school was Proclus' defense of the pagan philosophical tradition against Christianity. More than one Christian was a student of Neoplatonism, nevertheless, and even Porphyry found Christian readers and translators, by whom Neoplatonic ideas were co-opted into the teachings of the early Church.

Major Neoplatonic works survived intact, moreover, and by the end of the Middle Ages a handful of Europeans could read them in

Left, ancient religious manuscript illuminated in Coptic. **Above**, St Antony's Monastery.

the original. As knowledge of Greek began to extend outside the clergy, aristocratic study-groups sprang up, most notably in Florence, and Neoplatonism rapidly became a fashion, then a movement. Within a few years its influence had spread from Northern Italy throughout Western Europe, largely creating that cultural consensus we call the Renaissance. Thus a common element in the paintings of Botticelli or Titian, the engravings of Dürer, the sculpture of Michelangelo, or the poetry of Shakespeare, which distinguishes them from earlier European art, is their rootedness in Neoplatonic images and ideas. For two centuries or so, while a 1,000-year-old Christian orthodoxy came increasingly into question, these images and ideas were to be the conceptual currency of every educated European.

They were also modern man's first key to an understanding of the ancient pagan culture that the early Church, in Egypt and elsewhere, had conscientiously set out to destroy. As with most revolutionary groups, its motive was ideological zeal, which began with a sense of being persecuted.

Religious persecution: The first systematic attempt to put an end to Christianity by depriving the church of both its leaders and followers took place under the Emperor Decius (249–251), who ordered Egyptians to participate in pagan worship in the presence of Roman officers and to submit certificates of sacrifice. Those who refused were declared to be self-avowed Christians and were tortured. Some Christians sent in false certificates; others managed to escape to the solitude of the desert. Many, however, were willing to die rather than abjure their faith, and their martyrdom further accelerated the Christian movement.

Beginnings of Monasticism: St Paul the Theban, orphaned as a youth, and St Anthony, who came from a family of landowners with a certain status in society, were two of Egypt's earliest and greatest spiritual leaders. Both lived lives of meditation and prayer at about this time; each, unknown to the other, had chosen a retreat in the Eastern Desert in a range of mountains near the Gulf of Suez. St Paul, older than St Antony and with the gift of healing, is believed to have retired to the desert at the age of 16 to escape the persecutions of Decius. St Antony was born of fairly wealthy parents, but as a result of

visionary inspiration, sold his inheritance and gave his money to the poor, then retreated to the cliffs flanking the Nile Valley, later settling beneath a range of mountains known today as the South Qalala.

These two men became regarded as having special powers and a special relationship with the divine, attracting other eremites to draw near them. By this time thousands of ascetics, whose original models may be traced to pre-Christian times in Egypt, were living either alone or in small groups and were looking for guidance from masters, like St Paul and St Anthony, who would give instruction in an atmosphere of security and spirituality.

As with most great movements that spread beyond the borders of the country in which they first took root, contradictory traditions as to the origins of monasticism have emerged. St Jerome credits St Paul the Theban with being the first hermit. In both Coptic and Western tradition, however, St Antony holds a more prominent position, and Copts regard him as the prototype of the Egyptian anchorite. He took refuge from those who came to see him in a cave high up in the rugged mountains, while his disciples kept him supplied with provisions. The cave, which can still be seen, is situated at the end of a narrow tunnel approached from a ledge, below which is a small terrace believed to be the place where he used to weave baskets from palm leaves.

In 284 the Roman army elected Diocletian emperor and his reforms mark a turning-point in the history of Christianity. The appalling social and economic conditions throughout the Roman empire led him to reorganise it along military lines. He divided Egypt into three major provinces, separated civic and military powers, then imposed new methods of tax assessment based on units of productivity. Under Diocletian's reforms Egyptians were forced into public service and, to facilitate control, Latin was introduced as the official language.

Unification of the Roman empire was undoubtedly the reason for these reforms, but Egyptians had had enough. They rebelled so violently that Diocletian decided that if they could not be subjugated, they should be eliminated. They were dismissed from gov-

Modern Coptic painting, with Byzantine influence.

ernment service, their property was confiscated, and their houses levelled. Searches were made for Christian literature and copies of the scriptures, when found, were burned. Though thousands of people died during the terrible persecutions of Diocletian, unknown numbers escaped to refuge in the deserts, taking their zeal for Christianity with them, to create new converts.

The Christian church celebrates both martyrs and confessors. The latter are those who did not die for their faith but lived to spread it. In a world of want and violence, a religion that preached a message of common support and a blessed life after death was embraced with enthusiasm.

Early Monastic Reform: St Pachom (Pachomius in Latin, referred to as *Anba Bakhum* in Arabic), born about 285, first saw the benefits of organising the widespread anchoritic communities and therefore became the founder of a form of monasticism that took his name. A native Egyptian who only learned Greek late in life in order to communicate with strangers, Pachom established a community near Akhmin, where the caves in the hills flanking the Nile floodplain were populated with large numbers of ascetics. Pachom drew them together and introduced a schedule of activities for every hour of the day and night, emphasising that a healthy body provided a healthy spirit, and stressing that there should be no excesses of any kind, even in spiritual meditation.

Pachom's aim was to establish a pious, enlightened and self-sufficient community that would set an example to others. An applicant for admission did not have to exhibit spectacular feats of mortification of the flesh. Although there are numerous examples of physical self-torture in the lives of the Desert Fathers, a candidate for Pachomian monasticism merely had to undergo a period of probation, after which he was clothed in the habit of a monk and officially joined the community.

Leading disciplined lives, the monks brought productivity to the soil, revived crafts and, more importantly, were in communication with non-Christian neighbouring communities. There is abundant evidence in the surviving records of various monasteries that the monks aided the people economically by

Egypt's monasteries welcome visitors.

providing them with their crop surpluses, as well as products from craft industries. They supplied medication to those who came for a cure. They even played a role as mediators in popular grievances, whether between members of a single family, or, as was frequent, in disputes over land or water rights between neighbours. Pachomian monasteries were not isolated in remote stretches of the desert, but in many cases were within easy reach of valley settlements.

Pachom's first monastery was so successful that he moved on to found a second similar institution and yet another, until he had founded no fewer than 11 monasteries in Upper Egypt, including two convents for women. Not all the ascetic communities adopted St Pachom's Rule. Those that had grown up around spiritual leaders like St Antony or St Makarius, the son of a village priest, seem, on the basis of archaeological considerations, to have continued a semi-cenobitic form of monasticism: the monks only met once a week for mass and a communal meal, followed by a meeting at which work was allocated for the forthcoming week. St Pegol, founder of the White Monastery in Middle Egypt modified Pachom's rules and introduced a few more.

All Christian monasticism stems, either directly or indirectly, from Pachomian monasticism: St Basil, organiser of the monastic movement in Asia Minor, whose rule is followed by the Eastern churches, visited Egypt around 357; St Jerome, translator of the Bible into Latin, made it known to the West; and St Benedict who founded monasteries in the West in the 6th century, used the model of St Pachom, but in a stricter form.

Conversion and controversy: The famous revelation of the Emperor Constantine in 312, which resulted in his conversion to Christianity, was followed by the Edict of Milan, according to which Christianity became the favoured religion throughout the Roman empire. It was at last safe to admit to being a Christian in Egypt. Unfortunately, the theological disputes that had plagued the early Christian movement became even fiercer in the 4th and following centuries.

The controversies centred on the attempt to define the Incarnation: If Jesus was both God and Man, had He two natures? If so, what was their relationship? Defining the nature of Jesus of crucial importance to a new religion that attracted people from many backgrounds, with different traditions, concepts of godliness, and styles of worship, was extremely difficult. It concerned such definitions as "Father", "Son", "begotten", and "unbegotten".

The chief antagonists were the Arians, so called after Arius, an elderly Alexandrian presbyter, and the Monophysites, led by Alexander, bishop of Alexandria. The former held that "a time there was when He was not", in other words, that Jesus did not have the same nature as God the Father. The Monophysites regarded this doctrine as recognition of two gods and a reversion to polytheism. They believed that Father and Son were intrinsically

and Romans represented the West; and the Alexandrian delegation included the bishop Alexander, Athanasius his deacon, Arius his antagonist, and a large body of various monks and hermits.

Although Alexander officially led Egypt's delegation, it was his deacon, Athanasius, who was his chief spokesman. And it says a great deal for his eloquence, reasoning and persistence that the Nicene Creed, to the effect that Father and Son are of the same nature, was sanctioned and remains part of the Christian liturgy. Constantine formally accepted the decision of the bishops, and issued a decree of banishment against those who refused to subscribe to it.

of one nature, and that Jesus was therefore both divine and human.

The dispute was discussed in a highly charged atmosphere and reached such an impasse that Constantine felt impelled to define officially a dogma to unify Christian belief. The Council of Nicea, convened in Asia Minor in 325 for this purpose, was the earliest and most important church council, the first meeting between the Church and the State. It was attended by the Emperor Constantine and 318 bishops, with their delegations, from Egypt, Syria, Assyria, Asia Minor, Greece and the West. The Syrian and Assyrian delegations included bishops from Antioch, Jerusalem and Armenia; Goths

The decline of Alexandria: Soon after the Council of Nicea, Constantine moved his capital to the ancient Greek town of Byzantium, which became Constantinople or "Constantine's city", and was to gain much of the importance and prestige that had once belonged to Alexandria. The new metropolis was embellished with great monuments from many ancient cities, including an obelisk over 100 feet (30 metres) high shipped from Egypt. Known as "New Rome", Constantinople became a storehouse of Christian and pagan art and science and rapidly usurped the reputation Alexandria had held as a seat of learning since Ptolemaic times.

Thus began an era when ecclesiastical dignitaries excommunicated one another in Egypt and mobs sacked churches of opposing factions. Athanasius was driven into exile five times and sought shelter with hermits in their isolated caves, living with St Anthony near the Red Sea or in a monastery in Kharga Oasis. During his exiles, Athanasius successfully reconciled the differences between monks and hermits, some of whom did not want to join a monastic order.

Under Theodosius I Christianity was formally declared the religion of the empire and the Arians were again declared heretics. The Monophysite bishops of Alexandria were reinstated, but as a result of the partition of

pled. In Alexandria the famous statue of Serapis was burned and the Serapeum destroyed, along with its library, which had replaced the Mouseion as a centre of learning. It was a folly of fanaticism in the name of orthodoxy not, ironically, so different from that which had earlier opposed Christianity. In 415 under Theodosius II, Patriarch Cyril expelled the Jews of Alexandria from the city.

In the 4th and 5th centuries many ancient temples were converted into monastic centres – Dayr (monastery) al-Medinah and Dayr al-Bahri (Deir al-Bahari), both in the Theban necropolis, are two well-known examples – or churches, as in the second court

the empire between the Emperor Honorius of Rome and the Emperor Arcadius of Constantinople, their power was limited. Egypt fell under the jurisdiction of the latter and the so-called Byzantine rule of Egypt began.

Byzantine period: Theophilus was made Patriarch of Alexandria and displayed tremendous zeal in destroying heathen temples. A wave of destruction swept over the land of Egypt. Tombs were ravaged, walls of ancient monuments scraped, and status toppled.

Left, drawbridge leading to the keep at the Monastery of St Baramus, Wadi Natrun. Above, monastery of St Paul in the Eastern Desert.

of the mortuary temple of Ramses III at Medinat Habu and the Court of Amenhotep III in Luxor Temple. One of the earliest Christian buildings in Egypt was constructed between the Birth House and the Coronation House of the Temple of Hathor at Dendera, using some of the blocks from the Birth House. It is possible that this church was the famous Christian centre somewhere in the neighbourhood of Dendera that St Jerome alludes to as sheltering an assembly of 50,000 monks to celebrate Easter.

Pilgrims came from all over the Christian world to visit the monasteries in Egypt. The bishop of Bahnasa estimated the number of monks in Middle Egypt at 10,000 and nuns at 20,000, living in 40 monasteries and convents. Archaeology has revealed a huge monastic settlement in Kharga Oasis, in the Western Desert, dating from the 4th century, with a necropolis at Bagawat containing over 200 chapels. Wadi Natrun, recently revived as an important monastic centre, once had 50 monasteries and over 5,000 monks. East of Wadi Natrun, at Kelya (from the Latin for "cell"), a site described by such Christian writers as Palladius and Rufinus, there are more than 750 abandoned hermitages dating from around the 5th century. In the biography of St Macrufus, who lived in the 6th century, the village of Ishnin an-

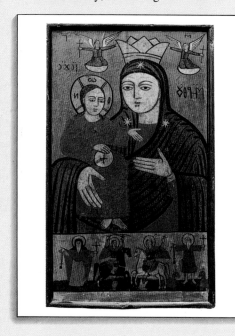

Nasarah is reported to have had "as many churches as there were days in the year".

Despite the growth of the Christian movement, factional disputes continued, especially when the see of Alexandria officially lost precedence to the see of Constantinople at the Council of Constantinople in 381. There had been riots so violent that the Catechetical School, a central force in the intellectual life of Alexandria for nearly two centuries, had been destroyed.

Foundation of the Coptic Orthodox Church: Convened in 451, the Council of Chalcedon showed Byzantine determination to exert authority in Egypt. A new statement of dogma declared that Christ had two Natures "concurring" in One Person. When the Egyptians refused to endorse this revisionist doctrine, their Patriarch was formally excommunicated. In the struggle that followed, several Egyptian leaders were killed, and Alexandria was pillaged by imperial troops.

From this time onward, Egypt generally had two Patriarchs, one representing the orthodoxy of Constantinople, the other upholding the "One Person" beliefs of the majority of Egyptian Christians, embodied in the Coptic Orthodox Church, the national Church of Egypt, which emerged as a separate entity. The English word *Copt*, meaning "Egyptian Christian", is derived from the Arabic *qibt*, which is derived in turn from *Kyptaios*, the Coptic form of the Greek word *Aigyptios*. It also designates not only the last stages of the ancient Egyptian language and script, but also the distinctive art and architecture that developed everywhere in Egypt except Alexandria – which remained attached to cosmopolitan forms – during the country's Christian era. It is used, finally, to refer to most of modern Egypt's Christian minority, who officially constitute about 9 percent of the population and who continue to be identified with the same intense patriotism that distinguished their forebears.

The Emperor Zeno's attempt in 482 to heal the breach between Churches was unsuccessful, but after strengthening his garrison and deporting the more outspoken Copts to Constantinople, he let matters rest. There were no more significant disturbances until the reign of Justinian (528–565).

The end of Byzantine rule: Under Justinian, the Copts were only saved from persecution by the interest of the Empress Theodora, his wife. After Theodora's death, however, Justinian sent Alexandria a patriarch-prefect determinedly armed with both civil and religious powers. Greeted by a mob, which stoned him when he attempted to speak in church, the new bishop retaliated by ordering the troops under his command to carry out a general slaughter. This act quelled immediate resistance, but completed the alienation of the Copts, who henceforward simply ignored any ecclesiastical representatives from Constantinople.

Left, Coptic icon showing Virgin and child. **Right**, cowled monk crossing drawbridge, Wadi Natrun.

The Arab Conquest: In the early 7th century, while the great rival Byzantine and Sasanian empires were exhausting themselves in a futile and costly struggle for supremacy, the Arabs were being spiritually and politically united by the Prophet Muhammad. His call for the creation of a Muslim community (the *Umma*) obedient to the commands of God, as revealed in the Holy Quran, cut across tribal conflicts and forged the Arabs into a single nation. Under the leadership of his successors, the Caliphs, the energy of the Arabs was directed outward against the contending empires of the north, who were too weak to resist an unexpected invasion from the heart of the Arabian Peninsula. Inspired by both the duty of waging *jihad* (Holy War) against non-believers and the promise of rich booty, the Muslim armies conquered all of Persia and half of the Byzantine empire between 636 and 649.

The Byzantine province of Egypt was invaded in 639 by 'Amr ibn al-'As, one of the ablest of the early Muslim generals, who had visited Alexandria in his youth and had never forgotten the Egyptian capital's public buildings, populous streets and obvious wealth. Acting on his own initiative, without the sanction of the Caliph in Madinah, 'Amr justified his actions by saying that the people of Egypt were sheep, that its land was gold, and that it belonged to whoever was strong enough to take it. Masters of hit-and-run tactics, his horsemen easily defeated by a Byzantine army near the ancient ruins of Heliopolis in 640, he then set about besieging both the fortress of Babylon, at the head of the Delta, and Alexandria itself. Paralysed by internal problems and foreign wars, the Byzantines were unable to reinforce their army in Egypt. Babylon fell in 641 and the rest of the country was formally surrendered soon after.

The Arabs were aided in their conquest by the indifference of the native Egyptians, the Copts, whose political and religious disputes with Constantinople, never resolved, had made them deeply hostile to Byzantine rule. Not yet interested in converting subject peoples to Islam, which they still viewed as a purely Arab religion, the Muslim conquerors favoured the Coptic Church over the Byzantine establishment and allowed it autonomy, using it to assist them in collecting the poll-tax levied on all non-Muslims.

During the siege of Babylon, the Muslims had camped to the north of the fortress and it was here that 'Amr founded Fustat, a garrison city for the control of the Nile Valley. Fustat was gradually transformed from a military base into the administrative and commercial capital of the Arab province of Egypt. Arabic began to replace Greek as the language of government, culture and commerce in the city and in time filtered down to the rural population, causing the local Coptic language to be all but forgotten.

The 'Abbasid Caliphs: The rapid growth of the new Islamic empire brought in its wake a host of problems. Tribal differences among the Arabs began to reassert themselves as various factions fought over the spoils of conquest and the leadership of the Umma. These conflicts, usually expressed in religious terms, deeply divided the Arabs and resulted in over a hundred years of rebellions and civil wars. A semblance of Muslim unity was reestablished in 750 when the 'Abbasid family seized control of the empire. Brought to power by a coalition of Arab and Iranian forces, they established a more international state, centred in Baghdad, that drew upon the services of all Muslims.

In Egypt, as a symbol of the new regime, a new administrative capital was built to the north of Fustat. Known as Al-'Askar or "the Cantonments", this military suburb became the official residence of the provincial governor, his army and bureaucracy. Never much more than an extension of Fustat, it was in time absorbed by the earlier town's own northern expansion.

During the first 200 years of Muslim rule, Egypt was a pawn rather than a true participant in the wider political issues that dominated the affairs of the Islamic empire. Controlled by a series of military governors appointed by the Caliphs in the East, most of the country's great agricultural wealth was channelled into the coffers of the central treasury. The power of these governors was severely curtailed by short terms of office and by restrictions placed upon their internal authority to prevent the establishment of an independent state in Egypt.

The result was oppressive taxation and widespread official corruption, which brought Egypt to the verge of economic collapse in the early 9th century. This state of affairs also reflected the progressive decline of 'Abbasid authority throughout the empire, which was simply too large to be effectively ruled by one man.

In order to hold their state together the who acted independently rather than as agents of the Caliphs.

Independence under Ibn Tulun: The most famous Turkish governor and the man responsible for the inauguration of Egypt's medieval era of greatness was Ahmad Ibn Tulun. The son of a Turkish slave, he had been raised and educated in the 'Abbasid court and was posted to Egypt in 868 at the age of 33. Taking advantage of rivalry amongst the 'Abbasid family and their Turkish armies, Ibn Tulun was able to gain total control of the provincial government, establishing the first autonomous Muslim state in Egypt. By drastically reducing the imperial tribute to Iraq and by reinvesting the coun-

Caliphs in Baghdad began to employ Turkish slave armies to act as a counterbalance to their turbulent Arab and Iranian subjects. Far from being slaves in the Western sense of the word, these Turks were groomed as a ruling caste, loyal only to the 'Abbasids. The power of the Turkish generals became so great and the upkeep of their armies so expensive that the Caliphs were compelled to distribute whole provinces to them in lieu of pay. In this manner Egypt became in 832 a private fief of the new Muslim military elite. Unwilling to leave the political nerve centre of Iraq, which might result in a loss of influence, the generals appointed their own governors to Egypt, try's wealth in his new domain, Ibn Tulun brought about a period of prosperity for ruler and ruled alike. One of his first actions as independent sovereign was the creation of a strong army made up of Turkish, Greek and Sudanese slaves, with which he conquered all of Syria in 878.

In order to celebrate his independence Ibn Tulun built a new royal city to the north of Al-'Askar called *Al-Qatai'* or "the Wards" after its division into separate districts, each housing a different contingent of his multiracial army. Situated at its centre was the great mosque of Ibn Tulun, completed in 879, the finest surviving example of Muslim architecture from the High 'Abbasid period in the world.

Ibu Tulun died in 884 and was succeeded by his 20-year-old son Khumarawayh. With his father's army he extended the borders of the Tulunid state to the Euphrates, forcing the 'Abbasids to recognise his sovereignty.

In 896 Khumarawayh was murdered by slaves from his harem and was succeeded by his two sons and a brother, noteworthy only for the extravagance of their life-style and incompetence of their rule. After exhausting the state treasury and alienating the army, they were deposed and murdered, one after the other, leaving Egypt too weak to resist the reestablishment of direct 'Abbasid rule

vaded Egypt during this period, however, demanded a more effective form of government in the Nile Valley. The 'Abbasids were therefore compelled to allow the establishment in 935 of a new semi-autonomous state in Egypt, founded by Muhammad Ibn Tuglij, known as "the Ikhshid", an ancient Central Asian royal title. His main task was the creation of a strong Egyptian buffer state to prevent further Fatimid eastern expansion.

On his death in 946, he was nominally succeeded by his young sons, but the real power was held by their regent, the Nubian eunuch Kafur. Kafur's strong rule held the Ikhshid state together, but on his death it fell in the face of the Fatimid invasion of 969.

in 905. As an example to future rebels against 'Abbasid authority, the city of *Al-Qatai'* was rased to the ground, only the mosque of Ibn Tulun being spared, while the surviving male members of the Tulunid family were taken in chains to Baghdad.

For the next 30 years Egypt was again ruled by a series of oppressive and ineffectual provincial governors, appointed from Iraq. The growing threat of the Shi'i Fatimid dynasty, centred in Tunisia, who twice in-

Left, engraving of the Mosque of Ibn Tulun from the *Description de l'Egypte*. **Above**, vaulted *Iwan* in the 14th-century Mosque of Sultan Hasan.

The origins of the Fatimids: The Fatimids were a radical Shi'i sect that believed their Imams (leaders) were the only rightful rulers of the Muslim world. Basing their claim on their direct descent from the Prophet Muhammad through his daughter Fatima, they viewed the 'Abbasids as usurpers, and dreamed of uniting all of Islam under the banner of Shi'ism.

The origins of this rivalry date back to the first years of the Islamic era, when the early Muslims were divided over who was to succeed Muhammad on his death in 632. The majority of his followers, who were to become the Sunnis, favoured the election of one of them as Caliph, while a minority, who became known as the Shi'a, supported a hereditary principle, which would preserve the Caliphate within the Prophet's family.

Among the most extreme of the various Shi'i sects that grew out of this conflict were the Isma'ilis, of whom the Fatimids were the most successful members. They attributed a semi-divine status to their Imams, the Fatimid Caliphs, believing that they possessed a special esoteric knowledge which made them infallible and thus the only men capable of leading the Umma to perfection. The Imams controlled a vast secret organisation, the Da'wa, which would send highly trained agents throughout the Muslim world, winning converts and preparing the way for the eventual takeover of the Isma'ili Caliphs.

The conversion of the Kutama Berbers of Algeria by an Isma'ili agent in the early 10th century supplied the Fatimids with an army and a North African kingdom, but their dreams were set on Egypt. The death of Kafur supplied the Fatimid Caliph al Mu'izz with the chance he had been waiting for.

The founding of Al-Qahirah: In 969 Egypt fell to general Jawhar, a military slave of European origin, whose first action was the construction of a new royal enclosure to house the victorious Al-Mu'izz and his Shi'i government. The new Fatimid capital was named *Al-Qahira*, "The Subduer", later corrupted by Italian merchants into *Cairo*.

Separated from the predominantly Sunni population of Fustat by a mile of wasteland, Al-Qahirah's high walls could only be penetrated by the Isma'ili elite. Within were two great palaces, the home of the Imam and his court bureaucracy. Its religious and intellectual centre was the mosque of Al-Azhar, the headquarters of the Da'wa and the main congregational mosque of the city. The rest of Al-Qahirah's 300 acres were filled with gardens, hippodromes and military barracks housing the Imam's army.

The initial military success of the Fatimids was short-lived. After gaining control of Palestine and the holy cities of Mecca and Medina, they encountered stiff Byzantine resistance in Northern Syria. Attempts to strengthen their army with Turkish slave soldiers only succeeded in fostering a dangerous rivalry between their original Berber supporters and the new Eastern recruits. To offset their military failure the Fatimids turned

to the realm of trade, creating a commercial empire with links stretching from China in the east to the Italian city states in the west. Fustat became a major trade emporium, as well as one of the principal centres of artistic production in the Muslim world. Fatimid Egypt became fabulously wealthy.

Secluded in the luxury of their fortress city, the Fatimid Imams underwent a dramatic change. Plans for the conquest of the 'Abbasid empire were postponed indefinitely and the more radical aspects of their esoteric teachings were toned down. Little effort was made to convert the predominantly Christian and Sunni Muslim native population to Shi'ism, while the external activities of the Da'wa were largely occupied with establishing trade connections with sympathetic foreign powers. As a minority Muslim sect in Egypt, unconcerned with proselytising, the Fatimids were extremely tolerant, employing Sunnis, Christians and Jews equally in the running of their state.

The mad Caliph: The shift to a conservative and materialistic state deeply concerned the third Fatimid Caliph Al-Hakim (996–1021). Universally described as insane by medieval Arab historians, Al-Hakim was preoccupied with revitalising the spiritual mission of the Isma'ili movement and with the maintenance of his personal power in the face of Fatimid governmental opposition. His measures were usually extreme, brutal and unpredictable, but not without purpose. His persecution of Christians and Jews was an attempt at breaking their governmental influence and a means of winning popular Muslim support.

Decrees aimed against women, forbidding them from leaving their houses or possessing independent wealth, besides being a concession to public morality, were probably directed against his sister, Sitt al-Mulk, an influential opponent of his policies. When he allowed a group of extremist Iranian Isma'ilis to proclaim his divinity in 1017, he was only carrying the spiritual pretensions of his family to their ultimate limits.

In this, however, Al-Hakim had gone too far. Riots of protest broke out in Fustat and his radical devotees were forced to flee to Lebanon where they founded the Druze reli-

gion, which still believes Al-Hakim to be the incarnation of God.

The Fatimid hierarchy, feeling threatened by Al-Hakim's eccentric behaviour, decided the unstable Imam had to go. While he was riding his donkey alone in the Muqattam Hills at night, as was his custom, Al-Hakim mysteriously disappeared, almost certainly murdered on the orders of his sister and the Fatimid elite, who now took charge.

Fatimid heyday: During the long reign of Al-Mustansir (1036–94), Fustat reached the peak of its prosperity. With a population of almost half a million living in 5-storey buildings, complete with running water and sophisticated sewer systems, it was one of the great cities of its age.

Despite Egypt's wealth the Fatimid state rapidly began to decline. The Turkish troops, who had largely replaced their Berber rivals, were unruly and a constant threat to internal security. A sequence of seven low Niles between 1066 and 1072 plunged the country into further chaos. Famine and plague spread throughout the Nile Valley, reducing the people of Fustat to cannibalism. The Turkish soldiers looted the Fatimid palaces on the pretext of arrears of pay, emptying the Caliph's treasury and dispersing his great library of 100,000 books. Al-Mustansir secretly called in Badr al-Jamali, the Fatimid's Armenian governor at Acre in Palestine, to restore order.

A surprise attack on Al-Qahirah in 1072 crushed all opposition and won Badr al-Jamali full dictatorial powers. He now had to face an impending invasion by the Seljuk Turks, masters of an empire stretching from Central Asia to Egypt's eastern border. The walls of Al-Qahirah, with massive new gates, were rebuilt to withstand the expected siege. A segment of these walls still survives in excellent condition on the northern side of the royal city.

The sudden break-up of the Seljuk empire after 1092 saved the Fatimids from certain defeat, but left the Middle East crowded with petty Muslim states. Their lack of unity facilitated the victories of the first Crusade of 1099, launched in response to the Seljuk conquest of Jerusalem a few years earlier. The crusaders were themselves divided into four, often hostile, principalities, more concerned with their individual short-term needs than with the establishment of a single strong Christian kingdom.

The rise of the Zangids of Mosul, who began absorbing their Muslim neighbours and preaching *jihad* against the crusaders in the first half of the 12th century, meant that it was just a matter of time before the Christians were encircled and picked off one by one. Both sides realised that Egypt, weakened by dynastic and military rivalries, yet incredibly wealthy, was the key to victory. Whoever controlled her vast resources could dominate the whole region.

Salah ad-Din takes power: The Fatimids tried to play one side against the other, but in 1169 were compelled to submit to the Zangid general Salah ad-Din, who abolished the Fatimid Caliphate in 1171, reestablishing Sunni Islam in Egypt. The Fatimids were the last Arab dynasty to rule Egypt. From this point on the country would be under the control of Turks and related peoples from the eastern Islamic world, a situation that would continue until the 1952 revolution.

In theory Egypt was now a part of the Zangid empire, ruled by Nur ad-Din, a man dedicated to *jihad* against the crusaders; in reality it was firmly in the hands of his Kurdish general Salah ad-Din. Refusing to leave Egypt until it was secure from crusader attack and Fatimid resurgence, Salah ad-Din fell out with his master who wanted Egypt's resources for his own war effort. Sending only apologies and excuses, Salah ad-Din set about building a power base. His enlarged army was stationed in the newly constructed Citadel, situated on an outcrop of the Muqattam hills, about halfway between Al-Qahirah and Fustat. The two urban centres were linked to the new fortress by a series of walls, to facilitate the defense of the Egyptian capital, setting the stage for the future development of one unified city.

In order to uproot the memory of Fatimid rule, Al-Qahirah was deprived of its royal status by being opened to the common people. A huge northward population shift followed, resulting in the decline of Fustat as the major centre of trade and production in Egypt. A new educational system, based upon the *madrasah*, a state supported institution for the teaching of Islamic law, was introduced from the east to ensure the establishment of an orthodox Sunni bureaucracy.

Traditional festive sugar dolls, called "brides".

Only *madrasah* graduates, well grounded in Sunni legal practice, would be employed in the new government of Salah ad-Din.

Resisting the Crusades: The death of Nur ad-Din in 1174 and the subsequent break-up of this empire left Salah ad-Din undisputed master of Egypt. He spent the next 13 years conquering the divided Zangid principalities of Syria and placing them under the control of his family, the Ayyubids. With Egypt and Syria once again united, Salah ad-Din turned his attention to the crusaders, who were decisively defeated in 1187.

The capture of Jerusalem and Palestine established Salah ad-Din as a champion of Islam, but also triggered off the Third Cru-struggles that dominated Ayyubid internal politics. As the head of the family, the Sultans of Egypt had the right to demand military aid from their brothers and cousins in Syria, but this was often reluctantly given, the minor princes being more afraid of their Ayyubid neighbours than of an external enemy. The Sultans, as a result, were hesitant about engaging in serious warfare, preferring to use diplomacy to achieve their aims. In particular, military conflicts with the Christians of the Palestinian coast were avoided as a matter of policy, out of fear of sparking off a new Crusade.

The Sultan Al-Kamil (1218–38) was able to defeat a Christian invasion of the Nile

sade in 1189. Led by Richard the Lion-Heart of England and Philip II of France, the Christians retook Acre, but were unable to advance further. The peace settlement of 1192 recognised Salah ad-Din's gains, leaving the crusaders in possession of a small coastal strip of Palestine. Salah ad-Din died the following year a satisfied man.

The Ayyubid empire created by Salah ad-Din was a federation of sovereign city states, loosely held together by family solidarity. The rulers of Egypt, the wealthiest and most centralised of the provinces, exercised a vague suzerainty over their kinsmen, which they used to limit the endless intrigues and power Delta in 1221, but to avoid a repetition of the experience came to a peaceful agreement with the Holy Roman Emperor Frederick II in 1229, whereby Jerusalem was declared an open city, accessible to Muslims and Christians alike. This solution to the crusading problem proved unpopular with religious fanatics on both sides and hostilities were soon resumed.

The last major Ayyubid Sultan, As-Salih (1240–49), whose ruthless rise to power had made enemies of most of his relatives, could

Brick architecture and lattice-work windows at Rosetta.

no longer rely on the support of his Syrian kinsmen. Faced with the growing threat of a Mongol invasion from the east, led by the sons of Jengis Khan, who had already devastated Iran and eastern Europe, As-Salih began building a Turkish slave army, loyal only to him, to defend the Ayyubid state.

The fighting abilities of As-Salih's new military slaves or Mamluks, who were known as the Bahris after their original barracks next to the Nile River (Bahr al Nil), were put to the test in 1249, when the 6th Crusade of St Louis IX of France invaded Egypt. During the course of the hostilities As-Salih died, but news of his death was concealed by his wife, Shagar ad-Durr (Tree of Pearls) and the Mamluk amirs, to allow his son, Turan Shah, to reach Egypt and claim the Sultanate. Turan Shah arrived in time to witness the defeat of the French king by the Mamluks in 1250. Alarmed by the power of the Bahris, the new Sultan began to replace them with his own men. But the Mamluks were not to be ousted so easily. Instead, they murdered Turan Shah and seized control of Egypt.

The Bahri Mamluks: To legitimise their *coup d'état*, the Mamluks proclaimed Shagar Ad-Durr Sultan on the strength of her marriage to As-Salih. The Ayyubid princes of Syria, refusing to accept the loss of the richest province of their empire to a woman, prepared for war. Needing a man to lead her army, Shagar ad-Durr married the Mamluk commander, Aybek, who now ruled as Sultan with this new wife. The Ayyubids were defeated in 1251 and Aybek, encouraged by his victory, conquered Palestine.

To strengthen his position, Aybek in 1257 began negotiating a second marriage with a princess of Mosul. Unwilling to share her power with another woman, Shagar Ad-Durr had her husband murdered in his bath. Aybek's Mamluks, enraged by the death of their master, seized his queen and handed her over to the former wife of Aybek, whom he had been compelled to divorce by Shagar Ad-Durr upon becoming Sultan. Egypt's only woman Sultan was then beaten to death with wooden bathclogs in front of her rival.

The Mamluks had proved their military prowess against the crusaders and the Ayyubids, but were now called upon to face a far greater threat, the heathen Mongols, who in 1257 swept through Iraq into Syria, brutally crushing all Muslim resistance.

Undefeated in battle and with the resources of an empire stretching from China to the borders of Egypt, the Central Asian hordes seemed on the verge of extinguishing Muslim civilisation in the Middle East. Only the Mamluks remained to stop them and at the battle of 'Ayn Jalut in 1260 they did, becoming the saviours of Islam.

Under their first great Sultans, Baybars al-Bunduqdari (1260–77) and Qalawun (1280–90), the Mamluks emerged as the foremost military power of their age. Kept in top fighting shape by the constant threat of the Mongols, now centred in Iran, the Mamluks recaptured Syria and expelled the last of the crusaders from the Palestinian coast.

The Mamluk system: The political system created by Baybars was based on a military slave oligarchy. Young Qipchaq Turks would be brought to Egypt as slaves, converted to Islam and given a thorough military training. On completion of their education they would be freed and enrolled in the private army of one of the great Mamluk amirs, who collectively controlled all of Egypt's resources and governmental positions. The most powerful amir would be chosen as Sultan. Although the position possessed certain military advantages, the Sultan was rarely strong enough to dispense with the services of the men who had brought him to power.

The foundation of the system was the intense loyalty the individual Mamluk felt for his military house (*bayt*). His political fortunes were linked to those of his amir, whose rise or fall in the state hierarchy would determine his own advancement. If his *bayt* was successful, the common Mamluk could expect to be promoted to the rank of amir and in time even to the Sultanate. Success required great solidarity, however, coupled with extreme ruthlessness in the struggle with the rival houses. The Mamluk political environment was therefore dominated by intrigue and the striving for power amongst the *bayts*. The Sultan tried to manipulate these conflicts to maintain his position, but if he was unsuccessful, he would be destroyed by the ambitions of his amirs.

Position within the Mamluk hierarchy was dependent upon slave origins. The children of Mamluks were prevented from following their fathers' military career and as a result the army required a steady flow of new Turkish slaves to replenish its ranks.

The reign of An-Nasir Muhammad: The one exception to this rule was that the son of a Sultan often succeeded his father as a stop-gap ruler without power, allowing the amirs time to determine who was the strongest without resorting to civil war. Once this issue had been decided the son was deposed and replaced by a Sultan with real authority. In this manner Qalawun's son An-Nasir Muhammad was made nominal Sultan by his father's amirs in 1294, at the age of nine. After ruling for a year he was deposed, but then reinstated in 1299, when the amirs fell out amongst themselves.

Having been raised in an atmosphere of intrigue and double-dealing, An-Nasir emerged at the age of 25 as a ruthless, suspicious and absolutely despotic Sultan. Resolving to rule alone after the miseries of his youth, he murdered the amirs of his father one by one, replacing them with his own men. Unwilling to trust even the amirs of his own *bayt*, An-Nasir inaugurated an era of peace to prevent arming a potential rival with the command of an army. A period of flourishing trade and great prosperity ensued, the apex of Muslim civilisation in Egypt.

An-Nasir was a great builder and patron of the arts; and it was under his rule that Cairo grew into a single unified city, filled with great palaces and splendid mosques. The mosque of Al-Maridani, completed in 1341, survives as a testimony to this golden age of Mamluk architecture.

An-Nasir's success in mastering the Mamluk system brought about the beginning of its decline. So firmly did he hold the reins of power that on his death in 1341, no amir was strong enough to replace him. Instead he was succeeded by a series of weak sons and grandsons.

His policy of peace, while filling the state treasury, caused the Mamluks to neglect their military training. A whole generation grew up without ever having fought a major war, a serious deficiency for a state founded on martial superiority. Instead the Mamluks devoted themselves to competing with each other for political and cultural preeminence. Their lust for power was matched only by their love of luxury and of grand buildings, with which they continued to beautify Cairo.

The reign of Sultan Hasan (1347–61) saw the outbreak of the Black Death, which rocked the economic foundations of Egypt by decimating its population. Whole districts of Cairo were wiped out, indirectly benefiting the Sultan, who inherited the property and valuables of the plague's victims. With this unexpected windfall Hasan financed his great mosque, completed in 1362, the grandest of all Mamluk buildings

The Circassian Mamluks: For 41 years after the death of An-Nasir, 12 of his direct descendants ruled Egypt as nominal Sultans. In 1382, however, the Amir Barquq (1382–99) seized control and began distributing all positions of power to his fellow Circassians. This second Mamluk dynasty maintained the same political system as the Qipchaq predecessors. An important difference, however, was that the Circassians were brought to Egypt not as boys, but as young men. Instead of being moulded by the rigours of a Mamluk education, they arrived in Cairo with clear ideas of how to manipulate the system to their own benefit. Ambitious, unruly and deficient in their military training, they were a terror to the inhabitants of Egypt, but poor soldiers.

Unable to defeat the invading Tamerlane in 1400, the Circassians watched helplessly as the new Central Asian conqueror devastated their Syrian province. Repeated outbreaks of plague throughout the 15th century decimated the ranks of the unacclimatised Mamluks, whose replacement was both costly and difficult. The threat of strong neighbours and the chronic outbreak of factional fighting at home further drained the treasury, forcing the Sultans to adopt the short-sighted economic policies of excessive taxation, debasement of the currency and the introduction of state-owned monopolies.

Despite the decline in their military and economic position, the Circassian Mamluks continued to live and build in the grand Bahri manner. The Sultan Qaitbay (1468–95), a master politician, managed to maintain the prestige of the Mamluk state, while devoting himself to his true love, architecture. His tomb complex in the Northern Cemetery is the most refined and elegant of his many great works.

The chief failing of the Circassians, however, was their refusal to adopt modern military methods. Bred to be a cavalry elite, they despised gunpowder as unmanly. Their major rivals in the early 16th century, the Ottoman Turks, had no such snobbish qualms.

When the two forces finally clashed at the battle of Marj Dabiq in 1516, the Mamluks were literally blown off the field by superior cannon fire. Following this victory, the Ottoman Sultan Selim the Grim conquered the Mamluk Sultanate and Cairo became provincial capital of a new Muslim empire centred in Istanbul.

Egypt as an Ottoman province: The Ottomans, engaged in continual warfare with Iran and the Christian West, could not afford to spare the necessary men to uproot the Mamluks from Egypt completely. Instead the Mamluks were incorporated into the Ottoman ruling elite and held in check by a provincial governor and a garrison of crack

ally transformed Ottoman Cairo into an economic backwater, sustained largely by a newly-developed trade in coffee.

In the 17th century, military defeats brought decline to the Ottoman empire. Rampant inflation, caused by the flood of Spanish silver from the New World, upset the balance of power in Egypt. The office of governor was now sold to the highest bidder, and then re-sold at the first opportunity, to supply the central treasury with a steady flow of cash. The governors, rarely ruling for more than three years, could never therefore establish effective control over Egypt. The Janissaries, forced into local trade by the steady devaluation of their salaries, became little more than armed shopkeepers

Ottoman troops, the Janissaries. The Mamluks were therefore allowed to maintain their *bayt* system, continuing to import new Circassian slaves, albeit on a drastically reduced scale.

Cairo, although no longer a major political centre, remained an important commercial emporium, despite the loss of much of its international trade to Europe. The Europeans had been forced by the high prices caused by the Mamluk monopolies to search for new routes to the East that bypassed Egypt. The discoveries of Columbus and da Gama gradu-

Above, painting on the wall of a house in Luxor.

and artisans.

The rise of 'Ali Bey al Kabir (1760–72) saw the remergence of the Mamluks as an international power. By destroying the rival *bayts*, the governor, and the Janissaires, 'Ali Bey became master of Egypt with the title "Shaykh al-Balad". While expanding his revitalised empire he was on the verge of reestablishing the Mamluk empire when he was betrayed by his lieutenant Abu'l-Dhahab, secretly in the pay of the Ottomans.

Deprived of its strong leadership, the Mamluk *bayt* of 'Ali Bey fragmented and Egypt was plunged into a devastating civil war which lasted until 1791. Although order was restored by the victory of Murad Bey and Ibrahim Bey, the economy of the country was in ruins. In this unsettled state, Egypt was invaded in 1798 by the French under Napoleon Bonaparte.

The French Expedition: On the morning of 21 July, 1798, not quite under the impassive gaze of the Sphinx, the combined musketry and artillery of 29,000 French troops smashed a headlong onslaught of Mamluk cavalry. Like Alexander the Great's conquests 21 centuries earlier, which led to a millennium of European dominance in the Mediterranean, the Battle of the Pyramids marked a turning of the tide against the East. It also roused Egypt from the slumber of 300 years as an Ottoman province.

The conquest of Egypt was ostensibly carried out on the orders of Bonaparte's superiors in Paris, whose overt objective was to threaten Britain's lucrative Indian trade from a Middle Eastern stronghold. In fact, however, the French expedition was largely inspired by irrational factors, of which by no means the least was Bonaparte's own romantic pursuit of glory, his notion of the inevitable triumph of will: like Alexander's Greeks and Macedonians, the new European invaders were led by a charismatic young fanatic who habitually confused his own lust for power with the destiny of his people.

A scientific mission comprised of 60 *savants* accompanied the expedition. Their task was to compile a complete dossier on Egypt's antiquities, people, topography, flora and fauna producing a massive *Description de l'Egypte*.

Bonaparte's expedition was doomed right from the start. Within just seven days of the raising of the *tricolore* over Salah ad-Din's Citadel, the British had summarily sunk the French fleet off Abu Qir and the Mamluks under Murad Bey had fallen back to Upper Egypt, from which they continued to conduct a successful guerilla war.

In Cairo, Egyptians meanwhile looked upon Bonaparte's attempts to clothe the ideals of *liberté, egalité,* and *fraternité* in the veil of Islam and to pose as the liberator of the country from the wicked Mamluks with equal scorn. While he strutted about in oriental garb, hobnobbing with the sheikhs of Al-Azhar, his officers, constrained by the loss of their gold with the sunken fleet, imposed extortionate taxes on the populace. Resist-

ance was met with the burning of villages and daily beheadings at the city gates.

Hoping to regain momentum and impress his constituency in France, Bonaparte decided to embark on a campaign in Palestine. Again, superior French artillery brought quick victories. Gaza fell within a few days, then Jaffa, where he had 2,000 Turkish prisoners herded down to the beach and shot in cold blood. These efforts to terrorise opponents into submission failed, however, and at the fortress of Acre in northern Palestine the French were brought to a halt. Reinforced from the sea by a British fleet, the Turkish garrison held out for two months, while Bonaparte's army was decimated by malaria and dysentery. By the time he opted for retreat, his force had dwindled to 15,000.

Despite the propaganda churned out in Arabic by his printing press – the first in modern Egypt – his attempt to portray the Palestine *débâcle* as a victory was not greeted with enthusiasm in Cairo. At last, with communications to Paris cut by the marauding British, his own troops disillusioned, he wisely concluded that his personal ambitions were unlikely to be served by further lingering. Fourteen months after his arrival, Bonaparte packed his bags and slipped home in such apparent haste that General Kléber, Bonaparte's second-in-command, received the first news of his appointment as the new General-in-Chief of the Army of the Orient scrawled on an abandoned scrap of notepaper.

Although the French remained in Egypt two more years, defeating two Turkish attempts to dislodge them, the hopelessness of their mission finally forced them to succumb. Kléber was assassinated at Azbakiyyah in June of 1800 and the task of negotiating with an Anglo-Ottoman force that landed in the Delta in the autumn of 1801 was left to his successor. Mercifully, the French, now numbering only 7,000 were allowed to return to France. In three years of occupation, they had failed to meet any of their strategic objectives. Britain still dominated the seas, the Ottomans had reinforced their hold on the Levant, and the Egyptians, though impressed by the power of European science, technology and military organisation, had rejected what little they saw of the infidel's civilisation.

Turco-Syrian tiles at Cairo's Mosque of Aqsunqur.

75

Muhammad Ali Pasha, who ruled for nearly half a century, is credited with having laid the foundations of modern Egypt. In addition to building an empire, he carried out reforms aimed at modernising Egypt and founded the dynasty that was to rule the country for a period of almost 150 years, until the revolution of 1952.

Muhammad Ali was born in 1769 in Kavalla, Macedonia, in what is now part of modern Greece, but then belonged to the Ottoman Empire. Early in his career he served as a tax collector, then obtained a commission in the imperial army, entering Egypt as second in command of an Ottoman army sent to join the British in expelling the French, who had occupied the country since 1798. After the French and British troops left Egypt, the Ottoman troops stayed on to reassert the Sultan's authority.

During the four ensuing years, however, Egypt was reduced to a state of anarchy, with Mamluk beys fighting among one another and against the Ottomans, who were divided along ethnic lines and fought among themselves. In 1805, having had enough of chaos, the people of Cairo finally turned to Muhammad Ali to restore order, naming Muhammad Ali the new viceroy. Such an appointment was the prerogative of the Sultan in Constantinople, but the Sultan, presented with the *fait accompli*, confirmed the Cairenes' choice.

Nevertheless, Muhammad Ali's position as viceroy was tenuous. Defeating a British force at Rosetta in 1807 consolidated his power, but bold steps were still required. Boldest and bloodiest was his extirpation of the rebellious Mamluk beys. On the 1st of March, 1811, he invited 470 Mamluks to a ceremony in the Citadel. Assembled to take their leave, the departing Mamluks had to pass through a narrow passageway to a locked gate, where the Pasha had arranged for their massacre. For the next 37 years his authority was absolute in Egypt.

Preceding pages: interior of the mosque of Muhammad Ali at the Citadel, Cairo. Left, a contemporary engraving of Muhammad Ali Pasha with his *shibuk*.

A new empire: Among Muhammad Ali's best known undertakings are his military conquests. In 1811, at the request of the Turkish Sultan Mahmud II, he sent troops into the Arabian province of the Hijaz to combat the Wahhabi movement, a fundamentalist sect of Islam that threatened the Sultan's authority. In 1816 Egyptian troops entered the Nejd, the Wahhabi's homeland, and by 1818 all of western and central Arabia was under Egyptian control.

After the Arabian campaigns, Muhammad Ali sent an expedition under one of his sons up the Nile to gain control of the Sudan's mineral resources and its active slave trade, which he saw as a possible source of manpower for the army. Next came campaigns in Greece. At the request of the Sultan, an army commanded by his son Ibrahim was sent to Crete in 1822 to quell an uprising against Ottoman control. In 1824 a second expedition, again commanded by Ibrahim, sailed from Alexandria for the Morea, now known as the Peloponessus. This reassertion of Ottoman power provoked the major European states, Britain, France and Russia. An allied fleet sent to mediate ended by sinking the entire Egyptian fleet at Navarino in 1827.

Muhammad Ali's last successful expansionist venture was his Syrian expedition of 1831. Using a quarrel with a governor as a pretext, he sent in Ibrahim with an army of peasant conscripts. At the end of 10 months all of Syria had acknowledged him as overlord. In 1832 Ibrahim pushed on into Anatolia, defeating the Ottomans at Konya. Before he could occupy Constantinople, however, Russian intervention again brought European interests into play; and in 1833 an agreement was signed between the Sultan and his unruly vassal, by which Egypt was formally accorded rule over Crete and Syria in return for an annual tribute.

With the Sudan, the Hijaz, and these new acquisitions, the Egyptian empire rivalled the Ottoman in size, although Egypt itself was still nominally a part of the Ottoman empire and Muhammad Ali still only a Pasha, the Sultan's viceroy. In 1839 the Sultan attempted to regain Syria by force. Ibrahim's own crushing victory over an Ottoman army at Nezib was followed by the desertion of the Ottoman navy to Alexandria and these two events led to a European crisis. Britain, Russia and Austria sided with the Sultan, while France supported Muhammad Ali. British and Ottoman troops invaded Syria, a British fleet anchored off Alexandria, a British squadron occupied Aden, and France mobilised for a European war. This catastrophe was averted when Muhammad Ali signed an agreement by which his rule was to be made hereditary, but which also confirmed the Sultan's suzerainty.

The terms of this suzerainty were agreed upon under European pressure in 1841: the Egyptian navy, forbidden to build new ships, the massive upgrading and extension of Egypt's irrigation system and the introduction of a multitude of exotic plants, many of them now naturalised in Egypt. Rice, indigo and sugarcane were massively encouraged, as well as the cultivation of long-staple ("Egyptian") cotton, which would later become the country's principal export. By 1840 he had planted more than 16 million trees and built roads and bridges where none had ever existed. Before Muhammad Ali, in fact, Egypt was a country where wheeled vehicles had long since passed out of use.

Land tenure and tax systems he reformed by nationalising all property and making himself titular owner of all land. Govern-

was virtually abolished; the Egyptian army was reduced to 18,000, who were to wear Ottoman uniforms and be led by Ottoman senior officers; all of Ibrahim's conquests were to become Ottoman provinces administered directly from Constantinople; and the viceregal succession would devolve upon the eldest male of the Muhammad Ali line.

Modernising on all fronts: Shorn of his acquisitions abroad, the Pasha turned his remaining energies back to the task of modernising Egypt. The ultimate aim of these endeavours may have been his family's aggrandisement, but the benefits to his country were enormous. They include, for example, ment monopolies marketed almost all important goods and agricultural produce, paying the peasants fixed wages calculated to encourage production. The new scheme eliminated the iniquitous tax farming system that had prevailed earlier; and it is generally agreed that the lot of peasants was somewhat improved, especially after 1841, when they could go back to tilling the soil. They still remained liable to the *corvée*, however, an obligation to provide labour for such public works as cleaning canals, which would become increasingly resented. The population nearly doubled during Muhammad Ali's reign, approaching 5 million in 1848.

Muhammad Ali also created modern industries in Egypt, initially to supply his army and navy, but later the whole country. Beginning with an industrial complex at Bulaq, the Nile port of Cairo, where the famous Bulaq Press was set up, he built shipyards, foundries and armament factories. Textile mills, the basis of the European Industrial Revolution, soon followed. Since a primary aim was to avoid dependence upon Europe, the infant textile industry was protected by embargoes and subsidies, but this step toward economic independence was foiled, like his foreign policy, by European interests: the provisions of 1841 made Egypt subject to the tariffs that prevailed through the Ottoman empire, allowing cheaper imports, mainly from Britain, to flood into Egypt.

created, the first in Egypt since the Ptolemies. Subsequently suppressed by the British, the system had already produced future leaders, who would not rest until it was revived, to become the core of the present Egyptian educational system.

The one subject on which Muhammad Ali is known to have been fanatical was public health. Swamps were drained, cemeteries were moved, hospitals, infirmaries and asylums were built, a school for midwives was established, and French-trained physicians were appointed as public health officers in all provinces to see that measures were carried out. In Cairo accumulated rubbish was cleared and seasonal ponds, like the famous

In other respects his efforts were more successful. The Bulaq Press was to become the most distinguished publisher in the Arab world. Its production of printed books was an essential element in the creation of a new intellectual élite, which would gradually replace the European experts recruited during his early years in power. To form this élite, new secular educational institutions were

Left, Muhammad Ali Square, Alexandria. **Above left**, Ibrahim Pasha; and **right**, Khedive Ismail, a spendthrift but a visionary ruler.

one at Azbakiyyah, were filled, while the beginnings were made of a new street system that would allow the use of wheeled vehicles. The city's dancing prostitutes, who appear to have fascinated European visitors of the period, were banished to Upper Egypt.

In Alexandria Muhammad Ali established a Quarantine Commission, thus identifying the city once again as the country's main port of entry. Shipyards, military bases and a new palace for the Pasha himself were made practicable by digging a new canal to link the city once again with the Nile. Entire new quarters would be laid out in the European style, as it became not only the country's summer capital, but also the home of its largest foreign enclave, enriched by the cotton trade. It was here that the Pasha died in 1849, 80 years old, but predeceased by his son, the gallant Ibrahim, to whom he had given the viceregal throne 11 months before.

Muhammad Ali's successors: Ibrahim's death was unfortunate, since he had shown himself to be a good leader. His nephew, Abbas, the only son of Muhammad Ali's second son, Tussun, became viceroy and immediately rejected all his policies. While Muhammad Ali had been eager for Western agricultural and technical ideas, particularly those of the French, Abbas was xenophobic, disliking the French in particular and favouring the

When Abbas was murdered in 1854 by two of his personal bodyguards, his uncle Said, 9 years younger, but the eldest of Muhammad Ali's surviving sons, succeeded him. Said again reversed the direction of the government, favouring a return to his father's programmes and to abandoned projects in irrigation, agriculture and education. The railway opened in 1855 and Said's private train is in Cairo's Railway Museum.

Open to European influences, Said is perhaps best known for his friendship with Ferdinand de Lesseps, to whom he granted a concession for the Suez Canal. As originally granted in 1854 this concession was one of the great swindles of all time, with terms

Le Caire
Ataba-el-Kadra

British, to whom he granted a railway concession. He summarily expelled all the French advisors upon whom his grandfather had depended, closed all secular or European schools, and turned for support to religious leaders. He was as autocratic as his grandfather, but earned the gratitude of the peasants by his negligence, which left them in comparative peace, even though he milked them by restoring the old tax-farming system. Apart from the British railway completed after his death, the sole positive relic of his 6-year rule was that he left full coffers and no foreign debt, an accomplishment that his two successors were unable to repeat.

extremely disadvantageous to Egypt. Recognising later the enormity of his error, Said managed to have it renegotiated and got somewhat more favourable terms, but only at the cost of an indemnity of more than 3 million Egyptian pounds. To pay this sum he was forced to take Egypt's first foreign loan, thus not only setting a dangerous precedent, but planting a time-bomb under his successor Ismail, the third of Ibrahim's four sons, who became viceroy on Said's death in 1863.

Ismail the Magnificent (1863–79): Under Ismail's rule the modernisation begun by Muhammad Ali moved forward with new dynamism. Reviving his grandfather's policy of independence from the Sultan, Ismail sought to transform Egypt into a country that Europe would respect in European terms.

In 1866, by payments to the Sultan and an increase in tribute, he secured a change in the hereditary principle from seniority to primogeniture, thus guaranteeing the throne to his own line, and permission to maintain a standing army of 30,000. The same year he summoned the first Chamber of Deputies, a move that pleased the Europeans as representing a step towards constitutionality. The following year he obtained the Persian title of Khedive ("Sovereign"), borne by his heirs down to 1914, as well as the right to create institutions, issue regulations, and conclude

the State Railways, Minister of Endowments and Minister of Public Works. Ismail and Mubarak had thus known Paris as it was before the Second Empire: an essentially medieval city, largely slums and only partially touched by modernisation under Bonaparte, dirty, ill-drained and picturesque, where noisy alleys overhung with washing wound among decayed palaces and townhouses, which now served the poorer part of the population as tenements.

When Ismail saw the transformation wrought by Haussmann – the new city, with its broad boulevards and parks – he was dazzled; and on his return to Egypt he sent Mubarak likewise to have a look, appointing him Minister of

The Suez Canal

administrative agreements with foreign powers without consulting Constantinople. His new independence was signalised in June 1867 by Egypt's autonomous participation in the Exposition Universelle in Paris.

Ismail had been sent as a student to Paris by Muhammad Ali in 1844, one of a delegation of 70 that also included a young man named Ali Mubarak, whose talents approached genius in several fields and who would later serve Ismail as Minister of Education, Director General of

Left, Ataba Square, Cairo, circa 1910. **Above**, before the advent of air travel, the Suez Canal was the main link between Europe and Asia.

Public Works in the meantime. The result was the transformation of Cairo.

The changes made in the city during the few months just before the opening of the Suez Canal, in 1869, were the culmination of five years of feverish modernisation throughout the country. Two other major canals, the Ismailia, connecting Cairo with the Great Bitter Lake, and the Sweetwater, joining it to supply the length of the Canal zone, had already been completed. Municipal water and gas companies had been set up in 1865 and Cairo's main railway station had been inaugurated in 1867, completing a system hundreds of miles long that included the new cities of Port Said and Ismailia. Telegraph linked all parts of the country.

Foreign debts come home: The Sultan's response to the festivities at the Canal opening, however, was to send Ismail a decree forbidding him to undertake foreign loans without approval. A massive bribe secured confirmation in 1873 of all the rights obtained earlier, as well as permission to raise a large army, for which Ismail had hired American officers, Northern and Southern veterans of the Civil War. The American war had already brought wealth to Egypt by raising the price of cotton, enriching the new class of landowners that Said and Ismail had created. Since the Khedive and his family still owned one-fifth of Egypt's cultivable land and managed it along the most up-to-date lines, much of the new wealth came Ismail's way. Not enough, however, even coupled with Egypt's tax revenues, to keep pace with his ambitions, his largesse or his financial carelessness. In the confusion of public and private exchequers, colossal debts had been run up, prompting professions of alarm in Paris and London, where Ismail's independence was already being regarded as a threat to the *status quo.* Meanwhile his country itself looked increasingly tempting, not only as a strategic base or a source of raw materials, but as an expanding market for European manufactured goods.

Most of the debt was the result of swindles, perpetrated by European adventurers who had been arriving in Alexandria since the reign began. The largest swindle, like the first of the debts, was an inheritance from Said: the Suez Canal, built using the *corvée,* at Egyptian expense. In 1875, after swinging another huge loan of which he saw only a third in cash, Ismail was forced to sell his shares in the Canal Company to Britain, which then sent out experts to look into his debts. An Anglo-French Dual Control set up to oversee his finances began creaming off three quarters of the annual revenues of Egypt to pay European creditors.

Ismail was forced to liquidate his personal estates, which included several factories, and to accept British and French ministers in his cabinet. Adroitly playing the few cards left to him, he evaded a complete takeover of his government until finally the Europeans lost patience. Putting pressure on the Sultan, they had Ismail deposed, the acting British and French Consuls-General delivering the telegram to him in person.

Intervention and occupation: His son Tawfiq, whom Ismail himself later described as having "neither head nor heart nor courage", was no match for adversaries who had defeated his father and thus broken the mainspring of Khedivial power. But the army made a stand. The chief spokesman, a senior officer named Ahmad 'Urabi, was appointed Minister of War and thus found himself at the forefront of Egyptian resistance to further European intrusion.

Presented abroad first as a military dictatorship, then as an anarchy dangerous not only to European interests, but also to the Sultan's, this situation provided the final excuse for intervention. Over the Sultan's protests, British warships bombarded Alexandria on 11 July, 1882. Hoping to regain status after repeated humiliations through the instrument of these invaders, Tawfiq abandoned his own government and put himself under their protection. Support for a provisional government also melted away. Near the end of August, 20,000 redcoats were landed on the supposedly sacrosanct banks of the new Suez Canal and two weeks later the Egyptian army under 'Urabi was crushingly defeated at Tell al-Kabir.

Thus ended 19th-century Egypt's double experiment at modernisation, twice halted by European displays of power, though the cultural, social and even physical marks left on the country by Muhammad Ali and Ismail have so far proven indelible.

British rule: Evelyn Baring, who became Lord Cromer in 1891, first came to Egypt in 1879 as the British financial controller during the Dual Control of France and Britain. He stayed only briefly in that capacity, but returned in 1882 as the Consul-General.

In 1882, the British government promised an early evacuation of its troops, but they lingered on and more and more British subjects arrived in Egypt to form a civil service corps. Since the British refused to formalise their presence, the British Consul-General, although officially vested only with the same powers as other consuls-general, became the *de facto* ruler of Egypt, with absolute authority in both its internal and foreign affairs.

Despite his high-handed manner, Cromer is generally credited with having believed that he acted with the best interests of the rural masses at heart. Declaring himself "a friend of the peasants", for example, he abolished the hated *corvée*. And as the country became financially solvent and even prosperous during the relative stability of the Pax Britannica, taxes were rationalised and eventually lowered. To other Egyptians, however, he was less sympathetic.

The most important achievements during this period were the completion of the Delta Barrage in 1890 and the building of the first Aswan Dam in 1902. Begun under Muhammad Ali, the Delta Barrage made double and triple cropping possible in the Delta, while the Aswan Dam, coupled with barrages at Asyut (1903) and Esna (1906),

Cromer therefore discouraged both industrialisation and higher education, putting an end to the kind of autonomous development that before the Occupation had made Egypt, with Japan, unique among countries of the non-Western world. It is therefore not surprising that the British occupation helped to solidify nationalist awareness in Egypt.

Abbas II Hilmi: This awareness received added stimulus after 1892, when Abbas Hilmi Tawfiq's 18-year-old son succeeded as Khedive. Educated at a Swiss school and at the celebrated Theresianum in Vienna, Abbas II was typical of the new Egyptian elite that had been created by Muhammad Ali's and Ismail's educational designs. In Egypt under

General view of the Nile Barrage.
Vue générale du Barrage.

extended the same system to Upper Egypt, reducing dependence on the annual flood.

By this time, cotton had become the mainstay of the Egyptian economy, accounting for 90 percent of foreign earnings in the period from 1900 to 1910. Other food crops, the most important of which was corn, continued to be grown and Egypt was still able to feed its growing population without depending on imports. Its role within the British Empire was essentially to supply raw materials and a market for manufactured items, like any other colony or possession.

Above, the Delta Barrage, completed in 1890.

Cromer, however, there was no real role for this elite or even for Abbas himself to play, as the Consul-General made humiliatingly clear to the young Khedive at the earliest opportunity. Abbas' response was to seek out the young nationalist leaders and provide them with financial support.

Al-Azhar, the great religious university founded by the Fatimids, which could claim to have served as the centre of Egyptian patriotism at many times in the past, was strangely quiescent during this period, though Cromer did not hesitate to raise the spectre of "Muslim fanaticism" with the politicians in London whenever it suited his purpose.

Egypt in the Gilded Age: Secular nationalism drew growing strength between 1890 and 1906 from the country's enormous prosperity, derived almost exclusively from cotton. Doubling production offset an initial fall in prices, which then nearly trebled. Despite the lack of an industrial base, real per capita income during the first decade of this period was to remain unsurpassed until the influx of petro-dollars in the 1970s. The land-owning class created by Said and Ismail grew even richer, merging with the old and new elites, and to share their wealth: Greeks and Italians chiefly, but also Britons, Frenchmen, Swiss, Germans and Belgians, all of whom received special privileges under the Ottoman Ca-

Europeans of another kind also flocked to Egypt during this period, but for briefer stays usually lasting only a single winter season: the aristocracy, for whom Egypt became, as Ismail had foreseen, the first of many playgrounds. Improved schedules and faster service had revolutionised steam travel well before the end of the century, making it possible then to get from London or Paris to Alexandria or Cairo with far more speed and ease by rail and ship than one can by the same means now. Shepheard's was already famous, but other celebrated hotels – the Savoy, the Continental, the Mena House, the Semiramis, the Heliopolis Palace – were all built between 1896 and 1910 to accommo-

pitulations, which granted them immunity to Egyptian laws and taxes.

In the last years of Cromer's proconsulship, as much as 50 percent of Cairo's population growth could thus be attributed to European immigration; and by 1914, more than 90 percent of the paid-up capital of all companies registered in Egypt would be in European hands. Cairo and Alexandria were irrevocably transformed by the real estate boom of 1896–1907 into European-looking cities, as Muhammad Ali and Ismail had intended, while European dress, already customary at the courts of Muhammad Ali's successors, became the middle-class norm, as it is today.

date the tastes of a rich and titled clientele.

The Dinshwai incident: As Cromer approached retirement from Egyptian service in 1906, he was contemplating changes to allow for more self-government, but his autocratic rule had left him few friends in the country. And in that year the Dinshwai Incident occurred. Casually shooting domestic pigeons that belonged to peasants in the Delta village of Dinshwai who tried to stop them, a group of British officers wounded a woman and four men. Outraged villagers

Above, a contemporary cartoon showing anti-British riots at Aswan in 1919.

86

surrounded them, beat them, then held them to await the arrival of the police. One of the officers escaped and ran through the noonday heat to a nearby British army camp, but collapsed and died of sunstroke just outside the camp entrance. A peasant who had tried to help him was beaten to death on the spot by British soldiers. This murder was subsequently forgotten. To consider charges of murder against the villagers of Dinshwai, however, a special Tribunal was set up.

Composed of two Egyptians and three Englishmen, the Tribunal met in Dinshwai for 30 minutes then, out of 52 accused, sentenced eight villagers to lashes, 11 to periods of penal servitude ranging from a year to life, and four – including a 17-year-old boy and a 60-year-old man – to hanging. Though public executions had been outlawed two years earlier, the villagers of Dinshwai were forced to witness the carrying out of these sentences.

No one connected with this incident – to which Egyptians could only respond with helpless grief – was ever forgiven.

Cromer's successor as Consul-General, Sir Eldon Gorst, spoke Arabic, having lived many years in Egypt, and was ready to effect change in British policy. He cultivated a friendship with the Khedive, whom he permitted to wield more power, and undertook several reforms. Egypt's first secular university was allowed to open in 1908 and provincial councils were encouraged towards more autonomy. Unfortunately Gorst's arrival coincided with a worldwide slump. Blamed for the ensuing crash, his policies were resented by British civil servants in Egypt and misinterpreted as signs of weakness by Egyptians. In 1910, recognising their failure, he resigned and Lord Kitchener succeeded.

Kitchener had served as Commander-in-Chief of the Egyptian army and knew Egypt well. He introduced new regulations for censorship, school discipline and the suppression of conspiracy. Once again the Khedive came under the Consul-General's strict authority. In 1913, however, he introduced what seemed to be a liberal reform: a new constitution that provided for a Legislative Assembly. It met only once before World War I broke out.

The Protectorate (1914–22): The outbreak of the war was the catalyst for a series of important events. Severing the 400-year-old Ottoman connection, Britain declared Egypt a protectorate, thereby finally formalising the authority it had had for the past 32 years. Martial law was imposed and Kitchener left to assume supreme command of the British forces. Abbas Hilmi, who had been in Constantinople when the war started, was forbidden to return, then declared a traitor and deposed. His two young sons being excluded from succession, his uncle, 60-year-old Husayn Kamel, was made ruler, with the title of Sultan, by the British. There was little enthusiasm in Egypt for either side in the war, but much resentment of the arrogance of British power.

At the end of the war, the nationalist movement was stronger than ever and a dynamic new leader had emerged to direct its efforts. Saad Zaghlul was an Azhar-educated lawyer of pure Egyptian peasant ancestry. Imprisoned briefly for his participation in the resistance of 1882, Zaghlul later practised law for several years. During this period he married the daughter of a pro-British Prime Minister, and was shown favour by Cromer, who appointed him Minister of Education. It was not until the Protectorate was declared in 1914 that, angry at Kitchener's treachery to the constitution he had supported in 1913, Zaghlul joined the nationalist ranks.

Emergence of the Wafd: As soon as the armistice was signed, Zaghlul requested the British government to be allowed to go to London to present Egypt's case for independence. Although High Commissioner Sir Reginald Wingate recommended that Zaghlul's request be granted, London refused. This uncompromising position only hardened nationalist sentiment, and by early 1919 they were demanding no less than complete independence, with representation at the Peace Conference in Paris. Following demonstrations in Cairo, Zaghlul and three other nationalists were exiled to Malta.

This provoked the successful uprising that Egyptians refer to as the Revolution of 1919. Violence was accompanied by a general strike that engaged Christians and Jews, as well as Muslims, of both sexes and all social classes. A Field-Marshal, Lord Allenby, was sent to replace Wingate, recalled because of his support of the Egyptians' demands. After appraising the situation, however, Allenby promptly brought Zaghlul home from exile, and gave him permission to go to Paris. With other members of the Wafd, as his followers had come to be called (*wafd* means "delegation" in Arabic), Zaghlul attended the conference, but failed to secure his major objective. On the same day that the Treaty of Versailles was signed Allenby issued a proclamation reaffirming the Protectorate.

The Wafd, headed by Zaghlul, came to speak for the whole country during this period. In fact, its ranks consisted mostly of Egyptian professionals, businessmen and landowners, whose interests the Wafd represented right up until the time all political parties were outlawed under Nasser.

In November 1919, the British government decided to send a mission to Egypt to study and make recommendations on the form of a constitution for the Protectorate. Acknowledging that "nationalism had established complete domination over every social and articulate element", however, the mission's report recommended that although Britain should maintain military forces in Egypt and retain control over foreign relations, the protection of foreign interests and the Sudan, Egypt should be declared an independent country. But the report was not published until the end of 1921, and meanwhile Zaghlul was arrested and exiled again.

For his part, Allenby had privately made conclusions similar to those of the mission though he did not hesitate to assert British authority by liberally using British troops to quell unrest. In February 1922, upon his return from a visit to England, he bore a proclamation unilaterally ending the Protectorate, but reserving four areas of British control. Three weeks later Egypt's independence was officially declared; and Sultan Fuad, chosen by the British from among several candidates to succeed his brother, Husayn Kamel, upon the latter's death in 1917, became King Fuad. A constitution based on Belgium's was adopted in 1923.

Fuad as King (1922–36): The Wafdists at first rejected this declaration of independence, with its four "reserved points". When Zaghlul was finally allowed to return, however, they sought to participate actively in the upcoming elections, which they won by an overwhelming majority. Zaghlul became the Prime Minister in early 1924.

As Prime Minister, Zaghlul gave up none of his demands connected with completing independence, which included the evacuation of all British troops and Egyptian sovereignty over the Sudan. His hopes for the fulfillment of these demands were raised, when a Labour government came to power in England. Less than a year after the Wafd's landslide victory, however, the assassination of Sir Lee Stack, the British Commander-in-Chief (Sirdar) of the Egyptian army and Governor-General of the Sudan, put an end to optimism. Allenby delivered an ultimatum to the Egyptian government, though it had clearly not been responsible, making punitive demands. Badly shocked, Zaghlul accepted most of them, but refused to agree to the withdrawal of Egyptian troops from the Sudan, the right of Britain to protect foreign interests in Egypt, or the suppression of political demonstrations. Defiance seemed impossible, however, and he could only resign, leaving it to a successor to accept all the British conditions.

During this crisis, in December 1924, King Fuad took the opportunity to dissolve the Wafdist Parliament and rule by decree. When elections were held in March 1925 and the Wafd again won by an overwhelming margin, the King again dissolved Parliament. A third set of elections in May 1926 also gave the Wafd a majority, but the British vetoed Zaghlul's reinstatement as Prime Minister. His health already shattered by the Stack murder, which had betrayed him, Zaghlul died a few months later.

Royal dictatorship: Mustafa An-Nahhas succeeded Zaghlul as the leader of the Wafd and during the following four years, the struggle between the Wafd and King Fuad took the same pattern, with the Wafd winning general elections and the King dissolving the Parliament to appoint his own ministers. In 1930, Fuad appointed Ismail Sidqi Pasha as Prime Minister and replaced the 1923 constitution with his own royally-decreed one. Sidqi's three-year dictatorship was outwardly a period of relative calm and stability in Egypt. Two successors managed to maintain Fuad's constitution until 1935, when nationalist, popular and British pressure combined to force him to restore the constitution of 1923.

Negotiations for an Anglo-Egyptian treaty concerning the status of Britain in Egypt and the Sudan had long been underway, and the

By the beginning of the 20th-century, European dress was the norm for middle-class Egyptians.

21-7-1914

treaty was finally signed in August 1936. It became the basis of the two countries' relations for the next 18 years. Britain agreed to withdraw its troops from everywhere except the Suez Canal Zone, to support Egypt's desire to end the Capitulations (the old agreements, dating from the Ottoman Empire, that gave foreigners special privileges in Egypt, including exemption from Egyptian law), and to back Egypt's application for admission to the League of Nations, of which it became a member in 1937.

Faruq: After 1936, political leadership and the internal political situation both deteriorated. King Fuad died in April 1936 and his son, Faruq, still a minor, succeeded him. The

During the inter-war period, agriculture remained the backbone of the Egyptian economy but the native Egyptian middle-class began to invest in factories and the process of industrialisation began again, albeit in a modest way. This process was greatly stepped up after World War II and again after the military came to power in 1952. Along with industrialisation inevitably came urbanisation. Population pressure in rural areas encouraged migration from the country to the city by the rural poor in search of jobs. Beginning in the inter-war period, this shift has since helped to make Cairo one of the most densely packed cities in the world. But two-thirds of Cairo's population

Wafd split, and a new party – the Saad Wafd – was formed. Extremist organisations also emerged, such as Misr Al-Fatat, an ultra-nationalist pro-royalist group that combined elements of religious fanaticism, militarism and a deep admiration for Nazi Germany and Fascist Italy.

In 1928, Hassan Al-Banna had founded the Muslim Brotherhood, the stated aim of which was to purify and revitalise Islam. But the Brotherhood had political aspirations as well and began to take an active part in politics in the late 1930s. It has since been a force with which every Egyptian government has had to contend.

growth has been indigenous, reflecting the same processes that are rapidly urbanising the rural countryside itself.

World War II and its aftermath: When World War II broke out, Britain took control, in accordance with the terms of the Treaty of 1936, of all Egyptian military facilities, although Egypt itself remained officially neutral for most of the war. The government necessarily supported the British, but many Egyptians did not, while clandestine army groups and Al-Banna's Muslim Brotherhood not only rejected the idea of cooperation but secretly plotted the government's overthrow. In February 1942, with tanks drawn up in front of Abdin Palace, the British installed their own candidate as Prime Minister at gun-point, the Wafdist An-Nahhas, thus not only poisoning Anglo-Egyptian relations for more than a decade, but also discrediting the Wafd itself.

At the end of the war, Egypt was in a precarious situation. Prime ministers and cabinets changed often; the Wafd, the Saadist party and the king (whose wanton behaviour now alienated the Egyptian people) were mutually hostile. The Muslim Brotherhood had created a terrorist arm during the war to undertake violent action against the government and the British, and even communist elements were gaining strength.

organisations plotted rebellion independently and clandestinely.

The disastrous defeat of the Arabs – the Egyptian army at their forefront – in Palestine in 1948–9 fed fuel to the Muslim Brotherhood, whose volunteers had fought bravely, and its membership rapidly increased. The defeat also increased the disaffection of the army with both the palace and the government, which it accused of complicity in a scandal involving defective arms. Both the Muslim Brotherhood and the Free Officers plotted to take power; and to this end the Brotherhood carried out a series of terrorist operations, including the assassination of the Prime Minister, Noqrashy Pasha, in Decem-

Wishing you a Happy Christmas and a Bright New Year.

In addition a new political force had appeared, the Free Officer movement in the army, led by Gamal Abdel Nasser. Fiercely nationalistic, completely disillusioned with the government, it denounced what it saw as Britain's humiliating occupation of Egyptian soil. The leaders of the Free Officers were in contact with the Muslim Brotherhood and although some of the two groups' aims coincided, the Free Officers refused Al-Banna's offer to join forces. So the two

Left, a 1933 advertisement for Cook's tours. **Above**, British servicemen had these cards printed to give their correspondence an Egyptian flavour.

ber 1948. By now aware of the danger that the Brotherhood represented, the government retaliated with massive arrests of its members and Al-Banna himself was assassinated in February 1949.

Black Saturday: In 1950, riddled with corruption and bad leadership, the Wafd was again elected to power. It instituted disastrous economic policies, but sought to hold onto popularity by releasing many members of the Brotherhood, abrogating the 1936 treaty, and calling for the evacuation of British troops from the Canal Zone. Resistance to British troops in the Canal area took the form of guerilla action with the tacit approval of the government. In January 1952, a second Dinshwai occurred when the British besieged and overran a post manned by Egyptian auxiliary police, who fought to the last man. Rioting broke out in Cairo, which the authorities either would not or could not control. On January 26, the day known as Black Saturday, foreign shops, bars and nightclubs were burned and British landmarks such as Shepheard's Hotel and the Turf Club disappeared forever.

The climax came in the night of 22 July, when the Free Officers took over key positions in a bloodless *coup d'état* engineered by Nasser and other members of his organisation. In the morning of 23 July, the Egyp-

Italy on the royal yacht. The constitution was repealed and all political parties were suspended. In June 1953, the monarchy was formally ended and a republic declared.

General Neguib, brought into the Free Officers' plans late to serve as a figurehead, an older and respected officer to command the confidence of the people, was declared President and Prime Minister of the new republic. Other Free Officers were installed as his ministers, Nasser becoming Deputy Prime Minister and Minister of the Interior. Neguib tried to assert the authority he only nominally held, but by May 1954 Nasser was Prime Minister and virtual dictator.

Nasser's first important public act as Prime

tians were informed that the army, commanded by General Mohammed Neguib, had seized power. Disillusioned by both their corrupt and impotent government and their dissolute king, the Egyptian people greeted the news with joy.

The Nasser Era (1952–70): Lacking a specific programme other than to wipe out government corruption and instability and affirm Egypt's independence from foreign domination, the young officers moved quickly to consolidate their power. On 26 July, King Faruq was forced to abdicate in favour of his son, only 6 months old, and the same day he left with his family for exile in

Minister was the amicable negotiation of a new Anglo-Egyptian treaty that provided for the gradual evacuation of British troops from the Canal Zone. The agreement was signed in October 1954 after six months of negotiations. Although his opponents grumbled that it was not favourable enough to Egypt, since it provided that the British could use the Canal base in times of war, Nasser was generally hailed as the leader who finally ended foreign occupation in Egypt.

In April 1955, Nasser attended the Bandung Conference of Afro-Asian states, announcing soon after Egypt's commitment to positive neutrality or non-alignment and its refusal to join the Baghdad Pact, a military alliance including Iraq and Turkey, which the United States and Britain hoped to establish in the Middle East as a way of maintaining Western influence. With Nehru and Tito, Nasser became one of the leaders of the Non-Aligned Movement.

The turning point in political orientation away from the West came in June 1956, after the United States withdrew its financing for the High Dam at Aswan. Nasser nationalised the Suez Canal and announced that he would use the revenues from it to build the dam. His charismatic declaration provoked the fury of France and Britain, whose nationals owned the Canal; and with Israel they launched a

alleged opponents of the regime, the state's intelligence apparatus became the most important centre of power next to Nasser.

On the economic front, one of Nasser's first important policies had been the institution of land reform. Ownership of land was limited to 200 acres per person. Holdings beyond this limit – subsequently reduced many times – were taken over by the government and redistributed among the peasants. Otherwise the new regime remained conservative, encouraging private enterprise during at least the first four years of the Revolution.

Arab socialism: It was not until July 1961, five years after the Suez War, that Nasser

tripartite attack on Egypt. The invasion was ended by the intervention of the United States and the Soviet Union, forcing the three aggressors to withdraw. Nasser had won an important victory with very little effort and became the symbol of the defiance of imperialist domination. His popularity in Egypt and the entire Third World was assured.

This popularity persisted despite increasing repression in Egypt after the Suez War. Arresting thousands of communists, socialists, "feudalists", Muslim Brethren, and other

Left, King Faruq admiring a bust of his father, Fuad. **Above**, President Gamal Abdel Nasser.

adopted a comprehensive programme of rapid industrialisation, to be financed in part by nationalisation of all manufacturing firms, financial institutions and public utilities. The July Ordinances also limited land holdings to 100 acres per person and put a ceiling on salaries. Meanwhile, private property was confiscated from foreigners, members of the royal family and the rich in general. Bank accounts, land, houses, furniture, clothing, jewellery and even books belonging to 4,000 families were seized, in an effort to deprive the old upper classes not only of their capital assets and political influence, but also of the private culture that had set them apart from the masses. Created to further the new programme decreed that year, the Arab Socialist Union was to remain the only legal avenue for political activity open to the Egyptian people for more than a decade.

As Nasser built respect for Egypt abroad, he began increasingly to wave the banner of Arab unity. This new facet of his foreign policy led in 1958 to a union between Egypt and Syria, later joined by Yemen, called the United Arab Republic, which it was hoped all the other Arab countries would eventually join. Initially more enthusiastic than the Egyptians, the Syrians were soon disenchanted, first by the Egyptian bureaucracy, then by the July Ordinances, which toppled

The Six-Day War: The Arab-Israeli war of June 1967 was a blow from which Nasser never really recovered. Following growing tension in the area, he demanded in May 1967 that UN troops stationed in the Sinai be withdrawn and announced a blockade of the Straits of Tiran. Probably only bluff on Nasser's part, these moves were quickly taken advantage of by Israel. On 5 June, it launched a sneak attack simultaneously on Jordan, Syria and Egypt, wiped out the entire Egyptian air force on the ground, and in 6 days had occupied the Golan Heights, Gaza, Jerusalem, the West Bank and the Sinai. Israeli troops crossed the Suez Canal and were ready to march on to Cairo. Only a

their government. A new military regime took Syria out of the Union in 1961. Egypt nevertheless retained the name of the United Arab Republic until after Nasser's death. The anniversary of the union is still celebrated and Syria still flies the UAR flag.

Nasser's next unfortunate undertaking in the name of Arab unity and socialist progress was his 5-year embroilment in Yemen. He sent troops to aid republican forces there in 1962, while Saudi Arabia aided the royalists. The two countries did not withdraw their troops until 1967, when they were forced to come to an agreement in order to face a common enemy, Israel.

cease-fire quickly worked out by the United States and the Soviet Union prevented further disaster. After the war Nasser resigned, but resumed his post the next day following mass demonstrations for his return.

However popular he remained, the old charisma was gone and Nasser himself was a broken man. His announcement of a War of Attrition against Israel in 1969 merely encouraged Israeli attacks on civilian targets. Efforts to salvage a wrecked economy, no longer even agriculturally self-sufficient, proved fruitless. His last important act was an attempt to reconcile King Hussein and the Palestinians after the bloody events of Black

September 1970, when the king tried to crush the PLO in Jordan. In later September, he helped to negotiate an accord by which Hussein, Arafat and other Arab leaders agreed to end the fighting. He died of a heart attack the day after the signing of the accord and was escorted to his grave by more than three million people.

The Sadat era: On Nasser's death, Anwar Sadat, his vice-president, succeeded to the presidency. No one expected Sadat to last long in this position, but he proved more skilful than his opponents. In May 1971, with what he called a "corrective move-ment", he consolidated power by dismissing high-ranking government officials who

claimed it one, but it did allow Egypt to regain its national pride.

It also gave Sadat enough prestige to ig-nore Arab unity and seek a separate peace with Israel. The dramatic opening of this process was his visit to Israel in November 1977 during which he addressed the Knesset. The treaty process resulted in the Camp David accords, signed under US patronage in March 1979. Furthered by massive infu-sions of US aid, the accords were greeted in Egypt with euphoria, but this mood rapidly dissipated as differences between Egyptian and Israeli interpretations of them became clear. Arab countries meanwhile denounced the Camp David accords as treachery and

openly or secretly opposed him. Another surprise move the following year was the expulsion of the Soviet technicians, teachers and advisors who had been in Egypt for more than a decade. After a long period of close relations with the Eastern bloc, Egypt was turning towards the West.

Sadat's boldest initiative was his launch-ing of the fourth Arab-Israeli war in October 1973. The outcome of this war was by no means a total victory, although Sadat pro-

Left, desert flowers bloom in the debris of a recent war, Sinai peninsula. **Above**, T-shirt souvenir of Sadat's dramatic presidency.

expelled Egypt from the Arab League.

Sadat's economic policies, encouraging foreign investment and private enterprise, also created high inflation and widened dif-ferences between the new rich and older salaried classes, as well as the poor. The drain of Egyptian brains and brawn to neigh-bouring oil-rich countries meanwhile be-came a torrent, which would continue more or less unabated even after Camp David, when all other links between Egypt and the rest of the Arab world would be broken. Remittances from abroad, long the mainstay of the Syrian, Lebanese and Jordanian econo-mies, began to emerge as the single most important factor in the Egyptian economy. Property prices soared as returning Egyptians sought to invest income earned in Libya, Iraq, or the Arabian Peninsula in something safe back home. The impact of these revenues were ignored by government planners, whose economic models were geared solely to public-sector revenues.

An experiment in January 1977 – withdrawal of long-standing subsidies on basic commodities, unaccompanied by any promise of higher wages or lower taxes – led to two-day riots among the salaried and unsalaried poor and had to be cancelled. Reminiscent of Black Saturday, the violence was clearly directed at newly acquired wealth

and demonstrated widespread alienation.

The Arab Socialist Union was abolished and the beginnings of new political parties were formed.

The high-handed style of Sadat's government, in an atmosphere of corruption and crony capitalism, alienated many followers. Overt opposition began to gather round the new political parties, including a revived Wafd, while less public opposition crystallised in Islamic revivalism. Thanks to Sadat's lifting of systematic repression and to his encouragement of religion, the Muslim Brotherhood had regained most of its freedom of action, but there were other more radical

groupings, one of which was responsible for Sadat's assassination on 6 October 1981 during a ceremony commemorating the crossing of the Suez Canal.

The Mubarak years: After nearly three decades of authoritarian rule, Vice President Hosni Mubarak, a powerfully built former air force commander, ascended to the presidency. While honouring commitments made under Sadat's liberalised economic policies and at Camp David, Mubarak's regime curtailed corruption and tried to promote more democratic government. However, faced with providing for a rapidly growing population, Mubarak introduced tough financial controls. His abolition of subsidies on basics such as tea, fish and meat (though significantly not on bread) angered the poor, and the better-off complained about the high level of graduate unemployment.

His greatest challenge was presented by the Islamic Group (el-Gama'a el-Islamiya), whose aim was to oust Mubarak and turn Egypt into a fundamentalist Islamic state. A new domino theory was propounded by international diplomats, envisaging the rapid collapse of secular governments in neighbouring countries if Egypt were to fall to the fundamentalists.

The Islamic Group's attacks on tour buses, Nile cruise boats and ancient sites caused tourism, Egypt's biggest foreign currency earner by far, to plummet, further increasing unemployment and social discontent. The government reacted with a harsh crackdown. Hangings of convicted terrorists – the first since the aftermath of Sadat's assassination – were resumed in 1993.

Egyptian society has become very complex. The population is now mostly urban rather than rural, eats and sleeps surrounded by walls of concrete rather than mudbrick, and works in industry, commerce, services, or the governmental bureaucracy rather than in agriculture. Authoritarian structures, frequently bolstered in the past by middle-class fears of the masses, have come to be seen as not only contrary to the dynamics of recent Egyptian history, but as wasteful and inefficient. Increasing democratisation therefore has become the centre of Egyptian hopes.

Left, Anwar al Sadat, Egypt's second president. **Right,** Presidents Sadat and Hosni Mubarak pictured on posters.

Until 1965, when the Aswan High Dam held back its first flood, very few of the millions of structures built by Egyptians throughout their history were ever intended to last more than a few months or at most a few years. Imhotep's architectural revolution at Saqqarah made the permanence of building in stone possible as early as the 3rd millennium BC, but for most of the ensuing centuries the idea of permanence was extended only to religious structures. Even the pharaohs' palaces, for example, which must have been delightful, were built of perishable materials, essentially no different from those that went into the making of any typical villager's house before 1965. Ancient dwellings have therefore disappeared, while ancient religious structures, the pharaonic tombs and temples remain, their survival an anomaly. They are the most tangible link between modern Egypt and its ancient past.

Apart from the obvious motives provided by the necessity for maintaining Egypt's cultural heritage, the question of conserving pharaonic monuments involves two major considerations: archaeology and tourism. Once a building has been thoroughly documented, its archaeological purpose has been fulfilled; and as far as archaeologists are concerned it can then be filed away for future reference. When the Secretary-General of the Egyptian Antiquities Organisation officially requested a distinguished Belgian expert in 1946 to outline the best method for conserving a pharaonic tomb or temple, the answer was that a well-sealed door should be installed and that the whole monument should be reburied beneath the sand. And this method has actually been used, not only between digging seasons, but as a long-range tactic. In 1969, for example, the French Archaeological Institute, working in collaboration with the Antiquities Organisation, excavated and cleared an extraordinary 6th-century monastic complex near Esna, secured the necessary data, then reburied it, publishing a

complete report three years later. The site has thus been saved for future generations.

Putting the Sphinx on show: The Sphinx, now an endangered monument, might have been preserved by this tactic. Though cleared many times in its earlier history, it had been allowed to rest safely under sand until 1925, when it was cleared again and repaired. Since its stone is very soft, however, it is subject, once exposed, to massive erosion by the sand-blast of Giza's incessant winds. Chemical injections, intended to harden and con-

solidate the stone, were made, though the long-term effects of this were still unknown. Unfortunately, it resulted in weakening the Sphinx rather than strengthening it; and subsequent erosion is such that there are now fears that its head may topple off.

The Sphinx, like the Solar Boat and many of the painted tombs at Luxor, is thus rapidly being sacrificed to tourism, which is not only an important industry in general for Egypt, but also specifically supports the Ministry of Culture and all the activities of the Antiquities Organisation, recently renamed the Supreme Council for Antiquities (SCA), including excavation, restoration and conserva-

Preceding pages: the Pyramids of Dahshur, photographed by Francis Frith. **Left**, paw and head of the Sphinx. **Right**, Cleopatra, detail from the Temple of Dendera.

tion. Egyptian archaeologists therefore face a dilemma: their source of funding is also the greatest source of destruction.

The problem of the Sphinx underlines some of the other ironies surrounding reconstruction of pharaonic monuments, more and more of which is being undertaken primarily for the sake of tourism, rather than for purely archaeological reasons. Reconstruction may be archaeologically desirable and even necessary at certain sites, such as Saqqarah or the great temple-sites of Upper Egypt, where much of what the contemporary sees is the result of painstaking reconstruction by archaeological experts, who cleared away sand and reassembled jumbled heaps of stones in

Philae was famous throughout the Mediterranean world in antiquity and could therefore exercise a special claim to "preservation", as representing a vital part of an international cultural inheritance. But motives for moving the rock-cut Abu Simbel temples, unknown until 1813, are best understood as a mixture of the aesthetic, the commercial, and the purely sentimental. There were eccentrics among the archaeologists, indeed, who argued that the best way to preserve both Philae and the Abu Simbel monuments within the cultural heritage was to let them drown, as Philae had done annually since completion of the first Aswan dam in 1902.

It was precisely for the benefits of tourism,

their search for knowledge. Once documentation has been finished, however, most archaeologists can bring themselves to accept even a building's complete destruction with a certain equanimity, as they have had to do at Kilya, the great Christian site in the Western Delta, or at Fustat on the edge of Cairo.

Philae and Abu Simbel: The archaeological outcry over the Nubian antiquities doomed by the construction of the High Dam at Aswan thus had less to do with the wish to preserve what had already been recorded, for example, than with the loss or destruction of vast amounts of physical data that had not yet been archaeologically surveyed.

however, that both Philae and the Abu Simbel temples were moved to their present positions. Though Egyptologists are even more thrilled than other people by these two sites, neither of them represents the cutting edge of modern archaeological research; and the sums finally expended on these two projects – nearly US$30 million for moving Philae and more than US$40 million for Abu Simbel – probably amounted to far more than the total that had been spent on archaeology itself since the beginnings of Egyptology.

Urban conservation: Generally standing on rural or desert sites in isolation from present-day communities, pharaonic tombs and temples have little significance for local people unless they can be exploited for immediate material gain. Living and working near these sites long before the emergence of such modern abstractions as "the cultural heritage", Egyptian villagers have therefore used them only for their own evolving purposes, ignoring them otherwise, as photographs and drawings from the 19th century clearly demonstrate. Local indifference allowed them to tumble or be buried under sand, but also created an absence of environmental complication that has since made many of them fairly easy to excavate, clear, reconstruct, record, restore and eventually conserve.

This situation contrasts totally with that of

has known earthquake, plagues and fires, but (uniquely among Middle Eastern cities) has never undergone the utter devastation that follows political, economic, or cultural irrelevance – these materials have ensured that Cairene buildings dating from the 7th century onward still remain more or less intact.

Secular buildings frequently fell victim throughout the middle ages to new architectural schemes, but street patterns were maintained and religious buildings were often restored by succeeding generations, embedding them so firmly in the urban environment that they largely define it. Conservation of Islamic streets and individual monuments thus involves not only questions of

Egypt's medieval and modern monuments, nearly all of which stand in the urban setting of Cairo. The ancestors of Cairo, moreover, were not only the mudbrick towns of the Old and New Kingdoms, but also the cities of the Hellenistic world, typified by Ptolemaic Alexandria, where the notion of architectural permanence had been extended for the first time in Egypt to secular buildings, making it a "city of marble". Burnt brick and stone thus became the materials of the new metropolis. Coupled with a remarkable history – Cairo

Left, scene at Karnak Temple, Luxor. **Above**, the Temple of Abu Simbel on Lake Nasser.

cultural heritage, archaeology and tourism, but also a host of other considerations, including all the usual concerns of the cityplanner, ranging from sociological issues to problems of rehabilitation, water-supply, electrification and sewerage.

Egypt's first conservation organisation, the Khedivial government's Committee for the Conservation of Monuments of Arab Art, was set up in 1881 specifically to protect medieval Islamic buildings, which had not only fallen into dilapidation, but were additionally threatened by new development. Many had in fact already been sacrificed to Ali Mubarak's master plan under the Khedive

Ismail, while work on reconstructing pharaonic monuments, by contrast, had hardly begun. The committee's criteria and techniques were identical with those of similar European organisations and are now quite out-dated, but during its 70 year existence it completed some remarkable tasks, beginning with an index of 800 buildings.

In 1952 it was absorbed into the Antiquities Organisation, under the Ministry of Culture, which carried out practically no urban or medieval restoration or conservation for nearly 30 years, largely because it had no access to its own revenues. The result, by 1980, was near-disaster. Apart from the conditions caused by modern traffic, industriali-

sation, declining cultural and economic levels, and increasing population density, the city's water delivery and sewerage systems had collapsed, raising the water-table in some places almost to the surface, well above the impermeable footings so cleverly installed by medieval builders. Walls soaked up water or drew it up by capillary action and began to disintegrate, while badly restored or un-repaired roofs began to collapse.

Great changes have taken place since 1981. There is no programme for urban rehabilitation, a normal component in any large-scale restoration scheme, but from 1982 onward the organisation at least tackled the problem of the medieval monuments themselves. Gaining access to its own revenues, it spent millions of pounds and was largely successful in carrying out not only restoration but urgently needed repairs. An earthquake in 1992 showed that there is still a great deal to be done, however, and some city areas have hardly been touched.

But Cairo's special favour comes from its combination of the medieval and the modern: its 19th and early 20th-century buildings are as important to its character as its great Mamluk monuments, to which they are often directly related. Many of these buildings, like Ismail's elegant streets, parks and squares, have already fallen victim to tasteless and shoddy development.

Awareness of their value to the city as a whole, however, has spread recently even into the public sector. A stiff new law passed in 1983 brought regulations up-to-date, covering all historic buildings and their environs with new protection but excluding those less than 100 years old from registration on the Index except by specific decree. The fate of Cairo's later neo-Islamic, Beaux-Arts, Art Nouveau, and Art Deco buildings thus still hangs in the balance. Moratoria on building permits, arising directly out of public dismay at what seemed to be the city's wholesale destruction, have slowed the pace of their disappearance dramatically, however, and a campaign mounted since 1985 has already succeeded in indexing a handful of the most important.

The conservation of entire areas, now the norm in European or American practice, has not yet been tried in Cairo except in limited zones – such as the Citadel or the enclosure of Babylon at Misr al-Qadimah (Old Cairo) – where the SCA has complete control.

Beyond all these concerns, of course, is the question of caring for the environment throughout Egypt as a whole. Today's tourist is attracted by precisely the same qualities that will make the country likewise attractive to future Egyptians themselves. To squander natural and cultural resources now is therefore to make the country not only less liveable in the future, but also less viable as a place anyone would want to visit. That fact is beginning to be thoroughly understood.

Left, Al Azhar, the world's oldest university and a centre of Islamic teaching, under restoration. **Right**, the mosque of Al-Hakim.

103

When God created the nations, so Arab wisdom has it, he endowed each with two counterbalanced qualities: to the intelligence of the Syrians he thus added fatuousness; to Iraq he gave pride, but tempered it with hypocrisy; while for the desert Arabs he compensated hardship with good health. And Egypt he blessed with abundance at the cost of humility.

It does not require a deep understanding of the past to feel that as far as Egypt is concerned God has withdrawn the first half of his covenant – or that, at any rate, He's made a new deal with the desert dwellers. As any Egyptian will explain, it is not many generations since Egyptian donations fed the poor of the holy cities of Mecca and Medina, in what is now Saudi Arabia. To the desert Arabs, however, God has recently given abundance, in the form of oil, while Egypt, formerly the land of plenty, has received unaccustomed hardship, in the form of war and overpopulation. Once the breadbasket of the Roman Empire, Egypt now follows only Japan and Russia as an importer of food and only India in the league of aid recipients.

Grace under pressure: Yet poverty is a relative thing and, perhaps because of their humility, Egyptians bear it with considerable grace. In the poorest hinterland of the south, a foreign traveller recently overhead a conversation between two venerable farmers: "These poor Europeans," said one, "They will do anything to escape their horrible climate. I saw one the other day who'd come all the way here on a bicycle." "Yes," replied the other, "their land is covered with ice all year round. Look at us. We've got sunshine, water, everything." "It is indeed terrible," concluded the first. "The *khawaga* I saw didn't even have money to buy proper trousers – he was riding about in his underwear!"

Egyptian humility takes many forms. One is a tragic sense of life, arising from a tragic view of history. While the West embraces the idea of progress as a solution to all man's ills, the Egyptians, who have a great deal more experience to draw on, have an impulse to turn towards a utopian past, perhaps to a time when Muhammad's successors, the four Rightly-Guided Caliphs, brought justice, prosperity, and true belief to the land.

The defeat suffered by Egypt in the 1967 war, one of the most humiliating in modern times, would have brought on a revolution in almost any other country. Yet when Nasser, in an emotionally charged speech, offered to resign, the response was dramatic: millions of Egyptians poured into the streets demanding that he stay. His willingness to share their humiliation brought forth instant sympathy from the Egyptian masses, who saw it as more important that his intentions had been morally right than that he had failed to realise them in actuality. His tragedy was, after all, theirs – the tragedy of decline that is repeatedly embodied in their history.

Islam and popular piety: Any visitor to Egypt will be struck by the piety of its people. Humility is inherent in the very word Islam, the religion of nine-tenths of Egyptians. Islam (from the Arabic root *salima*, to be safe; *aslama*, to surrender; *salaam*, peace) means "submission", whether it be to God, to fate, or to the social system framed by the Qur'an.

Most Westerners find the continuing dominance of Islam in what purports to be an age of reason perplexing. The important thing to recognise is that the Qur'an – literally, a "recitation" – is the word of God in Arabic as directly transmitted by Muhammad. The power of the Word thus has a strength in Islam unmatched by the literature of any other "revealed" religion; and the beauty of the Qur'an, by definition "inimitable", is cited as a miracle in its own right. It is not extraordinary that many modern Egyptian tastes, habits, and preferences are referred directly back to the Qur'an.

While there are many atheists and agnostics in Egypt, the vast majority stick tenaciously to belief in a supreme deity and the imminence of the Day of Judgement. The month-long, dawn-to-dusk fast of Ramadan, still officially observed by the entire country, bears witness to Islam's pervasiveness, but even the Coptic minority, conscious of being members of one of the earliest Christian sects, maintains a degree of devoutness that is often bewildering to Western Christians. Religious expressions of a kind that have almost vanished from European speech proliferate in everyday language. "God willing", "By God's permission", "Praise God", "Our Lord prevails" – all are as common as the word "Goodbye" is in English. But Goodbye long ago lost its original religious meaning while in Egypt such meanings have not been forgotten. The proper response to the greeting *Salam aleikum* (Peace be upon you) is thus *Aleikum as-salam wa rahmat Allah wa barakatu* (Upon you be peace and the mercy of God and his blessings).

temples; and magicians, witches and priests do a brisk trade in spells and potions.

Jest, gibes and practical jokes: Egyptian piety is also balanced by a deep love of mischief. If anything can compete in public esteem with holiness, it is wit; and Egyptian humour holds nothing sacred. Political jokes are particularly sharp and irreverent, but Egyptians make use of the smallest incident to provoke laughter. In a café or bar, wisecracks are fired back and forth with increasing hilarity until the whole company falls off their chairs.

Sages have often remarked that while the condition that formulates much of Western behaviour is the sense of guilt, arising from

Apart from piety, however, this exchange also reflects a point of Arab etiquette – any greeting must be followed by a response that outdoes the first speaker in politeness – and religiosity, though abundant, is not always heartfelt. The 19th-century chronicler Edward Lane observed that "it is considered the highest honour among Muslims to be considered religious; but the desire to appear so leads many into hypocrisy and pharisaical ostentation."

For many, particularly the poor, belief in the supernatural extends beyond orthodoxy to a world of genies and spirits of the dead. Fertility rites are still held in Upper Egyptian

an individual "conscience", in the East in general it is shame, arising from a sense of public disapproval or contempt. Egyptian children, raised with the idea that whatever you can get away with socially is morally permissible, must rank among the world's most naughty. This trait sometimes persists into adulthood, where it is reinforced by a cultural backlog of wise-guy folk-heroes such as the legendary Goha, whose countless exploits are marked by both asinine failure and impudent success. More locally and historically, Egyptian mischievousness has its roots in the legacy of centuries of repressive government. Numerous are the stories that celebrate the victory, through cunning and trickery, of the poor *fellah* over wicked pashas or foreigners.

This love of trickery has its drawbacks, as the 15th-century Egyptian historian Al-Maqrizi noted in an unflattering portrayal of his countrymen: "That which dominates in the character of the Egyptians is the love of pleasure... They are extremely inclined to cunning and deceit."

Maqrizi notes, among other things, that the Egyptians of his time showed a distinct disdain for study. This indifference to study, it must be said, is very pronounced to this day, in a tendency to attempt to achieve goals by means other than hard labour and careful

more than political exigencies, the heavy presence of police throughout the country. Belief in the need for coercion and forced restraint is strengthened by religious attitudes. It is commonly presumed that without the just guidance of Islam, society would fall apart. Yet many Egyptians rightly contrast the violence of American society and the high levels of suicide in other countries with the peace and security of Egyptian life. Where else in the world can two people let themselves go in argument and attack each other in the street, knowing that any passerby who is a good Muslim is duty bound to intervene? For this reason few arguments turn more than gently physical.

planning, a habit of mind that even President Mubarak castigates in his fellow citizens. Although much of it can be attributed to overcrowding and a faulty educational system, the degree of cheating in Egyptian schools and universities is scandalous.

Coercion and conformity: Shame has other manifestations. Unjustly, Egyptians are generally not trustful of one another, believing that it is only by overt pressure that people can be prevented from overstepping the bounds of morality. This attitude explains,

Attitudes to sex are also framed by the same phenomenon. Women are constantly pestered in the streets, largely because it is believed that really masculine men cannot resist the temptations of sex. The same is held to be true of women – perhaps even more so. Thus foreigners often find the Egyptian atmosphere highly charged sexually, which explains the Victorian view of Egypt as a land of licentiousness, a view that is still part of the Western mythology of the Orient in general.

Until the Western sexual revolution of the 1960s, Egyptian views of the issue were certainly far more healthy and uncomplex

<u>Left</u>, village girl. <u>Above</u>, desert-dwelling Bedouin gathering firewood.

than those prevailing in the West. Sex in all its aspects is openly discussed by both men and women, but also lurks at the edges of even ordinary conversation. Since the Arabic language itself is full of sexual innuendoes, its richness lends a wonderful bawdiness to Egyptian talk.

The mazes of matrimony: Marriage, however, is deemed an absolute prerequisite for sex, as well as for full adulthood and respectability. Particularly among women, whose freedom is still very much limited by rigid social norms, finding and keeping the right husband is thus the major focus of life. Since the 1920s, when the veil was finally discarded, substantial progress towards equality of the sexes has been made, but it is still the rule for a girl to remain in the care of her father until the day she is passed into the care of her husband.

Respect for parents and elders is so strongly ingrained that it is likewise uncommon for even a male child to leave home before marriage; and these days, few urban Egyptians can afford to marry before the age of 25. Despite Islam's flexibility on the subject – easy divorce and polygamy are both sanctioned – marriage is regarded as a binding agreement, made more absolute by economics. For this reason, young couples are expected to work out every detail of their future life – housing, furniture, a dowry for the wife as a form of divorce insurance – before signing the contract.

Extravagant weddings testify to the importance of the institution. Wealthy families will blow thousands of pounds on a binge in one of the five-star hotels, complete with a fanfare of trumpets, lurking video crews, famous belly dancers, singers and other entertainers. The weddings of poor families are equally extravagant – they too are expected to flaunt their pride and generosity – and much more fun. Whole streets are closed off and the affair takes place in the open air. Street musicians, acrobats, boy dancers, and slick masters of ceremonies keep things lively as the male guests tuck into the free beer, hashish, and opium.

"Money and children," the Qur'an says, "are the embellishments of life." Egyptians adore children, and large families are the norm. In many ways, the family is more important than the individual as a social unit, extending not only over several generations

but also to distant cousins. The fierce vendettas which still rage in Upper Egypt, often claiming dozens of lives over many decades, illustrate this point. Family honour and prestige are serious matters, particularly in the countryside. The crime columns regularly tell of adultery-related murders: a woman's honour, it is said, "is like a matchstick: it can only be used once."

In the cities, political and business alliances are often reinforced through marriage. Because numerous children enlarge the family's potential for wealth and influence, and also because it is believed that it is healthier for children to grow up with lots of brothers and sisters, family planners have had a hard time bringing down the birth rates.

Egyptian mothers are notoriously soft on their children. Centuries of high infant mortality, sexual roles that give house-bound wives complete responsibility for children, and lingering belief in the power of the evil eye mean that mothers are inclined to cater to their child's every whim for fear that some harm may befall him or her. This is particularly true in the case of favoured boys. It is not uncommon, in fact, for a woman's strongest emotional tie to be with her eldest son rather than her husband. As infants, children are wrapped up in swaddling and thoroughly doted upon. By the time they are old enough to walk, however, they are usually left to spend their time as they wish. This unorthodox combination of coddling and freedom is often cited as a reason for the strength, self-confidence and even obstinacy of the Egyptian character.

Life-support systems: Beyond the family, Egyptians have a strong attachment to their immediate community. Village solidarity – when not torn apart by blood feuds – is extremely strong. In the big towns the *hara* or alley is the main unit of social bonding. Partly because crowding in the poorer districts limits privacy, people help each other out in innumerable ways, lending money, sharing videos, and even testifying against strangers to the police.

The main function of *hara* solidarity is to defend the interest of the community. Gangs of local toughs, whose mandate varied from protection of neighbourhood women against strangers to simple extortion rackets, formed

Right, portrait of a man in full traditional garb.

part of the urban landscape until quite recently. One of the toughest gangs in Cairo ruled the neighbourhood around Bab Zuwayla and was run by a lady famed for knocking men out with a head butt. Such drama is rare nowadays, but it is true that strangers are carefully watched. Foreigners are deemed unworthy of this kind of attention, but young unmarried Cairene males seldom venture into a strange neighbourhood alone.

Peculiarities of places: Regional loyalties persist strongly as well. Each major town and province has its acknowledged characteristic, from Alexandria in the north to Aswan in the south. Like the inhabitants of other port cities, Alexandrians are known

sneer at less sophisticated compatriots, a Cairene habit that their country cousins do not find endearing. Caireness on vacation are apt to pine for the bustle and crowds of the metropolis.

The Saidis are the Polacks of Egypt, with the difference that the traits attributed to them – simple-mindedness, credulity, and impulsiveness – have a remarkable ring of truth. Saidis joke even about themselves, being too open-hearted to pass the buck. A sample joke: an Alexandrian, a Cairene and a Saidi are dying of thirst in the desert when a genie appears and allows each a single wish. The Alexandrian says, "I wish I were on the beach at Montaza surrounded by girls",

chiefly for their toughness and willingness to fight, but also for their cosmopolitan outlook and business acumen. The peasants of Lower Egypt and the Delta are regarded as hardworking, thrifty, and serious-minded. Rashidis, from Rosetta, are supposed to be kindhearted, while Dumyatis, from the town of Damietta at the Nile's eastern mouth, are reckoned to be untrustworthy. Menufis, from their province in the heart of the Delta, the homeland of Presidents Mubarak and Sadat, are renowned for their cunning.

Cairenes, like New Yorkers or Cockneys, are seen as slick, fast-talking and immoral. Simply being from the capital allows them to

and vanishes. The Cairene says, "I wish I were praying in the mosque of Hussein in Cairo", and vanishes. The Saidi, looking dismayed, turns to the genie and says, "I'm so lonely. Couldn't you please bring my friends back?" On the positive side, Saidis are noted for their generosity, courage, virility and sense of honour.

The dark-skinned Nubians of the far south, an ancient people with their own languages, are considered to be the most gentle and peaceful of Egyptians. Long isolated by the cataracts that made the Nile above Aswan impassable, Nubian life, relaxed and care-free, had a unique charm. Nubian villages are spotlessly clean, the spacious mudbrick houses always freshly painted, and both men and women are apt to be more enterprising than their Egyptian neighbours.

The desert Bedouin, of which there are numerous tribes, have not given up their ancient occupation of smuggling, and fierce tribal loyalty is still maintained. The Bedouin are feared, scorned, and envied for the wild aristocratic wilfulness of their ways. The old rivalry between these freewheeling bandits of the desert and the hardworking peasants of the valley has all but died out – largely through intermarriage – but their pure Arab blood and the beauty of their women still inspire admiration.

bourhood to the region to the nation and even beyond, is to prevent being pushed around.

It is characteristic of the Egyptians – with the exception, naturally, of the Saidis – that they prefer compromise to conflict. By inclination, habit and training, Egyptians are tactful and diplomatic, even to the point of obsequiousness. The proverb "Eat what appeals to you, but wear what appeals to others" embodies a cardinal rule. This rule governs not only what Egyptians wear – all but the poorest of the poor take care never to appear in public unless clean and neatly dressed – but also all but the most intimate of conversations: speech with a stranger should thus adhere to the traditional formulae of

Pride and prejudice: But this catalogue of accepted regional differences obscures an essential homogeneity of attitudes and feelings. Despite differences and despite the bitter legacy of imperialism – of defeat, occupation and dependence – pride in Egypt and "the Egyptian way" is fervent. An old Arab adage: "I and my brothers against my cousins, I and my cousins against my tribe, and I and my tribe against the world" serves to illustrate this point. The purpose of all allegiances, from the family to the neigh-

Left, three generations of a Cairo family. **Above**, man, beast and waterwheel.

flattery and light-heartedness.

Forms of address in Egypt are complex and varied, as befits a highly stratified society. A taxi driver may be addressed, for example, as "O Chief Engineer" or "O Foreman". (Note that, when sitting in a taxi, one is a temporary guest and not merely a fare; it is therefore insulting for a lone male passenger to sit in the back seat by himself.) A person of high social standing should be addressed as "Your Presence", while a person of respectable but indeterminate standing is "O President" or "O Professor". An older person is "O Teacher" or "O Pilgrim", the latter referring of course to someone who has made the pilgrimage to Mecca. Even Turkish titles – *bey, pasha, hanem* – survive, though they have no legal standing, and are used for courtesy's sake or alternatively for humourous effect.

This diversity, while lending a great deal of charm to the simplest exchanges, in fact underlines the cohesiveness of the society rather than its disparateness: the Egyptian world-view sees all men as equals, but allots to each a specific status and with it a role. It is often remarked how Egyptians act out these roles with a sense of the dramatic. Nowhere are bureaucrats so bureaucratic from head to toe, rich men so fat, criminals so comically sinister, movie stars so glitzy,

palling squalor, their homes nestled among putrid mounds of refuse, which they bring from the city, sort through and sell for recycling. The *zabbalin* represent the absolute bottom of the social pile, but their very existence testifies to general poverty. It would take the average worker a year to earn the price of a Cairo-New York round-trip ticket.

Display of wealth in Egypt is often, to Western eyes, vulgar. But the flaunting of riches only confirms that, in a society forced to count pennies, money carries a special prestige. As a rich merchant, whose lifestyle is otherwise modest, commented, "Yes, I would rather have spent my money on something other than a Mercedes. But you

intellectuals so full of *angst*, or mothers so haplessly maternal. Egyptians prefer to look like what they are.

Making do: As in many other Third World countries, sharp disparities of wealth exist. There are some 50,000 millionaires, and for a time in the late 1970s, poverty-stricken Egypt was importing more Mercedes cars than any other country in the world. On Cairo's streets the contrast between the elegance of imported luxury and the rolling slum of a packed bus or the pathetic heap of a trash-collector's donkey cart is shocking.

Trash collectors, known as *zabbalin* or "garbage people", live in conditions of ap-

wouldn't believe how much it saves me. I don't have to waste time – or money – proving myself. I get instant respect."

Open doors, closed options: Materialist ostentation has been particularly rife since the mid-1970s, when President Sadat reversed 20 years of socialist legislation with the announcement of his Open Door policy. Before him, Nasser had worked to redistribute the country's wealth, parceling out the great feudal estates, seizing the property of the richest families and reinvesting it in new state industries. Nasser's policies brought dignity to the majority at the expense of the few, but also frightened off private initiative.

Not many landlords bothered even to paint their houses, for fear of attracting the tax man. With the Open Door policy, the lid was abruptly removed; and luxury imports boomed as money came out of Swiss banks or from under the floorboards.

Allowing Egyptians underpaid at home to work profitably abroad, the Open Door policy has brought improved living standards in the form of more TVs, more cars, better clothing, and a richer diet, but it has also inflated expectations and undermined social cohesiveness. Neither the poor nor the old elites approve of the *nouveau-riche* of today.

A country without dreams can be a depressing place. The primary condition of

Four wars in 30 years, after three of which the army had to re-equip from bootstraps to fighter aircraft, imposed an immense sacrifice on the Egyptian people. Shortage of cash meant that no more than temporary relief could be found from the burdens imposed on an already inadequate infrastructure by a burgeoning population. Only when the flow of foreign aid began to pick up in the late 1970s could the government begin to tackle such basic and long-term problems as sewage, electricity, telephones, drainage, traffic and drinking water.

Products of a school system that stifles curiosity and promotes learning by rote, more and more young Egyptians feel a sense of

Egypt – too many people – doesn't help. In 1968, when Israel was revelling in its conquest of the Sinai peninsula and half a million inhabitants of the cities along the Suez Canal had been made homeless, a journalist asked President Nasser what his major worry was. Without hesitation, he replied, "The thousand new Egyptians born every day." A generation later, the population pyramid looms still more menacingly on the horizon. Schools in Cairo already operate three shifts and a new school must be built every day.

Left, funeral in the Fayyum. Above, native scene of a wedding. Tapestries are woven by children.

frustration regarding the future. Among men, those who do not go on to university or manage to obtain an exemption must face three years of military service, often under conditions of extreme hardship. In the bigger cities, many younger women find jobs before marriage, but the majority stay at home and hope for the best. Better prospects await the one in ten young Egyptians of both sexes who attend university, but the country's dozen institutions of higher learning are appallingly overcrowded, understaffed and disorganised.

Until recently, the government nevertheless followed a policy of providing employment for every university graduate. The result has been that the Egyptian bureaucracy and public-sector industry, which together employ half of the non-agricultural workforce, is catastrophically overstaffed. Various studies have shown that the average government employee actually works for between 6 and 30 minutes a day. Low salaries and lenient employment policies have encouraged apathy and abuses at every level – obstruction and obfuscation, absenteeism, corruption, or simply intolerable rudeness to the ordinary taxpayer, who foots the bills.

New anxieties: Low pay and a general loathing for the bureaucracy has meant that government jobs have lost must of their prestige. Increasingly one finds university graduates

working as taxi-drivers, plumbers, mechanics and the like. The money is better and tradesmen stand a likelier chance of saving in order to get married, though with inflation and the limited availability of decent apartments, many are obliged to scrimp for years before they can establish a household. In the past decade over three million Egyptians – a people famed for their love of home – have gone abroad, most of them with the sole purpose of saving enough money to get married. Since typical salaries in Egypt range from 75 to 150 pounds a month, emigrants can often earn as much in a couple of years in the oil-rich Gulf as they would in a lifetime

at home. Remittances from expatriates have become the key foreign currency earner for Egypt even above oil production but have also pushed up prices.

Universally aspired to in Egypt, marriage provides no passport to a life of ease. The typical lifespan is not long – perhaps 55 years – and many Egyptians appear to die of worry or grief before they reach the stage when they require medical care, which is frequently inadequate anyway. Money, in particular, causes endless anxieties; feeding, educating and underwriting the marriages of numerous children is not cheap, especially when respectability must be maintained at all costs. While families and neighbourhoods provide a degree of support unimaginable in the West, they also eliminate privacy; and the smallest problems quickly become everybody's business.

The housing shortage means that too many people are often cooped up in the same house, and there are districts of Cairo where the average density is three to a room. In such conditions, already living under constant emotional and physical strain, many Egyptians additionally face the sort of calamities that in other countries have been relegated to sensationalist fiction: collapsing buildings, bursting sewers, bizarre accidents caused by murderous traffic or industrial hazards, Kafkaesque lawsuits or impossible bureaucratic tangles.

Compensations: An atmosphere of melancholy pervades life, but strangely enough, the salient characteristic of the Egyptians is their cheerfulness. They are past masters at coping. All problems and situations are so endlessly discussed and analysed that they end by becoming mere topics of amusement. The tales of intrigue, frustrated love, good fortune or catastrophe that even the simplest people relate in connection with their own personal lives retain a quality of wonder reminiscent of *The Thousand and One Nights*. Everyone has a story.

The protective structure of society, based on the strength of family ties, allows Egyptian men and women to give free rein to their emotions. Families, neighbours and countrymen at large can all be relied on for compassion, commiseration or help. This solidarity makes Egypt one of the safest countries in the world. When someone shouts "Thief!" on the street, every shop empties as all and sundry help to chase the culprit, who is almost invariably caught and hauled off to the nearest police station by a gesticulating mob. Throughout Egypt, fewer murders are committed in a year than take place annually in any typical large city in America – a comparison reflecting the fact that Egyptian society allows fewer people to be marginalised. Every person has his recognised place in the scheme of things.

Among the few who are pushed to the margin are the intellectuals, those who take the facts of life or the issues of politics too seriously. Burdening oneself with principles runs contrary to Egypt's propensity for enjoying the moment. Laughter heals all wounds; and if Egyptian wounds are more

God), local kids try out the swings, shooting galleries and assorted tests of strength.

But even fun is not what it used to be. Respectable middle-class folk scorn the dowdy and unorthodox *mawalid*. Video tapes or television, with their fare of tinny, overdramatic soap operas, trashy foreign serials and official sloganising, now provide the entertainment of the majority. These appurtenances of modern life have a powerful effect in a largely traditional society. Glorifying the bourgeois and "liberal" attitudes of the city and thus homogenising Egyptian life, television has also deprived it of much of its vitality.

It will be a long time yet, though, before

than most other people's, so likewise are there few other peoples in the world who laugh so easily.

Time out: Egypt's true carnivals, in the form of *mawalid* or saint's days, offer a glimpse of this street energy in concentrated form. Push-carts hawking everything from plastic guns to chick peas sprout overnight, vying for space with the tents and sleeping bodies of country pilgrims. On the Big Night, while dervishes dance to exhaustion to the *dhikr* rhythms (chanting in remembrance of

Left, an *erqsusi*, a vendor of licorice drink. Above, Friday prayers at Al Hussein Mosque, Cairo.

the Egyptian people lose their appeal. Sensitivity and kindness still abound. Solicitous for the welfare of their fellows, Egyptians are invariably helpful, hospitable and friendly – indeed, almost to a fault: asking directions needs care, for example, since the response may be generated by a sense of social duty rather than by actual knowledge. Generosity is taken so much for granted that it is considered unseemly to offer thanks too profusely for a gift for fear of being insulting.

The warmth of human relations brings Egypt a *douceur*, a soft sweetness, even extended to visitors, that has always been the best part of its charm.

In crowded Egypt, Allah can be counted on for two great mercies: endless sunshine and abundant free time. Small wonder that the street café, where much of these two great resources is spent, is so ubiquitous an institution. Few men – for the café, like much else in Egyptian society, is a solidly male preserve – permit a day to pass without killing a few minutes in a café exchanging jokes that turn the trial of life into a spectator sport.

When Edward Lane wrote his sociological classic *Manners and Customs of the Modern Egyptians* in the 1830s, he judged the number of cafés in Cairo at over 1,000. Then, as now, the café was the centrepiece of street life, the axis of commerce and the vortex of opinion. Given a similar ratio of one café per 400 people, the megalopolis of today would contain over 30,000 such establishments.

Atmospheres: The *qahwa* – Arabic for both "coffee" and "café" – is defined loosely. It can be anything from a bench, a patch of charcoal, a tin pot and three glasses to a cavernous saloon reverberating with the clack of dominoes, the slap of cards and the crackling of dice. In Cairo, a café may serve as the headquarters of a street gang, the meeting place for homesick provincials, or the rendezvous of intellectuals. There are cafés for musicians, black marketeers, leftists, Muslim extremists, homosexuals, retired generals, pimps, and wholesalers. There is even a café for the deaf and dumb, where absolute silence belies the animated conversation conducted by gesture alone and where the waiter balances a tray in one hand and takes orders with the other.

The ideal café adjoins a small square in the back streets of a popular quarter. The simple decor of its exterior, replete with calligraphy and patterned tiles, will reveal the sense of style its patronage demands. The few outdoor tables will be shaded by a tree or vine, while the ground will have been sprinkled with water to keep down the dust. A pungent sweetness emanates from the interior, where sawdust covers the floor. An elaborate brass

Left, veteran smoker of the *sheesha* or water pipe. **Right**, the interior at Délices, a classically Alexandrine establishment.

sarabantina, a cross between a steam locomotive and a samovar, occupies pride of place on the counter at the back of the room, behind which striped glass jugs for water pipes line the walls. Just returned from the neighbourhood barber, the patron puffs judiciously as he takes in the crime column of the morning paper. The *qahwagi* or waiter keeps up a continuous banter between forceful shouts to the tea boy, meanwhile dodging the shoeshine man as he shuffles by, tapping his box suggestively with a brush.

Liquid incidentals: Atmosphere is only one of the pleasures the classier café offers. To begin with, of course, there is the pleasure of indulging in a hot drink. Tea, introduced in the 19th century has replaced coffee as the staple. The powerful Egyptian version of the brew takes some getting used to. Since cheap tea dust is the preferred variety, it is no use anticipating delicate flavour. Tea is drunk as a fix, as strong and sweet as possible. It is best to make no compromises with local taste: sugarless, Egyptian tea is unpalatable. Some connoisseurs say that the truly classic glass of tea should be only faintly translucent, with a mild aroma of kerosene from extended boiling on a Primus stove. In this form, tea is the perfect antidote to the hottest, dustiest, and most pestiferous of days.

Long used by the Arabian Bedouins, coffee was introduced to Cairo by Sufi mystics in the 16th century. The dervishes' adoption of the stimulant to prolong their ecstatic trances brought the wrath of the orthodox clergy down upon the bean. As with tobacco, controversy raged for years before the weight of popular taste concluded the debate.

Arabic coffee is still prepared and served in centuries-old style, without the fancy gadgetry of European invention. Sugar, then powdered coffee are added to hot water and brought to boil in a brass *kanaka*. The *qahwagi*

potations range from ginger, *ganzabeel*, which is recommended for coughs, *erfa* (cinnamon) and *yansun* (aniseed) for the throat, to *helba* (fenugreek) for stomach complaints. *Karkadé*, the scarlet tea of a hibiscus flower, is a specialty of Aswan. Packed with vitamin C, it is delicious hot or cold. *Sahlib*, a steaming cream, concocted from dried orchids and topped off with chopped nuts, is a winter favourite. In summer, cafés serve cooler drinks, ranging from lemonade, *tamarhindi* (tamarind), *erqsus* (licorice), and *farawla* (strawberry) to the ever more pervasive *Kukula*, *Bibs* and *Shwibs*, the commercially bottled soft drinks that have run old local brands off the market.

brings the *kanaka* and cup on a tin tray and pours the liquid with solicitude, preserving the *wish* – the "face" – the thick mud which sits on the surface before settling. In the better cafés, a dark blend spiced with cardamon is used. In all establishments, the customer must specify how he wants his coffee – *saada*, or sugarless, *'arriha*, with a dash of sugar, *mazbut*, medium, or *ziyada*, with extra sugar. In some "European cafés", *qahwa Faransawi* or French coffee is served.

Of far more ancient origin – and of more interest to the inquisitive traveller – are the hot medicinal infusions which can still be found in many cafés. The bases of these

A smoker's paradise: The Egyptian café is a paradise for the serious smoker and has perfected the ultimate tobacco tool. The *shiisha* or water pipe cools, sweetens and lightens the taste of burning leaves, makes a soothing gurgle and provides a pleasant distraction for idle hands. It is an instrument of meditation to be indulged in diligently and serenely.

Two kinds of tobacco are used. The most popular is *ma'assil*, a sticky blend of chopped leaf fermented with molasses. There are dozens of national brands of *ma'assil* and even more local varieties. It is pressed in small clay bowls which are fitted into the *sheesha* and lit with charcoal. *Tumbak*, the other variety, is loose dry tobacco wrapped into a cone with a whole leaf. While *ma'assil* is easy to smoke, a cone of *tumbak* may take an hour to exhaust, by which time the smoker may be ready for the cancer ward.

Until recently, hashish smoking was not uncommon in public places, especially at night. The *ghoraz*, or hash dens, of Cairo were famed throughout the Arab world. Official crackdowns, however, have relegated this once-popular entertainment to seedy back alleys and private homes.

Some of Cairo and Alexandria's grander cafés offer intoxication in the form of liquor, but with the post-Revolutionary departure of the large Greek and Italian communities,

ship – sports in which the sociable Egyptians notably surpass everyone else in the world – that draw the regular crowds. Despite the mass media and the telephone, average citizens still find that the best source of news – not to mention gossip, rumour, slander and fantasy – is among cronies at the local café. Formerly, any political candidate worth his salt began his campaign in the cafés, ordering drinks on the house for any and all.

With the penchant for nostalgia and complaint that characterises their country, afficionados will affirm that cafés are not what they used to be. Like the introduction of radio in the 1930s, which signalled the decline of traditional storytellers and poets, the

these café-bars have lost much of their former glory. Brandy on ice is the most popular of a bewildering array of potions, none of which exactly inspires confidence.

Live entertainment: Every café offers more innocent diversion in the form of cards (*kutshina*), backgammon (*tawla*) and dominoes. These games are not meant to be challenging to the intellect, but are played rather as an excuse for exchanging the insults and hyperbole for which the Arabic language is an unparalleled medium.

It is good conversation and companion-

more recent plague of television has led to a marked decline in public entertainment. Luckily, most café owners leave their sets off except during major football matches. At such times, when the two great teams of Ahli and Zamalek clash, the cafés are thronged with supporters. When a goal is scored, roars of applause echo across the whole country. Many cafés now have videos and offer a nightly dose of Indian romance, Egyptian humour, or American violence.

The best time for dropping in on a café is the late afternoon, when the sun's dying rays turn dun-coloured buildings to gold and smoke drifts skywards from the *sheesha*.

<u>Left</u>, café patrons. <u>Above</u>, a café in Luxor.

PLACES

Egypt occupies 385,000 sq. miles (1 million sq. km) of Africa's driest and most barren corner. It adjoins the Sinai peninsula, which is geologically African, but geographically belongs to Asia. South and west, beyond wide barriers of desert, stretches the great body of the rest of Africa, to which Egypt is umbilically connected, in addition, by the slender nourishing lifeline of the Nile.

As it crosses the Sudanese border into Egypt, the Nile has already travelled 3,000 miles (5,000 km). Leaving mountain lakes, it has roared down cascades, steamed through swamps, and finally carved a serpentine path through a thousand miles of rock and sand into a massive artificial lake, with the temple of Abu Simbel on one side.

The artificial lake, just south of Aswan, the world's largest, is Lake Nasser, a 20th-century achievement that has changed the face and pace of Egypt forever.

An ancient frontier town, where the colours and smells of Africa blend with those of the East, Aswan itself marks the southern limit of navigation from the Mediterranean. Graceful lateen-rigged *feluccas* swish around the rock islands of the First Cataract, on one of which the famous temple of Philae stands. Cruise ships stop here and return from here northward. At Luxor they pause in the centre of the largest agglomeration of ancient building the world can offer, anchoring between the East Bank's great temple complexes of Karnak and Luxor and the West Bank's vast funerary cities.

Further north, the river meanders timelessly on through fields fringed with date-palms, dotted with ambling water-buffalo. At length it swirls beneath the many bridges of Cairo. Fourteen million people inhabit this Arab-Mediterranean-African metropolis. Here the medieval glory of Islam is preserved in domes and minarets. To the west of Cairo the Pyramids of Giza continue to present their mountainous geometry as they have for 200 generations, while the Sphinx erodes impassively at their feet.

At Cairo the Nile exfoliates into the Delta, spreading itself lushly until, much diminished, it finally reaches the Mediterranean Sea. Joined to the Nile by canals is Alexandria, Egypt's most important coastal city, founded by Alexander the Great. From here a flat coastline of fine white sand stretches east and west.

The Nile and its Valley are not all there is to Egypt. Deep in the deserts and now accessible to the casual visitor lie miraculous islands of living green: the Oases. More life abounds in the salty depths of the Red Sea – which offers underwater sightseeing second to none, unsurpassed coral and teeming tropical fish – although it, too, is ringed by desert. And there is the Sinai peninsula, a landscape of striking beauty. God certainly showed his usual flair in choosing such a place for his rendezvous with Moses. What is harder to understand is why he ever commanded Moses to leave Egypt.

Preceding pages: the Queen's Temple, Abu Simbel; tourists; hobbled camel; street scene. **Left**, *felucca* and boatmen reflected in the Nile.

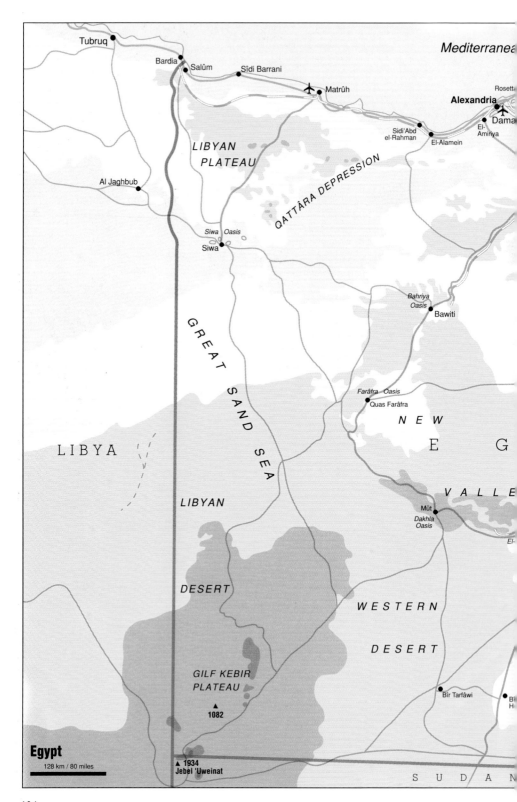

Tubruq

Bardia
Salûm
Sîdi Barrani
Matrûh

Mediterranea

Rosett
Alexandria
Dama

Sidi'Abd
el-Rahman
El-Alamein
El-
Aminya

*LIBYAN
PLATEAU*

Al Jaghbub

QATTÂRA DEPRESSION

Siwa Oasis
Siwa

*Bahriya
Oasis*
Bawiti

G
R
E
A
T

S
A
N
D

S
E
A

Farâfra Oasis
Quas Farâfra

N E W

E
G

LIBYA

LIBYAN

V A L L E

Mût
*Dakhla
Oasis*
El-

DESERT

WESTERN

DESERT

*GILF KEBIR
PLATEAU*
▲
1082

Bir Tarfâwi
Bi
H

Egypt
128 km / 80 miles

▲ **1934**
Jebel 'Uweinat

S   U   D   A   N

Sea

Damietta

El Mansura

Tanis

Tanta

Zagazig

Benha

Cairo

Helwân

Memphis

El Wasta

El Faiyûm

Beni
Suef

Wâdi Sannur

Minya

Necropolis of
Beni Hassan

Tel el-Amârna

airut

Wâdi Hubâra

ssiut

Tima

EASTERN

Sohâg

Y   P   T

Abydos

Nag Hammadi   Dendera

Qus

Valley of the Kings

Karnak

Thebes

Armant   Luxor

DESERT

harga

Esna

El-Kâb

Hierakonpolis

Edfu

Wâdi el-Miyâh

Kôm
Ombo

Gebel el Silsila

Elephantine   Daraw

Kalabsha   Aswan

Philae

Aswan Dam

Lake
Nasser

Abu
Simbel

Wadi Halfa

Wâdi el-Allaqi

Port Said

El-Arish

Suez
Canal

Ismâ'ilîa

Suez

Ras Zafarâna

Abu Rudeis

Monastery of
St. Catherine

Gebel Katherina
2642

Ras
Gharib

SINAI

Ashqelon   Jerusalem   Amman

Gaza

Dead Sea

Beersheba

ISRAEL

JORDAN

Petra

Ma' an

Elat

El-Aqaba

Nuweiba

Gulf of Suez

Gulf of Aqaba

2580

Sharm
el-Sheikh

Râs Muhammad

Hurghada

Bur Safâga

Wâdi Qena

Quseir

Wâdi 7 aidûn

Red

Sea

Marsa'Alam

Berenice   Râs Banas

Bîr Shalateln

Duba

SAUDI

ARABIA

Râs Hardarba

135

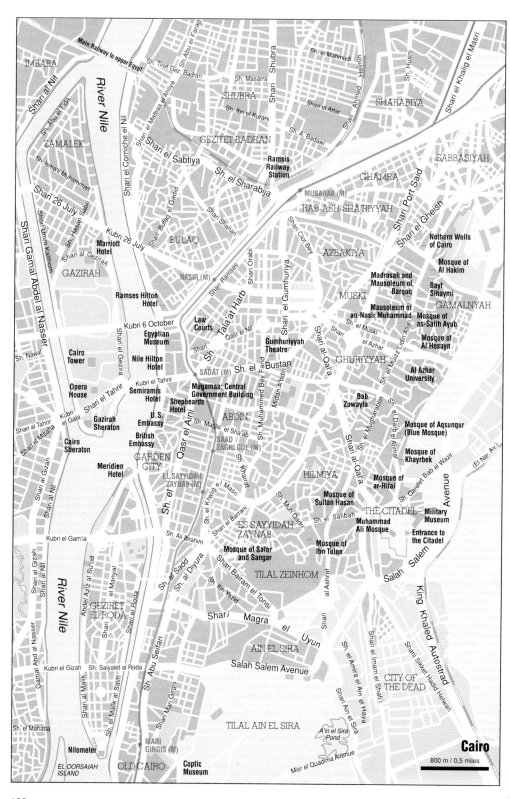

Cairo

800 m / 0,5 miles

138

CAIRO, MOTHER OF THE WORLD

"I can't believe this city!" a young American visiting Cairo for the first time said recently. "If I hadn't come here, I couldn't possibly have imagined anything of what it's really like." His reaction is typical and echoes a 600-year-old remark recorded by Ibn Khaldun, the great medieval Arab historian and social theorist, who reported a traveller telling him in 1384 that "what one can imagine always surpasses what one sees, because of the scope of the imagination, except Cairo, because it surpasses anything one can imagine." And when Ibn Khaldun finally came and saw the city himself, it certainly lived up to expectations: Cairo, he wrote, is "the metropolis of the universe, the garden of the world, the anthill of the human species, the throne of royalty, a city embellished with castles and palaces, its horizon decorated with monasteries and with schools, and lighted by the moons and stars of erudition."

What Ibn Khaldun was looking at was a city that had been devastated by the Black Death three decades earlier and had entered a long twilight of decline. It remained nevertheless the greatest metropolis on earth, still larger in both population and extent than any city west of China. Enriched by the spice trade, by traffic in luxury goods, and by re-distribution of urban and rural properties among the diminished population, its sultans and amirs continued to adorn the city with increasingly extravagant architecture.

City of 1001 Nights: It was during this period, sometime between 1382 and 1517, that the stories we know as *The Arabian Nights* were given their final form, not in the almost legendary Baghdad of Harun Al Rashid, but in the real Cairo of the Circassian Mamluks, a city of wonders, where miraculous reversals of fortune, as history records, were an everyday occurrence. "He who hath not seen Cairo," says a character in one of these tales, "hath not seen the world. Her soil is gold; her Nile is a marvel; her women are like the black-eyed virgins of Paradise; her houses are palaces; and her air is soft, as sweet-smelling as aloeswood, rejoicing the heart. And how can Cairo be otherwise, when she is Mother of the World?"

The Mother of the World is an old lady now, somewhat long in the tooth. The gold in her soil has ceased to glitter, her Nile has been thoroughly tamed; and though her women still have many admirers, her palatial houses are being rapidly demolished to make way for concrete high-rises, while her sweet-smelling air has achieved the highest pollution index in the world. She has become, in other words, a thoroughly modern metropolis.

The most radical changes have come within the past 10 years. In 1960 fewer than 40 percent of the Egyptian people were city-dwellers and only one out of every eight Egyptians was a Cairene. The city then had a population of less than 3.5 million. Today 80 percent of Egyptians live in an urban setting, one out of every three lives in Cairo, and the city's population has passed the 14-million mark, doubling every 10 years. In terms of population alone Cairo is the largest city in Africa, the Middle East and the Arab World.

Recent growth is clearly related to the population explosion taking place everywhere in the developing world. But the modern city occupies a position at the head of the Nile Delta that has been strategic for 5,000 years and that has consequently seen many urban foundations, of which Cairo itself is merely the largest and the latest.

Memphis: The most important of Cairo's predecessors was the city of **Memphis**, founded by Menes, traditionally regarded as the first king of the 1st Dynasty, on land reclaimed from the Nile in about 3100 BC. The site lies 15 miles (24 km) by road south of Cairo on the western side of the Nile. It can be reached by driving down the eastern band and crossing the bridge over the river south of Helwan; or by crossing the river directly into Giza and then driving south either along the main highway that goes from Giza to Upper Egypt, or along the far more attractive agricultural road that runs south from near the Giza Pyramids. The ruins of Memphis surround the village of **Mit Rahinah**, which derives its name from a temple of Mithras that was built here under the Romans, long after the days of the city's greatest glory.

There is very little to see at Memphis now except one of Ramses' two colossi (the other may be seen in front of Cairo's central railway station at Ramses Square where it was re-erected in 1955). More has been brought to light in the course of recent excavation and surveying by British, American and Egyptian experts, but the casual visitor is advised to enjoy the serenity of the surrounding groves of date-palms, meditate briefly on the perishability of power, then push on up the road. Ahead, on the desert plateau overlooking the green of Memphis, is a portion of the ancient capital's necropolis, the vast cemetery of **Saqqarah**, with religious and funerary monuments that span a period from the 27th century BC to the 10th century AD,

standing in the midst of an even larger pyramid field that stretches for miles to the north and south.

Saqqarah: The ticket office at the entrance to the Saqqarah necropolis stands above the valley temple attached to the **pyramid of Unas**, last king of the 5th Dynasty (c. 2375 BC–2345 BC), which houses the earliest Pyramid text: the ceremonial causeway linking the two has been excavated and the pyramid, visible at the end of it half a mile away, is one of the easiest for a visitor to enter. Dominating the whole area, however, is the **Step Pyramid** of Zozer (3rd Dynasty, 2668 BC–2649 BC), the earliest of all the pyramids and the first great monument in the world to be built of hewn stone.

The entire complex within the enclosure, including shrines, courtyards and the Step Pyramid itself, was the conception of a single man, Imhotep, Zozer's chief of works, who was perhaps the first recorded genius in history. An inscription left behind by a New Kingdom tourist venerates him as "he who opened

The Step Pyramid of Zozer at Saqqarah circa 3,000 BC.

the stone" and he was later identified with magic, astronomy and medicine, finally becoming deified in the 6th century BC. Translating motifs from more perishable materials, such as wood or papyrus reeds, into stone, the Zozer complex displays many features that became a permanent part of the Egyptian architectural vocabulary and a few that have apparently remained unique.

The Step Pyramid can be entered only with special permission; the tour takes several hours, and there is no lighting inside. A cross-section, however, would reveal its complexity, arising from the fact that it began as a *mastaba* (from an Arabic word that refers to the usual oblong shape), a one-storey tomb of common type. Even here Imhotep showed its originality, for his *mastaba* was square rather than oblong and built of stone rather than the usual mud-brick.

A conscientious visit to Saqqarah can take all day and the local tradition is to make the occasion an excuse for a picnic, usually eaten in the ruins of the **monastery of St Jeremiah**, which are quite close to the parking space below the enclosure on the opposite side of the causeway to the pyramid of Unas. Founded in the 6th century AD and destroyed in the 10th, it is this monastery that has supplied the objects in Rooms 6 and 7 of the Coptic Museum.

Cheerful realism: Not to be missed, no matter how short a visit, are two 6th Dynasty *mastabas*, the **tombs of Mereruka and Kagemni**, who were both viziers of King Teti (c. 2345 BC–2333 BC). Nestled next to the pyramid of Teti, northeast of the Zozer complex, these two structures promise nothing on the outside. The interior walls of both, however, are carved with lively scenes of domestic life, probably designed and executed by the same hands, showing the interests and pursuits of the Old Kingdom nobility: hunting, horticulture, husbandry, music and dancing, preparations to ensure that the next world would be as bountiful as this one. The artist's carved workmen exchange hieroglyphic one-liners; and such is the acuteness of his observations that over

Entrance to the funerary complex of Zozer at Saqqarah.

50 different species of fish have been readily identified by modern experts from these stone depictions. Almost as satisfying are the scenes in the 6th-century *mastaba* **of Ankh-ma-hor**, a few steps away in the same group of tombs, which show similar pursuits, but are particularly famous for their depictions of craftsmen (jewellers, metalworks, sculptors) and physicians.

Directly west of the pyramid of Teti, a kilometre away and connected with it by a dirt road parallel to what was once an avenue of sphinxes, is a rest house serving cold beer and soft drinks. Near the rest house, left of the dirt road, is the double 5th-Dynasty **tomb of Akhtehotep and (his son) Ptah-hotep**, high officials under the kings preceding Unas. To the right of the road is the **tomb of Ti**, their slightly older contemporary. Here too are remarkable scenes from daily life, including children's games (Ptahhotep) and boat-building (Ti).

Bulls and baboons: Below the rest house is the **Serapeum**, the catacomb of the sacred Apis bull, whose rites were witnessed by Herodotus during his sojourn in Egypt. A circle of statues representing Greek poets and philosophers set up by Ptolemy I (323 BC–282 BC) marks the entrance, but except for the size of the bull's sarcophagi, in which no taurine remains have ever been found, the Serapeum itself offers little to stimulate either logic or the imagination, though it makes a nice temporary retreat on a hot day. Situated immediately to the north are graveyards for the mummies of other animals: baboons, now actually extinct in Egypt, though they can still be found in the Sudan; and ibis (three species were known to the ancients, identified by modern experts as Sacred, Bald and Glossy), now extremely rare, though the name is often given locally to the cattle egret.

Just south of the Zozer complex, beyond the pyramid of Unas, is the recently discovered (1950) unfinished **Step Pyramid of Sekhemhet**, Zozer's successor (2649 BC–2643 BC), overlooking an area where there has been a great deal of archaeological activity.

A sphinx at Memphis near Saqqarah.

Here in 1975, while looking for the tomb of Maya, an official of Tutankhamen, the Egypt Exploration Society discovered a tomb prepared for Horemheb, Tutankhamen's general, who would become a pharaoh himself (1321 BC–1293 BC). Eleven years later, Maya's tomb was finally found, but not before an enormous amount from other burials had been revealed.

Further south, accessible on foot, by donkey, horse, or camel (which can be rented at the rest house) or by a vehicle with four-wheel drive, are several more monuments: the **pyramid complex of Pepi I** (2332 BC–2283 BC), the **pyramid complex of Djedkare Isesi** (2414 BC–2375 BC) with the pyramid of a queen nearby; the tomb of **Shepseskaf** (2504 BC–2500 BC); the **pyramid complex of Pepi II** (2278 BC–2184 BC); and three other pyramids, one of them identified as belonging to Userkare Khendjer (c. 1747 BC).

In the Saqqarah area alone, in fact, no fewer than 15 royal pyramids have been excavated, creating a zone more than 3 miles (5 km) long. And what has been discovered thus far is only a tiny fraction of what lies still buried under the sands which must cover innumerable unknown tombs, including – somewhere – that of Imhotep, the great architect.

The relationship of all these monuments to Memphis is made clear by the fact that "Memphis" is derived from one of them: the pyramid of Pepi I, which was called *Men-Nefer*, "Established and Beautiful". But the Saqqarah monuments themselves are only part of the Memphite necropolis as a whole, which extends north along the desert plateau beyond Giza to Abu Rawash and southward to Dahshur and Mazghuna, a total distance of about 20 miles (33 km).

Pyramids of Dahshur: Off-limits to foreigners for years because of a local military base, the peace and quiet beauty of the agricultural countryside around Dahshur have attracted many of Cairo's professional class, who have built rural retreats here. Failing an invitation from one of them, the most pleasant time of

A detail of he reclining statue of Ramses II, Memphis.

year to visit the seven royal pyramids of Dahshur is mid-winter, when a lake forms within an artificial embankment below the **Black Pyramid**, built of brick but unused by Amenemhet III (1832 BC–1797 BC), one of Egypt's most colourful kings. Amenemhet's pyramid and temple complex of **Hawarah** on the edge of the Fayyum was visited by Herodotus, who describes it as a wonder greater than the pyramids of Giza; and his building of another smaller pyramid here seems to have been a gesture, not uncommon, towards the old capital's prestige. The dark colour that gives it its name arises from the fact that it has been systematically stripped of its original white limestone covering. The view of it across the lake is one of the most charming in Egypt, worth the 3-mile (5-km) drive from Saqqarah. Its inscribed capstone is in the Egyptian Museum.

There are two other 12th-Dynasty pyramids here, another from the 13th-Dynasty, and a third not yet identified. Most striking, however, are two 4th-Dynasty pyramids, built by Snefru (2613 BC–2589 BC). The southernmost of these two pyramids is the third largest in Egypt and is easily distinguished, standing about 300 yards further into the desert beyond the pyramid of Amenemhet III, not only by its bulk, but by its peculiar shape, which has let it to be called the **Bent Pyramid**: the 54-degree slope of its sides changes halfway up to a shallower angle of 43 degrees, for reasons that may have to do with religious symbolism and aesthetics.

Visible a mile and a half away almost directly north is its companion, sometimes called the **Red Pyramid**, which uses a 43-degree angle throughout its height, the earliest known to have been completed as a "true" pyramid, built less than 60 years after Imhotep's great discovery.

The Bent Pyramid made internal use of cedar trunks imported from Lebanon, still intact, as beams, and is externally the best preserved of all the pyramids, thanks to an ingenious construction method that made stripping its surface difficult. About 650 yards northwest of

The Pyramids of Cheops and Khafre at Giza.

the Bent Pyramid, between it and the Red Pyramid, are the remains of Snefru's mortuary temple, re-dedicated to him during the Middle Kingdom and under the Ptolemies.

Snefru was the father and immediate predecessor of Khufu (2589 BC–2566 BC), better known by the Greek form of his name as Cheops, builder of the **Great Pyramid** at Giza. Khufu's own immediate successor, Djedefre (2566 BC–2556 BC) built a pyramid at **Abu Rawash**, 6 miles (10 km) northwest of Giza, which marks the northernmost limit of the Memphite necropolis; and 3 miles (5 km) south of Dahshur, at **Mazghuna**, are two ruined pyramids possibly marking its southernmost limit.

Pyramids of Giza: The **pyramids of Giza** (called *al-Ahram* in Arabic), the only survivors among the Seven Wonders of the World, are not hard to find. Standing at the end of a boulevard (Shari' al-Ahram) on the desert plateau above the western edge of Giza, across the river from Cairo, they can most usefully be seen in combination with a visit ei-ther to Saqqarah or to the modern villages of Kirdassah and Harraniyyah.

Kirdassah, situated at the end of an old caravan route to Libya, 3 miles (5 km) north of Shari' al-Ahram, formerly supplied goods for desert traders and has become a centre for weaving, textiles and ready-made clothing, including the typical flowing *gallibiyas*.

Harraniyyah, 3 miles (5 km) south of Shari' al-Ahram on the road to Saqqarah, houses the famous **Wissa Wassef tapestry workshops** in a group of buildings that have won international acclaim for their architecture. Now managed by the widow of founder Ramsis Wissa Wassef, the workshops export tapestries worldwide, usually made to order, though there is always a good selection on view. Half a mile or so farther down the same road, an outstanding collection of modern Egyptian painting and sculpture is visible at the **Aida Gallery**, which holds special exhibitions throughout the winter season.

At the foot of the pyramids, on the road leading up to them from Shari' al-

The Sphinx.

Ahram, is the **Mena House Oberoi Hotel**, one of the most celebrated hotels in the world. Connected by a tramline to Cairo in 1900 shortly after its opening, it soon rivalled the famous Shepheard's, entertaining statesmen at three historic international conferences, the latest in 1978. Its lavish neo-Islamic decor has been carefully preserved by its new managers.

The most striking thing about the Giza pyramids is their size. The **Great Pyramid of Khufu** was originally 480 feet (150 metres) high and incorporates 2.3 million stone blocks averaging more than 2½ tons in weight. Contrary to popular belief, however, it is neither the biggest pyramid in the world – that distinction belongs, according to the *Guinness Book of Records*, to the Quetzalcoatl pyramid at Cholula, south of Mexico City, which covers an area more than three times as extensive – nor was it built by slaves. Teams of skilled labourers on 3-month hire were supplemented by a permanent work force of local quarrymen. Other crews cut lime-stone and granite construction blocks at Tura and Aswan and transported them across or down the Nile to the building site. There was housing for 4,000 suggesting large and permanent administrative and support staffs.

Pyramid power: Climbing the Great Pyramid is strictly forbidden, which does not prevent local "guides" from offering their services. Illicit climbs have resulted in one or two fatalities annually for the past several years and are not recommended, though the task may look easy from a distance. Stripped of their smooth white Tura limestone upper casing and extensively quarried lower down for granite from the 11th century AD onward, its sides slope at an angle of 52 degrees, the normal gradient for all the pyramids built after Snefru's Bent Pyramid and Red Pyramid at Dahshur.

Except for their size, the isolated silhouettes of all the later large pyramids in Egypt would therefore have looked exactly like the Great Pyramid. Each, however, would also have stood within an enclosed complex, like Zozer's at

Open-air theatre at the Pyramids of Giza.

Saqqarah, and would have been further particularised not only by inscriptions, but also by a cap that was possibly either painted or gilded.

The interior of the Great Pyramid can be visited and includes a grand gallery with a corbelled roof that is itself regarded as one of the most remarkable architectural works of the Old Kingdom. East of the Great Pyramid is the site of Khufu's mortuary temple, identified by the remains of a basalt pavement, north and south of which are two boat pits. Near its base at the south are two more pits, one of which was excavated in 1954, when a complete dismantled river barge was found, probably secreted there to serve some purpose in connection with the sun cult. Beautifully re-assembled, it can be admired in the **Solar Boat Museum** on the site.

The causeway leading from the Great Pyramid's mortuary temple to its valley temple is largely ruinous and cannot be excavated at its lower end, thanks to the encroachment of modern buildings. But just south of it, close to a group of three subsidiary pyramids, the only undisturbed tomb thus far found of the Old Kingdom was uncovered in 1925. Although the sarcophagus in it was empty, it was identified as the tomb of Queen **Hetepheres**, wife of Snefru and mother of Khufu, and yielded extraordinary objects, including a carrying-chair and a portable boudoir, with its linen curtains as well as its gilt bed and chair, now in the Egyptian Museum.

The Sphinx: The pyramid of **Khafre** (Chephren 2589 BC–2566 BC), just south of the Great Pyramid and second to it in size, not only preserves a considerable part of its limestone casing at the top, but is also the most complete in relation to its surrounding complex, which includes the **Sphinx**. Intended originally to represent a guardian deity in the shape of a lion, the Sphinx had Khafre's face. It is disfigured and beardless, it is said, thanks to Mamluk artillery practice. Later associated with the sun god and with Horus of the Horizon, as a Greek drinking song scratched on one of its toes during the Ptolemaic

Tapestry in progress at the Wissa Wassef Art School, Giza.

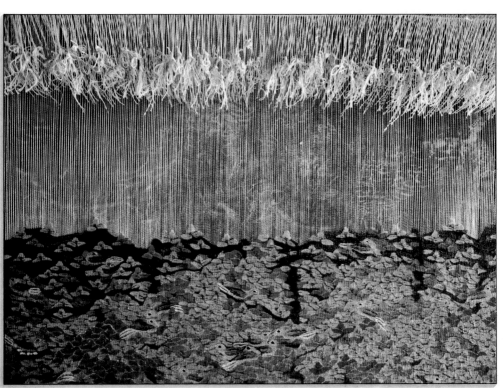

period attests, it was apparently the object of pilgrimages, especially during the 18th Dynasty. In front of it stands a granite stele set up by order of Tuthmosis IV (1423 BC–1417 BC), who records a dream he had while still a prince: while he was resting under its shade during a hunting expedition, the Sphinx appeared to him and spoke, promising Tuthmosis the kingdom if he would clear away accumulated sand from around its feet. The story has circulated for many centuries since as a folk tale involving later rulers: in one malicious 20th-century version the hero is Gamal Abdul Nasser and the boon the Sphinx asks for is an exit visa.

And baby makes three: The third of the royal pyramids at Giza was begun by **Menkaure** (Mycerinus, 2532 BC–2504 BC), Khafre's successor. By far the smallest, it was apparently left unfinished at Menkaure's death and hurriedly completed by his son, Shepseskaf, whose own tomb at Saqqarah has already been mentioned. There are signs of haste through the complex, even in the pyramid itself, which may have been intended originally to be encased entirely in red granite. Brick was used to finish off the mortuary temple, causeway and valley temple, though they had been begun in limestone and some of the blocks weigh as much as 200 tons, showing that the failure to complete it in limestone was by no means due to a decline in technical mastery. The ruins of the valley temple, now covered again with sand, were cleared many decades ago.

The City of the Sun: Clustered around the three great pyramids are scores of lesser tombs, some of them small pyramids, originally laid out in orderly rows along the same north-south axis as the tombs of the pharaohs. It seems clear that all the tombs at Giza, including the three great pyramids, were connected not only with Memphis but with the royal cult of Re, the universal sun god, centred at On, the city the Greeks called **Heliopolis** (City of the Sun). Heliopolis stood 15 miles (25 km) northeast of Giza and thus 20 miles (32 km) almost directly north of Memphis, at the edge of the plain on the opposite side of the

Nile, at a site that is now not easy to find in the modern district of Al-Matariyyah.

Mentioned in the Bible (Genesis 41:45, "And Pharaoh called Joseph's name Zaphnathpaaneah; and he gave him his wife Asenath the daughter of Potipherah priest of On"), Heliopolis was another of Cairo's ancient predecessors. The primary theological centre of Old Kingdom Egypt, it was finally displaced in importance by Thebes, but not before its priests had developed and written down elaborate rituals, liturgies and mythologies that revolve around the sun god Ra and a host of lesser deities known as the Great Company. Ramses III (1182 BC–1151 BC) the last of Egypt's great pharaohs, is recorded as endowing Heliopolis with over 12,000 serfs and more than 100 towns, not to mention buildings, statues, gold, silver, linens, precious stones, birds, incense, cattle and fruit.

Even in ancient times, Heliopolis had begun to suffer a decline that eventually led to systematic pillaging. Strabo, who visited the site in 24 BC, recorded its desolation and 14 years later a pair of obelisks erected by Tuthmoses III (1504 BC-1450 BC) were removed by the Romans to adorn their new Caesarium, the temple of the recently deified Julius Caesar in Alexandria. Some 19 centuries later, during the reign of Khedive Ismail, these two monuments found their way out of Egypt altogether and became the "Cleopatra's Needles" of London and New York, which have nothing at all to do with any of several Cleopatras. Only one obelisk, from a famous pair erected in the reign of Senusert I (1971 BC–1928 BC), survives on the site. Otherwise there is virtually nothing left of ancient Heliopolis. It is quite unconnected with the modern suburb sometimes called by that name.

"How many miles to Babylon?": Modern Cairo began at a point halfway between Memphis and Heliopolis, where a road crossed the river, using the present island of Rawdah as a stepping stone. Since there were no other roads across the Delta, this road not only connected the Old Kingdom's administrative and religious capitals, but was the main pas-

A hazy Cairo seen from the Pyramids of Giza.

sage into Egypt from the East, giving access to the rest of the country. During the Late Dynasty period a small fortress was built here and after a canal linking the Nile with the Red Sea was completed by the Persian occupiers under Darius I (521 BC–486 BC), the site became even more important. The Greeks called it **Babylon**, a name that should not be confused with Mesopotamian Babylon and that probably derives from some such Egyptian name as *Pi-Hapi-n-On* or *Per-Hapi-n-On*, meaning "The Nile House of On". Under the Emperor Trajan (98 AD–117 AD), after more than a century of Roman occupation, when Heliopolis had long been moribund, the old canal was reopened and a new fortress was built, one of three to control the whole of Egypt.

The Alexandrian astronomer and geographer Claudius Ptolemy recorded a visit he made to Babylon within the following half century, when he found a thriving town already established around the fortress with the canal running through it. Memphis still remained important, however, and one of its New Kingdom suburbs (*Hikuptah* – "The Temple of the Ka of Ptah") supplied the Greeks and Romans with *Aigyptos* as the name for the entire country.

Cairo's real name: Egyptians themselves knew their country by many names, of which the most common during the Roman period was probably *Kemet*, "The Black Land", from which the Arabic word "alchemy" is derived. Throughout the rest of the Semitic-speaking Middle East, Egypt was called **Misr**, the name it still bears in Arabic, which is, of course, the present language of the country.

When the Arabs conquered Misr in 641 AD and founded a new capital next to the walls of Babylon, this capital acquired the name of the country as a whole, which became more and more appropriate as new quarters with new names were added and it expanded to become the metropolis not only of Egypt, but of the Arab world, a huge city containing many distinct areas with their own lesser names. The Western name

Tents, sometimes still appliquéd by hand, are used for funeral wakes as well as festivals.

"Cairo" derives from "Al-Qahirah", the name of a single one of these later quarters as understood by medieval Italian merchants, who mistook it for a complete city like their little walled towns. Neither "Cairo" nor "Al-Qahirah" was ever used by Egyptians themselves to designate their capital city until recent decades, when "Al-Qahirah" was adopted, under Western influence, by the mass media. For the Cairene in the street and for most Egyptians, Cairo remains "Misr".

Foretaste of glory: The remains of Roman and Christian Babylon can be found in the area thus known as **Misr al-Qadimah**, which confusingly translates into "Old Cairo", though it is as distinct from Al-Qahirah as Misr al-Gadidah ("New Cairo") is from ancient Heliopolis, and should not be mistaken for representing more than a foretaste of Cairo's medieval glory. Here too are interesting remains from Egypt's Christian era, as well as one monument from the years immediately following the Arab conquest. Largely intact until the British occupation, what is left of the Roman fortress of Babylon can be visited conveniently in conjunction with the **Coptic Museum**, and can be reached by taxi or metro. The metro stop is **Mari Girgis** (St George) and stands opposite the modern Greek Orthodox church of the same name. The grounds of the museum begin immediately south of the tower and are entirely within the fortress walls.

Founded by private benefactors on land belonging to the Coptic Church, the museum was taken over by Egyptian government in 1931. Though there are hundreds of ancient Christian sites in Egypt, there are none in which the churches themselves have not been abandoned, destroyed, or extensively rebuilt inside and out. It is therefore only the Coptic Museum that can now give us some idea of what the interior of a 5th, 6th or 7th-century church was like. Objects which were excavated in Upper Egypt and in the ruins of the monastery of St Jeremiah at Saqqarah are of particular interest.

The mosque and tomb of a local holy man.

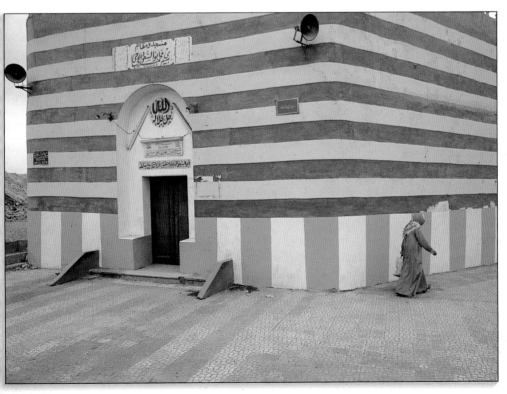

The museum's most prized relics, however, are the "Nag Hammadi Codices", a collection of nearly 1,200 papyrus pages bound together as books – the earliest so far known with leather covers – sometime soon after the middle of the 4th century. Written in Coptic, the Codices draw syncretically upon Jewish, Christian, Hermetic, Zoroastrian and Platonic sources and have thrown extraordinary light on the background of the New Testament, particularly the Epistles, by revealing that Gnosticism, hitherto supposed to be only a Christian heresy, was in fact a separate religion.

Ancient churches: Babylon is mentioned in St Peter's first epistle, most scholars now concede, in connection with St Mark's Egyptian mission, and local legend claims it as one of the many places in Egypt where the Holy Family rested. The monks and martyrs who elsewhere created the heroic age of the Coptic Church seem to have passed it by, and there are no specific documentary references to any church structure earlier than the Arab conquest. Babylon could not have had much importance as a Christian centre until four centuries later, when it had long since been absorbed into Misr. The **Patriarchate of St Mark**, robbed of the saint's relics by Venetians in 828, was transferred there from a declining Alexandria sometime after 1048.

Not only at Babylon, however, but all over the future site of Misr there were certainly scattered churches and monastic settlements. Many were later destroyed, but some were undoubtedly incorporated in later structures. Atop the two bastions of the southern gate of the Roman fortress, for example, is the **Church of the Virgin**, referred to locally as **Al-Mu'allaqah** ("The Suspended"), a seat of the Patriarchate for centuries, one portion of which is claimed to date to the 4th century; and within the walls are several others – the **churches of St Sergius and St Bacchus, St Barbara, St Cyril and St John**; a second church of the Virgin, known as **Qasriyyat al-Rihan** ("Pot of Basir");

The faithful at prayer in the 14th-century mosque of Mu'ayyad, Cairo.

and a **convent of St George** – with an almost equal claim to antiquity. Outside the fortress walls, but still within Old Cairo, are no fewer than a dozen more churches that were well documented in medieval times.

A visit to the churches within the fortress walls is made particularly pleasant by the fact that this enclosed area is entirely controlled by the Egyptian Antiquities Organisation, which has undertaken a great deal of cleaning and restoration. The interiors of the churches typically follow a basilican plan and cheerfully mix the ancient with the modern, between which local worshippers make little distinction. The use of pews, for example, is a 20th-century innovation inspired by Western Protestantism, but the use of cymbals or triangles in services may be traced back to the pharaohs. The oldest, finest and most portable objects have all been removed either to the Coptic Museum or to other collections around the world. One of the sanctuaries of the Suspended Church has the remains of some fine frescoes

attributed to the 7th or 8th century, however, and the buildings of the convent of St George include an intact reception hall belonging to a Fatimid-period house, with magnificent wooden doors 22 feet (7 metres) high.

These churches are all Coptic Orthodox, of course, but during Lent they become pilgrimage sites for Catholics as well. In the 17th and 18th centuries the Franciscan Friars had the right to celebrate mass in the sanctuary of the Holy Family at the church of St Sergius and St Bacchus, which marks a traditional resting-place of the Holy Family and is thus venerated by both Catholic and Orthodox.

Another people of the Book: Also within the walls is the **temple of Ben Ezra**, one of Cairo's 29 synagogues, a reminder of Egypt's role not only in fostering the Saphardic Rabbinical tradition, but also in providing a home for Karaite Jews (before the 10th century) and Ashkenazi Jews (from the 16th century onward). Originally a church dedicated to St Michael the Archangel, the building

was closed under the Fatimid Caliph Al-Hakim (996–1021), then sold to the Saphardic community. Among other functions it served as a *geniza*, a repository for documents made sacrosanct by being sworn under oath, which could not be casually discarded without sacrilege. Since these documents cover several centuries and include some mundane items as contracts, bills of sale and letters of credit, they constitute an extensive record of medieval Mediterranean trade and commerce, an invaluable prize for foreign scholars. Largely rebuilt in the 19th century, the building has been restored since 1980.

Beyond Old Cairo, 3 miles (5 km) to the southeast, reachable by car from the suburb of Maadi, is the **Rabbinical cemetery**, which is considerably older than the synagogue of Ben Ezra. Ya'kub Ibn Killis, the Jewish vizier of the Caliph Aziz (975–996), is buried there, as is Rabbi Hayim Kapusi, whose grave site, like that of Rabbi Ya'kub Abu Hasira in the Delta, continues to draw Saphardic pilgrims from Europe and North Africa.

The first Arab capital: Immediately to the east of Old Cairo, in an enormous area slowly being covered with new buildings, is the site of **Fustat**, the first Muslim capital at Misr, founded by Amr ibn al-'As in the course of the Arab conquest. Excavations here have uncovered the remains of elaborate water storage and drainage systems, the foundations of private houses and apartment blocks, and thousands of objects made of wood, paper, ivory, glass, metal, or ceramics, ranging in date from the 8th century to the 14th, and in provenance from Spain to China. The most significant of these objects may be seen in the **Islamic Museum**, including a sensational find made in 1980: block-printed papers which confirmed archaeologically the long-held belief that the art of printing was known in Fatimid Egypt within decades after its invention in China, at least four centuries before its adoption in Europe.

There is little to see at the site now to suggest the importance Fustat still had as a residential, manufacturing and in-

The 'Adli Street Synagogue built in 1905.

ternational trading centre even after the government had moved to new quarters farther north. One monument of the early period still remains in Old Cairo, however, and another, carefully preserved, stands at the tip of Rawdah Island, just across an intervening channel of the river.

The **mosque of 'Amr ibn al-'As** is 300 yards north of the Roman fortress on the main road parallel to the metro line. Erected in 641 or 642, it was rebuilt in 688, 710, 750 and 791, then doubled to approximately its present size in 827, thus testifying to Fustat's rapid growth. After several subsequent centuries of neglect, it was restored in the 13th century, rebuilt after the great earthquake of 1303, then partially rebuilt again a century later.

Near the end of the 18th century, just before the French invasion, the mosque again underwent massive rebuilding. After all this rebuilding, only an expert could now pinpoint older construction, but the site is important as marking that of the first mosque in Africa and in-

spired the building of Cairo's greatest mosque, that of Ibn Tulun.

The **Nilometer** at the southern tip of Rawdah Island is easy to see from across the river – it is distinguished by a conical cap – but not so easy to find from any point on the island itself; and even 19th-century travellers, who had no one-way streets to cope with, usually hired a guide. The only north-south street on the island giving access to the Nilometer is the easternmost, which can only be approached from the west. An ideal approach, often used in the 19th century and recently rediscovered by local yachtsmen, is by water.

The conical dome is a reconstruction made in 1893 of a 17th-century Ottoman dome that had been destroyed by the French in 1800; and its interior is covered with fine Turkish tiles. The substructure, however, which is the Nilometer itself, dates essentially from 861, which makes it the oldest intact Islamic monument in Cairo and the only survivor from the Abbasid period. Consisting of a calibrated stone column

Traditional *Mashrabia* woodwork in a modern apartment, Cairo.

standing upright in a stone-lined pit with a staircase, it is particularly notable for the pointed arches used at the highest intake level, three hundred years before the appearance of such arches in Europe.

The Mosque of Ibn Tulun: In 872 the Caliph's name was removed from the Nilometer by order of the city's 38-year-old Turkish governor, Ahmad Ibn Tulun, who would not only declare himself independent, but within 10 years would make Misr the centre of an empire stretching from southern Turkey to Sudan. Cramped by the growth of Fustat, the Abbasid caliphs had already built themselves a new military quarter, **Al-'Askar**, to the north; and Ibn Tulun felt the need for something grander. The result was **Al-Qatai'** ("The Wards"), a new town built over an entire square mile, large enough to include a walled hippodrome, a hospital, a menagerie, mews, gardens, markets, baths, residential quarters (classified by occupation or nationality), reception and *harim* ("harem") palaces for Ibn Tulun himself, and a large governmental complex, which was attached to a great congregational mosque. When the Abbasids repossessed Misr for the Caliphate in 905, this mosque, one of the architectural glories of the Muslim world, was the only building left standing in Al-Qatai'.

Though it is now approached by the narrow streets that grew up around it, most taxi drivers can find it, since it is situated between two landmarks, the Citadel and the popular modern mosque of Sayyidna Zaynab, just west of the Qasabah, the great north-south thoroughfare of Mamluk Misr. Several restorations – the earliest was in 1297, the latest in 1981 – have kept it in order without destroying its authenticity, though one must imagine its inscriptions and decorations as painted or gilded. Built in the imperial style of the Abbasid court at Samarra in Iraq, where Ibn Tulun had lived as a young man, it is constructed of red brick and stucco – original materials, rather than granite, limestone and marble borrowed from other sites, as is often the case in later

Four Cairene gentlemen.

mosques – and its courtyard covers 6.5 acres (2.5 hectares). The sycamore-wood frieze of Quranic verses surrounding the court is more than a mile and a quarter long.

The main street of Misr: Adjoining its northeastern corner is the **Gayer-Anderson Museum** (Bayt al-Kirid-lyyah): two houses, one of the 16th century, the other of the 17th, each comfortable by the standards of its time, have been delightfully joined together to create a single larger dwelling with a *salamlik* (reception suite) and *haramlik* (harem suite), both filled with antique furniture from all over the Middle East.

One entrance to the Gayer-Anderson Museum leads from the mosque of Ibn Tulun. Another entrance, opposite, can be used as an exit and gives on to a cross street called Shari' Tulun, which leads eastward (left) after less than 100 yards into the **Qasabah**, medieval Cairo's main street.

The Qasabah linked all the city's parts on a north-south axis; and at the height of Cairo's medieval prosperity it had become more than 8 miles (13 km) long, not only connecting the mosque of Ibn Tulun with older sites to the south, such as Fustat, and newer quarters to the north, such as Al-Qahirah, but also extending all the way into a suburban zone of villas and pleasure domes that lay beyond Al-Qahirah's northern walls. Changing its name as it moves from quarter to quarter, it can still be followed – on foot, of course – from Ibn Tulun northward for more than 3 miles (5 km) into the heart of modern Cairo's historic zone.

Shari' Salibah: There is so much to see of the rest of medieval Cairo however, that it is best to take the Qasabah piecemeal. The first major cross-street it intersects with, for example, about 300 yards up the Qasabah to the north, is **Shari' Salibah**, a special joy for the architect or city-planner. On the northeast corner of the intersection is delightful Ottoman-style *saabil-kuttab* ("fountain school") built in 1867 by the mother of Abbas I, the successor of Muhammad Ali, beautifully restored in 1984 by the

The courtyard of the 9th-century Mosque of Ibn Tulun, Cairo.

Egyptian Antiquities Organisation. There are many of these "fountain-schools" in Cairo, which were endowed by the pious for the public dispensation of the "two mercies" commended by the Prophet – water and religious teaching – and were consequently always constructed in two storeys, with a public water-dispensary below and a school for Quranic instruction above. Unmistakable just beyond the northeast and southeast corners of the intersection, one on either side of Shari' Salibah, are the massive facades of two "colleges" built by the Amir Shaykhu, commander of the Mamluk armies under Sultan Hasan ibn an-Nasir Muhammad ibn Qalawun (1334–61), who had him murdered in 1357.

Shaykhu's *madrasah* (built in 1349, on the left) and his *khanqah* (built in 1355, on the right) represent two classic Cairene architectural types, both introduced two centuries earlier by Salah-ad-Din. Persian in inspiration, the *madrasah* provided the perfect architecture for religious propaganda: a court-yard mosque made cruciform in plan by building into it four vaulted halls (*liwans*), where instruction could take place simultaneously in the four systems of legal thought regarded as orthodox by Sunni Muslims (Hanafi, Malaki, Shafi'i, Hanbali). A *khanqah* is a Muslim "monastery", a mosque with attached dwelling areas that are designed to serve as a hostel for Sufis (Muslim mystics). Sufis differ from Christian monks chiefly in not being sworn to celibacy and in being held on the whole by somewhat looser external discipline; Shaykhu's *khanqah* thus accommodated 700 Sufis, though it contains only 150 rooms surrounding a central mosque with a courtyard. These two buildings frame Shari' Salibah as one looks in the direction of the Citadel, creating a gorgeously "oriental" vista.

Farther up Shari' Salibah in the direction of the Citadel is the first free-standing *sabil-kuttab* in Cairo, built by Qaitbay in 1479, beyond which the street suddenly emerges into the **Qaramaydan** (Maydan Salah ad-Din). This enormous

Cluster of mosques seen from the Citadel.

158

square was the site of Ibn Tulun's hippodrome and the Mamluks' polo-ground, where their pageants, races, matches, musters and military displays took place under the gaze – and the guns – of the Citadel.

A masterpiece and its modern mate: At the northwestern corner of this square loom two colossal religious buildings, one on either side of the entrance to a street called Shari' Qal'ah (but better known under its old name as Shari' Muhammad Ali) confronting each other gatewise just as the Shaykhu *madrasah* and *khanqah* do in Shari' Salibah, though on a much larger scale: the **madrasah** of **Sultan Hasan**, Shaykhu's teenage master, built between 1356 and 1363; and the **Rifa'i mosque**, built to complement it architecturally between 1869 and 1912.

Visitors sometimes fail to understand that these two buildings were constructed more than five centuries apart, since the modern mosque shows perfect respect for its older neighbour across the street in fabric, scale and style.

Inside the Rifa'i mosque Mamluk motifs have been reproduced with luxurious fidelity, demonstrating recognition of the Mamluk style as Cairo's distinguishing trademark, an almost "official" style and thus particularly suitable in a mosque identified with the ruling dynasty. Originally endowed by the mother of the Khedive Ismail, it houses her tomb as well as those of the magnificent Khedive himself and four of his sons, including Husayn Kamil (1853–1917) and King Fuad (1868–1936). King Faruq's body was laid to rest here after temporary interment in the Southern Cemetery; and Muhammad Reza Pahlevi, the last Shah of Iran, whose first wife was Faruq's sister, was buried here in 1980.

A great parade of Sufi orders, with chanting, banners and drums, takes place annually in Cairo on the eve of the Prophet's Birthday. Despite the Revolution, it traditionally begins here at the Rifa'i mosque, marches down Shari' Muhammad Ali, up Shari' Port Said, then down Shari' al-Azhar – wide new

Twenty-seven varieties of marble were imported for the floors of the Mosque of Sultan Hasan.

European-style streets constructed by the Dynasty between 1873 and 1930 – to end at the popular **mosque of Sayyidna Husayn**, which was built by the Khedive Ismail.

Sultan Hasan's *madrasah*, across the street, provided a daunting model, since it is probably the greatest of the Bahri architectural monuments, second only to Ibn Tulun's mosque in grandeur of conception among all the buildings in Cairo. The walls are 117 feet (36 metres) high and so solidly built that it was used twice – in 1381 during a Mamluk revolt and again in 1517 during the Ottoman invasion – as a fortress.

It was originally planned to have four minarets, including two over the entrance portal, but in February 1360, while the building was still under construction, one of these two fell, killing 300 people, and the second was never built. One of the two remaining minarets collapsed in 1659 and was replaced by the present smaller version, an Ottoman construction in the Mamluk style, in 1672, when the dome was also replaced.

The architectural daring that caused the difficulties is made clear, however, by the sole original minaret, still standing at the western corner; it is over 265 feet (80 metres), taller and more massive than any other in Cairo.

The complex originally included a market, apartments and a well at its northern end, of which little now remains. The original wooden doors at the entrance, covered with bronze and filigree silver in geometric patterns, were removed by Sultan Mu'ayyad Sheikh in 1416 to be used in his own mosque situated near Bab Zuwaylah, where they are still visible; and the original marble floor was stripped by Selim the Grim for shipment to Istanbul after the Ottoman conquest. What is left, however, is stunningly impressive.

The Citadel: The **Citadel** was begun by Salah-ad-Din in 1176 as part of a plan to enclose all of Misr, for the first time, within a system of walls. By 1182, when he had gone northward again to fight his last series of victorious campaigns against the crusaders, it was vir-

The Citadel seen from the Sultan Hasan Mosque, Cairo.

tually complete; and though it was later modified in detail, it has never since been without a military garrison.

In 1218 Sultan al-Kamil, Salah ad-Din's nephew, took up residence in it and from that time until the construction of Abdin Palace in the mid-19th century, the Citadel was also the home and seat of government of all but one of Egypt's subsequent rulers, even Ottoman viceroys. The Lower Enclosure contains the famous gate-passage where Muhammad Ali conducted a massacre of Mamluks in 1811, which may be approached by an 18th-century gateway, restored in 1988. It is best seen, however, from the terrace of the Police Museum on the upper level, which contains the Southern and Northern Enclosures, nearly two-thirds of the Citadel's entire area.

The Citadel is maintained by the Egyptian Antiquities Organisation as a prime tourist attraction. A parking area, landscaping, plenty of historical interest and good public facilities have combined with cleaner air, more open space, less noise, and lower temperatures than anywhere else in Cairo to make this part of the Citadel a popular place.

Visible from nearly anywhere in the city below on its site at the highest point of the Southern Enclosure is the **Muhammad Ali** mosque. Built between 1830 and 1848, it was not completed until 1857. Designed by a Greek architect in accord with purely Ottoman models, it owes nothing to Egypt but the materials from which it is made and a few intermingled pharaonic and Mamluk decorative motifs, though it adds a wonderful picture-postcard element to the city's skyline. The clock in the courtyard, a charming touch of the period, was a gift made by Louis-Philippe of France in 1846, a belated exchange for the obelisk of Ramses II from the Luxor temple, now standing in the Place de la Concorde in Paris, which Muhammad Ali had given the French in 1831. The Pasha himself is buried here under a marble cenotaph.

The view over the city seen from the belvedere near the mosque is remark-

Festival decor at the Al Hussein Mosque, Cairo.

able on a clear day. Across a little court is the **Gawharah Palace**, built by Muhammad Ali in 1814, gutted by fire during a theft in 1972. The ruins have been intelligently refurbished and converted into a museum of the mid-19th century, when it served as a viceregal *salamlik* (reception) palace.

Below the Muhammad Ali mosque to the northwest, between it and the gateway to the Northern Enclosure, is the great 14th-century **mosque of An-Nasir Muhammad**, the father of Sultan Hasan. Built in 1318, enlarged in 1335, but stripped of its gorgeous marble by the Ottomans after 1517, it shows Persian-Mongol influence in its unique minarets, and an incredible variety of Egyptian sources in its columns: levied from pharaonic, Greek, Roman, and Coptic sites, they constitute a survey of Egyptian architectural styles.

North of the mosque of An-Nasir Muhammad are two gates: one downhill to the left leads into the Lower Enclosure; the other, around a corner to the right, leads into the Northern Enclosure. Within the Northern Enclosure are the Military Museum, which is housed in Muhammad Ali's Harim Palace, built in 1827, and an interesting small Museum of Carriages, displaying a few vehicles transferred here from the large collection of royal and viceregal conveyances at the **Carriage Museum** in **Bulaq**, which is worth a separate visit. In the far corner of the Northern Enclosure is the first Ottoman mosque built in Cairo (1528). Nestled next to an old Fatimid tomb, it is set in a small garden, which must have afforded a cool and leafy touch of the Bosphorus to the homesick Janissaries who lived there during the centuries after 1517.

Sultanic serendipity: The Citadel was remote from the city: what did a sultan do when he wanted to know what was really going on? Presumably he imitated the Harun ar-Rashid of *The Arabian Nights*, disguised himself, and went out to "wander through the streets and note the quality of people".

Certainly Cairo can only be known on foot: and one of its most magnificent walks begins at the **Bab al-Gadid**, the northern gate of the Citadel. From outside the Citadel this point can be reached by leaving a car near the Sultan Hasan mosque and walking up towards the Citadel, then turning left to climb a road that runs parallel to its walls, bearing on to the first intersection it makes with an old street running downhill.

This old street has other names – Al-Tabbana, Bab al-Wazir – but is best known as **Darb al-Ahmar**. Connecting the Citadel with Bab Zuwayla, the southern gate of Al-Qahirah, it runs through an area that had been cleared for pleasure-gardens by Salah-ad-din, then became fashionable during the reign of An-Nasir Muhammad, when many of his sons-in-law began building there.

First, on the left down a very short sidestreet, for example, are the ruins of a medieval hospital (1420), the *bimaristan* of Mu'ayyad Shaykh; while on the right appear the *madrasah* and tomb of Amir Aytmish al-Baghasi (1348), the remains of the tomb and *sabil-kuttab* of Amir Tarabay as-Sharifi (1503), and the tomb of Azdumur (early 16th century). A hundred yards farther down the street on the right (east) is the palace of **Alin Aq** (1293), later occupied and remodelled by the treacherous Amir Khayrbek, who built his tomb (1502), mosque and *sabil-kuttab* (1502) next to it, creating a northward view that is one of the most picturesque and frequently photographed in Cairo.

On the left (west) across the street from Khayrbek's mosque is the beginning of a 14-unit apartment house with several entrances, dating from 1522, which stretches along the street. Just beyond Khayrbek's mosque on the right (east), meanwhile, is a 17th-century house, with the mosque of **Amir Aqsunqur** (1347), one of An-Nasir Muhammad's sons-in-law, next to it, with tiles from Damascus installed in 1652 by Ibrahim Agha, the first owner of the House, which have inspired guides to call it the "Blue Mosque".

Across the street from Aqsunqur's mosque, next to the 16th-century apartment house, is a 17th-century *sabil* and tomb, then on the east side comes another of Ibrahim Agha's houses (1652)

Al-Azhar University, founded in 970 AD, and surrounding districts. On the far left are the twin minarets of Bab Zuwayla, one of the city's ancient gates.

with his adjoined *sabil* (1639); and beyond the *sabil* is a small Ottoman religious structure, with an Ayyubid minaret (1260) behind it. A little farther down the street, after an intersection, another 17th-century *sabil-kuttab* appears on the left, then a 14th-century tomb on the right.

Jutting into the street from the left, next comes the **mosque of Altanbugha al-Maridani** (1340), notable for its woodwork and marble, which give some idea of what An-Nasir Muhammad's mosque at the Citadel must have been like before the Ottoman conquest; and farther along on the same side of the street is the **mosque of Ahmad al-Mihmandar** (1325) with still another 17th-century *sabil-kuttab* next to it. Finally, on the right as the street turns a corner and Bab Zuwayla comes into view, stands the exquisite funerary mosque of **Amir Qijmas al-Ishaqi** (1481) connected with his *sabil-kuttab* by a bridge over a sidestreet.

Darb al-Ahmar now runs east and west and appropriately leads past **Bab Zuwayla** and the Tentmakers' Bazaar – after a change of name – to the **Islamic Museum**, Cairo's great storehouse and display-case of medieval treasures, which lies 494 metres (1,620 feet) straight ahead, on the northwestern corner of Shari' Port Said and a cluster of cross-streets, at Maydan Ahmad Maher.

Street life: All this monumentality, however, represents only a small fraction of what the Misr of *The Arabian Nights* still has to offer: there are hundreds of medieval buildings in Cairo, dotted and clustered over an area that is larger than Venice.

In Cairo even more than other Arab cities, noise is a measure of life. Commerce hums in one-room shops and buzzes around pushcarts selling everything from fresh fruit to second-hand clothes; bakers and tailors ply their own quiet trades to an obbligato of banging hammers, as neighbouring tinsmiths and furniture-makers carry on their percussive craft, turning out the aluminium buckets or the gilded chairs that are modern necessities of the traditional

The Mosque of al Mu'ayyad makes a quiet sanctuary from the bustling traffic outside.

life. Schoolrooms roar through open windows with mass recitation, everyone's transistor radio blares orgasmic *fioriture*, and five times a day loudspeakers crackle cassettes of the call to prayer from every working minaret. Housewives shriek chit-chat at each other from second and third-floor latticed windows on opposite sides of the street. Chickens cackle from roofs overhead and donkeys bray from the street below. Every few minutes, the scene is punctuated by the growl of a lumbering bus or the wild report of a two-stroke propelling its goggled rider and his overloaded sidecar to someone else's probable death and destruction.

The pungent sweetness of incense wafts from everywhere. It is one of the simple means by which this heavily-peopled street constantly reclaims its own original spirit. Universally believed to dispel all malignancy, whether human or supernatural, incense, like courtesy, does not cost much, but is worth a lot. It gratifies friends, wins strangers, and softens the hearts of enemies.

Street crimes, of the kind so familiar in New York, Stockholm, or Rio, are virtually unknown here, largely because it is inconceivable that passers-by would not come instantly to a victim's aid.

Bab Zuwayla and beyond: Built in 1092 as the southern gateway of Al-Qahirah, **Bab Zuwayla** is the most distinguished of all these old quarters. Originally a palace enclosure, it was opened to commercial development by Salah-ad-Din. Most of the Fatimid buildings disappeared in the course of new construction; and Al-Qahirah rapidly displaced Fustat as the focus of the city's trade and commerce. Through its heart still runs the Qasabah, at once the main artery of the whole medieval city and a single enormous bazaar, straddled momentarily at either end of Al-Qahirah by massive Fatimid gates.

High up on the wall next to the gate at Bab Zuwayla hangs a mysterious trophy of metal objects – weapons, tools, or Sufi instruments – which no one has ever convincingly identified. Directly on top of the gate are two minarets,

An 18th-century *sabil kuttab* in the Ottoman Baroque style.

which have given it such a specific identity that depictions of it were once used as logo-symbols for the modern city. Belonging to the mosque of **Sultan Mu'ayyad Sheikh** (1420), which stands just inside the gate to the left, they also demonstrate that by the end of the 14th century Bab Zuwayla had ceased to be regarded as primarily military.

It is in this mosque that the splendid doors of Sultan Hasan were finally hung and can still be seen. Across the street, with an attached *sabil-kuttab*, is the facade of a caravanserai-emporium called **As-Sukkariyah** (from the Arabic *sukkar*, the source of the word meaning "sugar" in every European language), which has given this district just within the southern Fatimid walls its name.

Cruising up the Qasabah: The Qasabah from here northward has been devoted for eight centuries to buying and selling; 450 yards up the street is another famous commercial district, the **Ghuriyyah**, named for Qansuh Al-Ghuri, one of the last Mamluk sultans. His *madrasah* and mausoleum (1505)

stand on the site of the **Silk Merchants' Bazaar**, a covered street-market that was once the most famous in Cairo. The place is still bursting with trade.

At this point the Qasabah's north-south axis is suddenly sliced by the modern east-west traffic of **Shari' al-Azhar**, cut through old Misr in 1930 to provide tram service for the greatest and most long-lived of the Fatimids' foundations, the **University of Al-Azhar**, which continues to attract Muslim students from around the world. Lying a short distance down Shari' al-Azhar to the east, Al-Azhar's oldest buildings represent a variety of endowments from the 10th to the late-19th centuries.

On the other side of Shari' al-Azhar, which can now be crossed safely only by using a pedestrian overpass, the Qasabah continues north, but is soon interrupted, just beyond a 15th-century *madrasah*, by another modern street, **Shari' al-Muski**. Connected with old Christian and European quarters, it soon became favoured by foreign merchants and by the end of the 19th century was

The mosques of Rifa'i and Sultan Hasan at festival time.

lined from end to end with European-owned shops.

The Qasabah itself still maintains its traditional character. Around this intersection spices and scents are sold; beyond are goldsmiths; and the first major street off the Qasabah to the right (east) leads to the **Khan al-Khalili**, famous formerly for Turkish goods and now the tourists' bazaar, where locals also go to buy jewellery and antiques (*see "Markets and Bazaars"*). Best buys in ordinary brassware will still be found in the Qasabah itself, for at this point it becomes the **Suq al-Nahhasin**, the Coppersmiths' Bazaar, an identity it has had since the 14th century, where brassware is sold at local prices by weight, regardless of its age.

Between the Palaces: A few steps further along, the Qasabah makes a jog to the left around a *sabil*, added in 1326 by An-Nasir Muhammad to the great hospital-tomb-*madrasah* complex that had already been built here by Sultan Qalawun, his father, 40 years earlier. This section of the Qasabah was known

even then as **Bayn al-Qasrayn**, "Between the Two Palaces", in commemoration of the two huge Fatimid palaces that had stood facing each other on this site over a century earlier still. Here two *madrasahs* honouring Ayyubid sultans were built over Fatimid ruins; and one of them, the *madrasah* built to house his tomb by the widow of Sultan as-Salih Ayyub, the last real ruler of the Ayyubid line, would later become the seat of the Mamluk's supreme judiciary.

Incessant attacks by crusaders had led As-Salih to the wholesale importation of slave-cossacks from Central Asia. He could hardly have foreseen that in 1250, only weeks after his death, they would murder his son and heir and make themselves masters over their own new empire. Next to his tomb-*madrasah*, showing perhaps a kind of belated loyalty, Baybars, the greatest of As-Salih's Mamluks, the acknowledged founder of this empire, built another *madrasah*.

Appropriately, Cairo's principal slave market was also held here in the Bayn-al-Qasrayn, where Mamluks and girls,

mainly Circassian and Greek, continued to be bought and sold until the time of Muhammad Ali.

One should imagine the Bayn al-Qasrayn, however, as it might have been after business hours on the night of some Mamluk festival, when it would have been illuminated as high as the tops of its six minarets by thousands of lamps and cressets.

Silks and satins would have been hung from upper windows, with more spread over the dust of the street for the sultan's horse to tread upon as he came riding down the Darb al-Ahmar and the Qasabah from the Citadel. Preceded by an amir bearing the Saddle-cloth, the emblem of state, by two pages in yellow silk and gold brocade mounted on white horses, by a standard-bearer, and by a musician playing a flute, the sultan would have been surrounded by halberdiers uniformed in yellow silk. An amir bearing a Poniard of State accompanied him on either side, the yellow silk royal Parasol surmounted with its Golden Bird was held over his head.

To recall some semblance of this splendour, extensive repair work is being constantly carried out in the Bayn-al-Qasrayn by the Antiquities Organisation and the German Archaeological Institute, who are responsible for the restoration of both the delightful 18th-century *sabil-kuttab* that overlooks the area from the north, and the 14th-century palace on the corner nearby.

To the Northern Gates of Al-Qahirah: Farther north, in a stretch of the Qasabah where such items as copper bean-pots and finials for mosques are made, stands the **Aqmar Mosque**, one of the few remaining Fatimid monuments; and around the corner at the second turning afterwards, on a side-street called the Darb al-Asfar, stands one of the best examples of an 18th-century Cairene townhouse, the **Bayt as-Sihaymi**, a merchant's dwelling that was inhabited by the owners until 1961. More typical than the Gayer-Anderson house, it illustrates not only the standard division of rooms into a *salamlik* and a *haramlik*, but also the ingenuity with which archi-

The *Haramlik* or ladies' quarters of an 18th-century palace, the Bayt as-Sihaymi.

tects used courtyards, fountains set in sunken floors, high ceilings, and north-facing wind-catchers on the roof to counter the heat of a long Cairene summer.

Just before the Qasabah exits through Bab al-Futuh, one of the two northern gates of Al-Qahirah, a space opens out to form another market, where fine agricultural produce from what were formerly the royal family's experimental farms is sold in its various seasons, the garlic being especially priced. Overlooking this area on its eastern side is the congregational **mosque of the Fatimid Caliph Al-Hakim**, finished in 1013 and restored in 1980 by the Bohora, an Ismaili Shi'ite sect who are based in Bombay, but trace the ancestry of their leaders back directly to the Fatimids, and who have imported features that give the building a touch of India.

Bab al-Futuh, the great "Gate of Conquest", **Bab an-Nasr**, "The Gate of Victory", the other northern gate of Al-Qahirah, and the 1,080-feet (330-metre) stretch of wall between them – all built by the Fatimids' Armenian general Badr al Gamali in 1087 – have been restored and are worth touring. Few buildings testify better to the sweep of Cairo's cosmopolitan history: Badr's Armenian architects were skilled military specialists; and their work originally made use of blocks quarried and carved under the pharaohs, some of which were scratched in turn, more than seven centuries later, with Napoleonic grafitti.

Outside the two northern gates is an open area, beyond which the Qasabah moves off from Bab al-Futuh northward through the **Husayniyyah district**, known both as a butchers' quarter and as a hotbed of nationalist sentiment; its patriotic meat-cutters gave the French a great deal of trouble and were bombarded by them more than once from the Fatimid walls. Adjoining the Husayniyyah on the east opposite Bab an-Nasr is a famous cemetery. Ibn Khaldun, the 14th-century historian so dazzled by the city, is among the celebrated who are buried here, though the area is so built up with dwellings among the graves that it looks thoroughly residential.

Brass merchant in the Coppersmiths' Bazaar.

Living among the dead: This fact, however, makes it a good introduction to Cairo's great **Northern and Southern Cemeteries**, which Western journalists delight in calling collectively "The City of the Dead", though they grew up at different times and have always been separated from each other by the limestone spur on which and out of which the Citadel was built. People live in these cemeteries, a situation journalists explain by quotations from official statistics indicating that the modern city has a terrible housing shortage. Foreigners made the same observations and offered the same rationale, however, as long ago as the 15th century; and the fact is that these cemeteries, as far as anyone knows, have always had inhabitants, because many of the tombs they enclose are large permanent structures.

Permanent structures demand caretakers and guardians and soon have communities around them, the more so if they are used for occasional purposes other than merely housing the deal. The tombs of popular Cairene saints are always thronged, but on Thursday evenings, Fridays, and major feast days the living Cairenes frequently visit their family tombs – as ancient Creeks and Romans did or as modern Europeans used to on All Saints' Day – and have picnics among the graves.

This custom was elaborated by the Mamluk Sultans and amirs. Every guest wore his most extravagant clothes: silks from China (like the cups, bowls and serving dishes) embroidered by the ladies of local *harims*, brocades manufactured in the Mamluks' own workshops. Amidst an abundance of flowers, perfume and incense, eating, drinking and music received rapturous attention, but if the tomb-site was suitable, there might also be horse-racing, mounted archery, and even hunting expeditions. The Northern Cemetery actually began in the 13th century as a hippodrome with viewing stands, evolving into a royal necropolis only later.

The Southern Cemetery is larger – it begins as far north as the mosque of Ibn Tulun – and much older. Several of the

Turco-Syrian tiles at the Mosque of Aqsunqur.

tombs have been pilgrimage sites for centuries, particularly that of Imam as-Shafi'i, a descendant of the Prophet's uncle and founder of the most influential of the four orthodox schools of Sunni jurisprudence, who died in Egypt in 820. Nearby is the mausoleum built by Muhammad Ali in 1816 for his favourite wife, where her three sons and other family members, including King Faruq, are also interred, alongside many of their retainers. All around in every direction, interspersed with apartment blocks and ranging in date from yesterday to 10 centuries ago, are a multitude of other tombs. The most notable are those of Burgi Mamluk amirs, set within the remains of complexes that frequently included *khanqahs* and other large residential structures.

What these amirs built in the Southern Cemetery, however, can hardly compare with what their sultans built in the Northern Cemetery. The Burgi period marks the high point in the development of both the carved stone dome and the three stage minaret – with a square base, an octagonal second storey, and a cylindrical upper storey, elaborately carved and topped by a bulb set on colonettes – features that used to dominate Cairo's skyline.

Unhampered in this freshly opened necropolis by considerations of space, the Circassian rulers were free here to indulge their tastes for piety and pleasure to the full. The results still visible are the remains of five huge monuments that may represent an epitome in Mamluk architecture. The most important are the complexes built by Farrag, the son of Barquq, the first of the Burgi line, and Qaitbay, the longest-lived, most active, and most famous of these Circassians, whose *madrasah* and mausoleum, built between 1472 and 1474, are the jewels of the period.

The city's new centre: Maydan at-Tahrir was originally named Maydan Ismailiyyah, for the Khedive Ismail, whose statue was later supposed to be placed on the huge granite plinth at its southeastern corner. An open place, it demarcated one end of the new admin-

Houses encroach on a medieval cemetery. Debris is thrown on roofs because of inadequate refuse collection.

istrative, commercial and residential quarter of Maydan Ismailiyyah, laid out by the Khedive in 1865. Despite a strategic position near the Nile, however, Maydan Ismailiyyah did not achieve its present importance until after the July Revolution (1952). Its name was changed and the mid-19th century barracks on its western (Nile) side, occupied throughout most of their history by British Guards regiments, were demolished, to be replaced by the **Corniche**, two new administrative buildings, and the **Nile Hilton**, the first major hotel built in Cairo since 1910. On the south side of the Maydan the remains of a palace were removed and a gray concrete block was run up to accommodate those portions of several ministries that deal with the administration of permits, licenses, visas, expulsion orders and endless other bureaucratic forms: the **Mugama'a**, a Kafkaesque castle of red tape, notorious not merely for venality, insolence, entrapment, frustration, and delay, but also for the number of suicides that have made use of its 14-storey central stairwell. Situated across the street from this monster at the extreme southeastern corner of the Maydan is the only building left from Ismail's era, a small palace dating from 1878, which now houses the **American University**. On the north side of Maydan at-Tahrir is the **Egyptian Museum**.

The Egyptian Museum: Built in 1902 under Abbas II Hilmi and uniquely dignified with Latin inscriptions that may testify to his education at the Theresianum, the Museum holds the world's greatest collection of Egyptian artifacts. It should be an early stop for any intelligent visitor, who would also be well advised not to join a group or hire a guide, "official" or otherwise, but to walk slowly around the building on two or three different occasions. Displays on the ground floor are of large objects arranged more or less chronologically running clockwise, so that a left turn from the entrance foyer leads, for example, to the famous Menkaure triads from Giza, while a right turn leads to Hellenistic painting and statuary.

Qasr el Nil Bridge, circa 1910, Cairo.

172

No one should be advised to miss anything if possible, but visitors in a hurry might turn right and go immediately upstairs to the eastern and northern galleries on the upper floor, where the treasures from the tombs of Tutankhamen and Hetepheres are displayed.

Not to be missed, in addition, is Case H in the upper foyer, containing small masterpieces that are the pride of the Museum, many of them famous from photographs that give no idea of their diminutive size: the ivory statuette of Khufu from Abydos; the black steatite bust of Queen Tiyi; the statuette of a Nubian girl with a single earring; the gilded statuette of Ptah; the dancing pygmies carved from ivory, made moveable by an ingenious arrangement of strings; and the blue faience hippopotami of which reproductions have been made that are sold in boutiques all over the world.

The Egyptian Museum, Cairo.

Of special interest also are the models which are displayed in Room 27 on the upper floor, mostly from an 11th-Dynasty tomb in Thebes, showing daily life circa 2000 BC.

Vestiges of glamour: Running northeast from between the front of the Museum and Maydan at-Tahrir, its entrance demarcated on one side by TWA's main office and on the other by an apparently permanent triangular excavation – where, until 1961, Cairo's two most distinguished private houses stood – is **Shari' Qasr an-Nil**. Still the city's main shopping street, it has vestiges of the glamour that Ismail intended when he planned this part of the city. Up the street on the left is the **Automobile Club**, founded in 1924, a favourite haunt of King Faruq, who loved playing poker for outrageous stakes, and 100 yards further on, where the street enters a square, is **Groppi's Corner House** (1924), the second of two luxurious catering establishments founded in Cairo by an Alexandrian Swiss family.

In the years before World War II, this branch of Groppi's sold Sèvres, Meissen, Lalique and silver as well as afternoon teas, aperitifs, confectionery, patisserie and delicatessen items. In the rear were a garden and a rotunda with a

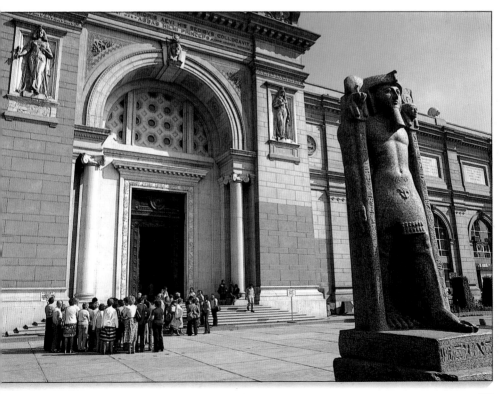

stained-glass ceiling, where concerts were given three nights a week during the winter season (November–April), with dinner and supper-dancing on the other four nights. But in 1952 the rotunda was burned, the dancing stopped, and Groppi's clientele began to change. A dwindling handful of old Turkish ladies, who still arrived for tea out of habit, bundled into pre-War furs, gradually found themselves elbowed out of the way by students, prostitutes, pimps and petty gangsters, though the bar remained popular with local businessmen until the whole place was sold to a teetotalling Arab in 1983.

The Revolution also changed the name and appearance of the square in front of Groppi's. Until then it had officially carried the Arabic name adopted by a Bonapartist officer, Colonel Anthelme Sève, who had entered Muhammad Ali's service after Waterloo, had converted to Islam, and as Sulayman Pasha al-Faransawi ("The Frenchman"), had distinguished himself brilliantly. The north-south street running through the square

likewise carried Sulayman Pasha's name, which is still used for both street and square by senior residents. A statue of the old hussar stood in this square until 1963, when it was replaced by the prosaic figure of a pre-Revolutionary nationalist banker.

Across the square, opposite Groppi's and on the same side of Shari' Qasr an-Nil, where a later building has been handsomely renovated by a foreign bank, stood the townhouse of one of Muhammad Ali's great-grandsons, which became the **Savoy**, second only to Shepheard's in glamour among the capital's hotels during the Edwardian era. Royalty stayed here, and several suites were taken every winter between 1898 and 1914 by Sir Ernest Cassel, the international financier, whose guests would include celebrities such as the Duke and Duchess of Devonshire, Sir Winston Churchill, or Mrs Keppel, King Edward's last *maîtresse en titre*. Evening dress was mandatory for late dining, as it was in all of Cairo's first-class hotels.

Banks and airline offices line most of

Groppi's, a centre of cosmopolitan life in the 1920s and '30s, is still a favourite Cairene meeting place.

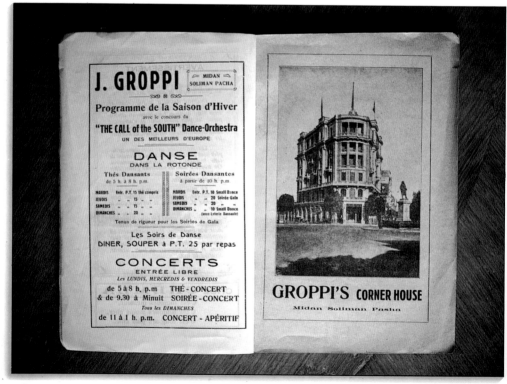

Shari' Qasr an-Nil in the stretch to the next square, with shops in between. Best buys are Egyptian yard goods – cottons, of course, printed and plain, but also silk and wool – and leather goods. Another nationalist adorns this second square and the north-south street that crosses Shari' Qasr an-Nil here again has two names – Shari' Emad ad-Din or Shari' Muhammad Farid – between which Cairenes choose according to age and politics. Down the north-south street to the right is **St Joseph's**, Cairo's biggest Catholic church, built in 1909; and nearly opposite is its finest neo-Islamic building, the main branch of **Bank Misr**, built in 1922, which has original woodwork and a particularly splendid Mamluk-style marble floor.

The pleasures of Azbakiyyah: Shari' Qasr an-Nil leads on into **Shari' Gumhuriyyah**, formerly Shari' 'Abdin, which runs north and south and connects **'Abdin Palace**, the Muhammad Ali family's chief residence, with the main railway station, where their private trains are now on display at a fine **Railway Museum**. An early 18th-century Ottoman mosque on the corner of Shari' Gumhuriyyah and Shari' Qasr an-Nil indicates the overlapping of Ismail's new quarter with old Misr as it was before the French marched in; and a left turn into Shari' Gumhuriyyah leads to **Azbakiyyah**, which was founded as a pleasure zone in the 15th century, but had evolved into an upper-class residential area by the time Bonaparte made his headquarters there in 1798.

When Napoleon moved in, the focus of the area was a picturesque seasonal lake that filled during the Nile flood. Local resistance and stern punitive measures soon reduced most of the luxurious dwellings along its southern and eastern shores to ruins; and during a revolt of Albanian troops after the French departure, Bonaparte's own palace overlooking the western shore, where his successor had been assassinated by an Egyptian patriot, was also burned.

Under Muhammad Ali, however, who established official residences here for himself and members of his family,

Traffic jams ensnarl in downtown Cairo.

Azbakiyyah was soon rebuilt and became dotted with new administrative offices. After 1837, when the lake was drained and its site converted into a park, hotels began to move their premises into Azbakiyyah from the old European quarter along Shari' Muski to the east. One of them, the New British Hotel, was to become world-famous under the name of its first owner – **Shepheard**'s. There was already a French theatre, which would soon be joined by restaurants and coffee-houses.

In 1868 Ismail reduced the park to an octagonal garden and the remainder of the old lake-site was opened for development. New squares were created in three of the four corner-spaces left by the octagon's shortest sides and new public buildings were erected, the most striking of which was a theatre for opera. Built entirely of wood and completed within five months during 1869, the **Cairo Opera House** saw the premier of *Aida* in 1871 and later became renowned for its collections of manuscripts, scores, costumes and sets, all of which were consumed by fire when the building burned in 1971. Its site is now identified by one of the city's few high-rise car parks. Commissioned by Ismail, later erected (1882) in the square in front of the Opera, and still standing on the same spot, is a heroic equestrian **statue of Ibrahim Pasha**, which has survived both fire and revolution.

Two of Ismail's new streets, both still fashionable – Shari' Abdel Khaliq Tharwat and Shari' 'Adli, where the largest of Cairo's synagogues stands – lead westward from Ibrahim's statue, while Shari' Gumhuriyyah continues north along the western edge of the **Azbakiyyah Garden**. Reduced in size again in 1872, but elegantly redesigned by Ismail's French city-planner as an enclosed English-style garden on the order of the Parc Monceau in Paris, the Garden at present retains its octagonal shape, but otherwise shows the devastating result of 20th-century priorities.

Public-sector construction, including a street driven through the octagon's heart has eliminated its central pond,

Posters on Opera Square.

destroyed its plan, perverted its intention, and occupied nearly a third of its green space, while Ismail's exotic trees and shrubs have been allowed to die. Only a few neglected 19th-century buildings suggest a time when joys were more elegant, plentiful and cheaper than they are in Cairo now.

Grand hotels: The **Continental Hotel** still stands overlooking the garden from the west, though it has been cut in half and concealed by a row of shopfronts. It was owned at an earlier stage (as the New Hotel) by Ismail himself and came to rank third among Cairo's hotels after the Savoy and, of course, Shepheard's.

Shepheard's itself, destroyed by fire in 1952 – the new Shepheard's on the Corniche has nothing in common with the old one but the name – stood at a site farther north on Shari' Gumhuriyyah now occupied by a highrise. In Ismail's time there were at least seven other hotels nearby, half a dozen restaurants, and a dozen foreign consulates.

The area had also been known earlier, however, for its prostitutes, pedlars, mountebanks, jugglers, acrobats and beggars, a reputation that deservedly did not diminish until long after the second of two world wars, during which the city was occupied by British and ANZAC troops who were eager for such diversions.

Shari' Clot Bey, ironically named for Muhammad Ali's chief advisor on public health, was famous until quite recently for its brothels. And there is still something raffish about other streets just north of the garden – where Bimbashi McPherson watched through an open window of the **Eden Palace Hotel** as Johnny Black made love to his Turkish mistress before going out on another murderous job; or where the runaway Princess de Caraman-Chimay (née Clara Ward of Detroit) sauntered on the arm of Janczi Rigo the gypsy violinist – something that breathes of mysterious *Arabian Nights* hugger-mugger despite the superficially European appearance of things.

A truly traditional quarter: Farther north and east of Azbakiyyah is an area where tourists never go and few Cairenes ever visit, the old **Bab al-Bahr quarter**, long identified with Christians, which probably exemplifies the meaning of tradition better than any other in the city. Though it contains very few historic monuments, its streets follow the 15th-century pattern surveyed in 1800 by Napoleon's *savants*, whose map remains the only accurate guide.

The whole district has always been maintained, as their own place, by its residents, who have rebuilt their houses continually on the old sites. Here, as in any truly Eastern city, distinct professions and trades cluster together, to create streets of shops selling and repairing sewing machines, for example, or making and selling electric lamps. Untouched by decay or redevelopment, the Bab al-Bahr quarter may represent the best of Cairo's old urban spirit.

Newer districts, however, still have some charm. **Al-Gazirah** (The Island), joined to the mainland by three bridges, two of them near Maydan at-Tahrir, offers not only **Zamalek**, a suburb popular among European residents, but also

Minaret and billboard compete for attention in central Cairo.

several individual attractions for tourists. The **Gazirah Exhibition Grounds**, for example, which were replaced in 1982 as the site of the city's international expositions by the new **Cairo International Fairgrounds** at Madinet Nasr, have since become instead the location of a Japanese-built cultural complex that Cairenes call the **Opera House**, seeing it as a replacement for the old Opera House in Azbakiyyah.

The **Museum of Modern Art** has meanwhile been moved from outmoded and overcrowded premises on Maydan Finney in Doqqi to one of the old permanent pavilions; and another permanent pavilion has been set aside for exhibitions of work by contemporary artists.

Finally, it was decided to construct a new **Museum of Egyptian Civilisation** here as well, to complement the displays of objects at the Egyptian Museum with working models and live demonstrations.

Across the road from the Gazirah Exhibition Grounds, in the park at the southern end of the island, is the **Mukhtar Museum**, housing works by Egypt's greatest modern sculptor, one of the handful of 20th-century Egyptian artists to achieve international recognition. North is the 500-foot-high (152 metre) **Cairo Tower**, erected in 1957, about which unkind jokes are made, but which is set in a beautiful garden and offers, when the lifts are working, a remarkable view of the city.

Farther north are the grounds of two clubs: the **National**, home of the national (*Ahli*) football team, with its own stadium; and the once-famous **Gazirah Sporting Club**, which offers a wide variety of facilities for tennis, riding, swimming and other sports. Temporary memberships are available at the Gazirah Club. This will especially attract keen bridge players, who may run into the likes of Omar Sharif at the club's tables. Arab horses from the best studs in Egypt, which race at the Gazirah track on alternate weeks in the season, offer another form of excitement.

Opposite the northern entrance to the Gazirah Club is the charming house

built in 1927 for *Nabil* (Lord) Amr Ibrahim, a great-great-grandson of Ibrahim Pasha, as a *salamlik* in the Khedival style. Confiscated after the Revolution, it now houses the Muhammad Mahmud and Emilienne Luce Khalil Collection of paintings and objets d'art, a bequest to the nation moved here when the Khalils' house on the Nile at Giza was absorbed into President Sadat's personal administrative complex.

Sixteen of the Khalil collection's Orientalist paintings, which now would evoke great interest, had meanwhile already been given to the **Muhammad Ali Club** near Maydan at-Tahrir, formerly Cairo's most exclusive private institution, rescued after the Revolution by the Foreign Ministry and transformed into a club for diplomats. They can still be seen there.

The **Amr Ibrahim house** is worth visiting for its own sake; for the Khalil collection, which is particularly strong in 19th-century French painting and sculpture and in chinoiserie; and for the **Al-Salam Gallery**, a small exhibition space in the basement where the Ministry of Culture stages one-man and group shows of contemporary artists.

Gazirah Palace: Immediately north, landmarked by a huge old banyan tree, one of Muhammad Ali's imported species, is the **Italian Cultural Centre**, outstanding among foreign institutions in Cairo for its support of the arts, where there are also exhibitions. The banyan indicates that the land the Amr Ibrahim house sits on formerly belonged to Ismail's **Gazirah Palace**, whose gardens stretched from one side of the island to the other.

The Palace's grounds now survive more or less intact only in two small portions: the **Fish Garden**, 350 yards to the west, between Shari' Gabalayyah and Shari' Hasan Sabri, a public park since 1902, which still has the original estate's grotto-aquarium as its most picturesque feature; and the enclosed garden attached to the **Marriott Hotel**, standing just across Shari' Lutfallah immediately to the east.

The central block of the hotel incorporates Ismail's Palace itself. Legend says it was built for the Empress Eugenie

The Nile in Cairo at sunset.

to reside in during the Suez Canal inaugural celebrations of 1869, but it was actually begun in 1863 and opened in 1868. Its chief architect was the German von Diebitsch, a pioneer in modular design, and its grounds were laid out by the Frenchman Barillet-Deschamps, who planned not only Ismail's final version of the Azbakiyyah Garden, but also every large green space that Cairo can still boast, including the grounds of the present zoo in Giza.

When the grounds were laid out in 1867, the Nile was diverted on the western side of the island and the resultant dry channel was turned into an irrigation canal for the gardens. Entire displays of masterworks were meanwhile being bought at the Exposition Universelle in Paris to serve as the palace's major furniture. Many of these pieces can be seen within the present hotel, having survived the palace's later history.

Although the Abdin Palace has been closed to the public for some years, two other palaces elsewhere in the city that once belonged to the Muhammad Ali family have been made into museums and can still be seen: **Shubra Kiosk** on the northern edge of the city and the **Manyal Palace** complex on Rawdah Island, now partially occupied by a hotel. Built in 1826, the Shubra Kiosk's plain square exterior conceals an Ottoman-Baroque fantasy within: an immense marble basin with a marble island in its centre, where it was later rumoured that Muhammad Ali sat cross-legged on silken cushions smoking a four-foot-long *shibuq*, while his *harim* cavorted naked in the water around him. The original Turkish glass chandeliers still hang throughout, though the surrounding gardens were illuminated with gas from their own plant as early as 1829, making them a great showplace.

The Manyal Palace complex was built between 1901 and 1929 and left to the Egyptian nation in 1955 by Prince Muhammad Ali, the younger brother of Khedive Abbas II Hilmi and a first cousin of King Faruq. It includes six separate structures, of which the most interesting are a museum exhibiting Faruq's game-

shooting trophies; the prince's own residence with its furnishings; and a 14-room museum housing his collections of family memorabilia. The banyan-shaded gardens, featuring dracaena and philodendron, are also worth a visit.

Zamalek and other suburbs: The name **Zamalek** covers all of Gazirah north of the Gazirah Sporting Club. Less green, less exclusively residential, and far more crowded than it once was, Zamalek now boasts on its western Nile-side a street (Shari' Abu 'I-Feda) of cheap night-clubs, which have replaced the old house-boat brothels that used to ply this stretch of the river.

Similar nightlife can be found along Shari' al-Ahram, the boulevard leading to the Pyramids, while more elegant diversion is available in the nightclubs of the city's major hotels, most of which also have good discos. Arabic-speaking seekers of down-market pleasure may prowl Azbakiyyah and adjacent streets in the centre of town, but those who are in the petro-dollar fast track simply order their fresh tarts by telephone.

For the more sober-minded, the **Akhnaton Gallery** on Shari' Ma'ahad as-Swissri' presents exhibitions of art. Zamalek also offers excellent shopping at a number of boutiques. Designer-models for women are a particularly good buy and reflect the conservative *chic* of a district where there are several embassies on every major street. Nearly a quarter of the 140-odd foreign missions in Cairo maintain their chancelleries or ambassadors' residences here. And most of the rest are scattered throughout areas on the Western bank, in Giza, Doqqi, Aguza, or Madinat al-Muhandesin, which were still rural hinterland as recently as 1970.

One or two embassies have installed themselves in **Heliopolis (Misr al-Gadidah)**, the new upmarket suburb laid out on the city's northeastern desert edge in 1906. Development of Heliopolis began at the wrong end of a boom in land and property values, but was so intelligently planned otherwise that its density has remained low, its traffic has not become unmanageable, its original

Central Cairo as seen from the Cairo Tower.

neo-Islamic architecture still predominates over new slabs of concrete.

Meanwhile the British and Americans have remained faithful to **Garden City**, laid out at almost the same time as Heliopolis, but on the site of an old estate of Ibrahim Pasha's south of Maydan at-Tahrir. The British Consulate-General – now the **Residency** – had in fact been there earlier, since 1893, and was restored in 1986 to its full late-Victorian splendour. Overcrowded with banks and their customers during the day, Garden City recovers some of its charm at night.

Towards the 21st century: Unlike the British Ambassador, most Cairenes live in relatively new "informal-sector" housing, which accounts for as much as 80 percent of all residential construction since 1965, when the city had less than a quarter of its present population of 14 million.

The result is that the built-up agglomeration we call "Cairo", only 6 miles (10 km) long in 1965, has been extended some 15 miles (24 km) and now covers the eastern bank of the Nile solidly for 21 miles (35 km). It has even begun to reach deep into the desert, and in many areas is without such basic services as running water, drainage, electricity, or paved roads. For political reasons, the government itself meanwhile created multiple disincentives to maintenance of public and private structures or systems that already existed, while undertaking new projects of its own that were often devastating to the environment. Pollution-heavy industrial zones were thus arbitrarily planted at either end of the new metropolis.

Thus the resort town of **Helwan**, at the southern terminus of the metro system, formerly a fashionable spa – an Egyptian Saratoga or Tunbridge Wells, famed for its baths, its Casino and its Japanese Garden – rapidly became a third-world industrial slum, sharing the fate that had already overtaken Shubra on the northern fringe, where Muhammad Ali's Kiosk is all that remains of an old and once popular summer retreat.

Midway between Helwan and Maydan

Boats in the rare yellow light of a sandstorm.

at-Tahrir, the planned residential community of **Maadi**, once identified by its groves of trees and the green fields that surrounded it, can now be picked out from any point in the city by 50-storey concrete apartment blocks, built on precious agricultural land in defiance of local ordinances.

Since 1975, and especially since 1980, the government has made huge efforts, mostly successful, to try to catch up with and correct the course of the city's growth, curtailing unofficial wildcat construction while installing new systems for telephones, electricity, water, drainage, traffic and even gas. Some small new green spaces have been created where rubbish was once dumped.

How such changes will affect the old spirit of the Mother of the World in the long run, only time, of which she knows so much, will tell. What is certain, however, is that the same qualities that have created her ramshackle charm and made her the most endearing city on earth have also made her the most humane; and that if these qualities are allowed to perish, Egyptians, and indeed the World, will have suffered a major loss.

Naguib Mahfuz, the great Egyptian novelist, winner of the 1988 Nobel Prize for Literature, is a true son of the city: he was born in the Gamaliyyah, less than a stone's throw from Bayn-al-Qasrayn. His most famous work, the *Cairo Trilogy*, is set in the heart of Cairo's historic zone, while later books have had settings in virtually every other part of the city. And all his novels radiate a sense that Cairo – the city itself – has its own special morale: not unlike the spirit that travellers and residents found in pre-war Paris or Berlin, but unique in its depth as well as in its appeal.

This morale is linked with Cairo's typical attitudes and lifestyles, which in turn have themselves been shaped and conditioned by the city's streets and monuments. Mahfuz is no longer alone in having seen that these streets and monuments therefore have a moral meaning; and one that is in danger of being obscured and even lost as they are transformed or disappear.

Frenetic construction testifies to Cairo's housing shortage.

MARKET AND BAZAARS

The best way to get a feel for the living energy of any city, beyond the epidermis of its monuments and museums or the skeleton of its streets, is to examine its circulatory system: the mainstream and tributaries of its economic life.

For Cairo, at the crossroads of continents and the nexus of the Nile, the function of marketplace has always been vital. Like Rome, the city's origin lay in its location at an easy crossing of the river. Commerce grew out of the transit of merchandise. Egyptian Babylon was already a settlement of buyers and sellers; and the coming of Islam in the 7th century brought a new impetus to business, for despite its Bedouin origins, Islam was an urban-centred religion. The prophet Muhammad had himself been a merchant; and the codes of his revelation called for fair play, respect for property and inheritance, and a communal spirit. Egypt, with the new city of Fustat as its capital, became the centre of an enormous area of free trade within the Muslim empire.

Throughout the Middle Ages, as it added more quarters and spread to the north, Cairo boomed. It was an international entrepôt for slaves, ivory, textiles, livestock, spices and luxury goods; and until the 15th century, the dinars and dirhams of the Cairo mint were the most stable currency in the Mediterranean. Long before the Mamluks' extortionate monopoly of the spice trade had pushed Europeans to search for new routes to the East and led indirectly to Columbus' discovery of America, crafts such as metalworking, ceramics, weaving and glass-making had also turned the city into an industrial centre. Fatimid lustre-ware, glass, and textiles were enlisted early among the treasures of European cathedrals, while Mamluk metalwork and carpets have become prizes for museums.

Egyptian taste, however, was even more sophisticated: as early as the 14th century, for example, the kilns of Cairo were turning out quantities of imitation Chinese pottery, a fact that shows not only the extent of Egypt's trading links, but also indicates the city's thirst for cosmopolitan luxury.

The coming of Ottoman rule in 1517 brought coffee to replace spices, but marked a rigidification of the economic structure and a slackening of the entrepreneurial pulsebeat. Guilds and other professional organisations came to dominate the city's economic life. Cairo was divided along ethnic and economic lines into strictly defined districts, each with its own specialisation. Over generations, trades were kept within the hands of a few families, so that by 1800 over 300 professional unions occupied 12 bazaars and 80 marketplaces.

The industrial age came to Egypt in fits and starts. The legacy of the medieval marketplace has therefore had time to adapt, as opposed to being swallowed up by, modern mass-production and marketing. It is this fact that makes Cairo's market life so interesting. Even Nasser's socialist experiment and mammoth bureaucracy spawned traditional offshoots, as the booths of photographers, scribes, and fixers outside many government offices attest. The zone of boutiques and department stores in the modernised centre of town is still ringed with distinct market areas catering to specialised trades. In this sense Cairo remains the Oriental City *par excellence.*

The Khan al-Khalili: At one corner of a triangle of markets that stretches south to Bab Zuwayla and west to Azbakiyyah is the Khan al-Khalili, a good place to begin exploring older parts of the city. Founded by a Mamluk amir in 1382, the original *khan* or caravanserai grew into the headquarters for merchants of Turkish wares. By the present century, it had become the centre for retailing the products of traditional crafts. Today, while souvenirs and trinkets continue to make headway on the shelves, the narrow lanes of the Khan still conceal articles of fine workmanship and occasionally true works of art, though many things, such as carpets, papyrus, antiques, appliqué work, and *gallibiyas* (caftans), are best procured elsewhere. Within the Khan, the better bargains are leather goods, inlaid boxes, silver, gold, jewellery (the stones are mostly artificial, as the dealers will tell you), brass and copper.

Haggling is called for in most transactions in the Khan, though not in all other *suqs*. Some people are born bargainers, while others botch the business miserably. A few tips: relax and take your time. Shop around and *never* spend money for politeness' sake. Keep up a cheerful banter and maintain eye contact as much as possible. In Egypt nearly everyone is a softy at heart, so charm is essential. Be sure of what you want and calculate how much it is worth to you before entering negotiations. Couples should be particularly prudent – best to let one person do the talking while the other maintains silence and a sour expression: when husband turns to wife and says, "Do you really think we should, dear?" the merchant has his cue to home in for the kill.

The Khan al-Khalili strictly speaking is bordered on the south by Shari' Muski and

Running left off the Qasabah at a small vegetable market is Shari' Amir al Guyushi, where the cacophonous bang and clash of hammers announces the presence of dozens of metalworking ateliers: this ancient street extends westward for 2 miles (3 km) through mat-makers, glass recyclers and dye-makers to Ramses Station. The Qasabah meanwhile leads on northward through garlic, onion and lemon markets to Bab al-Futuh. On Fridays a market for pigeons convenes outside this gate, while 5 minutes' walking further north along an insalubrious lane into the Husayn-iyyah quarter leads to a pair of traditional glass-blowing shops.

Southwards from the crossroads of Shari'

on the west by the Qasabah, the main street of medieval Cairo, here called Shari' Muizz il Din. Northwards along the Qasabah from the Khan are gold and silversmiths, then the Suq am-Nahhasin, the Brass and Copper-smiths Market.

Shops here cater more to local needs and much of the work is now done in aluminum, but better bargains are to be had than in the Khan. A zone of monumental buildings, Bayn al-Qasrayn, comes next, beyond which are a dozen shops specialising in water pipes, café accessories, and cooking pots.

Textile merchant in no hurry to sell his goods.

Muski and the Qasabah, a turning to the right alongside the mosque of Sultan Al-Ashraf Barsbay brings us into the Suq al-Attarin, the picturesque Spice Bazaar. Its flagstoned lanes are mere corridors among scores of tiny booths stocked with bottles of essences and bags of spices. Slats of sunlight pick out swirling spice dust kicked up by shuffling feet, as black-clad women of the older quarters procure herbal remedies, perfumes, aph-rodisiacs, and fertility potions.

A few shops further on, a pedestrian over-pass crosses bustling Shari' al-Azhar. On the other side, where the Qasabah plunges into what was the famous Silk Merchants' Bazaar, is the Ghuriyyah. Passages to the right under the mosque of al-Ghuri lead to a lane parallel to the Qasabah. On this tiny street, more of the Spice Bazaar, truncated with the cutting of Shari' al-Azhar, merges with a market selling carpets, blankets and finally shoes, all at fixed prices.

Bab Zuwayla: Southwards towards Bab Zuwayla, the shops along the Qasabah bulge with all manner of useful household goods, from teapots and brooms to prayer mats. One of the few remaining manufactories for tarbooshes stands here: new fezzes can be bought or old ones reblocked. Beyond the massive 11th-century gate of Bab Zuwayla itself, with its spectacular twin minarets, lies a

through an assortment of saddles and bridles, colourful tin lamps, butchers' blocks, garden chairs, rat-traps, beach umbrellas, marble and pesticides to Shari' Port Said and the Islamic Museum.

Maydan al-Atabah: Following one of the small streets between Shari' Port Said and Maydan al-Atabah provides a fascinating glimpse of the internal mechanics of Cairo's furniture industry: wholesale wood merchants give way to vendors of upholstery, stuffing and springs until, towards Atabah, the final flashy product emerges.

Maydan al-Atabah itself is the true hub of Cairene market life. In its vicinity just about anything from transistors to bulk paper, tim-

charming square where the Qasabah is crossed by Darb al-Ahmar, which changes its name here to Shari' Ahmad Maher. On the far side of this square the Qasabah dives into the tunnel of the Khayamiyyah, the covered Tentmakers' Bazaar. A shop on the right just at the entrance specialises in colourful canvas bags, one of the best bargains in Cairo. Under the bazaar's wooden roof, the only one currently surviving, are the alcoves where artisans fashion appliqué tent panels, cushion covers, bedspreads and wall hangings. The most beautiful are the calligraphic and geometric designs.

To the west, Shari' Ahmad Maher leads

ber, or a whole side of beef can be found. Shari' Muski leads from it eastward parallel to Shari' al-Azhar back to the Khan al-Khalili. Its length crawls with shoppers and wares, street hawkers, porters and black marketeers in a ceaseless buzz of commerce. Just off Shari' Muski, beginning at the Atabah end, are watches, shoes, paper, confectioneries, hardware, pipes and hoses, luggage, beads, buttons and textiles.

Bulaq: Far from the crush of central Cairo, on the Nile north of Shari' 26th of July, lies the district of Bulaq. Untouched by the tourist trade, this former river port, transformed into an industrial centre by Muhammad Ali, offers an exemplary microcosm of a traditional economy's adaptation to modern needs. Still dotted with Mamluk warehouses as well as small machine works and welding shops, Bulaq is also a huge junk market, which found its niche during World War II dealing in military surplus.

The alleys back from the main streets are crammed with arm's-width stalls, selling car parts which have been cannibalised from wrecks. An astonishing degree of specialisation has been achieved, so that a shop may stock only 1950 Cadillac fenders or a variety of radiator caps. Further inside is the used clothing market, a jumble of colourful streets packed with America's and Europe's cast-

The Camel Market: Students of native life may find the Suq al-Gimal, or Camel Market, more diverting. It is held early on Friday mornings on the edge of the city beyond the west bank district of Mohandiseen.

Though some of the camels come from the Western Desert – small Bedouin herds may be seen there and in the Eastern Desert and Sinai – the majority come from the Western Sudan and used to be herded north on an arduous 40-day trek called the *arba'in*. Nowadays only the first 30 are done on foot or hoof, bringing the animals as far north as Aswan, where they are loaded onto trucks for a 24-hour ride to the Cairo market. Here hundreds of the noble yet troublesome beasts

offs, which are auctioned daily.

Further northward is the Wikalat al-Balah, a district named for a former date warehouse, which now serves as a market for all kinds of refuse, from bits of old iron grillwork to antiques pilfered from collapsed buildings. Nowadays the rich don blue jeans to pick through the junk, so prices are not what they used to be. Beyond Wikalat al-Balah is the district of Rod al-Farag, which houses Cairo's wholesale fruit and vegetable market.

Left, some rustic types in a rustic setting. **Above**, boxes made from palm fronds carry fruits and live animals.

are hauled off the trucks, examined, and haggled over by dozens of rustic traders, most of them either Nubians or hot-headed Upper Egyptians.

Once sold, some of these beasts will be loaded back on trucks, while others will be herded across one of the city's southern bridges, all of them destined for Cairo's abattoirs. Adventurous tourists who make their way out to the camel market are therefore not expected to buy the merchandise there, but to wait until it emerges in finished form: camel flesh is closely textured but prized as *basturma*, the dried spiced meat that is apparently the origin of pastrami.

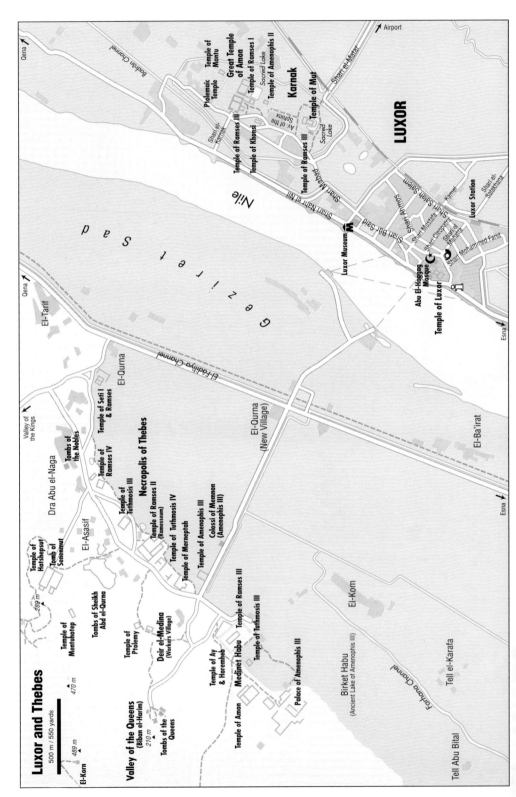

Luxor and Thebes

500 m / 550 yards

Airport

Karnak

Temple of Montu
Great Temple of Amon
Temple of Ramses I
Temple of Amenophis II
Sacred Lake
Ptolemaic Temple
Temple of Khonsu
Temple of Ramses III
Temple of Mut
Av. of the Sphinx
Sacred Lake
Temple of Ramses III

Shari el-Karnak
Shari el-Matari

LUXOR

Nile
Shari Nahr el-Nil
Shari Madina
Shari Bur Said

Luxor Museum
Shari Cleopatra
Shari Mustafa
Shari Ammos
Shari el-Mahatta
Kamel
Shari Salah Salem
Luxor Station
Shari el-Sciakhana

Abu El-Haggag Mosque
Shari Mohammed Farid
Temple of Luxor

Esna

Qena
El-Tarif

Gezîret Sâd

Qena

El-Hadithy Channel

El-Qurna

Valley of the Kings

Dra Abu el-Naga

Tombs of the Nobles

Temple of Sefi I & Ramses

Temple of Ramses IV

El-Asasif

Temple of Tuthmosis III

Necropolis of Thebes

Temple of Ramses II (Ramesseum)

Temple of Tuthmosis IV

Temple of Merneptah

Temple of Amenophis III

Colossi of Memnon (Amenophis III)

El-Qurna

El-Qurna (New Village)

El-Ba'irat

Esna

Temple of Hatshepsut
Tomb of Senenmut
209 m

Temple of Mentuhotep

Tombs of Sheikh Abd el-Qurna

470 m

Temple of Ptolemy

Deir el-Medina (Workers Village)

Valley of the Queens
(Biban el-Harim)

210 m

Tombs of the Queens

Temple of Amon

Temple of Ay & Horemheb

Medinet Habu

Temple of Ramses III

Temple of Tuthmosis III

Palace of Amenophis III

Birket Habu (Ancient Lake of Amenophis III)

El-Kom

Fadliyya Channel

Tell el-Karafa

Tell Abu Bital

489 m

El-Korn

UPPER EGYPT

If one thinks of Egypt as a lotus flower with the Delta as the blossom, Upper Egypt is the long narrow stalk, extending from Lake Nasser in the south to Cairo, with the oasis of the Fayyum growing out to the left like a leaf. This stalk is 550 miles (800 km) long, and never more than 12 miles (20 km) across. Throughout its whole length are remains of Egyptian civilisation including such famous sites as **Abydos**, **Karnak**, the **Valley of the Kings** and **Philae**, dating from the very earliest times. To explore it properly would take months.

During the 19th century, as more and more archaeological discoveries were being made and the mystery of hieroglyphics unravelled, wintering in Egypt became fashionable for the well-to-do. They would hire a private sailing houseboat, complete with crew and cook, at the port of Cairo, and proceed upstream, stopping here and there to explore the ruins and visit local dignitaries. Their impressions were conscientiously set down day by day in letters home or in morocco-bound diaries, as they sat under the awning on deck, glancing up every once in a while to watch the palm-fringed shore slipping peacefully by.

A river trip between November and March is still the ideal way to visit the magnificent monuments of Upper Egypt. Sightseeing can be interspersed with delicious idleness. Most of the luxury cruise boats run 3-, 5-, or 8-day trips starting from either Luxor or Aswan. Passengers fly or take the train to meet the boat and go straight on board. Facilities and services are comparable to those in the best hotels and most boats have well-trained guides speaking several languages. For the Egyptology buff, there are select tours led by university lecturers and archaeologists.

True romantics can hire a *felucca* (the indigenous sailing boat with tall lateen rig) for the trip from Aswan to Luxor for a fraction of what tourist steamers charge, but these boats are more picturesque than comfortable.

There are certain advantages, however, to seeing Upper Egypt by private car or by taxi. Out-of-the-way sites can be visited and alternate routes can be taken for the return trip, either through the Western Oases or over the mountains and up the Red Sea coast.

Whichever way the visitor may choose to travel and whatever his particular predilections, the monuments of Upper Egypt are breathtaking. They have to be seen to be believed. They also require a certain amount of study beforehand.

Sightseeing can be both exhilarating and exhausting, so be prepared. Comfortable shoes, not sandals – there are too many stones to stub the toes – a hat, sunglasses, and a flashlight for dark corners, are useful additions to light cotton clothes. Sweaters and wraps may be needed for evenings, which can be cold. Parties in the big hotels and cruiseships can be dressy and romantic, but not risqué – remember Egypt is a Muslim country.

Luxor: 420 miles (675 km) south of Cairo, **Luxor** is the most important and dramatic site in all Egypt. *Al-Uqsur* (the Palaces) is the Arabic name for Thebes, the capital city of the New Kingdom (1550 BC–1070 BC), whose glory still glowed in the memories of classical writers a thousand years after its decline. Here the booty of foreign wars, tribute and taxes poured into the coffers of the pharaohs of the 18th and 19th Dynasties, each of whom surpassed his predecessor in the construction of gorgeous temples and tombs, creating a concentration of monuments that rivals that of any imperial city before or since.

Amon, once just a local god, took on the qualities of Ra, the sun god of Heliopolis, when Thebes became the seat of power, becoming Amon-Ra and rising to a position of ascendancy over all the multifarious gods of Egypt. With his consort Mut and his son Khonsu he formed the Theban Triad.

Two tremendous temple complexes were established in honour of these gods, the temple of Karnak and the temple of Luxor. Both were built over extensive periods of time and were constructed from the inside outwards; the original founders built sanctuaries on spots that had probably been venerated for centuries, and successive pharaohs added progressively more grandiose courtyards, gateways and other elaborations.

Cosmic symbolism: Temples in general all followed the same principles. For the ancient Egyptians the precinct represented a little replica of the cosmos at the time of the creation. It was set apart from the everyday world and demarcated by a mudbrick girdle wall. Usually, but not always, the temple had an east-west axis, so that the rising or setting sun could strike right into its innermost recesses. Giant wedge-shaped pylons or gateways flanked tall gold-plated doors and were decorated on the outside with enormous reliefs of the pharaoh symbolically subduing his enemies and safeguarding the sacred place from malevolent forces.

Within the gates were courtyards, with small kiosks or barque-stations (storage places for the boats of Egyptian gods) for visiting gods. Other shrines appeared in later times, including the birth-houses in which the divine progeniture of the pharaoh was established. Before the entrance of the covered part of the temple stood enormous statues of the pharaoh in human or animal form and/or obelisks. Inside was a hypostyle hall, where giant columns, usually with vegetal bases and capitals shaped like papyrus reeds or lotus buds, clustered thickly together to represent the marsh of creation. The conception was completed by the ceiling overhead which was adorned with depictions of heavenly bodies, to recreate the sky. All was lavishly decorated.

In the outer parts of the temple, the reliefs record historical events: the foundation and dedication of the temple itself and details of processions and ceremonies. The pharaoh is very much in evidence, leading the activities. He always faces the interior, while the resident god or goddess, often shown together with a consort and attendant gods, faces the outside world.

Proceeding through a vestibule into the offering court and then the inner

Upper Egyptian elegance on the Luxor Corniche.

194

parts of the temple, the ground rises by degrees, the roof gets lower, the brilliant daylight is shut out, until the sanctuary, which represents the mound of creation, is quite dark. Only the pharaoh and the priests were allowed into this holy of holies, where a gold-plated image of the presiding god was kept.

From time to time the god would be brought out from his seclusion, suitably dressed and perfumed, to receive offerings of bread and beer, or to pay visits to other gods carried on his sacred barque. Probably the image could be made to move its hand or bow its head, and its movements were no doubt accompanied by mysterious sounds.

The rooms surrounding the sanctuary were used as storerooms for cult furniture, vestments, perfumes and incense, as laboratories and as libraries. Some temples had crypts and secret passages and ducts under the floor.

Karnak: The temple complex of Amon-Ra at Karnak and its concomitant accretions constitute the most overwhelming of all the Egyptian monuments. Apart from the immense conglomeration of elements that make up the temple proper, the vast precinct covers an area of 60 acres (25 hectares) and contains no fewer than 20 smaller temples and shrines. It incorporates 10 pylons, six on an east-west axis and four on a north-south axis, which, together with intervening courts, halls and enclosures, surround the nucleus of the sanctuary. Behind the sanctuary to the east is a great festival hall; to the north is a temple of Ptah and an older enclosure of Montu, and to the south are a sacred lake, temples of Mut and Khonsu, and avenues of sphinxes connecting the enclosures with each other and with the Luxor temple.

The origins of the Karnak temples as we now see it are attributable to the royal family of the 18th Dynasty, whose rise to power brought Thebes to the heights of glory. Three Tuthmoses and Hatshepsut, whose relationships are still not satisfactorily sorted out, were responsible for most of the inner parts of the temple. Hatshepsut dominated the family from the time of Tuthmoses I's

The Temple of Karnak seen from across the Sacred Lake.

death in 1492 BC. She was Tuthmosis III's unfavourite wife/aunt, however, and as soon as she was out of the way he proceeded to hack her name away from cartouches, substituting his own, and to wall up the chamber and the bases of the 320-ton obelisks that she had had erected. Thus unwittingly he preserved her work in pristine condition.

The third Tuthmosis (1479 BC–1425 BC) proceeded to reign long and brilliantly, waging 17 successful campaigns and extending the Egyptian empire from Syria to the Sudan. He brought back thousands of prisoners and immense quantities of booty, as well as new varieties of trees and plants, new ideas, new fashions. The annals of his career are inscribed on the walls surrounding the sanctuary and extend to his great Festival Hall and to the southern courts.

Succeeding generations added new pylons, new courts and subsidiary temples, all lavishly and colourfully illustrating their conquests, like a great stone history book. Amenhotep III added a pylon and the temple of Mut.

The complex was thus already enormous at the advent of the 19th Dynasty, when Seti I (1306 BC–1290 BC) conceived the idea of constructing the **Great Hypostyle Hall** with its 137 huge columns, covering an area of 6,000 sq. metres. This mighty work was completed by Ramses II (1290 BC–1224 BC), who placed the appropriate colossi of himself at the entrance.

Though the capital moved away to the Delta and the importance of Thebes declined thereafter, Karnak continued to be expanded and embellished, such was the awe in which Amon-Ra was held. Ramses III added a complete small temple and at the end of the Ramesside line the temple of Khonsu was built, in which reliefs show clearly the rise to kingly status of the priests.

In the 6th century the Persians did a certain amount of damage when they sacked Thebes, but the incoming Greeks set things to rights. Alexander, his brother Philip Arrhidaeus (who replaced the original sanctuary with one of rose-granite), and subsequently the Ptolemies

Hypostyle hall of the Temple of Amon, Karnak, Luxor.

196

restored and continued to make additions to the temple. The entrance pylon by which it is approached from the west today, and the enclosure of the first great court were their work.

Luxor temple: The Luxor temple is relatively long (780 feet/230 metres) and narrow. It is also dedicated to the Theban Triad, but Amon of Luxor had a slightly different form and function, as a divinely fertile figure. The temple was built on a north-south axis, sometimes off kilter to accommodate older structures. The major part was built by Amenhotep III (1414 BC–1397 BC) with substantial later additions by Tutankhamen (1333 BC–1323 BC), Horemheb (1319 BC–1307 BC), Ramses II (1290 BC–1224 BC), and Alexander the Great (332 BC–323 BC).

The sanctuary area dates from the reign of Amenhotep III. In the Birth Room, his mother Mutemwia is shown being impregnated by Amon and giving birth to the infant pharaoh, whose body and spirit are formed on the potter's wheel by the ram-headed creator-god Khnum. The facts of life are indicated with delicate symbolism. The inner parts of the temple issue into an extensive peristyle court from which a tall processional colonnade with papyrus-bud columns leads northwards.

Amenhotep was succeeded by his son, the revolutionary pharaoh who took the name of Akhenaten (1353 BC–1335 BC) and rejected all forms of religion except the worship of the Aton, symbolised by the sun disc, and moved the capital away from Thebes to Tell el-Amarna. His reforms collapsed immediately after his death, however, and the capital returned to Thebes, the old hierarchy of priests was re-established, and his successors Tutankhamen and Horemheb dutifully took up the embellishment of the Luxor temple again.

On the walls of the colonnade their skilful sculptors depicted the annual Opet festival, showing the gods of Karnak, accompanied by a cheerful procession of priests, musicians, singers, dancers and sacred cows, parading down to Luxor on the west, and going back to

A medieval mosque, known as Abu el-Haggag, left high and dry by 20th-century excavation of the temple it sits on.

their own temple on the east. The great peristyle court, which today incorporates a medieval mosque, was added by Ramses II, who redefined the structure in his usual Cecil B. de Mille style, with a gigantic pylon on which were displayed his triumphs. He also had vast colossi of himself erected within the gates.

The invading French and 19th century diarists noted the glorious city of Thebes had shrunk to a miserable cluster of villas and squalid mudhuts on top of the metres of dirt and debris which cluttered the Luxor temple. Only the heads of the colossi of Ramses, half the granite obelisk of Amenhotep, and the capitals of the columns were visible; and these remains were battered and blackened with smoke.

The riverside road called the **Corniche**, along which the cruise boats tie up and the ferries to the West Bank dock, runs parallel to the courts and colonnades of the Luxor temple.

Strung out to the north are hotels, shops, an excellent small museum and other public buildings. To the south are bigger and more luxurious hotels, some old and venerable and others very up-to-date. The rest of the town spreads to the east towards the station, and the small international airport.

Dilapidated old calèches clatter up and down the Corniche, the drivers cracking their whips and vociferously soliciting business. The sound and smell of the horses and some of the old facades give Luxor a faintly raffish air.

The West Bank: The Nile valley is wide at Luxor and the mysteriously pink limestone mountains hovering to the west above the lush green plain are so honeycombed with treasures and secrets, legends and curiosities, that the average day or two spent among them is not enough.

An early start is recommended. For one thing the mornings are crisp and delicious, the ferries are less crowded then, the donkeys are fresher, the bicycles have not been picked over, and the monuments themselves are better seen by oblique sunlight rather than direct vertical rays. Taking advantage of the

The Valley of the Kings and, beyond it, the Nile Valley, seen from the desert.

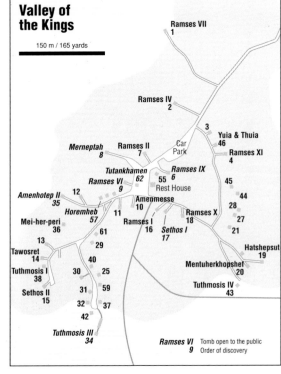

Valley of the Kings

150 m / 165 yards

Ramses VII
1

Ramses IV
2

3

Yuia & Thuia
46

Ramses XI
4

Merneptah
8

Ramses II
7

Car Park

Ramses IX
6

45

Tutankhamen
62

55

Rest House

44

Ramses VI
9

Amenhotep II
12

28

Amenmesse
10

Horemheb
57

11

Ramses X
18

27

Mei-her-peri
36

Ramses I
16

Sethos I
17

21

61

Tawosret
14

29

Hatshepsut
19

40

Mentuherkhopshef
20

Tuthmosis I
38

30

25

Tuthmosis IV
43

Sethos II
15

31

59

32

37

42

Tuthmosis III
34

Ramses VI Tomb open to the public
9 Order of discovery

cool crystalline air, one can savour the sounds and scents of the countryside: beanfields, cassias and acacias in bloom, birds twittering and singing, and children wandering along to school.

The fringes of the desert hills lie about 2½ miles (4 km) to the west of the Nile across the plain; and here the great mortuary temples of the New Kingdom pharaohs are spread out over a shallow arc. The **Valley of the Queens**, the **Tombs of the Nobles** and the **Workers' Village** are in the foothills behind them. The road leading to the **Valley of the Kings** skirts the cliffs before climbing a rocky defile to the northwest.

Mortuary temples: The innovative pharaohs of the 18th Dynasty broke with the pyramid tradition and began to have their tombs tunnelled deep into the mountainside, hoping that they would thus avoid the depredations of tomb robbers. On the edge of the valley, at some distance from their final resting places, each pharaoh constructed his individual mortuary temple. Those of Hatshepsut, Seti I, Ramses II, and

Ramses III still stand. Two colossi in the fields by the side of the road are all that remains of the Temple of Amenhotep III, the famous Memnon.

The architecture and decoration of these mortuary temples follows essentially the same lines as those of the temples already described, except that in the sanctuary area there is a false door through which the *ka* or spirit of the deceased king (he became a deity after his death) could pass freely back and forth to enjoy the offerings and ceremonies in his honour.

Questionable queen: The **Temple of Hatshepsut** (1492 BC–1458 BC) is somewhat different from the others, being set back in a spectacular natural amphitheatre of soaring pinkish purple cliffs. Three gracefully proportioned and colonnaded terraces are connected by sloping ramps. The sanctuary areas are backed right up against the mountain and partially hollowed out of the rocks.

Probably the daughter, sister/wife and aunt of the first three Tuthmoses, Hatshepsut was a lady of great character.

The Temple of Hatshepsut, Deir al Bahari, Luxor.

She succeeded her father when she was 24 years old and assumed royal powers and regalia, including the false beard, reigning until her death 34 years later. Her divine birth and exploits are recorded on the walls behind the colonnades. They include a famous expedition to Punt in Somalia, whence incense trees, giraffes and other exotica were brought back to Egypt. The cutting and transportation of the two great obelisks set up by Hatshepsut at Karnak are also recorded. The temple was designed by an architect named Senenmut, evidently a great favourite of the queen. His portrait is discreetly hidden behind a door; and his own tomb is nearby.

Ozymandias, king of kings: A large part of Ramses II's (1290 BC–1224 BC) mortuary temple, the **Ramesseum**, is in ruins, but like other monuments of this long-lived and most prolific pharaoh, who reigned for over 60 years and had no fewer than 80 children, what remains is majestic indeed. Parts of what is the largest granite colossus on record lie collapsed before the entrance of the hypostyle hall. One foot alone measures 11 feet (3.3 metres). The famous battle of Kadesh is depicted on the pylons. More interestingly there is a representation of Thoth, the ibis-headed secretary-god writing Ramses' name on the leaves of the sacred tree. Both here and at Ramses III's temple, there are vestiges of adjoining palaces where the kings came to spend a few days supervising work on their "Mansions of Eternity".

Ramses III (1194 BC–1163 BC), however, is not eclipsed by his famous forebear. His mortuary temple is the largest building in a complex surrounded by a massive mudbrick girdle wall, known as **Medinet Habu**. The battle reliefs on the exterior of the Ramses temple are particularly interesting: this pharaoh fought off invading sea peoples from the west and vivid naval engagements are depicted.

Valley of the Kings: After being embalmed and mummified, the New Kingdom pharaohs were transported in solemn cortège to the Valley of the Kings. Gorgeously bedecked with gold and jew-

The Temple of Medinet Habu. The niches in the facade were for huge banners.

els, surrounded with treasures and replicas of all they would need in the afterlife, they were buried in their rock-cut tombs.

There are 62 of these sepulchres, though only a few are open to the public. In most, long, elaborately decorated corridors lead down through a series of chambers and false doors to the burial vault. The entrance passage is painted with texts and illustrations from mortuary literature and the Book of the Dead. As the pharaoh takes his last journey he passes through the 12 gates of the 12 hours of the night, beset by serpents, crocodiles and other malevolent beings. He arrives at the Court of Osiris where he is met by a delegation of gods; he makes his confession and his heart is weighed for its truthfulness and purity. A hideous monster waits to devour him should he fail the test, but evading the torments of hell, he is at last received into the company of heaven.

The tomb of Tutankhamen: Only one of these tombs miraculously escaped the attention of the tomb robbers, who were already ransacking them, sometimes within a few years of their construction. The famous small tomb of the boy-king Tutankhamen (1333 BC–1323 BC) was not discovered until 1922, when Howard Carter, under the patronage of Lord Carnarvon, chanced upon it after a search of seven long years. The dramatic story has been told many times. A breathtaking treasure of over 5,000 precious objects was buried with the young pharaoh, whose embalmed remains were still in situ in a complex system of gold and jeweled mummy cases and coffins within coffins. A gilded chariot, beds, chairs, stools and headrests covered in gold leaf, alabaster lamps and vases, weapons, sandals, statues of servants, and all manner of other objects in perfect condition were crammed into the relatively small space of the tomb. The majority of the treasure is in the Egyptian Museum in Cairo.

Valley of the Queens: The royal wives were buried in the Valley of the Queens in the hills behind Medinet Habu. Very few are open to the public. The nine-

Feet of a colossal statue of Ramses II at the Ramesseum, Luxor.

year-old son of Ramses III is buried in the same valley. The young boy is shown being led by his father to meet the gods.

Tombs of the Nobles: Unlike royalty, who were buried with somewhat ominous solemnity, the scribes and dignitaries of the court, whose tombs are scattered in the sandy foothills, departed this world surrounded with scenes of the joyous good living to which they had apparently been accustomed during their lifetime. There are 414 private nobles' tombs, from the 4th Dynasty to the Roman period, but the majority are from the New Kingdom. Compared with the tombs of the kings they are small. Many of them are vividly painted with naturalistic scenes of agriculture, fishing, fowling, feasting and junketing, and they constitute a fascinating record of everyday life. One lady diarist, Amelia Edwards, was so delighted when she visited them that she wrote: "It seemed to me that I had met those kindly brown people years ago, perhaps in some previous existence; that I had walked with them in their gardens, listened to the music of the lutes and tambourines; pledged them at their feasts."

Workers' village: There are records of more humble workmen's lives in the tombs of the village of **Deir al-Madina**, where the masons, painters and decorators were kept segregated from the rest of the population for generations, in an effort to keep the whereabouts of the treasure-filled royal tombs a secret. They prepared their own tombs in advance.

Even today the country folk on the West bank, known for their independence and their secretiveness, cannot be persuaded to move down from the hills to the plain. World-famous architect Hassan Fathi designed a model village for them at **New Qurna**, but they would have none of it. It still stands beside the road, rather the worse for wear, and the wily villagers still guard their secrets.

Abydos: Since there are no accommodations or facilities for tourists in the immediate vicinity of Abydos, one of Egypt's most spellbinding spots, it is usually visited on an all-day excursion from Luxor or from one of the longer

Titi alabaster shop, painted by a local talent, Luxor.

cruise trips. The earliest known tomb of a pharaoh, dating to around 3150 BC, was discovered here in 1993, containing some of the oldest examples of hieroglyphic writing.

In the dawn of history, Wepwawet, the jackal deity, roamed the desert's edge guarding the ancestral burial grounds below the dip in the western hills. At sunset the ancients imagined it to be the dusty golden staircase to the afterworld and they wished to be buried at its foot.

The Osiris legend: Later Abydos became closely associated with the legend of Osiris. The story relates how the just ruler Osiris was killed by his evil brother Seth. Isis the weeping sister/wife faithfully searched the banks of the Nile for his dismembered body, which she at length managed to reassemble. He revived sufficiently for their son Horus to be conceived. Thereafter the pieces of Osiris were buried at different places in both Upper and Lower Egypt, but his head was supposed to have been buried at Abydos; and it was at Abydos that he was resurrected and assumed his powers as the lord and judge of the afterlife. His son Horus grew up and resumed the struggle with Seth.

Every January the great drama was reenacted as a sort of miracle play with a cast of thousands and crowds of pilgrims came from all over Egypt to participate. A gold-plated image represented Osiris, the pharaoh himself took the part of Horus, and the priests and priestesses masqueraded as Wepwawet, Seth, Isis, Nephthys and supporting cast.

From the Middle Kingdom onwards, every pharaoh as well as hundreds of thousands of pilgrims left some token of their presence at Abydos, hoping to gain favour for themselves and their relatives with Osiris in his capacity as Judge of the Court of the hereafter. The area is a mass of funeral stelae, burial grounds, former temples and memorials. But it was Seti I (1306 BC–1290 BC) of the New Kingdom who was responsible for the most beautiful tribute to Osiris in his seven-sanctuaried temple.

Seti came to power in 1306 BC, just 29 years after the monotheistic regime

Inside the Temple of Ramses II at Abydos.

of Akhenaten at Tell el-Amarna, some miles to the north, had collapsed. The nation was still recovering from the shock of this apostasy, and Seti wished to reaffirm his faith in the traditional gods and restore them to their former reeminence. To this end he rallied all the resources of the land to build and adorn a new temple at Abydos, in which he recorded his devotion to Osiris and his wife and son, as well as to Amon-Ra, Ra-Hor-Akhty and Ptah. He also honoured his forebears by recording their names in a List of Kings, an assemblage of cartouches which has been of immense importance to subsequent researchers and historians.

Exquisite reliefs on fine white limestone, which has sometimes taken on the shade of old ivory, show Seti engaged in performing a multitude of rites in honour of Osiris and the company of gods. Seti himself died before the temple was completed, leaving his son Ramses II to finish the decoration of the courtyards and colonnades.

The cult of Osiris and Isis later moved south to the Cataract Region, but the annual festival of Abydos continued through Egyptian history, lingering for almost 400 years into the Christian era. It was the Christians themselves who finally sacked the temple in 395 AD, but mercifully failed to spoil its essential beauty. Vestiges of powerful magic still cling to the sacred precincts. Local women can be seen circling the pool of the mysterious building, probably the burial place of Osiris, called the **Osireion**; and quite recently an English mystic deeply versed in Egyptian history and religion spent the last 25 years of her life living at Abydos and working daily in the temple. She was known as Umm Seti, or the Mother of Seti.

Dendera: The longer cruises visit the **Temple of Dendera** on a bend in the river about halfway between Abydos and Luxor. Like those of Esna, Edfu, Kom Ombo and Philae, and others lost under Lake Nasser, the temple is about a thousand years younger than the New Kingdom temples, and its construction was initiated by the Ptolemies.

The Sacred Lake at the Temple of Dendera.

Dendera is dedicated to Hathor, the cow goddess, known as "The Golden One", goddess of women, who was also a sky and tree goddess, sometimes equated to Aphrodite by the Greeks and a great favourite with them. She was supposed to have had healing powers, and the sick journeyed here, as to Kom Ombo and Philae, to be cured.

Despite being damaged by the Christians, who chipped out the faces and limbs of many figures, Dendera is one of the best preserved of all Egyptian temples and its adjunct structures can all be easily identified. It has retained its girdle wall, its Roman gate, two Birth Houses and a sacred lake, as well as its crypts, stairways, roof and chapels.

Its most immediately distinctive feature is its hypostyle hall, with its 24 Hathor-headed columns and a ceiling showing the out-stretched Nut, the sky-goddess, swallowing the sun at evening and giving birth at morning. The hall was decorated during the reign of Tiberius and is dated 34 AD. The dark courts and crypts in the interior give evidence of various festivals in which Hathor was involved. The most important of these feasts was the annual New Year Festival, during which the goddess was carried up the western staircase to the roof for the ritual known as the "Union with the Disc", returning down another staircase to the east. On the walls of the stairways the order of procession of the gods in full regalia is clearly shown. There are interesting graffiti on the roof including names of Napoleon's soldiers. On the back of the temple is one of the very few contemporary representations of Cleopatra with Caesarion, her son by Julius Caesar.

Esna: The town of Esna lies 30 miles (50 km) south of Luxor and is built over the ruins of the **Temple of Khnum**. Only the hypostyle hall has been excavated and its foundation level is 27 feet (8 metres) below that of the street. It contains most interesting reliefs and inscriptions, however, and is of great historic importance. The names and activities of Ptolemies and Roman emperors up until the time of Decius, who was

The Northern Palace at Tell el-Amarna.

murdered in 249 AD, are recorded. French archaeologists have recently deciphered many details of the rituals of the worship of Khnum, as well as a precise calendar specifying when and how they should be celebrated.

Edfu: By contrast, the Ptolemaic **Temple of Horus** at Edfu, another 30 miles to the south, is the most completely preserved in Egypt and is in near-perfect condition, with its great pylon, exterior walls, courts, halls and sanctuary all in place. Its walls are a veritable textbook of mythology and geopolitics. Building is recorded as having begun in 237 BC by Ptolemy III Euergetes (246 BC–221 BC), and continued until the decoration of the outer walls was finally finished in 57 BC. Several great annual festivals are depicted; the mock battle commemorating the victory of Horus over Seth; the joyful annual wedding visit of Hathor, who journeyed upriver from Dendera to be reunited with her spouse, and the annual coronation of the reigning monarch, identified with Horus, which took place in the great forecourt.

Regal carved-granite sparrow-hawks still stand sentinel at the doors.

Kom Ombo: The Temple of Horus, dedicated jointly to Horus the sparrow-hawk and Sobek the crocodile, is situated right on a sweeping bend of the Nile 24 miles (40 km) north of Aswan, near a sandy bank where crocodiles used to sun themselves. Part of the front of the temple has fallen into the river and the back parts are roofless. It is built on a double plan with twin sanctuaries for Horus to the north and Sobek to the south. Each has a black diorite offering table. Most of the reliefs were executed by Ptolemy XII (80 BC–58 BC and 55 BC–51 BC) and have some fine details including the personifications of the four winds and an interesting set of medical instruments. At one side a small shrine is used for storing some rather unpleasant crocodile mummies.

The Ptolemies evidently had more than religion in mind when they subsidised the building of these temples, as each one is placed in a strategic position both economically and militarily.

Heads of the goddess Hathor at the Temple of Dendera.

Aswan: Ivory, ebony, rose, and gold are the defining colours of **Aswan**. Here, a wild jumble of glistening igneous rocks, strewn across the Nile, suddenly create narrows between the highlands of the Eastern Desert and the sandy wastes of the Sahara. The barrier to navigation is known as the First Cataract, and was once where the civilised world stopped.

During the Old Kingdom a few travellers ventured further up the Nile in quest of gold, slaves and the occasional pygmy, leaving records of their mis-

sions inscribed on the rocks among the islands, but most expeditions were to **Elephantine**, the island in the middle of the river at the foot of the cataract, which was the first capital.

Quarries: Coloured granites, greywacke, syenite, alabaster, ochre and other minerals were quarried and transported down the Nile when the river was in flood to the royal cities of the north. Obelisks that later made their way to Rome and Istanbul, Paris, London, or New York, were ingeniously cut from Aswan granite. In a quarry just south of

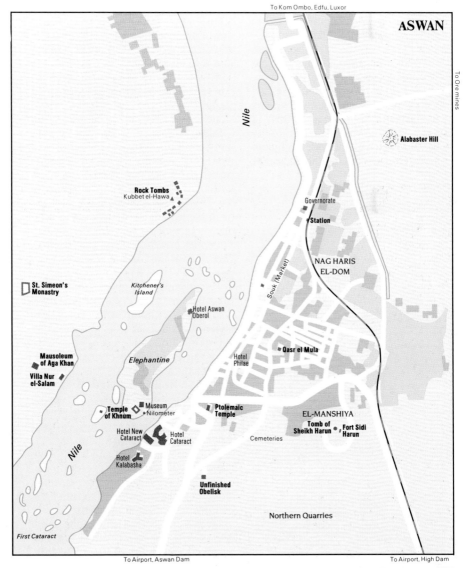

To Kom Ombo, Edfu, Luxor

ASWAN

To Ore mines

Nile

Alabaster Hill

Rock Tombs
Kubbet el-Hawa

Governorate

Station

NAG HARIS
EL-DOM

Souk Market

St. Simeon's
Monastry

Kitchener's
Island

Hotel Aswan
Oberoi

Mausoleum
of Aga Khan

Elephantine

Qasr el Mula

Hotel
Philae

Villa Nur
el-Salam

Temple
of Khnum

Museum
Nilometer

Ptolemaic
Temple

EL-MANSHIYA

Tomb of
Sheikh Harun

Fort Sidi
Harun

Hotel New
Cataract

Hotel
Cataract

Cemeteries

Hotel
Kalabasha

Nile

Unfinished
Obelisk

Northern Quarries

First Cataract

To Airport, Aswan Dam

To Airport, High Dam

the present town of Aswan, an unfinished obelisk can still be seen, attached to the bedrock. It would have weighed an incredible 1,100 tons had it ever been completed, but it developed a crack.

Nilometer: From the Old Kingdom onwards a strict watch was kept on the rise and fall of the Nile. Its measurement was one of the important functions of the resident governor of Elephantine and later Aswan. Up until the last century, when western technology started to revolutionise the management of the water, frequent and regular readings were taken from the Nilometer at the southern end of Elephantine Island and the information was communicated to the rest of the country. Those responsible for the cultivation of crops and the maintenance of embankments and canals would thus know in advance what to expect; and other administrators could calculate tax assessments.

According to an interesting text at Edfu, if the Nile rose 24 cubits at Elephantine, it would provide sufficient water to irrigate the land satisfactorily.

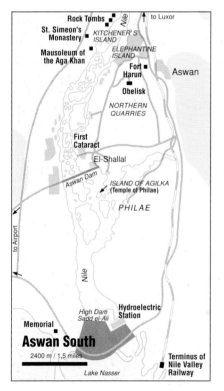

If it did not, disaster would surely ensue. Just such a failure, which lasted for seven years – though it is not the drought mentioned in the Bible – is recorded on a block of granite a short way upstream: "By a very great misfortune the Nile has not come forth for a period of seven years. Grain has been scarce and there have been no vegetables or anything else for the people to eat."

Archaeological remains of the temples on the southern end of Elephantine are sketchy, but there is evidence that Tuthmosis III, Amenhotep II, Ramses III, Alexander IV (the son of Alexander the Great), Augustus Caesar and Trajan all had a hand either in their construction or maintenance. Parts of them were still standing when the French expedition arrived in 1799, but were demolished about 20 years later by Muhammad Ali's son Ibrahim, at this time viceroy at Upper Egypt, who used the fine white stone to build himself a palace.

Outpost of empires: The excellent winter climate and beautiful setting of Aswan were well-known in the classical world and were described by several writers. They mentioned the temples, the garden and the vineyards of Elephantine, which were supposed to produce grapes all the year round. Both the Ptolemies and the Romans maintained garrisons at this distant southern outpost.

The greatest geographer in antiquity, Eratosthenes (c. 273 BC–192 BC) who held a post as librarian in Alexandria under the Ptolemies, established the approximate circumference of the earth from astronomical observations made at Elephantine and Alexandria. He noted that the sun's rays fell vertically to the bottom of a well at Elephantine at the summer solstice, whereas on the same day in Alexandria an upright stake cast a shadow indicating that the sun was 7 degrees from its zenith. Since he knew the distance between the two cities, he could then proceed to work out the total circumference of the earth; and he came within a few miles of the truth.

Juvenal, the satirical Roman poet, died here in exile at the age of 80 towards the end of the 1st century AD. But it was the merchants rather than the scholars, scientists, poets and soldiers, who left the greatest quantity of humble reminders of their passage, in the form of *ostraka*, or potsherds, inscribed with records of their commercial transactions. Nineteenth-century travellers were able to pick up a pocketful within minutes.

Some of these remains can be seen in a small **museum** on Elephantine, which is to be replaced by a more ambitious one just south of Aswan. A gold-plated ram, ram mummies, precious stones, jewellery and amulets, as well as artefacts salvaged from sites in Nubia, are on display.

Dome of the Winds: As in so many places in Egypt, there are a multitude of burial grounds and memorials from the different eras of Egyptian history. The hereditary governors of Aswan and other highranking officials and their tombs cut out of the cliffs on the west bank of the Nile at a spot called Qubbat al-Howa in Arabic, or **Dome of the Winds**. They were decorated in traditional style, and combined with the Aga Khan's mauso-

leum and the Coptic Monastery of St Simeon, make a good expedition.

Aga Khan III, the grandfather of Kerim Aga Khan and distinguished leader of the Ismaili sect of Islam for many years, loved Aswan for its timeless tranquillity and had his domed mausoleum built high up on the bluffs overlooking the river. He was buried there in 1957. The building is a close relative of those of his ancestors the Fatimids, whose followers' mausoleums are on the east bank. There are also many gravestones from the long period of Turkish occupation.

In February 1799, a contingent of Napoleon's invading army arrived, footsore and exasperated, having chased the Mamluk Murad Bey, a survivor from the Battle of the Pyramids, all the way up the Nile Valley. He infuriated them further still by slipping away up the cataract under cover of darkness. The French occupation lasted for less than two years, but it nevertheless brought a long era of somnolence to an end. Aswan was to wake up to great schemes,

Aswan seen across the Nile from the west.

envisioned by Napoleon and started by the reforming Muhammad Ali.

Aswan from a *dahabeyya*: In the second half of the 19th century tourists began to arrive by way of Thomas Cook steamers and *dahabeyyas*; and there were plentiful observations to be noted in morocco-bound diaries. Amelia Edwards describes the hustle and bustle of the waterfront, which probably had not changed much in hundreds of years, although slaves and gold were no longer the chief items of merchandise: "Abyssinians like slender-legged baboons; wild-looking Bishariya and Ababdeh Arabs with flashing eyes and flowing hair; sturdy Nubians… and natives of all tribes and shades, from Kordofan to Sennar, the deserts of Bahuda and the banks of the Blue and White Niles. Some were returning from Cairo; others were on their way thither… Each was entrenched in his own little redoubt of piled-up bales and packing cases, like a spider in the centre of his web; each provided with his kettle and coffee pot, and an old rug to sleep and pray upon…

great bundles of lion and leopard skins, bales of cotton, sacks of henna-leaves, elephant-tusks swathed in canvas and matting, strewed the sandy bank."

Elegant hotels were built to accommodate the fashionable travellers who came to spend the winter at Aswan or to plan the future development of Egypt and the Sudan. The terraces of the **Cataract Hotel** must have been the scene of many a portentous discussion by cigar-smoking Victorian empire-builders. The construction of the first **Aswan Dam** was successfully financed and the project completed in 1902. King Edward VII's younger brother, the Duke of Connaught, came out from England for the opening with Lord Cromer and a host of onlookers, among whom was the young Winston Churchill.

Modern hotels have replaced the grand old ladies of the past, though the Old Cataract survives and the happy hour can still be enjoyed, to the accompaniment of splendid sunsets from its terrace. Below on the shore, the *feluccas*, which are one of the prettiest sights of

Elephantine Island, Aswan.

Aswan, tie up for the night after a busy day sailing around the islands.

The *suq* retains a hint and a whiff of Africa, where small shops sell cotton, baskets, dates, hibiscus-blossom tea (*karkadé*), ebony canes and crocheted skull caps. Soft-spoken Nubians while away their time in front of coffee shops, and shy women carry home the day's shopping on their heads, still wearing the thin black dresses with flounces that trail behind them. Not so long ago, when they walked across the Nubian sand-dunes, these flounces used to brush away their footprints in the sand. Nowadays they return to their neat stone-built villages in the area, which are quite a contrast to the untidy-looking mudbrick and brick villages further north.

Rescued from a watery grave: During Ptolemaic times the cult of Isis and, to a lesser extent, that of Osiris moved south and were established on the islands of **Philae** and **Biggeh** respectively lying at the head of the cataract about 5 miles (8 km) south of Aswan. A particularly beautiful temple was built and dedi-cated to Isis on Philae; and many subsidiary temples, shrines and gateways were added to enhance the glory of the original. Pilgrims came from both north and south to invoke the healing powers of Isis and continued to come long after Christianity had been adopted.

The construction of the first Aswan Dam in 1902 resulted in the partial submersion of Philae during eight months of the year. There had been strong objections by the conservation-minded but, as Winston Churchill caustically observed, to abandon plans for the dam would have been "the most senseless sacrifice ever offered on the altar of a false religion". The dam was built, Philae was indeed inundated, and more so in 1932, when the dam was heightened for the third time. But visitors were able to row and even swim about among the foliated capitals of the long colonnades and glimpse the ghostly reliefs on the walls in the water below.

Sixty years later, when the **High Dam** went up, Philae was threatened with total and permanent immersion. This

Tomb of the Aga Khan at Aswan.

time it was rescued by a huge international mission. A mile-long coffer dam was constructed round the island, and all the water within was pumped out. Stone by stone the temples were dismantled, and transported to nearby **Agilkia Island**, which had been levelled and remodelled to receive the masterpiece of reconstruction that visitors see today. The total cost was in the area of US$30 million.

The massive bulk of the **High Dam** straddles the Nile 8 miles (13 km) south of Aswan. Beyond it **Lake Nasser** stretches for 500 miles (800 km) deep into the Sudan. The dam was built with help from the Russians between 1960 and 1971, after negotiations with the United States had broken down, and it was hoped that it would be an answer to many of Egypt's economic problems.

Taming the Nile: The taming of the river's unpredictable moods, sometimes bountiful and sometimes enraged, and the year-round conservation of its waters has been at the core of Egypt's history and civilisation since its earliest beginnings. In primeval times, the unharnessed flood roared down annually from the Ethiopian Highlands, swamping the valley for three months before it receded, leaving behind the thousands of tons of fertile silt, which, accumulating over millennia, created the 10-metre-thick blanket of soil which constitutes the Valley and the Delta.

The flood, however, was unpredictable and occasionally failed to appear. The consequences were disastrous; and the coordinated planning required to deal with the recurring problem was an important factor in the development of ancient Egyptian civilisation. By systems of dykes and channels, water could be trapped in basins. These systems were improved by waves of conquerors who tried their hand at governing Egypt.

Barrages and dams: In the 19th century Muhammad Ali set about repairing and extending the canals and building barrages, which conserved enough water for a limited year-round supply. They made feasible the production of summer cash crops such as sugar, rice and

Toothache victim and the colonnade at Philae near Aswan.

cotton, which enormously increased the country's revenue.

Continuing this pattern of development, the British in their turn built the first Aswan Dam in 1902 at the head of the Cataract, creating a reservoir 140 miles (225 km) long. At the time it was acclaimed as a great feat of engineering, and there was another marked increase in the well-being and prosperity of the country. It was heightened twice, in 1912 and 1932.

With the demise of the British occupation and the takeover of Egypt by Colonel Nasser's revolutionary government in 1952, the Nile Valley became a testing ground for international rivalries. The new regime focused its aspirations on the construction of a High Dam that would generate enough electricity for new industry, as well as for wide rural electrification, and provide enough water to bring millions of new acres under cultivation, but they needed financial and technical assistance to realise the project. The United States was ready to help, but withdrew its offer abruptly when Nasser refused to compromise his non-aligned status. The Soviet Union stepped in with the necessary loans and technology.

For 10 years 30,000 workers laboured on the enormous dam, which was built on a new principle of soil mechanics. Hundreds of tons of rubble and rock were shovelled into the Nile to make a barrier 2.5 miles wide and 300 feet (92 metres) high. Four huge channels were cut through the granite on the west side to divert the water while 12 turbines (which have since had to be replaced with the help of the United States) were installed on the east. By 1972 the dam was finished; and at last Egypt had a predictable water supply.

The beneficial effects of the dam were immediately apparent, though it has fallen short of being the hoped-for panacea for all Egypt's ills. Had it not been for the water stored up behind it, however, Egypt would have suffered as disastrously as Ethiopia and the Sudan during the droughts of 1972 and 1984.

The hydroelectricity produced was

The Kiosk of Trajan, Philae.

sufficient to power new fertilizer, cement, iron and steel plants, and to make electricity available throughout rural areas, though it is recognised that the dam will not be able to produce enough to satisfy the country's ever-increasing demands in the future.

New lands: The addition of 3 million *feddans* (1.2 million hectares) to Egypt's cultivable lands, irrigated by the new assured water supply, was planned. But the leaders were so closely identified with the project that they turned a deaf ear to seasoned advice. The new lands were on poor soil, which took years to attain marginal productivity at exorbitant cost. Eventually Sadat had to admit that grandiose schemes for land reclamation were unrealistic.

The total containment of the flood has other results. Houses can now be built in places that used to be under water for three months of the year; and as a result of vastly improved incomes from the oil boom, together with the pressure of the population explosion, the private sector has responded by a rash of building on precious agricultural land. Moreover other land is being lost through the constant use of excessive amounts of water, causing waterlogging and salinity, and the projected drainage system that would remedy this defect is proving to be more costly than the dam itself.

Middle Egypt: Cruises generally pass through **Middle Egypt** only twice a year, at the beginning and end of the winter season, on their way between Cairo and the more glamorous sites of Upper Egypt. Except for Tell el-Amarna, there are few royal monuments in this region, but there are some very interesting tombs of provincial governors and dignitaries, best reached by car.

Minya, which is a sizable town with an important university, is 153 miles (245 km) south of Cairo. The Nile is not visible from the road, for between it and the river are the railway and the Ibrahimiyyah Canal.

Minya has a couple of decent hotels and is a good place from which to make various excursions. Crossing the Nile by a ferry, and driving 12 miles (21 km)

north on the east bank of the river brings the curious traveller to an extraordinary monastery, the **Deir al Adhrah** (*Monastery of the Virgin*) perched on top of a cliff and approached by 66 steps hewn into the rock. It is said to have been founded in 328 AD by St Helena, a dubious attribution, but one that corresponds in date at least with the archaeological evidence and the plan of the church. Coptic pilgrims flock here on the feast of the Virgin every 22 August and make the precipitous ascent.

On the east bank of the Nile 11 miles (18 km) south of Minya, approached by a battered old ferry with a competent young man of about nine as a pilot, is the village of **Beni Hassan**, above which 39 Middle Kingdom tombs have been cut in the cliffs. One can ride up through the clover fields on a donkey to visit them. The view itself is worth the effort.

Powerful feudal lords, who ruled almost independently of the Middle Empire, were buried here. Twelve of the tombs are decorated with scenes similar to those at Saqqarah, but painted in fresco rather than carved in relief. Biographical accounts describing the military and administrative pursuits of the aristocratic owners are depicted, as well as occupations and trades such as hunting, fishing and dyeing cloth.

Ten miles (16 km) further south is the site of the town of **Antinoe** (*Antinopolis*), founded by Hadrian in memory of his friend and favourite, the beautiful boy Antinous, who was drowned here, perhaps willingly, as a human sacrifice.

At **Mallawi**, a few minutes further on, a road leads to the right, bending northwards through fields of sugarcane, where a little railway runs in and out to transport the crop to a smoky redbrick Victorian molasses factory nearby. The road passes through the village of **Ashmunayn**, which partially covers the ruins of ancient **Hermopolis**, city of the moon god Thoth, the reckoner of time, and therefore equated by the Greeks with Hermes. It is worth taking the time to wander around the rather confusing overgrown hummocks, which are all that remains of this once flourishing

Mudbrick domes of a cemetery in Middle Egypt, near Minya.

provincial capital. The ruins of a huge temple of Thoth and a church of the Virgin are about all that can be identified. Across the fields on the edge of the desert is the necropolis called **Tuna el Gebel** with some interesting graves, in particular that of a man named Petosiris, the decorations of whose family tomb provide a vital link between Egyptian and Greek art.

Petosiris belonged to a family of high priests of Thoth during the time that Alexander liberated the Egyptians from the hated Persians at the end of the 4th century BC. In the decoration of his fine tomb he chose to have the conventional offering scenes depicted in the fashionable new Greek style. The stiff virgins of the New Kingdom are replaced by a parade of buxom young matrons in fluttering see-through draperies, the men in hitched up *gallibiyas* and straw hats.

Similar figures, in fact, are visible on the road today, but the countryside is changing fast. For the last 25 years electricity has been reaching nearly every village of any size; and with the influx of money from labour in other Arab countries, families are now able to buy washing machines and television sets, to set up small workshops with power tools, or at least to throw parties with strings of lights and amplified music. A century of change is being telescoped into a dozen years.

Tell el-Amarna: Returning to the main road and heading south, another 6 miles (10 km) will bring the motorist to the turn-off for **Tell el-Amarna**, the open plain on the east bank of the Nile where Akhenaten and Nefertiti made their brief bid to escape from the stuffy and overbearing establishment at Thebes in the 14th century BC. Though their story is appealing, the hot dusty bowl of the Amarna plain is rather a disappointment. Archaeologically, however, it has yielded a great deal of information and some beautiful objects, including the famous head of Nefertiti now in the Berlin Museum. Since their time there has been no further building of any significance on the site, so that the original outlines are still discernible.

Ping pong on the Nile, somewhere between Luxor and Aswan.

From what remains of buildings and frescoes, Akhetaten seems to have been a bright and cheerful place reflecting the king's delight in his family and the everyday world. "Because Thou has risen," he says in his wonderful *Hymn to the Sun*, "all the beasts and cattle repose in their pastures; and the trees and green herbs put forth their leaves and flowers. The birds fly out of their nests; and their wings praise Thy Ka as they fly forth. The sheep and goats of every kind skip about on their legs; and feathered fowl and birds also live, because Thou hast risen for them."

The city of Akhetaten was spread out over a distance of 9 miles (14 km) from north to south. To the north, outlines of a palace and courtiers' villas can be traced. Incorporating reception rooms, bedrooms, bathrooms with basins and toilets, kitchens, and storerooms, the houses were surrounded by gardens with trees and pools. Air conditioning was effected by wind catchers which faced the northerly breezes. These architectural details can be seen in paintings in the Egyptian Museum. Remains of the official palace and the **Temple of Aten**, situated in the middle of Tell el-Amarna, are discernible south of the present day village of **El Till**.

A few miles further on, **Asyut**, the most important town in the region, stands on a bend in the river. Thanks to the cotton boom during the late-19th and early-20th century, its millionaires built themselves palatial villas and lived on a grand scale, with black-tie dinners and weekly races. Most of these families eventually moved north, however, and Asyut is now rather provincial, though it has a university, a huge cement plant and rug factories. A Presbyterian Mission has been established here for over a hundred years and there are many Coptic churches and communities.

Continuing southwards through what is the heartland of the Nile Valley, one passes early monasteries and many ancient remains, arriving eventually at Sohag, Akhmim and Baliana, the turn-off place for Abydos, a standard stop for the longer tourist cruises of Upper Egypt.

Aswan ferry.

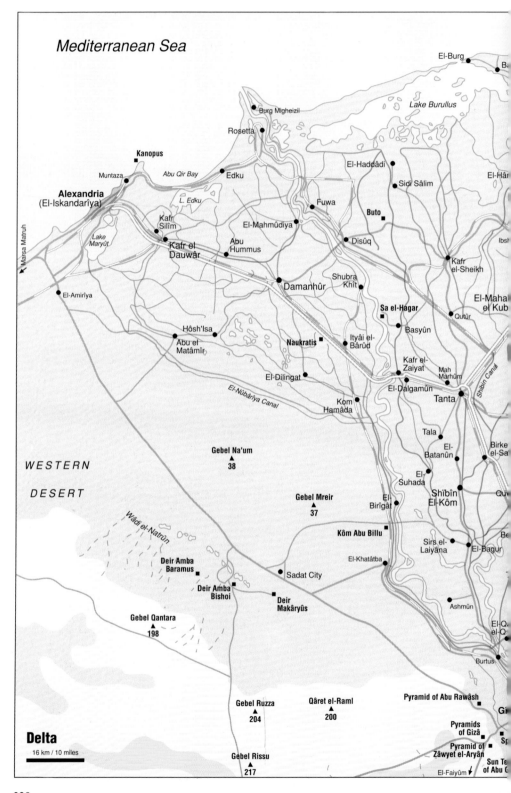

Mediterranean Sea

El-Burg

B.

Lake Burullus

Burg Migheizil

Rosetta

El-Haddâdi

El-Hâr

Kanopus

Abu Qir Bay

Edku

Sidi Sâlim

Muntaza

Alexandria
(El-Iskandarîya)

L. Edku

Fuwa

Buto

Ibsh

Kafr
Silîm

El-Mahmûdiya

Disûq

Kafr
el-Sheikh

Lake
Maryût

**Kafr el-
Dauwâr**

Abu
Hummus

Damanhûr

Shubra
Khît

Sa el-Hagar

El-Maha
el Kub

El-Amirîya

Basyûn

Qutûr

Hôsh'Isa

Naukratis

Ityâi el-
Bârûd

Abu el
Matâmîr

Kafr el-
Zaiyat

Mah
Marhûm

Shîbîn Canal

El-Dilingat

El-Dalgamûn

Tanta

El-Nûbârîya Canal

Kôm
Hamâda

Tala

El-
Batanûn

Birke
el-Sa

WESTERN

Gebel Na'um
▲
38

El-
Suhada

DESERT

Gebel Mreir
▲
37

El-
Birîgât

Shîbîn
El-Kôm

Qu

Wâdi el-Natrûn

Kôm Abu Billu

Sirs el-
Laiyâna

B

El-Bagur

Deir Amba
Baramus

El-Khatâtba

Deir Amba
Bishoi

Sadat City

Deir
Makâryûs

Ashmûn

Gebel Qantara
▲
198

El-Q
el-Q

Burtus

Pyramid of Abu Rawâsh

Gebel Ruzza
▲
204

Qâret el-Raml
▲
200

Gi

Delta

16 km / 10 miles

Pyramids
of Gizâ

Sp

Pyramid of
Zâwyet el-Aryân

Gebel Rissu
▲
217

El-Faiyûm

Sun Te
of Abu (

Marsa Matruh

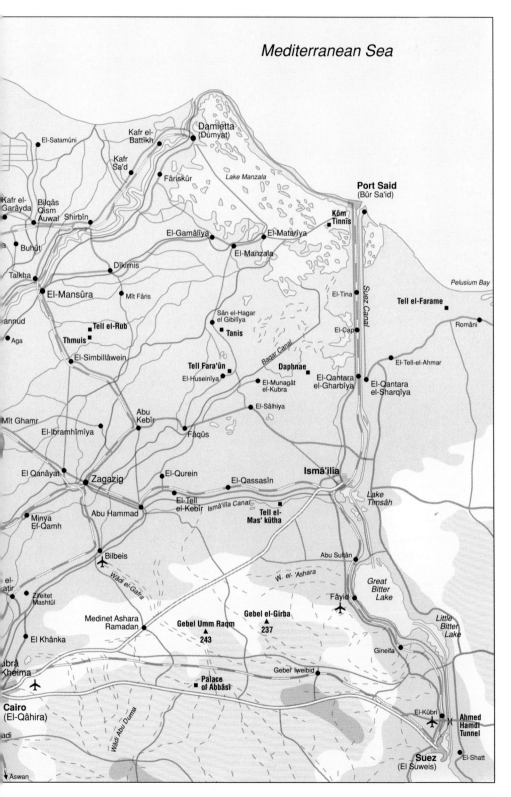

Mediterranean Sea

El-Satamûni

Kafr el-Battîkh

Damietta (Dumyat)

Kafr Sa'd

Fâriskûr

Lake Manzala

Port Said (Bûr Sa'îd)

Kafr el-Garâyda

Bilqâs Qism Auwal

Shirbîn

Kôm Tinnîs

Buhût

El-Gamâlîya

El-Matarîya

Dîkirnis

El-Manzala

Pelusium Bay

Talkha

Mît Fâris

El-Tina

Suez Canal

Tell el-Farame

El-Mansûra

San el-Hagar el Gibillya

El-Cap

Români

ânnûd

Tell el-Rub

Tanis

Aga

Thmuis

El-Simbillâwein

Bagar Canal

El-Tell-el-Ahmar

Tell Fara'ûn

Daphnae

El-Huseinîya

El-Munagât el-Kubra

El-Qantara el-Gharbîya

El-Qantara el-Sharqîya

Mît Ghamr

Abu Kebîr

El-Sâlhiya

El-Ibramhîmîya

Fâqûs

El Qanâyat

Zagazig

El-Qurein

El-Qassasîn

Ismâ'ilîa

Lake Timsâh

Minya El-Qamh

Abu Hammad

El-Tell el-Kebîr

Ismâ'ilîa Canal

Tell el-Mas' kûtha

Bilbeis

Wâdi el-Gafra

W. el-'Ashara

Abu Sultân

Great Bitter Lake

el-atîr

Zifeitet Mashtûl

Fâyid

Little Bitter Lake

Medinet Ashara Ramadan

Gebel Umm Raqm
▲
243

Gebel el-Girba
▲
237

El Khânka

Gineifa

ubrâ Kheima

Gebel Iweibid

Cairo (El-Qâhira)

Wâdi Abu Duma

Palace of Abbâsi

El-Kûbri

Ahmed Hamdi Tunnel

adi

Suez (El Suweis)

El-Shatt

Aswan

ALEXANDRIA AND THE NORTHERN COAST

When Emperor Alexander died in 325 BC, his mortal remains were brought to Memphis for burial, but the priests of Memphis sent the funeral cortège away. "Do not settle him here," they said, "but at the city he built at Rhakotis. For wherever his body must lie, that city will be uneasy, disturbed by wars and battles." So the conqueror of Asia was returned to the city he had established eight years earlier, where he was buried in a grave now lost somewhere below the foundations of modern Alexandria. And the priests were wrong: Memphis today is a sand heap waiting for future archaeologists, while Alexandria, although buffeted by many wars and battles, has somehow managed to stand the test of time.

Visitors to modern Alexandria must be prepared, however, for some disappointment. A search for physical testimonies to the Alexandria of antiquity will be largely in vain. There is very little left of the buildings and monuments that graced it during the Hellenistic and post-Hellenistic period, making Alexandria the most renowned city of the ancient world after Athens and Rome. An odd column or two on the skyline, dank catacombs deep under modern pavements, a Roman pillar propping up the gateway to some pre-Revolutionary patrician villa are all that is left of this glorious past.

Modern Alexandria is the second largest city in Egypt, with a population of about six million inhabitants. Set as it is on the shores of the Mediterranean, it has long been a summer holiday spot, a refuge from landlocked Cairo's searing summer heat. During the summer season, which begins in June and ends in September, two million more visitors crowd into the city, filling the beaches, taking over apartment blocks especially built for their needs and haunting the streets in the cooler hours between dusk and dawn. As autumn heralds winter, however, and the vacationers depart, the Mediterranean churns crossly against the littoral, hotels pull in their awnings, and outdoor cafés retreat indoors. Then the city takes on a resigned air and seems to go back into hibernation, tired, it would appear, of competing for prominence in a changed world. Having twice been the busiest and most cosmopolitan commercial centre in the Eastern Mediterranean, Alexandria now seems to exist largely as a city of memories.

A magnificent entry: E.M. Forster observed that "few cities have made so magnificent an entry into history as Alexandria." When the 25-year-old Macedonian conqueror Alexander the Great arrived in Egypt in 332 BC, he realised that he needed a capital for his newly conquered Egyptian kingdom and that, to link it with Macedonia, it would have to be located on the coast. Early in 331 he sailed northward from Memphis down the Nile, then westward along the coast. At a small fishing village called Rakofi, on a spit of land between the sea and a freshwater lake, with limestone quarries and easy access to the Nile, he founded his city, gave orders to build it, and promptly departed. He never saw his new metropolis.

After Alexander's death in 323 BC, Egypt fell to a Macedonian general named Ptolemy who had been present at the foundation of Alexandria. He made it his new capital and founded a dynasty that ended only in 30 BC when Octavianus Ceasar defeated Cleopatra VI and replaced her as ruler of Egypt.

As is so often the case with a post-conquest generation of rulers, the first Ptolemies had busily set about adorning their city. They also encouraged scholarship; and under their rule Alexandria became a haven and refuge for intellectuals. It nurtured not only outstanding scientists and mathematicians, such as Archimedes, Aristarchus, Hipparchus, Hierophilus, Erasistratus, Ctesibius, Euclid and Eratosthenes, but also poets like Callimachus, Apollonius Rhodius and Theocritus. The first two Ptolemies meanwhile decided that they needed a great monument in their new city, which could be seen by ships at sea and provide a guide for sailors through the limestone reefs that line the shore. Thus the lighthouse on the island of Pharos, one of the Seven Great Wonders of the ancient world, came into being. A fortress as well as a beacon, this huge lighthouse stood at the eastern end of Pharos, where it dominated both the Eastern Harbour, which sheltered the royal fleet, and the Western Harbour. Nothing remains of the lighthouse but a few Aswan granite blocks, far longer than any used in the Pyramids at Gizah.

The Mouseion: The Ptolemies' intellectual achievement was epitomised by the Great Library attached to the Mouseion in Alexandria. The Alexandrian Mouseion was founded by Ptolemy I Soter, who invited an Athenian intellectual to organise an institution on the lines of the Lyceum in Athens, Aristotle's school, where a *mouseion*, a shrine to the Muses, had contained his library. The Mouseion developed quite differently from its Athenian model. Essentially a courtly institution, it enjoyed both the advantages and disadvantages of royal patronage. In many ways, it resembled a modern university, but the scholars, scientists and literary men it supported were under no obligation to teach. They could devote their entire time to their studies. The Great Library, alas, was burned during Caesar's wars and the Mouseion's buildings have disappeared under subsequent rubble.

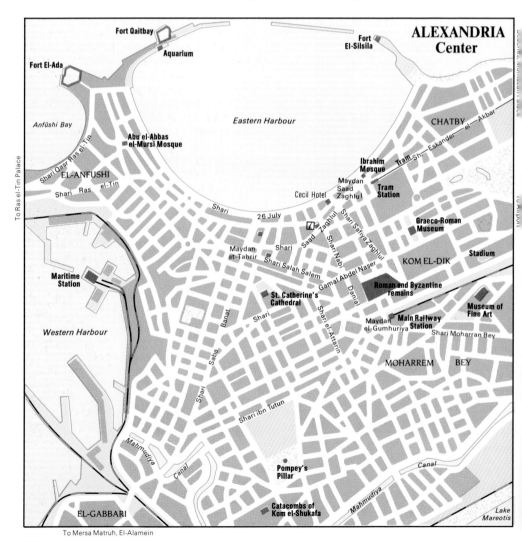

External threat, nationalist rebellion, intrigue at court, and family strife made the Ptolemaic dynasty dependent on Rome. By 89 BC, thanks to the debts it owed to this new power, the Ptolemaic dynasty was under Roman control. In 51 BC, while rivals squabbled in the Roman Senate, a 17-year-old girl was crowned queen in Alexandria as Cleopatra VI. Three years later she was ready to play the temptress, first at Caesar's, then at Mark Anthony's feet. Whether she loved them or not, but her dalliances with powerful Romans were the shrewd and calculated moves of a politician attempting to thwart the ambitions of men who had designs on her kingdom. And as long as she lived, Alexandria preserved its autonomy. At her death, it became a Roman city.

Centuries of decline: As Rome acquired increasing sway over its new colonies in the East, Christianity, a brand new religious movement, began to find disciples. More than any other city in the Roman Empire, Alexandria was the intellectual capital of the new religion.

Alexandrian converts raised its doctrines to the level of a philosophy, while Egyptian tradition provided the new faith with some home-grown images.

Depictions of the god Osiris or the goddess Isis with her child, Horus, for example, parallel the images of Christ on the one hand, and the Virgin and Child on the other; and the Pharaonic *ankh*, which reminds one of a looped cross, actually appeared on many early Christian gravestones.

The conflict between the Church and State came to its height in the first years of the 4th century under the emperor Diocletian, who demolished churches, demoted all Christian officials and enslaved or killed the rest, as many as 60 a day for a period of five years, according to the traditions of the Coptic Church. This persecution prompted flight to the desert, which led to the founding of the first monasteries, and made such a strong impression on the Egyptian church that it dates its calendar from the Era of Martyrs.

Although the Emperor Constantine

Alexandria in a 19th-century engraving.

soon made Christianity the official state religion, centred in his new city of Constantinople, Alexandria still thought of itself as the spiritual capital of the East, where bishops, priests and monks vied to have the last word in doctrinal disputes. This displacement of Alexandria was in part the source of the Monophysite controversy, a disagreement over the nature of Christ. Alexandrian theologians decided that although Christ had been born of Mary, the man in him had been entirely absorbed into the divine.

Adherents of this view were Monophysites and "single nature" became the national cry of Egypt. Accepted at Nicea in 325, the Egyptian view was condemned at the Council of Chalcedon in 451, where a majority of churchmen agreed that Christ had two natures, unmixed and unchangeable, but at the same time indistinguishable and inseparable. This is the definition officially accepted by Western Christians. The Copts and Ethiopians are still Monophysites, though these days the issue doesn't receive much discussion.

In 641, Alexandria fell to the Arab General Amr, who rode into Egypt with 3,500 Bedouin horsemen. Islam, the new religion that Amr brought with him, would have been hostile to a pagan Alexandria and was uneasy with a Christian one, but the Arab Conquest was a humane affair and no damage was done to property. The two great libraries, which the Arabs are often accused of destroying, had already been burned by pagans and Christians. It was Cairo that would develop and blossom under Egypt's Arab masters, however, while Alexandria gradually dwindled, especially after a Frankish raid in 1365, when all the public buildings were destroyed and 5,000 people were carried off to slavery.

Renaissance and revolution: Modern Alexandria really dates from the early 19th century and the reign of Muhammad Ali, who was responsible for introducing cotton and for building the Mahmudiyyah canal, which once more linked Alexandria to the hinterland, forcing Egypt to look not only towards the **The Mosque of Abul Abbas.**

Mediterranean again, but beyond it, to Europe. The later 19th century witnessed the creation of extensive wealth in the cotton trade and a steady influx of Greeks, Italians, French and English, who turned Alexandria into a pseudo-European city, complete with wide, grid-planned streets, foreign schools, clubs, restaurants, casinos, businesses and banks. It is hard today, strolling down the pocked and dusty boulevards of the city, to actually believe that behind the grimy, peeling walls of what were once elegant buildings the aspirations of a whole cosmopolitan society were played out in vast, ornate rooms lit by pendulous chandeliers.

The 1952 Revolution changed all that. The new government eventually expelled most foreigners and confiscated their lands or nationalised their businesses, while Egyptian capital and enterprise fled abroad.

Using the mind's eye: Modern visitors to Alexandria will get the most out of the city if they possess lively imaginations. That is not to say that there isn't plenty to look at, for the city is still enchanting, but the visible glories of its past are few and far between and for the most part must be almost reconstructed in the mind's eye. The city is best explored on foot, but taxis, painted in distinctive black and orange, are plentiful and cheap and can be hired by the hour or the day.

A good place to begin is the **Cecil Hotel**, located at the heart of the former European zone, overlooking the sea. The entrance to the hotel is on the west side of **Maydan Saad Zaghlul**, a large square between **Ramleh** (*Ar-Raml*) **tram station** and the **Corniche**. Here, in the lee of a few straggling palm trees, where the Romans built a temple to honour Julius Caesar, Cairo buses disgorge their passengers. The two obelisks that once stood here, the famous "Cleopatra's Needles", are now in London and New York. In the centre of the *maydan* is a **statue of Saad Zaghlul**, the nationalist hero who tried to negotiate the independence of Egypt after World War I. As you stand facing the

The Eastern Harbour and the 15th-century Fortress of Qaitbay, which stands on the site of the ancient lighthouse.

sea, let your gaze follow the sweep of land to your left and come to rest on the solid mass of the **Fort of Qaitbay** at the western tip of the headland. The best time to see the fort is just before the sun goes down, when the warm reds and oranges of an Alexandrian sunset turn the old sandstone building the colour of rich honey.

The Fortress and the Pharos: The trip out to the tip of the promontory where the fort of Qaitbay stands is of no particular interest. On the Corniche side, you pass some dilapidated apartment buildings, gaily festooned with washing. On the sea side is the modern Yacht Club and a small fishing port, where brightly painted boats bob up and down on a dirty-looking sea and nets are hung along the jetty to dry. The fort is at the end of a breakwater and has been restored since the British bombardment of Alexandria in 1882, the preliminary to their invasion and occupation. It stands on the site of the ancient **Pharos lighthouse** and, if only for this reason, draws the curious.

The lighthouse took its name from the island of Pharos, where it was built in around 279 BC. It gave its name in turn to future lighthouses, beacons and headlights, called *phares* in French, *fari* in Italian, while its form inspired the classic Cairene minaret.

The Pharos was a marvel of its day. It was over 400 feet (120 metres) high and hydraulic machinery may have been used for hauling fuel to the top. Within its square base were as many as 300 rooms, to house mechanics and operators; above were an octagonal storey and a circular storey, topped by a lantern with a beacon and devices that are still a mystery. One was described as a mirror of polished steel, to reflect the sun by day and a fire by night, or as made of glass or transparent stone, so fashioned as to enable a man sitting under it to see ships at sea that were invisible to the naked eye. This description suggests a kind of prism, the secret of which Alexandrian mathematicians might well have discovered, only for it to be lost or destroyed when the Pharos fell.

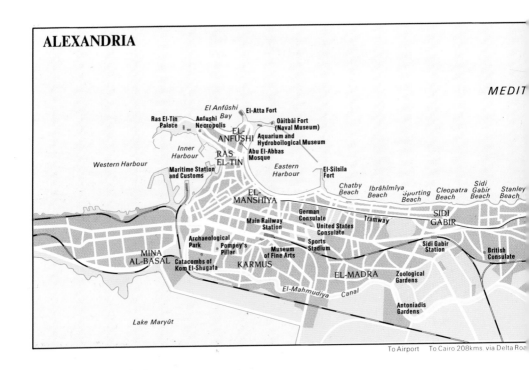

The lantern collapsed as early as the 8th century, followed by the circular storey. In 881 Ibn Tulun did some restoration, but in 1100 an earthquake toppled the octagonal storey and nullified his efforts. The Pharos still served as a lighthouse, however, until the square base was finally ruined in another earthquake in the 14th century. Enter Sultan Qaitbay, who in 1480 built the fort that still stands on the site, which incorporates some of the debris from the Pharos. You can make out granite and marble columns, for example, in the northwest section of the enclosure walls. The fort itself is an impressive piece of defensive architecture and inside is a newly revamped **Naval Museum**.

Ras at-Tin and Anfushi: Westward along the sea front, 1½ miles (3 km) from the Fort, is the **Palace of Ras at-Tin** (Cape of Figs). Built by Muhammad Ali, but altered by later rulers of Egypt, it is the site where King Faruq abdicated on 26 July, 1952, and from which he embarked a few hours later to sail away on his yacht, *Mahrusa* – just as his grand-father, the Khedive Ismail, had done in the summer of 1879. This enormous pile is still used for official Egyptian government functions and cannot be visited. East of the Palace on Shari' Ras at-Tin, near the end of the tramline, and worth a look, are the **tombs of Anfushi**. Ptolemaic, with decorations that marry Greek and Egyptian styles, their stucco walls are painted to imitate marble blocks and tiles.

At this point, you can turn into the old Turkish quarter of **Anfushi** at the heart of what was once the island of Pharos.

Continuing southeast along Shari' Ras at-Tin you will reach **Shari' Faransa** (*Rue de France*). You are now in one of the most "native" parts of the city, where you may stop briefly to look at the 17th-century **Tirbana mosque**. It has a pale yellow exterior, plaster overlying a red and black Delta-style facade of bricks and wooden beams. On the left side note the ancient columns at the entrance to the cellars. Two huge Corinthian columns mark the entrance to the mosque itself and support its minaret.

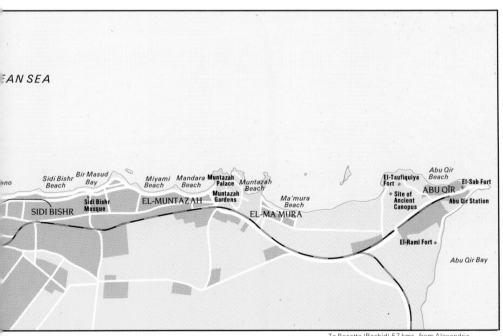

To Rosetta (Rashid) 57 kms. from Alexandria

In ancient times Pharos was connected to the mainland by a causeway called the **Heptastadion**, which gradually became a permanent broad neck of land. Along it to the south Shari' Faransa runs into **Maydan at-Tahrir**, formerly Place Muhammad Ali. A statue of the Pasha on horseback (by Jacquemart) still graces the *maydan*. The southern end of the square marks approximately the former mainland coastline and the seafront of the village of Rhakotis.

The southern quarter: To reach the centre of **Rhakotis**, the hub of ancient Alexandria, you must be prepared for a detour, armed with a map and on foot, through a particularly insalubrious part of town. Rhakotis is about a mile southwest from the Corniche along Shari' Salah ad-Din and Shari' 'Awud as-Sawari. Simplest, perhaps, is to hail a taxi and tell the driver to take you to **Pompey's Pillar** (*Al-'Awud as-Sawari*, "The Horseman's Pillar"). If you survive the drive, which bumps over busy tram tracks, you will reach the bottom of a rather shapeless hill surrounded by a wall. Believe it or not, this is what is left of the acropolis of the Ptolemies.

Long before Alexander arrived on the scene, this hill was the citadel of Rhakotis, dedicated to the worship of Osiris. The Ptolemies in their turn constructed a temple of Serapis on its summit. Here, with a collection of around 200,000 manuscripts given to her by Mark Anthony, Cleopatra endowed the second great Alexandrian library, which was to remain attached to the **Serapeum** until the temple itself was destroyed by a Christian mob; and thus here, for almost half a century, was the most learned spot on earth.

Today not much of the Serapeum remains: some tunnels in the rocks with crypts and niches and a few marble pillars. What the Christians wiped out in 391 AD later vicissitudes have put paid to. But the principal attraction, a solitary 72-foot (22-metre) high pillar of pink Aswan granite, seems to touch the sky defiantly and when European travellers arrived in the 15th century it caught their attention. No scholars they, but

Late Roman council chamber excavated in downtown Alexandria.

since they had heard of Pompey, they named the pillar after him and said his head was enclosed in a ball at the top. It actually has nothing to do with Pompey: according to an inscription on its base, it was dedicated to the Emperor Diocletian in 297 AD and it may once have had an equestrian statue on top, which would explain its Arabic name.

This once famous site has been encroached upon by a brash and often ugly modern city: hideous buildings loom around its perimeter, trams bump, screech and grind their way noisily along the street below. But a certain sense of dignity and charm lingers.

The Catacombs: A short distance south of the site of Pompey's pillar and not to be missed are the **catacombs of Kom esh-Shawqafa**. Come out of the enclosure of Pompey's pillar, turn right up a small crowded street and at the top you will come to a small crossroads. Just beyond it is the entrance to the catacombs. Immediately inside the entrance are four very fine sarcophagi of purplish granite. You are now on the Kom

esh-Sahwqafa (Hill of Tiles) and the tombs here are the most important in the city and quite unique. They also constitute the largest Roman-period funerary complex in Egypt. They date from about the 2nd century AD, when the old religions began to fade and merge with one another, as demonstrated in the curious blend of classical and Egyptian designs.

The catacombs are on three different levels, the lowest being flooded and inaccessible. The first level is reached by a wide circular staircase lit by a central well, down which the bodies were lowered by ropes. From the vestibule you enter the Rotunda, with a well in its centre upon which eight pillars support a domed roof. To the left is the Banquet Hall.

From the Rotunda, a small staircase descends to the second level and the amazing central tomb is revealed. Here the decorations are fantastic and in a hodgepodge of styles. Bearded serpents on the vestibule wall at the entrance of the inner chamber hold the pine-cone of Dionysus and the serpent-wand of Hermes, but also wear the double crown of Upper and Lower Egypt, while above them are Medusas in round shields. Inside the tomb chamber are three large sarcophagi cut out from the rock. Roman in style, decorated with fruits, flowers, Medusas and filleted ox-heads. None of them has ever been occupied and their lids are sealed on. Over each of the sarcophagi is a niche decorated with Egyptian-style reliefs.

Turn and face the entrance. On your right stands the extraordinary figure of Anubis – with a dog's head, but dressed as a Roman soldier, with sword, lance and shield. Left is the god Sobek, also dressed in military costume, with cloak and spear.

In search of Alexander: Start at Maydan Saad Zaghlul and walk south along Shari' Nabi Danyal. The point where it meets Shari' Harriyyah has been the chief crossroads of the city for over 2,300 years. Here, from east and west, the Canopic Way (Shari' Hurriyyah) once ran from the Gate of the Sun to the Gate of the Moon. From north to south ran a street joining the harbour and its

Strange mixture of styles at the Catacombs of Kom esh-Shawqafa testifies to the cosmopolitan nature of ancient Alexandria.

docks with Lake Mareotis, now Shari' Nabi Danyal. In ancient times both were lined from end to end with colonnades.

A short walk up Shari' Nabi Danyal will bring you to the mosque of that same name, on the left side of the street with an entrance somewhat set back. Mistakenly believed to be the tomb of the prophet Daniel, it is named for Shaykh Danyal al-Maridi, who died in 1407. It is also mistakenly believed to be the site of Alexander's tomb, the Soma, where he and some of the Ptolemies were buried in the Macedonian manner.

Inside the mosque, an ancient caretaker will beckon you over to peer down a great square hole into the crypt where Danyal and one Luqman the Wise lie, keeping company (it is alleged) with Alexander and some of his successors. The cellars have never been properly explored, although there is the dubious account of a dragoman named Ambroise Schilizzi attached to the Russian consulate, who claimed in 1850 to have descended into the gloom and seen through a hole in a wooden door "a human body in a glass cage with a diadem on its head, and half bowed on a sort of elevation or throne."

Almost immediately opposite the mosque are some antique columns propping up the gatepost of what is now a French Cultural Centre.

Kom ad-Dik and the Greco-Roman Museum: One block east of Nebi Danyal, on the south side of Shari' Hurriyyah lie the **excavations of Kom ad-Dik**. Here, Polish archaeologists have been digging up Alexandria's past since 1959. Below Muslim tombs dating from the 9th to 11th centuries, they have found baths, houses, assembly halls, and the site where Christian mobs burnt objects from the Serapeum. Continue east along Shari' Hurriyyah and you will come to the Rue du Musée and the entrance to the **Greco-Roman Museum**.

For visitors satiated with the hieratic wonders of ancient Egyptian civilisation, the Greco-Roman Museum can only come as a delightful relief. Filling the historical gap between the country's

Monument to the Unknown Soldier was a gift from the Italian community in Alexandria.

several museums of pharaonic antiquities and Cairo's museums of Coptic and Islamic art, it has recently been renovated and a charming new sculpture garden has been laid out in its grounds. Among its many treasures are some spectacular pieces of Hellenistic sculpture, but special attention must be paid to the wonderful collection of Tanagra figurines. Likewise not to be missed is a masterpiece of fresco-painting that is also the earliest depiction of an ox-powered waterwheel.

Modern pleasures: This might be the time to take a break from sightseeing and to stroll back down Shari' Hurriyyah towards the sea, stopping off at **Pastroudis**, one of the last Greek cafés. Here you can sit at a sidewalk table overlooking the ruins of Kom ad-Dik and ponder Alexandria's more recent cultural past.

During the earlier part of this century a literary revival took place. Its luminary was Constantine Cavafy, called "the poet of the City" by Lawrence Durrell. E.M. Forster, who lived in Alexandria and wrote its history, first met Cavafy in 1917 and was responsible for introducing him to the English-speaking world. The Greek poet's apartment at 4 Sh. Sharm ash-Shaykh became a museum open to the public in 1993.

Lawrence Durrell's *Alexandria Quartet* was to a large extent inspired by Cavafy's poetry. All the characters in the *Quartet* meet at least once at Pastroudis for an *araq*.

Alexandria is a Mediterranean city and still has a Mediterranean café life. **Pastroudis**, the **Trianon** and the **Delices** (the last two are on Maydan Saad Zaghlul) are fine examples, if somewhat down at heel, of fin-de-siècle coffee houses.

Alexandria has a reputation for serving up good food, particularly seafood. Greek *tavernas*, such as the **Diamantakis Taverna** on the south side of **Maydan Rami** (*Ramleh Square*), offer fried or grilled fish and Greek salads. The **Santa Lucia** is the best known restaurant: the food is good and the atmosphere lively. It is on Shari' Safiyya Zaghlul, not far from Pastroudis. A relic

Alexandria in 1930.

Alexandria — The Boulevard Fouad I   106

of the past is the **Union**, on Shari'al-Bursa just off Maydan Muhammad Ali near where the charming Anglican **church of St Mark's** is situated. As for hotels, romantics will probably favour landmarks such as the Cecil or the **Windsor Palace**, overlooking the sea.

West to Burg al-Arab: Although a train runs westward just inland from the Mediterranean coast, it is unreliable and anyone interested in exploring the region west of Alexandria would do best to hire a car by the day.

The coast road is unprepossessing for the first 18 miles (30 km) until you pass the resort town of **Agami**, which began some years ago as a few bathing huts and simple beach houses in a grove of trees, but has now mushroomed into the Marbella or St Tropez of Egypt's Mediterranean coast, complete with swimming pools, discotheques, fast-food joints and a section of villas known as "Millionaire's Row".

Before the turnoff to the **village of Burg al-Arab** on the hill on your left, is the ancient **temple of Taposiris Magna**, whose name is preserved in the modern Abu Sir. It is contemporary with the founding of Alexandria and was dedicated to the cult of Osiris. The ruined tower to the east is a Ptolemaic lighthouse, the first of a chain that stretched from Alexandria all the way down the North African coast. It looks, in miniature, very much as its big brother, the Pharos, would have looked.

It is no longer possible to ascend to the top of the lighthouse – a great pity, as the view is magnificent: To the north, the brilliant turquoise blue of the sea is offset by its bleached white beaches, while to the south lies the dun-coloured **lake-bed of Mariut** (ancient Mareotis), vibrantly alive with wildflowers in the spring. If you leave the coast and drive south across the lake-bed, you will be able to make out the remains of the ancient causeway, to your left, which connected ancient Taposiris with the desert.

Over the crest of the hill, you will come to the curious little village of Burg al-Arab, the brain child of W.E. Jennings-Bramley, governor of the

Alexandria – The Bride of the Sea – across the Eastern Harbour.

Western Desert under the British, who decided in the early '20s to build a Bedouin capital, using stone from the ruins of Roman villas, which dotted the area. Modelling his village as a fortified medieval Italian hill town, he invited friends to build vacation houses within its turretted walls. Today the village looks like a crumbling set for a remake of *Beau Geste*, though one or two of the houses are still in private hands and the Egyptian president has a rest house there at his disposition.

From here, you may want to continue inland and visit the ruins of the **monastery of Abu Menas**. Drive south out of Burg al-Arab through an industrial development and turn left at the first crossroads you come to. This road will take you to the turnoff to the monastery. Before long you will spot the twin towers of the new monastery, founded in 1959, on the horizon, an ugly concrete pile much favoured as a pilgrimage spot by modern Copts. Drive on by and very shortly you will see a low line of hillocks to your right. You have arrived at the site of the ancient monastery of Abu Menas and the hillocks are the scrap heaps left behind by several generations of enthusiastic archaeologists.

Menas was a young Egyptian officer, martyred in 296 AD during his service in Asia Minor because he would not renounce Christ. When his troops returned to Egypt, they carried his remains with them, but at this spot a miracle occurred: the camel carrying the remains of the saint refused to go any further. Here, then, he was buried and forgotten for a while. Some time later, a shepherd noticed that a sick lamb passing over the burial spot became well; so did another sick lamb, then a sick princess.

The saint's powers were quickly recognised. A church was built over his grave by Athanasius in the 4th century and was incorporated into a great basilica, erected by Emperor Arcadius, at the beginning of the 5th century. For pilgrims, the site became the Lourdes of the Western Desert.

The reason for this rapid popularity

The Palestine Hotel at Muntazah, Alexandria.

was probably the local water, which must have possessed real curative powers, for in the shrine's heyday pilgrims flocked here by the thousands, filling little flasks, stamped with the saint's image, from the sacred source by his tomb. Houses sprang up, baths were built, the land nearby was irrigated, and the settlement soon grew big enough to need its own cemeteries.

The cult of Menas was meanwhile carried across the desert by traders and over the Mediterranean by sailors, extending as far afield as France and Spain, where the distinctive little flasks have also been discovered, with their stamped depictions of the saint standing between two kneeling camels.

Conversions to Islam eventually put an end to the cult, but as late as the year 1000 an Arab traveller saw the great double basilica still standing in the desert: lights still burned day and night at the shrine and there was still a trickle of "the beautiful water of St Menas that drives away pain".

The site has been excavated and the foundations of the primitive church and the basilica of Arcadius may be clearly discerned. The crypt where St Menas was buried lies at the foot of a marble staircase in the church, which was incorporated into the portico of the basilica, but his relics rest in the modern monastery. A baptistry with a font can be seen to the west. North of the basilica are the hospice and the baths, with cisterns for hot and cold water.

Pursuing the Desert Fox: Further along the coast road is **Al Alamayn** (*Alamein*) the site of a series of battles that began in the summer of 1942 and turned the tide of war in favour of the Allies. When the Africa Corps under Rommel pushed as far as Al Alamayn on 1 July, 1942, the British fleet left Alexandria and withdrew through the Suez Canal to the Red Sea. But Rommel had problems of his own: his troops were exhausted and the British navy had succeeded in torpedoing ships carrying badly needed supplies. In October 1942, Britain's General Montgomery launched a third and final counteroffensive against Rommel, **Near Alexandria.**

defeating the German army and driving it westward out of Egypt.

Of the three main war cemeteries in Al Alamayn, the British is the first one you come to. It is on your left as your enter the town from the east. A walk around the simple tombstones, each of which carries an inscription, cannot fail to move.

In the centre of town is a **Military Museum** housing numerous artifacts of the battle. Beyond stands the massive stone monument to Germany's fallen in a beautiful setting which overlooks the sea. Further on down the coast is the Italian memorial, a huge impressive white marble pile, and curiously reminiscent of a railway station in a provincial Italian city.

From this point on, the coast is startlingly beautiful. On the left are the duns and ochres of the desert, enlivened by an occasional flash of colour from a gaily painted house or a Bedouin tent; to the right, the sea and sand stretch towards infinity.

If you long for a day on the beach,

keep going to **Sidi Abd ar-Rahman**, about 15 miles (25 km) beyond Al-Alamayn: some people claim it's the best beach on the coast. There is a perfectly adequate hotel here with camping facilities.

Or, alternatively, you can go all the way to **Marsah Matruh**, 45 miles (72 km) farther, 175 miles (280 km) from Alexandria, which has long been a seaside resort and has some fine beaches. Its hotels are simple but good and the town is still picturesque. There you can visit **Rommel's Cave**, now a museum containing, amongst other things, the Desert Fox's own armoury, donated by his son.

Eastward to Rosetta: Alexandria's **Corniche** extends some 10 miles (16 km) eastwards and there are a number of public beaches along the seafront between the Eastern Harbour and Muntazah. But they are crowded and often dirty and incessant building has turned most of the Corniche into an ugly string of high-rise buildings, lashed into premature decrepitude by salt sea-winds.

Girl near the desert monastery of Abu Menas. Tracks head to excavations of a 5th-century AD city.

At Muntazah is a former summer residence of the royal family, set within extensive closed grounds planted with Italian pines. No longer open to the public, **Muntazah Palace** was built in the Turco-Florentine style by Khedive Abbas II and E.M. Forster worked there when the Red Cross took it over as a hospital during World War I. A walk in its gardens, open to the public for a small fee, is very pleasant.

Five miles (8 km) east of Muntazah is **Abu Qir**, famous for battles fought here in 1798 and 1799. The first was the Battle of the Nile, Nelson's great victory, which destroyed Napoleon's fleet and left the French army stranded in Egypt. The battle was so named because Nelson reported that the engagement had taken place not far from the Rosetta mouth of the Nile. Underway since 1985 has been a joint Franco-Egyptian project aimed at raising the sunken French fleet from the seabed. The second battle took place on land a year later under the command of Napoleon himself, who had rushed down from Cairo with 10,000 men, mostly cavalry, to repel an Ottoman force of 15,000.

Abu Qir therefore ought to be a romantic spot, but it isn't. The only real reason to come to this seaside shanty town is its excellent seafood restaurants. One, the **Zephyrion**, bears the ancient name of the site. It is a large barn-like structure with an open air terrace right on the sea. The fish is fresh and best eaten grilled or fried. Wash it down with the local anise drink, *zibib*, or cold bottles of Stella beer.

Nearby is the site of ancient Canopus, but there is little to see. The next spot of interest is **Rosetta** (*Rashid*), 40 miles (65 km) from Alexandria on the western branch of the Nile near the sea. It was here that the Rosetta stone, which enabled Champollion to decipher the language of the pharaohs, was discovered by a French soldier in 1799. Rosetta is famous for its 17th- and 18th-century houses, built during prosperity under the Ottomans when it was the busiest port in Egypt. The finest example, the house of 'Ali al-Fatali (1620), has been

Italian War Cemetery at Al Alamayn, one of the key battlefields of World War II.

destroyed but there are 21 others, of which three may be visited. Several 18th-century mosques may be toured, as well as a mill and a *hammam*. There is also a small museum in the *house of Aralo Kulli*, where coins, metalwork and ceramics are displayed.

The Delta and Wadi Natrun: Lush with vegetation and veined with canals, the **Nile Delta** is the flower of the Egyptian lotus. From the Barrage at **Qanater al-Khayriyya** in the south, where parks surround locks and sluices built under the British occupation, to the marshy waters of lakes **Edku**, **Burullus** and **Manzala**, where smugglers and fugitives live among the reeds, the Delta fans out like a broad palm reaching for the Mediterranean. To both the west and the east, deserts are receding in the face of vast land reclamation projects, while in the Delta *felaheen* pack their bags for Cairo or the oil-rich Gulf.

The *Saidis* or people of Upper Egypt are renowned for their pride, generosity, spontaneity, and hair-trigger tempers. Their Delta cousins, less independent, more attuned to the hard labour of perennial irrigation, and lacking the wild inspiration that may come from living close to the desert, are sober, thrifty and sharp-witted. Natives of **Menufiyyah** in particular – among them Presidents Sadat and Mubarak – the Delta's richest orchard country, are famed for their craftiness.

Indeed, each section of the Delta has its recognised particularity. **Mansurah**, the "victorious" city, was founded on the site of the Mamluks' triumph over invading Crusaders under Louis IX. With its elegant Nileside villas from the age when cotton was king and its light-skinned, fair-haired inhabitants, the city is regarded as Queen of the Delta.

The men of **Mahalla al-Kubra**, the centre of the textile industry, are known for their hardworking habits, while the women of **Zagazig**, capital of Sharqiyyah Province and home of a university, are famed for their "gazelle-like" eyes and classic Bedouin beauty. **Dumyat** (*Damietta*), an ancient port that rivalled Alexandria in the Middle Ages,

Sunbathing cows, Mersa Matruh.

is recognised as being the home of Egypt's furniture industry; and **Disuq**, on the same branch of the Nile as Rosetta, is identified with the famous annual festival, or *mulid*, it stages in honour of its patron saint, Ibrahim ad-Disuqi. But it is the Delta's largest town, sprawling **Tanta**, that is renowned as the home of Egypt's greatest *mulid*. In the month of October, as many as two million thrill-seekers gather for the festival of Ahmad al-Badawi.

The prehistoric Delta was a swampy tidal estuary interspersed with islands. Centuries of Nile effluvia built up a silty land mass that eventually split the river in two. Diligent canal building, after the union of Lower and Upper Egypt in the Old Kingdom, tamed the swamp and sedentarised the region's original inhabitants. With the growth of Mediterranean trade and rivalry between Egypt, Phoenicia, and the Greeks, the Delta grew in importance, encouraging later Pharaohs to abandon the old capitals of Thebes and Memphis and establish headquarters in the Delta near the sea.

The region's muddy soil and lack of solid building materials made its ancient cities perishable; and their sites have been additionally threatened in recent decades by a population explosion in rural Egypt. Of **Buto**, **Leontopolis**, **Mendes**, **Naukratis**, **Piramesse** and **Athribis**, little now remains but mounds of earth. **Bubastis**, near the modern town of Zagazig, once the home of the cat goddess Bastet, is now reduced to a few chunks of stone. **Tanis**, which was a great port long before Alexander founded his city, is today nothing but a huge mound. The need for archaeological investigation is urgent everywhere in the Delta; and multinational teams are hard at work.

The monasteries of Wadi Natrun: To the west of the Delta, beyond the ridge of desert and just off the Cairo-Alexandria desert road, the **Wadi Natrun**, or *Valley of Natron*, snuggles below sea level. It was once home to over 50 monasteries. Hundreds more monks lived in the total isolation of desert caves.

Europeans who are unused to seeing

One of King Farouk's palaces at Montazah, Alexandria.

Christianity as a vital, living faith, will find the *wadi* a strange, perhaps even unsettling place. Dour, bearded monks in black robes with gilt-embroidered hoods appear in the middle of the waste atop shiny new Massey Ferguson tractors. On the occasion of religious festivals, hordes of devout pilgrims descend on the valley's four extant monasteries. A religious revival has swept across the Middle East in recent years; and Coptic Christians like everyone else, have been caught up in the religious fervour.

Deir Abu Maqar, the largest and most active of the monasteries, has in recent years been the seat of the Coptic Pope, who was exiled to the desert by the late President Sadat. Its oldest remains date to the 9th century. **Anba Bishoi**, founder of another monastery, was a disciple of Abu Maqar (St Macarius). A third monastery, **Deir as-Suryan**, has some of the best preserved buildings. Its church of al Adhra' has 10th-century paintings and ivory panels. **Deir Baramus** is the smallest and most remote of the four.

Although the monasteries' foundation dates all the way back to the 5th and 6th centuries, extensive restorations throughout their history have left very little of the original work and indeed testify more to the decline in taste that has beset Egypt since the Ottoman occupation. Note that Wadi Natrun's Coptic churches, like Pharaonic temples, have three distinct areas. The outer is reserved for laymen, the middle for initiates, and the inner for clergymen.

Ordinary visitors to the monasteries should therefore on no account venture into the curtained inner sanctuaries. Aside from numerous churches and chapels, each monastery has a hospice, living quarters for monks, a refectory and a keep where monks could shelter from Bedouin raids.

Monasteries are closed to members of the public during periods of fast: Sexagesima Monday to Orthodox Easter (61 days), Advent (25 November–6 January), before the Feast of the Apostles (27 June–10 July), and before Assumption (7–21 August).

By the sea at Damietta.

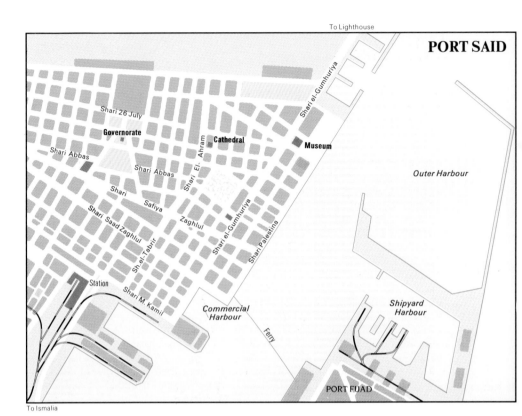

PORT SAID

Shari 26 July

Governorate

Shari Abbas

Shari Abbas

Shari

Safiya

Shari Saad Zaghlul

Zaghlul

Sh. el-Tahrir

Shari El- Ahram

Cathedral

Shari el-Gumhuriya

Shari el-Gumhuriya

Shari Palestina

Museum

Outer Harbour

Station

Shari M. Kamil

Commercial Harbour

Shipyard Harbour

Ferry

PORT FUAD

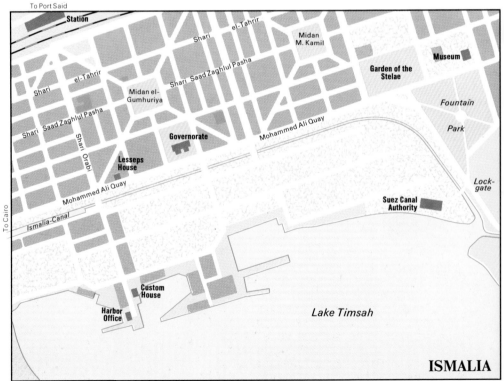

Station

Shari

el-Tahrir

Midan M. Kamil

Museum

Shari

el-Tahrir

Shari Saad Zaghlul Pasha

Garden of the Stelae

Shari Saad Zaghlul Pasha

Midan el-Gumhuriya

Fountain

Park

Shari Orabi

Governorate

Mohammed Ali Quay

Lock-gate

Lesseps House

To Cairo

Mohammed Ali Quay

Suez Canal Authority

Ismalia-Canal

Custom House

Harbor Office

Lake Timsah

ISMALIA

SUEZ CANAL

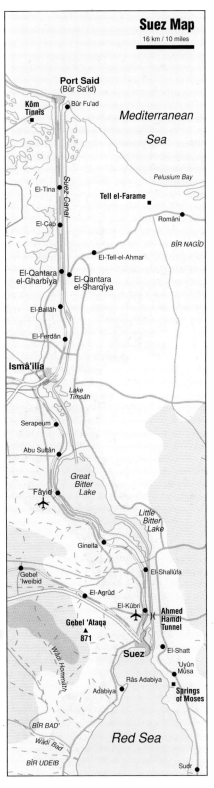

Picture a huge ocean-going ship drifting through a sea of sand. Seen across flat desert, the hallucinatory effect of the Suez Canal underlines the revolutionary impact the waterway has had not only on Egypt, but on the structure of international commerce. The Canal is arguably the single most vital traffic artery in the world.

Labouring for the barbarians: The idea of building a canal that would link the Mediterranean with the Red Sea is ancient indeed. The 26th Dynasty pharaoh Necho II first aired such a proposal at the end of the 7th century BC, with a project to join the Gulf of Suez to the Nile, down which ships could continue to the Mediterranean. According to Herodotus, an oracular pronouncement that he would merely be "labouring for the barbarians" dissuaded Necho from completing excavations. The job was therefore left to Egypt's Persian conquerors a century later; and their work was followed by Ptolemaic and Roman re-excavation.

During the centuries before the Arab conquest, however, this old canal silted up and the Muslims' brilliant general Amr ibn al-'As suggested that a new and better one should be cut across the narrow isthmus of Suez. Cautioned by the Caliph Omar that it would be hard to defend and that Greek pirates might use it as a route to attack the holy city of Mecca, he had to be satisfied instead with renovating the exisiting canal. It flourished for another century before being blocked on orders of the Abbasid Caliph al-Mansur.

It was not until the 19th century, with the growth of European power and the energetic promotion of a French engineer, Ferdinand de Lesseps, that Amr's idea could be brought to fruition. A Suez Canal Company was opened by public subscription in Europe and an agreement was reached with the Viceroy Said and his successor the Khedive Ismail whereby Egypt provided both capital and labour for the job itself.

Construction began in 1859. It took 10 years, with 25,000 labourers working 3-month shifts, to cut the 100-mile (160-km) channel. The total cost, including the building of the Sweetwater Canal for drinking water from the Nile, reached £25 million, of which Egypt put up more than two-thirds.

Amidst extravagant fanfare, with assorted European royalty in attendance, the Canal was opened to shipping in November of 1869, transforming trade and geopolitics as dramatically as the Portuguese and Spanish discoveries of the 15th century. Distances from Europe to the Far East were cut by a third, distances to India by half. However, Egypt's debts forced the sale of its stake to the British government for a paltry sum of £4 million sterling. As London's *Economist* drily commented in the year of its opening, the Canal was "cut by French energy and Egyptian money for British advantage". The strategic importance of the Canal to Britain's empire was one of the excuses for occupying Egypt in 1882.

The fortunes of five wars: Britain imposed draconian measures on Egypt while fighting to defend the Canal in both World War I and World War II. For Egyptians, foreign possession of the Canal came to represent the major reason for anti-imperialist struggle. Not until 1954 did Nasser arrange for the withdrawal of British troops occupying the Canal Zone.

In 1956, hard up for cash and seeking to finance the High Dam, Nasser turned as a last resort – having been refused financing at the last minute by the United States – to nationalising the Canal, from which Egypt received only a tiny portion of the revenue. Unreconciled to the rapid decline of its empire, Britain responded by invading, with the collusion of Israel and France. Only the intervention of the two superpowers resolved the crisis, which marked a turning point in world affairs. Ten years later, all that remained of Britain's empire were Gibraltar, Hong Kong and a few remote islands, while Egypt had become dependent upon the Soviet Union.

Mecca-bound pilgrims relax by the Suez Canal.

In 1967, the Israelis again attacked Egypt, and held the Sinai Peninsula up to the edge of the Canal. Heavy bombardment during the "War of Attrition" that followed the Israeli conquest shattered the canal cities and made refugees of their 500,000 inhabitants. For six years, until the successful Egyptian counterattack of 1973, the waterway was closed to traffic. Reopened in 1975, it has since been widened and deepened.

The canal cities: Port Said sits on an artificial landfill jutting into the Mediterranean. From here convoys of ships pass the green domes of the Suez Canal Authority building to begin the journey to the Red Sea. Once the major point of entry for tourists stepping off the great Peninsular and Orient ("P and O") passenger lines, Port Said is now the Hong Kong of Egypt, where Cairo consumers flock for duty-free goods. Despite the damage of three wars and the current emporium atmosphere, this resilient town retains a good deal of character.

Situated on **Lake Timsah** halfway between Port Said and Suez, **Ismailia** is the queen of the Canal cities. With its tree-shaded avenues and genteel colonial-style houses, it is the cleanest city in Egypt. There are a number of fine hotels and restaurants; and from uncrowded lakeside beaches ships transiting the Canal can be watched.

South of Ismailia the Canal enters the **Great Bitter Lake**, a small inland sea bordered by holiday villas and military installations. Halfway between the lake and Suez, the 3-mile (5-km) long **Ahmed Hamdi tunnel** provides the only permanent bridge across the Canal.

Suez, the Canal's southern terminus, was Egypt's major Red Sea port for hundreds of years. Its harbour is now at **Port Tawfiq**, an artificial peninsula where the Canal meets the **Gulf of Suez**. Israeli bombardments flattened the town in the 1967 war; and hasty rebuilding after 1973 has not enhanced its beauty. Suez is best observed from the Sinai side of the Canal, where scores of ships can be seen lining up in the turquoise waters of the Gulf ready to make the northward passage.

Wreckage from a recent war in the Sinai Desert.

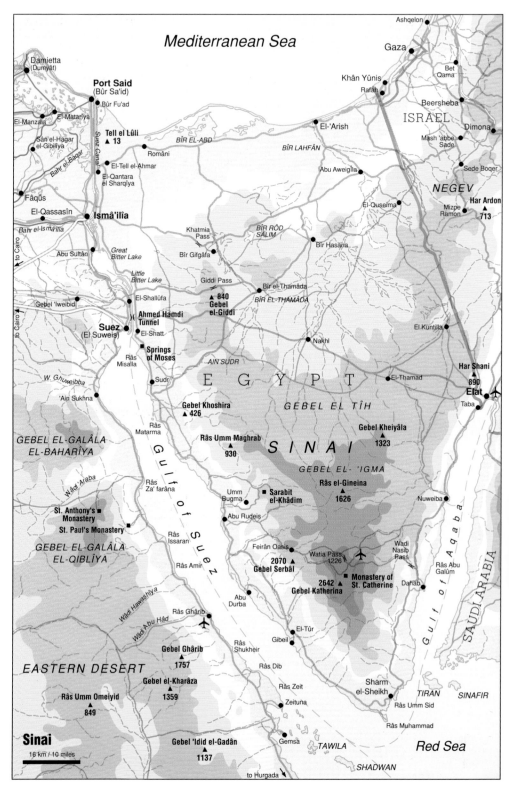

Mediterranean Sea

Damietta
(Dumyât)
Port Said
(Bûr Sa'îd)
Bûr Fu'ad
El-Manzala
El-Matarîya
Suez Canal
Tell el Lûli
▲ 13
San el-Hagar
el-Gibillya
El-Tell el-Ahmar
Români
El-Qantara
el Sharqîya
Fâqûs
El-Qassasîn
Bahr el-Baqar
Ismâ'ilîa
Bahr el-Ismâ'ilia
to Cairo
Abu Sultân
Great
Bitter Lake
Little
Bitter Lake
Gebel 'Iweibid
El-Shallûfa
Ahmed Hamdi
Tunnel
Suez
(El Suweis)
El-Shatt
Springs
of Moses
Râs
Misalla
Sudr
W. Ghuweibba
to Cairo
'Ain Sukhna
Râs
Matarma
GEBEL EL-GALÂLA
EL-BAHARÎYA
Wâd 'Arâba
Râs
Za' farâna
St. Anthony's
Monastery
St. Paul's Monastery
GEBEL EL-GALÂLA
EL-QIBLÎYA
Râs
Issaran
Râs Amîr
Wâdi Hawashiya
Wâd Abu Hâd
Râs Ghârib
EASTERN DESERT
Gebel Ghârib
▲ 1757
Gebel el-Kharâza
▲ 1359
Râs Umm Omeiyid
▲ 849
Sinai
16 km / 10 miles
Gebel 'Idid el-Gadân
▲ 1137

BÎR EL-ABD
BÎR LAHFÂN
El-'Arish
Abu Aweigîla
Khatmia
Pass
BÎR RÔD
SÂLIM
Bîr Gifgâfa
Bîr Hasana
El-Quseima
Giddi Pass
▲ 840
Gebel
el-Giddi
BÎR EL-THAMÂDA
Bîr el-Thamâda
AIN SUDR
Nakhl
EGYPT
Gebel Khoshira
▲ 426
GEBEL EL TÎH
El-Thamad
Gebel Kheiyâla
▲ 1323
Râs Umm Maghrab
▲ 930
SINAI
GEBEL EL- 'IGMA
Umm
Bugma
Sarabit
el-Khâdim
Râs el-Gineina
▲ 1626
Abu Rudeis
Feirân Oasis
Watia Pass
1226
Wadi
Nasib
Pass
▲ 2070
Gebel Serbâl
▲ 2642
Gebel Katherina
Monastery of
St. Catherine
Dahab
Abu
Durba
El-Tûr
Gibeil
Râs
Shukheîr
Râs Dib
Râs Zeit
Zeituna
Sharm
el-Sheikh
Râs Umm Sid
Râs Muhammad
Gemsâ
TAWILA
SHADWAN
to Hurgada
Red Sea

Ashqelon
Gaza
Khân Yûnis
Rafah
Bet
Qama
Beersheba
ISRAEL
Dimona
Mash 'abbe
Sade
Sede Boqer
NEGEV
Mizpe
Ramon
Har Ardon
▲ 713
El-Kûntilla
Har Shani
▲ 890
Elat
Taba
Nuweiba
Râs Abu
Galûm
Gulf of Aqaba
SAUDI ARABIA
TIRAN
SINAFIR

SINAI

"Put off thy shoes from off thy feet, for the place whereon thou standest is holy ground," the Lord admonished Moses (Exodus 3:5). And ever since, whether treated as holy ground or as battleground, fought over by people of different religions, classical empires, and modern nation-states, the Sinai peninsula has been special.

Volumes have been dedicated to this small jewel of a desert poised delicately but obstinately between two continents. As a passage between Asia and Africa, it has weathered as many military crossings as it has peaceful occupations, thanks in part to a climate that precludes all but the sparsest settlement. Even its few prehistoric, ancient and medieval remains, however, have only been scratched at by archaeologists, while Biblical geographers' controversies over problematical routes and sites have created an academic kaleidoscope of fact and fantasy.

It is only in the years since the latest of more than 50 recorded invasions that Sinai has ceased to be regarded by non-inhabitants as an empty buffer zone, as a dangerous crossroads where native Bedouins or foreign powers controlled all access, or as a barrier separating the two halves of the Arab world.

Sinai's 10,000 sq. miles (25,000 sq. km) of desert, ranging from the spiky granite mountains of the south to the central plateau of At-Tih, then to the rolling dunes of the northern coastal plain, are now fair game to backpackers, camel trekkers and camera-happy busloads of tourists. The shock of the recent occupation and the Israelis' opportunistic development of the peninsula's tourist potential prodded Egypt towards a fierce determination to bind Sinai once again to the Nile Valley, this time inextricably. Although some of the hotel infrastructure, originally geared to low-budget kibbutzniks rather than staid middle-class Cairenes, has grown a trifle rusty, the Sinai now boasts Egypt's best maintained roads and most efficient bus services. Daily flights connect the capital to Al-Arish, St Catherine's and Sharm ash-Shaykh. While public transport is reliable, there is no substitute for having one's own car – preferably with four-wheel drive.

North Sinai: Aside from seasonal Bedouin encampments, North Sinai's population is concentrated around the provincial capital of **El-Arish**. From Cairo the main Ismailia highway leads to the Suez Canal. At **Qantara**, north of Ismailia, crossing to Sinai is made by ferry. The road continues across the desert to the northeast, skirting the marshy lagoon of **Lake Bardawil** to reach Al-Arish after 85 miles (130 km). This town of 40,000 is the biggest in the peninsula and much recent effort has been made to turn it into a palm-fringed and unspoiled beach resort with plenty of reasonably priced hotels and restaurants. Bedouin crafts and jewellery are on display at the local museum.

Just east of the town, the bare dunes begin. A few olive trees appear, marking the decline of the desert and the beginning of the fertile Palestine coastal plain. At 30 miles (50 km) the town of **Rafah** marks the current border. Beyond lies the **Gaza Strip**, a Middle Eastern Soweto occupied by Israel since 1967. Rafah's population is a mixture of local Bedouin and Palestinian refugees. Their camp – built with Canadian government aid and consequently called "Canada" – was brutally bisected by the border fence erected after the area's return to Egypt in 1983.

Between El-Arish and Rafah a number of *wadis*, seasonal watercourses, lead back from the sea into the desert interior. The laid-back Bedouin graze their goats and camels extensively in this region. Friendly and hospitable, they are wont to invite travellers into their ramshackle settlements – shacks slapped together with cans, boxes and the debris of four wars – for a glass of tea. The desert-dwelling women of North Sinai wear gorgeous embroidered dresses and heavy silver jewellery, so the opportunity to mingle should not be missed.

South Sinai: With its two coasts, oases, mountains and historic sites, the South

Preceding pages: view from Mt Sinai.

Sinai is a more popular destination. North of Suez, the **Ahmed Hamdi tunnel** carries traffic under the Canal. Turning south, the main road follows the Canal, veering eastwards opposite Suez. From here it descends 200 miles (320 km) along the breezy Gulf of Suez to Sharm ash-Shaykh.

Along this route are **'Uyun Musa**, the "Springs of Moses" where the prophet is said to have rested with his flock, a palm grove fed by brackish water reached after 25 miles (40 km). Twenty miles (33 km) farther on, the road nears the coast at the wide sandy beach of **Ras-as-Sidr**, a favourite stopping place, and for some people worth the day trip from Cairo. Unlike the Gulf of Aqaba on Sinai's east coast, the Gulf of Suez is shallow and sandy-bottomed; the marine life is abundant, but there are no major coral reefs this far north.

Beyond Ras as-Sidr the road bends away from the coast up into the mountains. A track to the right at this turn leads after a few hundred yards to **Hammam Fara'un**, the hot spring known as the *Pharaoh's Bath*. The spring's boiling hot waters, said by local Bedouin to cure rheumatism, bubble from the base of the mountains right into the sea.

About 10 miles (16 km) into the mountains above Hammam Fara'un, a track leads left among palm trees. Negotiable only by four-wheel drive vehicles, it continues for 20 miles to the site of **Sarabit al-Khadim**, a 12th-Dynasty temple that serviced workers in the region's mines and was dedicated originally to the goddess of Hathor. A second shrine, for the patron god of the Eastern Desert, Sopdu, was later added. Dozens of New and Middle Kingdom stelae commemorate Egyptian rule. Among them are those dedicated to Hatshepsut and Tuthmosis III. Inscriptions at the **mines of Wadi Maghara**, south of Sarabit al Khadim, date back to the 4th Dynasty and the reigns of Snefru and Khufu (Cheops), builder of the Great Pyramid. Turquoise, malachite and copper were mined in the region.

From Wadi Maghara a track running

Preceding pages: the view from Mt Sinai. **Below**, Bedouin in the northern Sinai.

down the **Wadi Sidri** for 15 miles (24 km) rejoins the main road at **Abu Zeneima**, where it descends again from the mountains to the coast. Beyond this ramshackle frontier settlement, where manganese from local mines of recent date is processed, the road continues to **Abu Rudeis**. The Gulf of Suez is at this point dotted with beetle-like rigs shooting flame into the haze: this is the centre of Sinai's oil fields, most of them offshore. Pipes, fences, tanks and prefabricated housing clutter the shore town to **Balayim** 30 miles (50 km) farther on.

The road again leaves the coast, heading inland towards the high mountains of the Sinai range. A checkpoint marks the turnoff to St Catherine's monastery, while the main road continues south to **Al-Tur** and Sharm ash-Shaykh. Tur, the capital and largest town in South Sinai, is reached after 45 miles (75 km) of hot driving through a wide valley. Settled in ancient times because of its good water supply and excellent harbour, it was the chief quarantine station for pilgrims returning to Egypt from Mecca. Modern Tur, despite scattered palm groves and a beautiful beach, retains this way-station atmosphere. A peculiarity of the town is the racial mix of its inhabitants, many of them descended from Berber and African immigrants. From Tur it is 60 miles (100 km) to Sharm ash-Shaykh.

Going to St Catherine's: Turning instead up towards St Catherine's, you enter the **Wadi Feran**. Narrowing as it mounts, after 20 miles (33 km) the dry gulch suddenly blossoms into a river of date palms. This is the **Oasis of Firan**, the largest patch of cultivation on the peninsula. Parched for most of the year, winter rains and melting snow send down short-lived torrents to water the valley. Scattered throughout the palm groves are clusters of Bedouin huts. Colonies of Christian anchorites inhabited the oasis long before the foundation of the monastery at St Catherine's, and the remains of their constructions abound. South of the oasis, approached most easily up the **Wadi 'Aleayat**, rises the peak of the **Jabal Sirbal**. At 7,000 feet

Lithoglyphs at Ain Hora, Sinai.

(2,100 metres) it is not high for the Sinai range, but its isolation makes the view from its summit extensive. One school of Biblical speculators claims it as the true **Mount Sinai**.

From Feran the road climbs into an open plain and after 20 miles reaches the settlement of **Santa Katarina**. Here there are numerous hotels, a campsite and the bus stop. The famous monastery sits in a *wadi* between **Jabal Musa** – most popular candidate for the site of the delivery of the Ten Commandments – and the **Jabal ad-Dayr** just up the hill to the south.

The Roman emperor Justinian ordered the building of a fortress monastery on the site in 537 AD in order to protect the Sinai passes against invasion. Originally dedicated to the Transfiguration of Christ, the church built within the fortress was renamed St Catherine, a 4th-century Alexandrian martyred for her derision of Roman idol-worship. Her body miraculously appeared atop the Sinai's highest peak five centuries later, apparently looking none the worse for wear. This miracle, coupled with the Crusaders' occupation of nearby Palestine, ensured the support of Christian rulers. The monastery's fame spread, so much so that by the 14th century up to 400 monks lived there, as the grisly collection of skulls in the ossuary attests. In recent centuries Russia was the chief benefactor. The dozen or so monks who now inhabit the monastery are mostly Greek.

The monastery and its treasures: The path to St Catherine's leads past a walled orchard and an outer complex of buildings before reaching the monastery itself. An old basket-and-pulley system of entry has been abandoned and visitors now enter by simply walking through a portal. (Note that the monastery is closed on Friday and religious holidays and that modesty of attire is required. The best time for a visit is between 9.30 am and noon.) A small building on the left inside the wall is one of the original structures, diplomatically converted into a mosque in the 12th century. The **Church of St Cath-**

The Church of St Catherine's, founded by the Emperor Justinian.

erine is down the steps to the left just behind the mosque.

Inside, the church is basilical in form, with great granite columns supporting the nave. The marble inlay floors will be familiar to anyone who has visited the mosques of Cairo. The wooden bracing beams of the reconstructed ceiling are original and beautifully carved, one of them with a foundation inscription dating to Justinian. The doors leading to the sanctuary are flanked by two silver chests inlaid with precious stones. Both were donated by members of the Russian royal family, one in the 17th century, the other in the 19th. The sanctuary is adorned with 6th-century mosaics that are the monastery's greatest treasure. Within the a؟ ؟ and semi-dome of the apse is a portrayal of the Transfiguration of Christ. To his left stand Moses and St James, and on his right are Elijah and St John the Apostle.

Side aisles lined with chapels dedicated to varied saints and decorated with ancient and modern icons lead off from either side of the church. At the sanctuary end of the building a small alcove opens into the **Chapel of the Burning Bush**. Here, on a site marked by a small silver plate God spoke to Moses disguised as a flaming shrub.

The monastery's other treasures are off limits to run-of-the-mill tourists. They include a library of manuscripts and a museum stocked with a superb collection of icons. Enthusiasts should arm themselves with a letter of introduction from the Greek Patriarchate in Cairo to gain admittance.

Just behind the monastery a well worn path begins, leading ultimately to the summit of **Jabal Musa**. Steps mounting the cliff to the right should be avoided for the ascent. Instead, continue on the gently sloping main track, which curves behind the southern slope. All but the most feeble should be able to manage the way up – coming down is trickier, and care needs to be taken. The view from the top is magnificent, particularly at dawn or sunset. **Jabal Katarina**, the highest point in Egypt at over 8,500 feet (2,600 metres), has an even better

The Ossuary at St Catherine's houses the skulls of former monks.

view. It is approached up the *wadi* on Jebel Musa's western side.

Sinai's mountains are very ancient, and their variety, in terms of texture, colour, shape and vegetation, is fascinating. The descent from St Catherine's to the east traverses enthralling landscapes all the way to the sea. Here along the **Gulf of Aqaba** one of the earth's most dramatic interfaces has yet to be ruined by commercialisation. The Gulf itself, only 10 miles (16 km) wide, is in places as much as 6,000 feet (1,800 metres) deep. Indeed, it marks a long geological fault, running from the Dead Sea in the north to Africa's Great Rift Valley in the south.

Coral reefs line the shores of the Gulf from Ras Muhammad at the peninsula's extremity to Taba on the Israeli border. Teeming with life and colour, they provide a striking contrast to the desolation of the land.

The Gulf of Aqaba: Ras Muhammad, a peninsula jutting into the Red Sea, has the best diving of all. Fortunately for the ecology of the area, it has been declared a nature conservation area. Anyone wishing to camp there will require a permit. **Shark Reef** off the eastern shore is the favourite swimming hole.

North of Ras Muhammad, on a beautiful natural harbour much damaged by the ill-planned building of successive occupants, is the town of **Sharm ash-Shaykh**. Five miles farther on, **Na'ama Bay** is the local tourist centre, with hotels, restaurants, camping grounds and diving shops. Over-developed, it makes a good base for visiting local beaches. Some of the best for diving and snorkelling are **The Tower**, **Ras Umm Sid**, **Ras Nasrani** and **Nabq**. Equipment can be rented at one of several diving centres, where boat trips to **Gazirat Tiran**, an island in the middle of the straits with superb corals, can also be arranged.

The next coastal settlement lies 56 miles (90 km) north at **Dahab**. Sediments washed down from the mountains have created a broad sandy plain here. A model Israeli-built town on a sandy cove, it boasts a hotel, a cafeteria, and camping and diving facilities.

Across the plain a to the mile west, the Bedouin village of Assalah sits next to a palm-lined horseshoe bay. Here low-budget travellers stay in reed huts on the beach and live on grilled fish. The locals are very laid-back – frequently horizontal in fact – so outsiders are often surprised to find that many of them speak perfect English. Camel treks into the interior can be arranged here. Many of Dahab's fertile *wadis* are stunningly beautiful.

Nuwayba is 45 miles (75 km) further north, a slightly up-market resort, although the reefs are not as good as farther south. There is a wide sandy beach, a hotel and a campsite. The hotel offers tours by Land Rover to the **Oasis of 'Ayn al-Furtaga**. If the preferred vehicle is the camel, arrangements can be made with the Bedouin at their settlement a few miles south of the hotel, where palms mingle with shacks along the beach. Ferries from Nuwayba's new port leave daily for Aqaba in Jordan, a journey taking three hours. At Aqaba excursions to the rock city of **Petra** can be arranged.

Taba is 38 miles (60 km) north of Nuwayba and offers a five-star hotel with international telephone lines. Two hundred yards (185 metres) beyond the hotel is the Israeli border. **Gazirat Fara'un**, an island just offshore, is a recently-restored 12th-century fortress. Smack in the middle of the peninsula and difficult of access lie the ruins of a second medieval fortress, **Qalaat al-Gindi**. Built by Salah-ad-din to protect trade and pilgrimage routes, these fortifications attest to the importance Muslim rulers attached to Egypt's Asian gateway.

Although no one needs to be warned of the danger of sharks, swimmers should be aware of a few facts. Coral reefs can hide unpleasant as well as pleasant surprises. The spine of a sea urchin is most unfriendly on the feet and the sting of the well-camouflaged stone fish can be fatal. Wear shoes or flippers in the water at all times. Always swim in pairs and keep calm in the water no matter what happens. Above all, be aware that corals take thousands of years to form and so should be handled with due care and respect. They should not be removed.

Ancient steps to the summit of Mt Sinai.

255

THE RED SEA AND EASTERN DESERT

The **Red Sea coast** of Egypt runs for 1,000 miles (1,600 km) in a south-easterly direction from Suez. Despite the many offshore oil wells and frequent oil depots, gas-stations are few and far between and trips by car must be planned with foresight. Once assured of freedom from mechanical worries, however, the happy motorist is rewarded with a glorious sense of infinite space. For most of its length, beautiful but desolate limestone and granite mountains border the coast. Range rises upon range as a thousand peaks harmonise their purples with the blue of the sky. Sandy coves and beaches edge a brilliant sea. Within its coral reefs the water is a light blue-green, while beyond them a deep dark blue shimmers to the distant coasts of Sinai and Arabia, even further away.

In the vicinity of Suez, this deep dark blue is rather liberally strewn with tankers and other ships converging on the Canal, and the road along the coast has received a good deal of wear and tear from heavy trucks. Both sea and land traffic soon thin out, however, and the beaches improve near 'Ayn Sukhna.

South of 'Ayn Sukhna the rocky skirts of the North Galala Plateau come right down to the edge of the sea and the drive is spectacular. A new highway has recently been constructed on which one can proceed comfortably and swiftly to **Zafarana** (50 miles/80 km) south of 'Ayn Sukhna, the checkpoint and junction for a good road coming across the desert from the Nile Valley 180 miles (290 km) to the west.

Hurghada (Arabic *Ghardaqa*), 250 miles (420 km) south of Suez, is Egypt's most popular seaside resort. Its pleasures are the ideal antidote to an overdose of monuments. It has none. Instead it offers golden sands and a sea full of exquisite tropical fish, which swim in and around the plentiful coral beds. The water is warm all the year round except for a few weeks in December and January; the sun is always shining and even in the hottest months there is a breeze.

Giza
Pyramids of Giza
Birket Qârûn
Sphinx
Cairo
Ismâ'ilîa
Memphis
Helwân
Suez (El Suweis)
El Faiyûm
El Wasta
Beni Suef
Ain Sukhna
Beni Mazâr
GEBEL EL-GALÂLA EL-QIBLIYA
Nile
W. Araba
Wâdi Sannur
Râs Zafarâna
Gulf of Suez
Necropolis of Beni Hassan
Ras Gharib
Wâdi Hubâra
Tima
Sohâg
Wâdi Qena
Abu Sha'r
EASTERN
Hurghada
GIFATIN
Abydos
Qena
Bur Safâga
Dendera
SARFAGA
Valley of the Kings
Qus
W. Qal
Armant
Luxor
Wâdi Zaïdûn
Quseir
Red Sea
Esna
El-Kâb
DESERT
Edfu
Wâdi el-Miyâh
Kôm Ombo
Gebel el Silsila
Daraw
Aswan
Marsa'Alam
Philae
Wâdi Gimal
Trans East African Highway
Berenice
Râs Banâs
Bîr Shalatein
N
Red Sea
80 km / 50 miles
Bîr al Hasa
Râs Abu Dâra

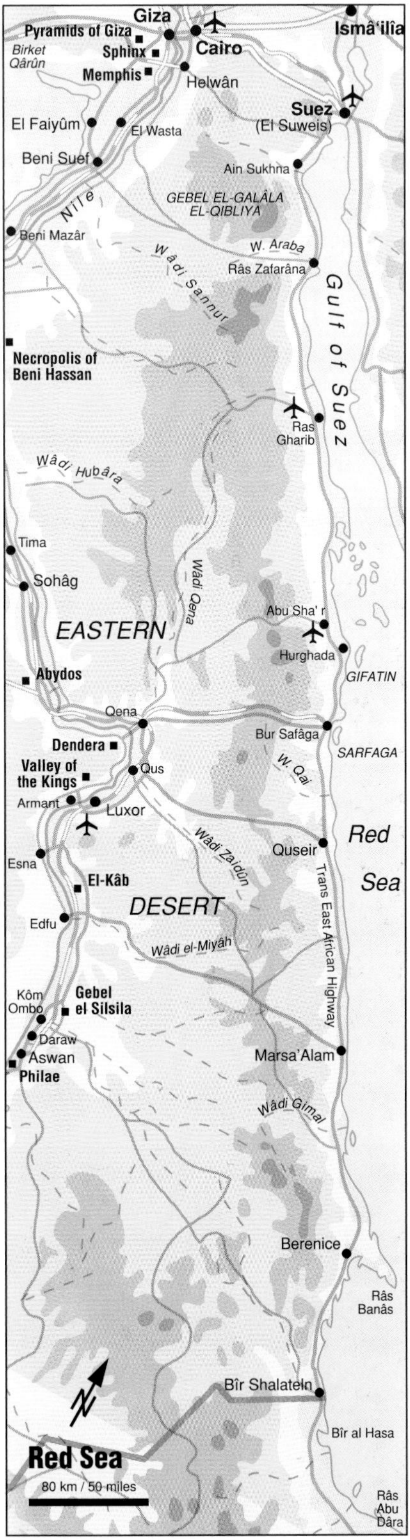

Hurghada has an airport and is only an hour's flight from Cairo. Its hotels vary in the accommodation they offer, from basic and cheap to luxury-class. There is a cluster of four- and five-star hotels overlooking a magnificent bay; and several hospitable tourist villages, with chalets and buffet meals, are staffed by cheerful youngsters of many nationalities. These young people do double duty as instructors in diving, snorkeling, sailing, surfing, archery and other sports. For the fisherman, all-day or overnight fishing trips to the offshore islands can be arranged through the hotels or privately with individual boat owners at the harbour.

Further on down the coast the famous ancient ports, which were thriving even after the discovery of the Cape route in the 15th century, have largely fallen into disuse since the inauguration of the Suez Canal. Some are still visible as little ghost harbours with the skeletal hulls of old wooden boats whitening in the sun; and others have completely disappeared under the sand.

Safaga, however, which is 45 miles (70 km) south of Hurghada, is still very much alive. Its deepwater facilities have recently been expanded and it has retained the role it played in the past as the nearest port to **Qena** (110 miles/177 km) to the west. The old caravan trail leading through the mountains is now replaced by an excellent paved road to the Nile Valley that carries truckloads of wheat and raw aluminium off-loaded at Safaga. It is also convenient for those who want to make the round trip from Cairo down the Nile to Luxor, across the mountains to the sea, returning north up the coast.

"Where my caravan has rested": In antiquity and even in Ottoman times the ports of **Qusayr**, **Marsa Alam**, **Berenice** and **Halayib** were of more importance than they are today. Like Suez and Safaga they were connected to important points in the Nile valley by caravan routes, along which laden pack animals brought spices, silks, pearls and precious woods from Arabia, Persia, India and the East African coast. Muslim pilgrims from the hinterlands thousands of

Windsurfing at Hurghada on the Red Sea.

miles away, sometimes en route for years, embarked at these ports for Mecca. One can still see traces of graffiti carved on the rocks.

Except for the remote mountainous area known as Gebel Elba on the Sudanese border in the far south, which receives monsoon rains and has a unique ecosystem supporting forest and pasturage, the coastal plain and the Red Sea mountains are almost entirely devoid of vegetation. What rain there is falls only a few times a year and then often in the form of violent storms, which carry all before them as water pours off the mountains into the sea.

Some water gathers in pools and potholes among the granitic rocks and together with the ancient wells amounts to enough to support the scattering of *bedu* and animals that live there. Until very recently freshwater for the villages along the coast had to be shipped in, and the natives lived on a diet of bread and fish.

Realms of gold: In pharaonic times the Eastern Desert, particularly the mountains, was thoroughly searched for gold and other precious metals, for ornamental stone and for building materials. These resources contributed greatly to the wealth and prestige of the pharaohs and were later coveted by Assyrians, Persians, Greeks and Romans.

Thousands of prisoners in chains were used for the extraction of these riches. More often than not they died in the mines and quarries. The gold was arduously mined and smelted, and the limestone quarried and transported to Thebes for the construction of temples and other monuments.

The indefatigable Romans established permanent quarrying camps in the mountains, visible from the stretch of road between Hurghada and Safaga. They were particularly partial to the purple stone known as porphyry, which comes from **Gabal Abu Dukhan** ("Father of Smoke"). It was in great demand for the adornment of palaces and temples and was brought out of the Egyptian mountains until as late as the 5th century AD. Great blocks were quarried and then dragged the 112 miles (180 km) through

Tourists at sunset, Hurghada.

the mountains and over the desert to Qena, whence they were transported down the Nile and then across the Mediterranean to Rome.

Another famous mountain nearby, known as **Mons Claudianus**, yielded superlative white granite. Remains of animal stalls in the ruins of a quarry indicate that the huge lumps of stone were hauled out by bullocks.

Ships of the desert: Desert roads that we now speed across in vehicles were once laboriously traversed by camels. For the amateur this mode of transport would be tiresome. One enthusiastic but baffled traveller commented of camel travel: "It is unpleasant to ride an animal which not only objects to being ridden but cherishes a strong personal antipathy to its rider… His paces are more complicated than his joints and more trying than his temper. He has four: a short walk, like the rolling of a small boat in a chopping sea; a long walk which dislocates every bone in your body; a trot that reduces you to imbecility; and a gallop that is sudden death."

Not everyone found the desert unpleasant, however. "Only those who have travelled in the desert," wrote an English devotee at the beginning of this century, "can understand the joy of returning there; a joy which, strangely enough, has only one equal and that is the pleasure of returning to water, to flowers and trees after a spell of some days or even weeks in the wilderness."

The transition from the teeming green valley is abrupt: suddenly the lush green cultivated land gives way to stony wilderness, where the rocks rise up in extraordinary formations, strangely reminiscent of the pyramids and sphinx, the sand blows and spills, and there is scarcely a sign of life for hundreds of miles. The one exception to this dramatic change is east of Cairo, where semi-suburban industrial zones sprawl out to the east, eventually joining up with the pock-marked battlegrounds of recent wars in the Canal area.

Desert flora and fauna: Interesting excursions can, however, be made from Cairo into the Eastern Desert. The geo-

Keep at the Monastery of St Antony's near the Red Sea in the Eastern Desert.

logical formations are endlessly various and strange, yielding stones and sands of amazing shapes and colours. The flora and fauna, though sparse and timid, are all the more wonderful for their tenacious hold on life. A variety of plants, some of them aromatic, grow on the flanks and bottoms of the *wadis*; once in a while a lone tamarisk or wild fig casts a bit of shade.

There are numerous species of birds, some resident and some migratory, and occasionally in spring and autumn a skein of migrating cranes can be seen high overhead, their conversations with each other quite audible. Once in a while a gazelle or a wild goat streaks across the open plain and disappears among the rocks; and often a sandy picnic place is crisscrossed with the embroidery of bird and animal tracks. Jerboas, jackals and foxes leave dainty padmarks, while rabbits, gazelles and hyenas leave heavier prints.

One hundred and thirty-one miles (200 km) east of Bani Suwayf in the rugged hills at the foot of the South Galala Plateau, looking out over the desolate Wadi Araba stands the **Monastery of St Antony**, the 4th-century Christian hermit, whose temptations are so enthusiastically illustrated by European painters of the Renaissance. An hour's drive further on by car brings one to the Monastery of his contemporary **St Paul**, which is tucked into a fold of the Red Sea Mountains.

These two monasteries are the object of pilgrimage for thousands of Egyptian Christians on certain feast days during the year and are also visited by many curious tourists. Both were founded on the sites chosen by the hermits in the 4th century AD, when Egyptian Christians were being persecuted by the Romans, and the influence of their way of life spread far and wide throughout the Christian world.

The monks here today lead a quiet life of work and prayer, very much as they did 15 centuries ago, when the original Desert Fathers retired from the fever and injustice of the world to seek a better way of life.

Service in progress at St Antony's Monastery.

SCUBA DIVING AND WATER SPORTS

Egypt is only just waking up to the marvels that fringe her Red Sea Coast, the eastern coast of Sinai, and the handful of scattered islands offshore. Snorkeling and scuba diving are becoming increasingly popular with young Egyptians as more hotels and facilities are opened up.

Coral reefs: The climatic and geographic position of Egypt's eastern coasts is ideal for the formation of coral, which cannot grow at temperatures of less than 18.5°C or at depths of more than 70 feet (22 metres). Though the Gulf of Aqaba and the Red Sea attain a depth of 6,000 feet (1,850 metres) in the middle, where the tectonic plates of Africa and Asia have drawn apart to form a great rift, relatively shallow seas cover the continental shelf that runs along the shores, which are interrupted only by occasional *wadis*, formed by infrequent but torrential rains. The sunshine that penetrates the very salty water for many hours each day enables the coral to build up its formations.

There are basically four types of reefs. Fringing reefs and barrier reefs run parallel to the coast, usually with shallow sandy-bottomed lagoons between the land and the coral, which then drops steeply as much as 70 feet (22 metres) in a cliff-like formation. There are no atolls in the Egyptian part of the Red Sea, but the fourth type of reef, roughly distinguished as a patch formation, occurs quite frequently. Mounds of coral build up on the sandy floor of the sea like islands, the tips of which are barely skimmed by the waves. Patch formations occur at Nuweiba on the Sinai coast, off Hurghada and at other spots further south.

Living on skeletons: Each coral accretion consists of numerous minute anemone-like individual polyps, growing together in a colony. When one colony dies, a new colony grows on top, attached to the skeletons of their defunct ancestors, so to speak. Two thousand species have been identified and christened with complex names. Even the amateur can find as many as 100 types.

Delicate pinks, purples, yellows and beiges

Left, the coral reefs of the Red Sea are rivalled only by the Great Barrier Reef in Australia.

are dappled by the flitting shadows of waves. Some corals are soft and undulating, like the sea anemones; some are hard and solid, squat and rounded like brains or mushrooms; some branch like elkhorns, or stack up like fortifications, spires and pinnacles; others are fanshaped and perforated like Elizabethan lace collars. The almost miraculous forms are at the same time familiar and strange.

Ecosystem: The corals feed, mostly at night, on organisms trapped on their multiple surfaces. These organisations in turn are nourished by sunlight, which is the base of an ecosystem that supports a rich variety of marine life and furnishes a living laboratory for both professional and amateur biologists. Some creatures live off algae and plankton trapped by the coral, others actually eat and digest the coral itself. These characters are in turn hunted and eaten by a progressive chain of predators, the biggest of which are the prowlers of the open sea.

Slugs, snails, shellfish, shrimps and crabs live in the nooks and crannies of the coral or in the sandy patches within the lagoons. But it is, above all, the fish that liven the coral beds, with their beauty and variety, their curious relationships and habits, as they suddenly dart about or circle, idly waving their fins, either singly, in pairs, or in schools.

The most common inhabitants of the reefs are the thousands of little damsel fish, including green chromis and blue fusiliers, which graze peacefully or shoot up suddenly in a great sparkling cloud. Flame-coloured coral fish, only about an inch long, hover close to the shadows in ones and twos. Butterfly and angel fish form a large and easily distinguishable family because of their oval shape, snub noses, and gorgeous lemony colouring, enhanced with blue and black stripes and patches: they swim in pairs and stick to the same territory. Other easily distinguishable types are the disc-shaped sergeant-major, who sports appropriate stripes, and his cousins the dascylus and bi-colour chromis, who parade in regiments, turning together like lazy pieces of a Calder mobile.

More gorgeous greens and blues occur in the families of wrasses and parrot fish, which can reach a fair size if they manage to survive the hazards of predatory society; the giant humphead wrasse can be as big as 5 feet (1.5 metres) long. These families actually eat coral with their beaks and the crunching of their nibbling jaws can be heard as they chew up the madrepore. Grinding plates in their throats break down the coral; and once the nourishing material is extracted, great quantities of coral sand are excreted.

The parrot fish also have a very noisy sex life, in which dominant males preside over a harem of females. Something very curious happens when the boss of the harem succumbs or is eaten by a passing prowler: rather than a younger male taking his place, the leading lady in his entourage changes

toral fins and hovering steadily, ready to pounce on their prey.

The more scary monsters of the deep are not normally encountered by the ordinary snorkeler and rarely by a prudent scuba diver. Only experienced professionals engage in debates with moray eels, lionfish, barracuda, sting rays or sharks.

Whales and sea-cows (or dugongs) rove the deep sea and are not carnivorous, but ingest gallons of plankton. The only danger from these species is that they may accidentally give a small boat a mighty wallop.

In spring one may observe some extraordinary aspects of the mating season from a boat or even from the beach. The sea may sud-

sex, and with it her colours, assuming the leadership of the pack. Shades of that other great Egyptian lady, Hatshepsut!

The adaptive and dissimulating mechanisms of other varieties of small fish are just as fascinating, but too numerous to mention here. Each one has his distinctive character, colouring, shape and habits.

Predators: Next up the ecological ladder come the groupers, jacks, skates and other predators, who feed on the little fish. Their bodies are usually mottled or blotched brown, red, or blue, and they have big mouths, which can stretch wide to swallow their dinner. They hunt singly, swimming with their pec-

denly boil with a million sardines laying eggs, or one may be lucky enough to see the dance of the manta rays, who compete for the favours of the female and court her by making great leaps out of the water.

Diving centres: Several of the modern hotels on the Sinai and Red Sea coasts have affiliated diving centres with resident diving instructors, boats and equipment for hire. Nuwayba, Dahab and Sharm el Sheikh, for example, have diving centres with hotels and camping grounds in the vicinity. The Hurghada Sheraton, Jasmine Village, Sonesta, Magawish Village, Giftun Village, and other hotels are all well-equipped. Diving and fishing trips are organised daily as part of these hotels' sports programmes: the trained professional supervisors can initiate the novice into what to look for, where to see it, and how to manage his gear.

Gear: Reasonably efficient snorkeling equipment – mask, snorkel and flippers – can be rented or purchased. For those who want to take the sport seriously, it is advisable to buy and test out gear before coming. Old tennis shoes are useful if one simply wants to put one's feet down and peer at the wonders from a more static position.

Scuba: An acronym for "self-contained under-water breathing apparatus" *scuba* enables the diver to submerge completely for up

Training: No one should attempt to scuba dive who has not completed a course of proper training consisting of at least 15–20 hours of theoretical study, followed by 20–30 hours of diving experience with an expert. There are dangers of running out of oxygen, going too deep, and coming up too suddenly, all of which can be fatal. Certificates of competency are granted after a sufficient course of training. For those who are able to invest enough time and money, the Red Sea is an ideal practice ground for gaining mastery of scuba diving.

Trophy-hunting is severely discouraged, as every effort is being made to protect the delicate environment, which has already suf-

to 30 minutes at a time, to depths of 70 feet (22 metres) or more. Besides the mask and flippers, a dive tank, consisting of two cylinders of compressed oxygen, attached to a harness generally worn on the back and connected to the mouth by tubes, a regulator, and a weight belt, comprise the essential equipment. A wet suit, or part of one, is advisable, particularly during the winter months, when the water can be chilly and the wind cold. It has the added advantage of protecting the wearer from the coral.

Left, delicate aquatic exotica. **Above**, diver with friend, the Red Sea.

fered from fishing with explosives, vandalism and oil spills. The best souvenirs of snorkelling and scuba diving are photographic. Special high quality waterproof cameras are available, enabling divers to share their unique experiences.

For the less adventurous there are trips in glass-bottomed boats, sailing, wind-surfing and fishing, not to mention beachcombing, sunbathing and just doing nothing. The Red Sea beaches are a wonderful playground and can be enjoyed by everyone throughout the entire year, though the optimum months in which to visit are October, November, February and March.

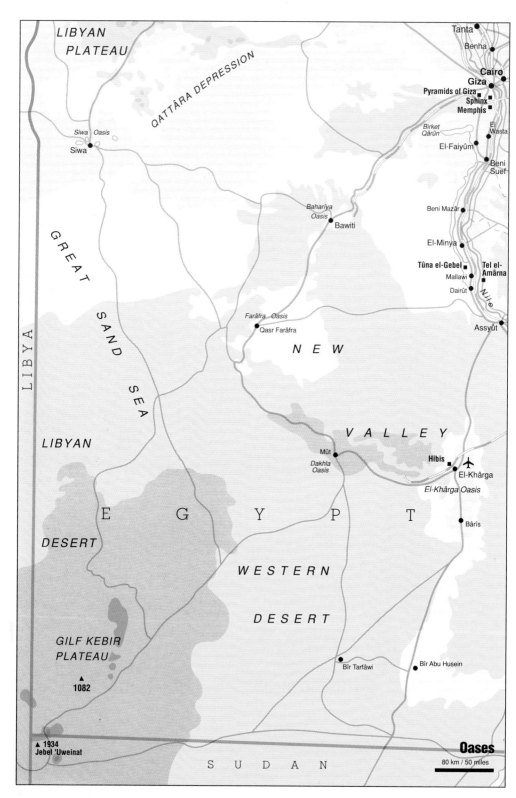

LIBYAN
PLATEAU

QATTÂRA DEPRESSION

Tanta

Benha

Cairo
Giza
Pyramids of Giza
Sphinx
Memphis

El Wasta

Siwa Oasis

Siwa

Birket Qârûn

El-Faiyûm

Beni Suef

G
R
E
A
T

S
A
N
D

S
E
A

Bahariya Oasis
Bawiti

Beni Mazâr

El-Minya

Tûna el-Gebel   **Tel el-Amârna**
Mallawi
Dairût

Farâfra Oasis
Qasr Farâfra

N E W

Assyût

LIBYA

LIBYAN

E   G   Y   P   T

DESERT

V A L L E Y

Mût
Dakhla Oasis

Hibis

El-Khârga

El-Khârga Oasis

W E S T E R N

Bâris

D E S E R T

GILF KEBIR
PLATEAU

▲
1082

Bîr Tarfâwi

Bîr Abu Husein

▲ 1934
Jebel 'Uweinat

S   U   D   A   N

Oases

80 km / 50 miles

Nile

THE OASES AND
THE FAYYUM

The very word "**Oasis**" conjures a string of images – swirling sands, blue-veiled Tuaregs, mirages, the thirsty caravan stumbling into a pool of sweet water set amidst swaying palms.

As always, little of this vision has any foundation in modern reality: the caravans have all but vanished, banditry has been suppressed, and the Bedouin have traded their camels in for Toyotas. Not even the vestiges of modern man, however, in the form of asphalt, high tension wires and water pumps, are capable of concealing the truths of a harsh climate, where shifting sands can block roads for days and where the foolhardy can still meet death by thirst, exposure, or the sting of a scorpion. Nor have 20th-century wonders obscured the essential miracle of water, gushing hot or cold from barren rock to irrigate acres of garden in the midst of a wasteland.

From the Nile, the Sahara stretches 3,000 miles (5,000 km) westward to the Atlantic. The world's greatest expanse of desert is broken only by some several score dots of green, where human habitation has survived the spread of sands. Contrary to popular imagination, which sees verdure sprouting incongruously from dunes, oases generally lie in rocky lands where wind and time have scratched out vast depressions whose depths allow natural underground aquifers to reach the surface.

In Egypt's Western Desert a single aquifer flows north from Sudan, running in an arc of five oases roughly parallel to the Nile. Prehistoric remains show that man has been exploiting nature's gift since at least 5000 BC. Under the pharaohs the four Nileward oases – Kharga, Dakhla, Farafrah and Bahariyya – formed a line of defense against marauding Libyan tribes.

The camel, the only beast capable of five days' march without water, was introduced by invading Persians in the 6th century BC and provided the oases with their first great leap forward, matched in importance only recently with the introduction of electricity and the automobile. The camel helped to revive the desert economy. The new beast was no help to the Persian emperor Cambyses, however, when he dispatched his army from Kharga across the desert to Siwah in 525 BC. According to Herodotus, all 50,000 men were buried in a sandstorm.

The Ptolemies, who administered the country like a vast estate, set about improving desert agriculture. Archaeological remains show that cultivation grew to its furthest extent under their rule; new wells were dug with Alexandrian technology and the complex systems of water distribution that still persist were brought into use. Roman conquest led to a reversal of fortunes. The internal unrest of the late Roman period saw banditry increase at the expense of sedentary agriculture, while persecutions forced Christians into desert refuge, as the many Christian remains in the oases testify. Wells that had been regularly repaired and cleaned were allowed to dry up, as a general

Preceding pages: Siwah Oasis. **Right**, a lone tree in the desert.

decline in population, lasting up to the present century, set in.

Although the date of the last Christian conversions to Islam is not known – the present inhabitants of the oases being solidly Muslim – it is likely that the new religion, so well suited to desert ways, made easy headway in the oases. The charm, generosity, and peaceability of the inhabitants owe much to Islam. In a landscape seemingly touched by God – abundance amidst waste – a touching humility of outlook is so appropriate as to seem unsurprising.

Al-Kharga (The Outer) Oasis is the most frequented of Egypt's oases, by virtue of its proximity to the Nile and because it is the seat of the New Valley Governorate. Although it is linked by twice-weekly flights from Cairo and Luxor, most travellers prefer the overland route. Three miles (5 km) north of Asyut, a fine paved road leads past a new industrial complex up into the desert. One hundred and twenty miles (200 km) of barren gravel later, the road descends suddenly down a magnificent

cliff into the **Kharga Depression**, which extends southwards, narrowing at its extremity, for 60 miles (100 km).

As one crosses the flat bottom of the depression, a few straggly trees appear on the roadside, inauspiciously announcing the beginning of cultivation. Then Nasserite housing blocks begin to sprout, marking the entrance to **Kharga** town. Visitors to the oases should not be too disappointed by the town. It is merely an administrative centre and a showpiece of the New Valley project, initiated by Abdul Nasser in the later 1950s. The project, the aim of which was to use the vast potential of the oases' waters for land reclamation and new settlement, has met with notable success. Much of Kharga's population consists of resettled Upper Egyptians; and the new hotels, duck farms, and packaging industries point to a fair degree of prosperity. However, with the exception of its old market there is not much to see here.

Just northeast of the town, not far from the main road, lies a cluster of monuments. Chief among them is the **Music of the desert.**

Temple of Hibis, important as one of the few remnants of Persian rule. Built of local sandstone, it was begun under Cambyses' successor Darius I, but not completed until the reign of Nectanebo II in the 4th century BC. The temple lies in a palm grove beyond the remains of a ceremonial pool and an avenue of sphinxes. The carving style within shows local influence, while the content of the reliefs – deities, the burial of Osiris, a winged Seth struggling with a serpent – follows a standard pattern.

At the edge of cultivation to the north of the temple lies the Christian necropolis of **Al-Bagawat**, a huge area of mudbrick domes and vaults, some of which preserve decoration. A kilometre's hike across the sand leads to the ruins of a fortified monastery.

South of Kharga town a paved road extends through a string of smaller oases, past some minor antiquities, to **Baris**, the village designed by renowned architect Hassan Fathi.

Dakhla Oasis: With 30,000 acres (12,000 hectares) under cultivation and a population of 60,000, **Dakhla** (*The Inner*) is the largest of the oases. The New Valley project has more than doubled its size in recent years, but Dakhla retains more of its original charm than Kharga, to which it is connected by a 120-mile (200-km) road and daily buses.

The first village of importance in the depression is **Balat**. Here a direct caravan route from Asyut had its terminus and a hive of mudbrick dwellings testifies to medieval prosperity. Using only mud and straw, builders attained a sophistication in architecture that combines utility, beauty and harmony with natural surroundings. Balat was the seat of the oases' pharaonic governors; and a French expedition is currently excavating the extensive remains to the northwest of the village.

Dakhla's current capital is at **Mut**, some 18 miles (30 km) farther west. The town contains Dakhla's only hotels, as well as the police station where foreign visitors must register. Most necessities may be obtained here and there are a number of decent restaurants, but little

Coptic cemeteries at Al Bagawat in the Kharga Oasis.

to see – the old town's mudbrick citadel has been allowed to fall into ruins. Outside the town to the northwest are the **Tourist Springs**, which visitors are expected to admire. In fact many of the other springs – most in Dakhla are warm – are equally pleasant.

No trip to Dakhla would be complete, however, without a walk through its fields and gardens. The main field crop is wheat, while in the gardens grapevines vie for space with date palms, mulberry trees, figs and citrus. Dakhla is the only place in Egypt where new *saqiyas* – huge buffalo-driven waterwheels constructed of palm timber and clay jars – are still made.

Eighteen miles (30 km) beyond the Tourist Springs, the town of **Al-Qasr ad-Dakhla** perches on a mound between the desert and the fields. Like Balat, Al-Qasr is a honeycomb of little lanes that run between multi-storied mudbrick houses. Although cement is gaining ground, many locals still prefer the older material, since mudbrick walls retain heat at night and coolness in the day.

In the desert beyond Al-Qasr to the west are some well preserved Hellenistic tombs, one with a brightly painted zodiac on the ceiling. Farther along the main road lie the ruins of the Roman temple at **Deir al-Hajar**. This 1st-century wreck is a picturesque landmark.

Farafrah is the farthest of this group of oases from the Nile valley. Although it is also the smallest, with little over 2,500 acres (1,000 hectares) under cultivation, it has the greatest potential for land reclamation.

Only recently has Farafrah been connected to the rest of Egypt by decent roads. One now leads south, past the isolated settlement of Abu Mungar and through a 120-mile (200 km) stretch, justifiably called the Sand Sea, to Dakhla. The other, a more travelled route, goes northeast, through 150 miles (250 km) of some of Egypt's most spectacular desert, to the Bahariyya Oases and then to Cairo.

Al-Qasr al-Farafrah is the only town in Farafrah. It has a three-room resthouse, one shop and a coffeehouse: note

Wind sculptures in the Western Desert.

274

that food here is not obtainable. The village, many of its houses gaily painted by a talented local artist, clusters on the leeward side of a hill. Farafrah's beautiful gardens, famous for apples and apricots, lie on the windward side. A small natural bath-house at the gardens' edge is a good place for a scrub, while a Roman well within the gardens is of archaeological interest. At the bottom of the hill is a small lake stocked with river fish. The gentle *Farfuris* are not entirely accustomed to foreigners and prefer to avoid them.

The **Bahariyya Oases** are reached from Cairo by an excellent road that leads westward off the Fayyum desert road behind the Giza pyramids. About 200 rather dull miles later we reach the new settlement attached to Egypt's only iron mines. Not far beyond the mines the road descends into the **Bahariyya Depression**. The major town, **Al-Bawiti**, lies in the centre of the depression, which measures 45 miles (75 km) from north to south. Visitors should not be put off by Bawiti's uninviting aspect,

as the town has only very recently emerged from being a self-sufficient agricultural village and is suffering growth pangs brought about by the arrival of electricity in 1986. Accommodation at the town's only hotel leave much to be desired, but there are some decent eateries.

Bawiti sits atop a rock outcrop. To the north, cliffs drop abruptly into a sea of palms. Bawiti's gardens, spread for 3 miles (5 km) along the base of this cliff, are among the most beautiful in all the oases. The view from the cliffs at the spring called **'Ayn Bishmu** is breathtaking. Here the water emerges from a gorge to flow into the orchards. Within the gardens, land is so precious that there are few walkways and one must often paddle through the irrigation channels. Dates, olives, oranges, apricots, lemons, pomegranates and tiny apples grow in jungle-like proliferation, set in gardens fenced with mud walls and palm fronds.

Around Bawiti and its sister village of Al-Qasr are numerous ancient sites, not

A casualty of the desert.

all accessible and not all interesting. More to the taste of tourists are likely to be the hot springs, which range in temperature up to a scalding 115°F (47°C). The waters vary in content, some reeking of sulphur, others tinged with iron ore. Few things in life are more memorable than a moonlit bath under palm trees in the crisp air of the desert.

Siwah: The most mysterious, the most remote, and until recently the least visited of Egypt's oases, **Siwah** has been off-limits to tourists thanks to troubles along the Libyan border, to which it is adjacent. At present, half an hour's bureaucratising at **Mersa Matruh** is all that is required to obtain a visitor's permit. Daily buses now ply the tarmacked 190 miles (300 km) between Siwah and Matruh, while 10 years' heavy military presence have contributed to gradual Egyptianisation. A number of shops now cater to basic needs, while a large government-run hotel provides lodging.

Siwah is unique in Egypt in that it has a distinct culture and its own language.

The *Siwi* dialect, related to the Berber languages of North Africa, still holds out against the inroads made by Arabic through state education and military service. Unusual customs, such as homosexual marriages, have altogether died out, although the reclusive women of the oasis cling to traditional dress.

The oasis' main population centre is in **Siwah town**, to which the Siwis moved from the **fortress of Aghurmi** in the earlier part of this century. On the rock of Aghurmi, 2.5 miles (4 km) distant from the town centre, sit the remains of the **Temple of Jupiter-Amon**, home of the famous oracle which confirmed Alexander the Great in his status as a god. In the palm groves below the rock stood a second temple, unfortunately destroyed by dynamite in 1887. The other major historical site is at **Gabal al-Mawta**, a mile or so northeast of Siwah town. Here tombs have been cut out of the rock of a conical ridge. Paintings cover some of the walls, especially in the tomb of Si-Amon, but much was destroyed when the tombs were used as **Lake Qarun.**

276

shelters during the Italian air raids of World War II.

The most impressive sight in the oasis, however, is undoubtedly its agriculture. Siwah is the major producer of dates in Egypt. Some 250,000 palms fill the cultivated area; and their production is prized as the finest in the country. Olives also grow in abundance, as well as various other fruits and vegetables. Among the groves lie numerous springs, such as the 'Ayn al-Gubah, the ancient **Well of the Sun**, whose waters were said to have purifying properties. Indeed, water is in such abundance that large salty lakes have formed and drainage is a major problem.

Fayyum: Sprouting from the west bank of the Nile like a tender leaf, the **Fayyum** is referred to by some as Egypt's largest oasis. Others deny that it is an oasis at all, fed as it is by the **Bahr Yusef**, an ancient canal flowing from the Nile.

In prehistoric times the Fayyum was a marshy depression that collected the Nile's overflow in flood season. Its wetlands were a favourite hunting ground of the Old and Middle Kingdom Pharaohs until the 12th Dynasty's Amenemhet I (1991 BC–1962 BC) drained the swamps, building a regulator at Al-Lahun, the point where the river periodically breached its banks, and allowing a permanent reservoir to form, Lake Moeris, to the Greeks, now called **Lake Qarun**.

With this lake at the depression's northern end stabilised, agriculture could be introduced; and the Fayyum began to flourish. It received a further boost under the Ptolemies, who reclaimed more than 450 sq. miles (1,200 sq. km) of fertile land, reducing the lake to about twice its present size. Improved agricultural methods were introduced and new-fangled Greek hydraulics – waterwheels of a unique type still in use today – permitted extensive terracing.

The Fayyum, then, was an early and highly successful effort at land reclamation. Further improvements in the 19th century turned it into the "Garden of Egypt". This century has unfortunately brought with it the twin evils of

The collapsed pyramid of Meidum.

over-population and salinisation. Lake Qarun now measures only 24 by 5 miles (40 by 9 km) and is as salty as the Mediterranean, while the population surge has transformed Madinat al-Fayyum, the capital city, into a slum.

Day trips from Cairo to the Fayyum (2 hours away) are practical and pleasant as an excellent road connects them across the desert, leaving Cairo from behind the Giza pyramids, but the main road along the Nile to Upper Egypt is more attractive. Thirty miles (48 km) south of Cairo's edge the road draws parallel to the **Pyramid of Maydum**, a huge two-stepped tower silhouetted on the western horizon. A signposted turn-off leads up to the pyramid.

Dating from the end of the 3rd Dynasty, Meidum represents the transition from the Saqqarah-type step pyramid to the "true" pyramidal forms of Giza. Its present shape resulted from the collapse of the smooth outer casing; it is sometimes called the Collapsed Pyramid. A descent into Meidum's murky interior will charm the non-claustrophobe.

Continuing southwest for 10 miles (16 km) across the desert the road leads over train tracks and along the edge of an army camp. Eventually it forks: the road to the right enters cultivation and ultimately goes to Madinat al-Fayyum; the road to the left goes on towards the **pyramid complex of Amenemhet III** (1832 BC–1797 BC) at Hawarah. Having lost its outer casing of limestone, Amenemhet III's pyramid survives as a huge pile of mudbrick. It is easily climbed and the view from its top is superb. Below the pyramid are a number of ruinous tombs and very patchy remains of a mortuary temple. This was the great Labyrinth, which received a rave review from that globe-trotting Greek of the 5th century BC, Herodotus.

Southwest of Hawarah the road crosses a canal to reach the main Fayyum-Bani Suwayf road. Five miles (8 km) to the left, on a peninsula of desert, stands the 12th-Dynasty **Pyramid of Al-Lahun**, the southernmost in the Fayyum pyramid field. Turning right we reach **Madinat al-Fayyum** after 6 miles (10 km).

This town of half a million is the site of ancient **Crocodilopolis** and the hub of Fayyum province. Strung out along the Bahr Yusef, it has lost most of its evidently considerable former charm. In the central square a fine example of the Fayyum waterwheel groans away, bemoaning its fate. The main *suq*, its lanes cluttered with wares, has an untouched rustic simplicity surpassing that of any other major provincial market.

Lake Qarun itself is the Fayyum's greatest tourist attraction. It has a peculiar aura of mystery, especially at dusk on a windless day, when the pale sky and stripe of sand on the far side melt into their own reflection. The beaches at its eastern end, where the hotels and an excellent fish restaurant on a pier are located, fill up with mobs of Cairenes on holidays. The western end, approached through the villages of **Sanhur** and **Ibshawai**, is more peaceful: the Ptolemaic **temple at Qasr Qarun**, the site of ancient Dionysias, is an attraction and the lovely countryside makes the drive worthwhile.

Right and left, transport in the desert.

ABU SIMBEL AND NUBIA

Nubia, the arid sun-seared land of about 8,500 sq. miles (22,000 sq. km) between Aswan and the northern Sudan, now lies beneath the waters of the High Dam reservoir. Nubia's entire population of some 100,000 people were uprooted from their ancestral homes, half to be relocated in Egypt (in Kom Ombo, about 9 miles (14 km) north of Aswan), the other half in the northeastern Sudan (in Kashem el-Girba).

Nubia's major monuments, like its people, were transported to new locations, one as far afield as New York. Both the tragedy of the uprooting of the Nubian people and the technological achievement in saving the monuments can best be understood in the context of Nubia as it was before the deluge.

Old Nubia: Nubia was the link between Egypt and Africa, but it was not a regular trade corridor because of its inhospitable environment. It was a largely barren land, while Egypt, on the other hand, had an abundant agricultural surplus. Even in ancient times Nubians turned to their rich northern neighbour for vital food supplies, especially grain. And Egypt was ready to fulfil the Nubians' requirements in return for the right to exploit their rich mineral resources.

Despite its stark and barren nature the Nubian people had a strong attachment to their land. In the 20th century their working men went northwards to Egypt to find employment as bargemen, doorkeepers, cooks, or government clerks, but they seldom married Egyptians and inevitably returned to Nubia, bearing cloth, clothing and food for their families, as well as pictures cut out of magazines and newspapers – mostly portraits of political leaders, athletes and film stars – which were used to adorn the walls of their houses.

In the years before the High Dam, Nubian houses were made of sun-baked brick, a mixture of clay and straw. The facade of each house was different from the next. Houses were painted, both inside and out, with finger paintings of

trees, chickens, boats, flags and sacred symbols, and most had porcelain plates (brought from Cairo) inserted into the clay before it dried. Nubia's date-palm groves provided the people not only with food, but also with no fewer than 40 other commodities, such as fibre for ropes, timber for heavy construction, and palm "spears" for a variety of uses.

Sailing southwards from Egypt before the land was flooded, one could see Nubian settlements grouped near the banks of the river. Whitewashed shrines of local saints and sheikhs broke the skyline. In the vast distances from village to village, ancient temples could be seen: the great fortress of Kubban which once guarded the Wadi Alaki, one of the richest gold-mining areas in Nubia; the temples of Debod and Tafa, now reassembled in Madrid and Leiden, or the temples of Kirtasi, Kalabsha, and Bayt el Wali, now re-assembled on a new site near the High Dam, all originally built atop jutting sandstone cliffs. And, of course, the great Temple of Ramses II at Abu Simbel, a symbol of Egyptian power in Nubia in ancient times.

The end of Old Nubia: The trauma for the Nubians, faced with the news that their land was doomed, was compounded by the fact that this was not the first, but the fourth time they had watched their homes being submerged by the River Nile. An old man at Darau, near Kom Ombo, for example, recalled when the first Aswan dam was built, between 1899 and 1902. It formed an artificial lake 140 miles (225 km) upstream and the Nubians had to move back from the fertile strip at the edge of the river to rebuild their homes.

Less than five years after the dam was completed, it was seen to be inadequate to meet the growing needs of the country and was heightened by about 15 feet (5 metres). The reservoir now created by the thwarted Nile backed upstream 185 miles (300 km) and the Nubians had to move a second time. Between 1929 and 1934 the Aswan dam was raised again, and this time the water extended as far south as Wadi Halfa in northern Sudan. When the Nubians were told that a new dam would be built and that they would have to move again, this time out of Nubia completely, some of the older generation refused to leave; and with the water lapping at their feet they finally had to be helped or even carried bodily to the waiting vessels.

Saving the Nubian monuments: Meanwhile, the Egyptian and Sudanese governments launched an international appeal to save and record as many of the monuments of Nubia as possible. The response was immediate and Nubia was subjected, between 1960 and 1970, to the most concentrated archaeological operation ever mounted. Scholars, engineers, architects and photographers from over 30 countries fought against time to preserve what they could. Twenty-three temples were saved. Many of them were left in Nubia but moved or lifted out of harm's way: the **temple of Amada**, for example, was raised as a unit of 800 tons, put on rails and dragged up a hill to safety, while the **temple of Derr** was re-assembled nearby. A temple built by Queen Hatshepsut was dismantled, crated, loaded on 28 lorries, and transported to the Su-

dan, where it was rebuilt in the National Museum at Khartoum.

The temples of Abu Simbel: The famous **Temple of Ramses II** at Abu Simbel, the largest and most magnificent monument in Nubia, presented a formidable challenge. Unlike other temples, Abu Simbel was not freestanding. The temple facade was, in fact, the cliff face itself hewn in imitation of a pylon, dominated by four seated statues of a youthful Ramses II. The central hall was flanked by eight more statues of the king in a double row facing each other, against a corresponding number of square pillars. The northern wall of the hall was decorated with the Great Battle Scene, which is one of the most extraordinary and detailed reliefs to be found in the Nile Valley.

There are over 1,100 figures and the entire wall, from ceiling to bedrock, is filled with activity: the march of the Egyptian army with its infantry and charioteers, its engagement in hand-to-hand combat, and the flight of the vanquished prisoners, leaving overturned

The Temple of Abu Simbel before excavation.

284

chariots behind them. There are also scenes of camp life.

Beyond the court, carved out of the mountain to a depth of 180 feet (55 metres), was the sanctuary, which contained seated statues of four gods, Ptah of Memphis, Amon-Ra of Thebes, the deified Ramses II and Ra-Harakhte, the sun-god of Heliopolis.

Countries from all over the world offered technical and financial aid to save this unique monument. The project finally chosen entailed sawing the temple into over a thousand transportable pieces, some weighing as much as 15 tons, and placing them safely above the water level until they could be reassembled at a new site 200 feet (60 metres) higher than their original site.

While the stone blocks were being treated and stored, the new site on top of the mountain was levelled. Explosives could have ruined the temples, so compressed air drills were used instead. Studies were carried out on the bedrock to ensure that it could support the huge weight it was destined to bear forever,

The Queen's temple at Abu Simbel.

not only the mass of the reconstructed temple, but also a great reinforced concrete dome that would cover it. The dome would be 400 feet (125 metres) high and the cylindrical part was designed with a free span of some 200 feet (66 metres), which would have to bear a load of about 100,000 tons.

The small **temple of Queen Nefertari**, which lay to the north of the Great Temple at Abu Simbel, was also saved. Nefertari was the most beloved of the wives of Ramses II; and throughout the temple, on pillar and wall, even in the sanctuary, the names of the royal couple are linked.

Salvage archaeology: By 1970, with the water of the High Dam reservoir constantly rising, engulfing more and more of what had once been Nubia, considerable portions of known temples and shrines had been salvaged. But how much more archaeological evidence, in the form of town sites, tombs, temples, churches, and documents, had been lost to the world forever under the waters can never fully be ascertained.

Ironically, however, it is due to its disappearance that we now know more of Nubia than we do of many important sites in the best of Egypt. We know, for example, that when the civilisation of ancient Egypt was in its decline, a kingdom of Upper Nubia prospered, and that around 600 BC the Nubians moved their capital from Napata southwards to Meroe (Shendi). In the fertile bend in the river, free from invasion, well-placed for trade, rich in iron ore and in wood for iron-smelting, they developed a culture that was at once a continuation of the Egyptian-influenced Napatan culture and a totally individual African culture.

The Meroitic Kingdom spread northwards until, by the reign of Ptolemy IV (181 BC), the king of Meroe, Argamanic, controlled the Nile to within sight of Elephantine. There the Nubians remained until the Roman conquest of Egypt in 30 BC, when the Romans signed a treaty with them, turning all northern Nubia into a buffer zone.

Nubia embraced Christianity between the 5th and the 6th centuries, when numerous churches were built and some ancient temples were converted into churches. When Egypt was conquered by the Arabs in the 7th century, they concluded a treaty with the Christian Nubia king and Nubia officially remained Christian until the 12th century, when many Nubians embraced the Muslim faith. Mass conversion to Islam came when tribes from Arabia settled in Lower Nubia and began to impose their religion and their political organisation on the people. They intermarried with Arabs and their children came to be called *Bani Kanz*, or the Kenuz tribe. Most of the resettled Nubian population in Kom Ombo belong to this tribe. By the end of the 15th century, Nubians, with the exception of only a few settlements, were Muslim.

Digging at Qasr Ibrim: Surviving documents in a host of languages, including "Old Nubian" (which has yet to be deciphered), Arabic, Coptic and Greek, provide a wealth of information about the Nubian people in the form of private and official letters, legal documents, and petitions, which date from between the end of the 8th to the 15th centuries. Most of these documents come from a site about 9 miles (15 km) north of Abu Simbel called **Qasr Ibrim**. Now an island, it was situated on the eastern bank of the Nile where three massive peaks of rock rose from the river. Crowning the middle peak was a ruined town and fortress, whose imposing position commanded the valley for miles around in all directions.

This *qasr* (castle) is all that emerges above the level of the lake today and it must have been a striking landmark in Roman times when the first fortress was built. It is the only site in Nubia where archaeologists are still at work. A joint American/British excavation started in 1986 and aims to restore its major monuments, including a cathedral.

Luxuriously outfitted cruise ships ply the waters of Lake Nasser, the High Dam reservoir in the winter season (15 November–15 March), offering splendid views of restored monuments and African wildlife. Reservations must be made a year in advance.

Left, the draping of a turban shows a typically Nubian casualness. **Right,** inscriptions on a boulder at Sehel Island, Aswan. **Overpage:** skull caps for sale, Aswan.

INSIGHT GUIDES
Travel Tips

FOR THOSE WITH MORE THAN A PASSING INTEREST IN TIME...

Before you put your name down for a Patek Philippe watch *fig. 1*, there are a few basic things you might like to know, without knowing exactly whom to ask. In addressing such issues as accuracy, reliability and value for money, we would like to demonstrate why the watch we will make for you will be quite unlike any other watch currently produced.

"Punctuality", Louis XVIII was fond of saying, "is the politeness of kings."
We believe that in the matter of punctuality, we can rise to the occasion by making you a mechanical timepiece that will keep its rendezvous with the Gregorian calendar at the end of every century, omitting the leap-years in 2100, 2200 and 2300 and recording them in 2000 and 2400 *fig. 2*. Nevertheless, such a watch does need the occasional adjustment. Every 3333 years and 122 days you should remember to set it forward one day to the true time of the celestial clock. We suspect, however, that you are simply content to observe the politeness of kings. Be assured, therefore, that when you order your watch, we will be exploring for you the physical—if not the metaphysical—limits of precision.

Does everything have to depend on how much?
Consider, if you will, the motives of collectors who set record prices at auction to acquire a Patek Philippe. They may be paying for rarity, for looks or for micromechanical ingenuity. But we believe that behind each $500,000-plus bid is the conviction that a Patek Philippe, even if 50 years old or older, can be expected to work perfectly for future generations.
In case your ambitions to own a Patek Philippe are somewhat discouraged by the scale of the sacrifice involved, may we hasten to point out that the watch we will make for you today will certainly be a technical improvement on the Pateks bought at auction? In keeping with our tradition of inventing new mechanical solutions for greater reliability and better time-keeping, we will bring to your watch innovations *fig. 3* inconceivable to our watchmakers who created the supreme wristwatches of 50 years ago *fig. 4*. At the same time, we will of course do our utmost to avoid placing undue strain on your financial resources.

Can it really be mine?
May we turn your thoughts to the day you take delivery of your watch? Sealed within its case is your watchmaker's tribute to the mysterious process of time. He has decorated each wheel with a chamfer carved into its hub and polished into a shining circle. Delicate ribbing flows over the plates and bridges of gold and rare alloys. Millimetric surfaces are bevelled and burnished to exactitudes measured in microns. Rubies are transformed into jewels that triumph over friction. And after many months—or even years—of work, your watchmaker stamps a small badge into the mainbridge of your watch. The Geneva Seal—the highest possible attestation of fine watchmaking *fig. 5*.

Looks that speak of inner grace *fig. 6*.
When you order your watch, you will no doubt like its outward appearance to reflect the harmony and elegance of the movement within. You may therefore find it helpful to know that we are uniquely able to cater for any special decorative needs you might like to express. For example, our engravers will delight in conjuring a subtle play of light and shadow on the gold case-back of one of our rare pocket-watches *fig. 7*. If you bring us your favourite picture, our enamellers will reproduce it in a brilliant miniature of hair-breadth detail *fig. 8*. The perfect execution of a double hob-nail pattern on the bezel of a wristwatch is the pride of our casemakers and the satisfaction of our designers, while our chainsmiths will weave for you a rich brocade in gold *figs. 9 & 10*. May we also recommend the artistry of our goldsmiths and the experience of our lapidaries in the selection and setting of the finest gemstones? *figs. 11 & 12*.

How to enjoy your watch before you own it.
As you will appreciate, the very nature of our watches imposes a limit on the number we can make available. (The four Calibre 89 time-pieces we are now making will take up to nine years to complete). We cannot therefore promise instant gratification, but while you look forward to the day on which you take delivery of your Patek Philippe *fig. 13*, you will have the pleasure of reflecting that time is a universal and everlasting commodity, freely available to be enjoyed by all.

Should you require information on any particular Patek Philippe watch, or even on watchmaking in general, we would be delighted to reply to your letter of enquiry. And if you send us

fig. 1: The classic face of Patek Philippe.

fig. 4: Complicated wristwatches circa 1930 (left) and 1990. The golden age of watchmaking will always be with us.

fig. 2: One of the 33 complications of the Calibre 89 astronomical clock-watch is a satellite wheel that completes one revolution every 400 years.

fig. 5: The Geneva Seal is awarded only to watches which achieve the standards of horological purity laid down in the laws of Geneva. These rules define the supreme quality of watchmaking.

fig. 3: Recognized as the most advanced mechanical regulating device to date, Patek Philippe's Gyromax balance wheel demonstrates the equivalence of simplicity and precision.

fig. 6: Your pleasure in owning a Patek Philippe is the purpose of those who made it for you.

fig. 7: Arabesques come to life on a gold case-back.

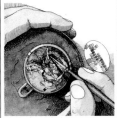

fig. 8: An artist working six hours a day takes about four months to complete a miniature in enamel on the case of a pocket-watch.

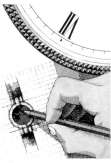

fig. 9: Harmony of design is executed in a work of simplicity and perfection in a lady's Calatrava wristwatch.

fig. 10: The chainsmith's hands impart strength and delicacy to a tracery of gold.

fig. 11: Circles in gold: symbols of perfection in the making.

fig. 12: The test of a master lapidary is his ability to express the splendour of precious gemstones.

PATEK PHILIPPE
GENEVE
fig. 13: The discreet sign of those who value their time.

your card marked "book catalogue" we shall post you a catalogue of our publications. Patek Philippe, 41 rue du Rhône, 1204 Geneva, Switzerland, Tel. +41 22/310 03 66.

THOMAS COOK
MASTERCARD
TRAVELLERS CHEQUES...

...HOLIDAY ESSENTIALS

Travel money from the travel experts

THOMAS COOK MASTERCARD TRAVELLERS CHEQUES ARE
WIDELY AVAILABLE THROUGHOUT THE WORLD.

Getting Acquainted

Area: 626,000 sq. miles (1,002,000 sq. km).
Capital: Cairo.
Longest River: The Nile.
Population: 62.3 million.
Language: Arabic (official), English and French are widely understood by the educated classes.
Religion: Muslim (mostly Sunni) 90%, Coptic Christian and other 10%.
Time Zone: GMT plus 2 hours.
Currency: Egyptian pound of 100 piastres. UK£1 = 5 Egyptian pounds; US$1 = 3.5 Egyptian pounds.
Weights and measures: metric.
Electricity: Power supply in Egypt is 220 volt.
International Dialling Code: 20.

Egypt links the northeastern corner of Africa and the southwestern edge of Asia. Its longest distance north-south is 640 miles (1,025 km) and widest distance east-west is about 775 miles (1,240 km).

The **deserts** of Egypt comprise over 90 percent of the land surface. They are part of an arid region that stretches from the Atlantic coast in the west to Central Asia in the east. Though extremely sparsely populated (they are inhabited by less than 1% of the population), they contain six inhabited depressions known as oases.

The **Eastern** or **Arabian Desert** is east of the Nile Valley and extends to the Red Sea. It is far higher than the Western Desert, rising to a series of ranges, parallel to the sea, called the Red Sea Mountains. It covers approximately 86,101 sq. miles (223,000 sq. km), or 21 percent of the land mass of Egypt. The Arabian Desert has two distinct areas, the northern Al Ma'aza Plateau, which is composed primarily of limestone, and the southern Al 'Ababda Plateau. Water is very scarce in these areas.

The **Western** or **Libyan Desert** is much larger than the Arabian Desert, covering 332,434 sq. miles (681,000 sq. km) and comprises two thirds of Egypt. It is separated from the North African or Great Sahara by highlands and is composed primarily of Nubian sandstone and limestone. South of the Qattarah depression there is a band of north-south sand dunes that continue as far south as the Kharga Depression, where they flatten out. The Western Desert is the most arid region of Egypt.

The **Red Sea** is 7,785 feet (2,359 metres) deep, 1,207 miles (1,932 km) long from north to south and 191 miles (306 km) from east to west. Cutting through the Gulf of Aqaba from the Dead Sea and continuing south through the Red Sea and on into East Africa is the **Great Rift Valley**, the juncture of the African and Arabian Tectonic plates. The Red Sea is highly saline with small tides and exquisite coral shelves and reefs.

Climate

Summers are hot and dry in Upper Egypt, humid in the Delta and along the Mediterranean Coast. In recent years the humidity has spread to Cairo and the city swelters in August. Winters are mild with some rain, but usually there are bright, sunny days and cold nights.

Spring and autumn are short, and during the 50 days (*khamseen*) between the end of March and mid-May, dust storms can occur sporadically.

Average Year-round Temperatures
(max/min, in Fahrenheit)

	winter	summer
Alexandria	69/51	86/69
Cairo	69/51	96/68
Luxor	79/42	107/72
Aswan	79/49	108/77

The Economy

Since 1979 there has been a massive influx of foreign aid into Egypt. As a result of this there are new roads linking all areas of the country, villages up and down the Nile and in the deserts have been electrified, new schools, hospitals, and other services have sprung up by the dozen, telephone systems continue to undergo massive renovation and expansion, and the private sector has been encouraged to invest heavily in Egypt's future. The change in Egypt has been dramatic. Everything connected with infrastructure has improved.

For the tourist there are dozens of new hotels and restaurants, monuments have been restored and their environments spruced up, tour guides are licensed, and retail shops are bursting with good quality products.

The Egyptian pound has been floated, with an exchange value fixed daily and has shown itself to be remarkably stable. For Egyptians, however, life is expensive. Rents are high, food though abundant is costly, and salaries lag behind the cost of living.

The major source of income for the country as a whole has been remittances from Egyptians working abroad. Domestically, tourism has become vitally important and visitors are encouraged to spend freely.

The Government

Egypt is officially known as the Arab Republic of Egypt (ARE). Its capital city is Cairo and other major cities include Alexandria, Giza, Port Said, Asyut, Suez, Minya, and Aswan. It is a republic with an elected president, who is commander in chief of the Army, and leader of the National Defense Council. The prime minister and cabinet are appointed by the president.

There is one legislative body: the National Assembly, composed of elected representatives from all districts of the country, 50 percent of whom must be from the working class or farmers. Copts and women are elected according to a quota. The Shura Council is an advisory body with 140 elected members and another 70 appointed members.

Culture & Customs

Whether Muslim or Copt, the Egyptians as a whole tend to be religious, and piety is important in their daily lives. So is commitment to the extended family. Each family member is responsible for the integrity of the family and for the behaviour of other members. Certainly, one result of these concerns is that the city of Cairo is safer than any western metropolis.

Yet when westerners visit Egypt they are often apprehensive. Their views of Egyptians and Arabs, fomented by unkind and untrue media stories, often bear no relation to reality at all. Travellers normally receive friendly, hospitable treatment everywhere and take home with them good feelings about the warmth and good will of the Egyptian people.

Women

Before the famous Egyptian feminist Hoda Shaarawi deliberately removed her veil in 1922, veils – which had no religious significance – were worn in public by all respectable middle-class and upper-class women, Muslim, Jewish, or Christian. By 1935, however, veils were a comparative rarity in Egypt, though they continued to be worn as an item of fashion in neighbouring countries like Syria and Jordan for 30 more years and have remained obligatory in the Arabian Peninsula to this day.

Nowadays in Egypt, veils are worn only by Bedouin women, who are the inheritors of the urban fashions of a century ago, or by younger middle-class urban women demonstrating either modesty or Muslim piety. Feminine modesty alone – not necessarily identified with any religion – is shown by wearing a covering over the head or even a sort of wimple. One reason for the latter, favoured by many young professional women, is that it tends to discourage male advances, either of a physical or verbal nature.

From the 1930s onwards, Egyptian women began to enter into businesses and professions. Thus by 1965, thanks in part to social changes effected in the course of the July Revolution, Egypt could boast a far higher proportion of women working as doctors, dentists, lawyers, professors, diplomats, or high officials than might have been found in the US or in any European country outside of Scandinavia. Egyptian women still do not have equality with Egyptian men, however, either in law or by custom; and no matter how much they may rule within the bedroom, the kitchen, the shop or even the office, Egyptian public places, including streets, coffeehouses, and popular cinemas, are still fundamentally male preserves.

Planning the Trip

What To Bring

Almost everything is available in Cairo, but may be cheaper at home. Special medication should be brought with you. A small supply of plasters, antibiotic ointments and anti-diarrhoea tablets may well come in handy. If you have a favourite sun lotion, make-up, toothpaste, or shampoo that you cannot possibly live without, bring some with you.

What To Wear

Be modest, be sensible, and travel light. Egypt is a conservative country. It is an affront to your hosts to appear in a mosque or even on the street in clothing that is considered immodest. Women should keep shoulders and upper arms covered. Neither men or women should wear shorts except at resorts or on the tennis court. No topless or nude bathing is permitted.

On the practical side, leave your synthetics at home as they will prove to be too hot in summer and not warm enough in winter. Cotton is suitable for all seasons; wool for winter and many summer nights.

Loose and flowing garments are not only modest, but also practical in a hot climate. Hats are vital and necessary, to protect against heat stroke and so are sunglasses, to defend the eyes against the glare.

Bring stout, comfortable shoes. You will be doing a lot of walking and neither Cairo's streets nor Luxor's temple floors are friendly to feet.

Entry Regulations
Visas & Passports

All travellers entering Egypt must have the appropriate travel documents: a passport or other legal pass and a valid visa. Lost or stolen passports must be reported to the police immediately. New passports can be issued in a matter of hours at the consular office of your embassy in Egypt but procedures will require a copy of your police report. Tourist visas are also routinely issued at the Cairo International Airport and the Port of Alexandria, but may be acquired in advance of your visit at any Egyptian consulate.

Types of Visas

Single entry visas are good for one entry into the country for one month. If you require a longer stay, request it at the time of application.

Multiple entry visas should be requested if you plan to exit and re-enter Egypt during your visit.

Student visas for people studying in Egypt are valid for one year and are not issued until the student can verify registration at an Egyptian university.

Business visas are issued to persons with business affiliations in Egypt.

Tourist Residence visas are extended to persons wishing to visit Egypt for an extended period of time. They are not permitted to work in Egypt and must be prepared to present evidence of having exchanged $180 a month for up to six months at a time. This type of visa is only issued in Egypt at the Passport Department of the Mugama'a (central administrative building). Persons holding a Tourist Residence visa must apply for a re-entry visa whenever they plan to leave the country.

All visas may be renewed up to 15 days beyond their expiration date. If not renewed during that time a fine is imposed and a letter of apology from your embassy must be taken to the Mugama'a.

On Arrival

A notice stamped in passports on entry into Egypt says "registration within 7 days" but arrivals in Cairo should in fact be registered within 48 hours, either at the nearest police station or at the Mugama'a, with re-registration at each new city visited. Hotels perform this service routinely, but visitors staying in private houses, must make other arrangements to be registered. Their hosts may be held responsible for failure to do so.

Extension Of Stay

Visas may be renewed at the Mugama'a, usually after a long wait. They are valid for 15 days after the expiry date, but if not renewed a letter of apology from your embassy must be presented to the Mugama'a or you will have to pay a small fine.

Customs

A visitor is permitted to enter the country with 250 grammes of tobacco, or 50 cigars, one litre of alcohol and personal effects. Animals must have a veterinary certificate attesting to their good health and also a valid rabies certificate.

Duty-free purchases of liquor (3 bottles per person) may be made within a month of arrival twice a year at ports of entry or at the tax-free shops in Cairo.

Persons travelling with expensive electronic equipment such as cameras, video cameras, or computers may be required to list these items in their passports to ensure that they will be exported upon departure.

Porter Service

For a rental of one LE, baggage trolleys are available at Cairo International Airport. There are also porters with larger trolleys to service individuals and groups. Porters should be tipped.

On Departure

Although the traveller is free to buy and export reasonable quantities of Egyptian goods for personal use, the export of large quantities of items requires an export license. Egyptian-made items over two years old are not permitted to leave the country. Nor are foreign-made items deemed to have "historic value". Exportation of carpets, Egyptian-made or not, is restricted. Travellers may be requested to show bank receipts as proof of payment for other valuable items. Egyptian currency may not be taken out of Egypt. Travellers may exchange their extra pounds at the airport provided they have valid bank receipts.

Animal Quarantine

It is not wise to bring a pet to Egypt on vacation. Rabies is a problem in the country and very few hotels have facilities for animals.

Health

Evidence of yellow fever and cholera immunisation may be required from persons who have been in an infected area within six days prior to arrival.

Money

Airport Exchange: Banks are available at the airport for currency exchange. Egyptian money, with both Arabic and English numerals, consists of these denominations:
Pound notes: 100, 20, 10, 5, 1.
Piaster notes: 50, 25.
Coins: 20, 10, 5.

Credit cards are used in most major hotels, but not always in shops. Bring some traveller's checks.

Public Holidays

There are currently six official government holidays a year when banks, government offices, many businesses, and schools are closed. In addition there are Islamic and Coptic holidays spread throughout the year.

New Year's Day. Public holiday.

Coptic Christmas, January 7. Copts observe the birth of Christ on the same date as all other Orthodox churches except the Armenian. Prior to the feast they abstain from animal flesh and animal products for 43 days.

Feast of Breaking the Fast, Id al-Fitr, celebrates the end of Ramadan, the month of fasting. During daylight hours, Muslims will have abstained from food, drink, sex and violence for some 30 days. Business hours are shortened during Ramadan and social life, centering on the meal eaten after sunset, called *iftar*, becomes nocturnal and intense. The Id al-Fitr is a happy celebration with new clothes, gifts, and plenty of good food. Festivities usually last for three days.

Feast of the Sacrifice, 'Id al-Adha, begins approximately 70 days after the end of Ramadan and commemorates Abraham's sacrifice of a sheep in place of his son, Isaac. It is traditional to kill a sheep and share the meat with the extended family, neighbours and the poor. Festivities last for four days.

Coptic Easter ends the Coptic Lenten season. It is usually celebrated one week after Western Easter. Coptic businesses are closed.

Sham an-Nissim, "sniffing the breeze", is a holiday celebrated the Monday after Coptic Easter. Dating from Pharaonic times, it is celebrated by all Egyptians regardless of their religious affiliation. The entire population goes to the countryside or to some urban green space for a day-long outing, with picnic baskets filled with hard boiled eggs and pickled fish. Businesses are closed.

Liberation of Sinai Day, April 25. Public holiday.

Labour Day, May 1. Public holiday.

Islamic New Year, Ras al-Sana al-Higriya. Public holiday.

Anniversary of the 1952 Revolution, July 23. Businesses are closed.

Prophet's Birthday, Mulid eh-Nabi, is celebrated in honour of the Prophet Muhammad. A traditional parade complete with drums and banners is held in the historic zone of Cairo. Public holiday.

Armed Forces Day, October 6. Public holiday.

Calendars

The business and secular community in Egypt operates under the Western (Gregorian) calendar. But other calendars have official status in Egypt. The Islamic calendar is used to fix religious observances, and is based on a lunar cycle of 12 months of 29 or 30 days. The Muslim year is thus 11 days shorter than the year according to the Gregorian calendar and months move forward accordingly.

In the Gregorian calendar, for example, April is always in the spring, but in the Muslim calendar all months move through all seasons in a 33-year cycle.

The Coptic calendar is the Julian calendar, which was replaced in the West by the Gregorian calendar between 1582 and 1752, but the months carry their current Egyptian names. The Coptic year consists of 12 months of 30 days and one month of 5 days. Every four years a sixth day is added to the shorter month. An adaptation of the Coptic calendar is used by many farmers for planting and harvesting crops. It is used by the authorities of the Coptic Orthodox Church.

Muslim	Coptic
Muharram	Toot (begins Sept 11 or 12)
Safar	Baaba
Rabi' il-awal	Hatour
Rabi' it-tani	Kiyaak
Gamada-l-uula	Tuuba (mid-Jan)
Gamada-l-ukhra	Amshir
Ragab	Baramhat
Sha'aban	Barmuda
Ramadan	Bashans
Shawal	Bauna
Dhu'l	Abiib
Dhu'l	Misra
	Nasi (5–6 days)

Getting There

By Air

Egypt is served by international airports at Alexandria, Cairo, Luxor, and Hurghada on the mainland, and at Sharm el Shaykh on the Sinai peninsula. The largest and most active airport is in Cairo.

There are non-stop flights from African, Asian, and European cities. Return tickets must be confirmed before departure. Check with a travel agent in your hotel or contact the airline office in Cairo. Most major airlines have offices located at the Cairo International Airport and downtown in and around Midan Tahrir.

In recent years **Cairo International Airport** has expanded into a first class facility. Despite the fact that it is located to the north of the city, most airlines from Europe approach the air field from the south. In daylight passengers are offered a magnificent view of Cairo, the Nile, and the Giza pyramids.

Terminal 1: Egyptair domestic and international flights.
Terminal 2: International Airlines.
Terminal 3: Saudia Arabia Airline.
Terminal 4: International cargo.
English language information, Tel: 291-4255, 291-2266.
Quarantine, Tel: 666-688.

Alexandria airport is served by Olympic Airlines and Egyptair. **Luxor** Airport now has direct flights from several European cities via Air France and Lufthansa. **Hurghada** Airport is also serviced by Lufthansa while **Sharm el Shaykh** Airport receives charter flights from Germany and France.

Other airports in Egypt are Asyut, Aswan, Abu Simbel, Al Arish, St Catherine's, Kharga Oasis, Siwa Oasis.

DOMESTIC AIRLINES

Egypt has two national carriers for internal flights, Egyptair and Air Sinai. Egyptair flies daily from Cairo to Alexandria, Luxor, Aswan, Abu Simbel, and Hurghada and twice a week to Kharga Oasis. Air Sinai flies from Cairo to Hurghada, Al Arish, Taba, Sharm el Shaykh, St Catherine's Monastery, El Tor, and to Tel Aviv, Israel.

Egyptair Offices
Alexandria: 19 Midan Zaghloul. Tel: 492-0778.
Cairo: 6 Adli Street. Tel: 920-000; 12 Qasr el Nil Street. Tel: 750-600; Nile Hilton Hotel. Tel: 759-703; Cairo Sheraton. Tel: 985-408.
Heliopolis: 22 Ibrahim el Lakani. Tel: 668-552.
Luxor: Winter Palace Arcade.
Aswan: Corniche.

By Sea

Alexandria and Port Said on the Mediterranean Sea, and Suez and Nuwayba on the Red Sea are ports of entry. For sailings, check with your travel agent or the following operators:

Adriatic Lines, Castro and Company, 12 Talaat Harb. Tel: 743-213, 743-144 (passengers and shipping).
The Egyptian Navigation Company, 26 Sherif. Tel: 393-8278; 1 Hurria, Alexandria. Tel: 472-0824.
Favia Shipping Lines, 18 Adli. Tel: 393-8983.
Federal Arab Maritime, 27 Gazirah el Wosta, Zamalek. Tel: 341-5823, 340-6351.
The International Agency for Tourism, Navigation and Trading Services, 13 Midan Tahrir. Tel: 762-892, 779-452.
International Transport & Maritime Service Co., 26A Asma Fahmi, Kulliet el Banat, Heliopolis. Tel: 661-783.
Misr Edco Shipping Company, Menatours, 14 Talaat Harb. Tel: 776-951.
North African Tourist Shipping, 171 Muhammad Farid. Tel: 391-3081, 391-4682, or el Takkadom, Madinat Nasr. Tel: 608-417 (only from Port Said to Cyprus and Haifa).

By Land

With some restrictions all borders are now open to travellers.

From Israel: Private vehicles are not permitted to enter Egypt from Israel; however travellers may use public transport and enter Egypt via Rafah on the northern coast of Sinai or from Eilat on the Red Sea. Buses run regularly from Tel Aviv and Jerusalem to the border at Rafah. At the border passengers disembark from the Israeli vehicle, go through customs, and take an Egyptian bus or taxi. There are no facilities for issuing visas at the Rafah border. In Eilat, Israeli buses are permitted to enter Egypt and travel as far as Sharm el Shaykh at the southern tip of Sinai.

From Sudan: There is a twice-weekly steamer that ferries cars the length of Lake Nasser, from Wadi Halfa in the Sudan to Aswan in Egypt. Information is available from the Nile Navigation Company Limited, Ramses Square (in the train station), and Nile Maritime Agency, 8 Qasr el Nil, both in Cairo; and the Nile Company for River Transport, 7 Atlas Building, Aswan. All arrangements to enter Sudan, including visas, must be made in Cairo. You must have a valid passport and either a transit or tourist visa to Sudan. If you plan to pass through the Sudan you must have a valid visa for your next destination.

From Libya: The border with Libya is open and buses and taxis make regular runs between Alexandria and Sollum. There are some travel restrictions for Westerners. Consult your embassy or the nearest Libyan Embassy for details.

MOTORING TO EGYPT

All private vehicles entering Egypt must have a *triptyque* or *carnet de passage en douane* from an automobile club in the country of registration or pay customs duty which can be as high as 250 percent. Emergency *triptyques* are available at the port of entry via the Automobile and Touring Club of Egypt. This permits a car to enter Egypt for three months with one extension. The extension is available from the Automobile and Touring Club of Egypt, Qasr el Nil, Cairo. All persons travelling in the vehicle must have a valid passport and the driver must also have an

International Driver's Licence. The latter is available from automobile clubs in the country of registration. (See *Getting Around*, *Private Transport* for additional details on driving in Egypt.)

Special Facilities
Disabled
Few hotels or cruise boats and no public buildings, restaurants, theatres or historical sites provide any facilities for the infirm or disabled. Major airlines, however, provide services both entering and leaving the country that match worldwide standards.

Useful Addresses
Egyptian Tourism & Information Centres
Athens: 10 Amerikis St. Tel: 360-6906.
New York: 630 Fifth Ave. Tel: 246-6960.
San Francisco: 323 Geary Street. Tel: 433-7562.
London: 168 Picadilly, W1. Tel: 493-5282.
Rome: 19, Via Bissolati. Tel: 475-1985.
Geneva: 11, Rue de Chantepoulet. Tel: 3291-32.
Paris: 90, Avenue de Champs Elysees. Tel: 562-9442.
Frankfurt: Kaiserstrasse 64, Bürohaus A. Tel: 25-23-19.

Egyptian Consulates Abroad
Canada: 3754 Côte de Nièges, Montreal; 454 Laurier Ave, M.E. Ottawa.
France: 56 Avenue d'Iena, Paris.
Germany: Taunusstrasse 35, Frankfurt.
Greece: 3 Vassilissis Sophias Ave, Athens.
Italy: 19 Via Bissolati, Rome.
Spain: Alcala 21, Madrid 14.
Switzerland: 11 Rue de Chantepoulet, Geneva.
United Kingdom: 19 Kensington Palace Gardens, London W8.
United States: 2310 Decatur Place, N.W. Washington, DC 20008; 1110 Second Ave, New York, NY 10022; 3001 Pacific Ave, San Francisco, CA 94115; 505 N. Lakeshore Drive, 4902, Chicago, IL 60611; 2000 West Loop So., Houston, TX 77027.

Practical Tips

Business Hours
Banks: 8.30am–1.30pm daily, closed Friday, Saturday and most holidays.
Businesses: Business hours throughout the week are flexible. Few businesses function before 8am; many are open until 5pm, but some close during the afternoon and then re-open at 5pm. Clinics are customarily open from 5pm to 8pm.
Government offices: 8am–2pm daily, closed Friday, Saturday, most holidays.
Shops: Shops keep hours according to demand. In central Cairo, many shops, including those owned by Muslims and Jews, are closed on Sunday.

Khan al-Khalili bazaar is open 10am–7 or 8pm daily and most shops close Sunday.

Religion & Religious Services
Islam is the official religion of Egypt, but there is a large Coptic community and other Christian sects represented in the country. There is also a small Jewish community. Islam is part of the Judaeo-Christian family of religions and was revealed to the Prophet Muhammad in what is now Saudia Arabia.

Islam has five major principles, known as "pillars", which form the foundation of the religion. The first principle is the belief that there is only one God and that the Prophet Muhammad is the messenger of God. The second is prayer, which should be performed five times every day. Almsgiving is the third principle and Muslims often donate a percentage of their earnings to others.

The fourth pillar is fasting during the holy month of Ramadan. The fifth pillar is pilgrimage to Mecca, *haj*, which all Muslims hope to perform at least once. The pilgrimage is performed during the month of Dhu'l-Higga, which begins 70 days after the end of the Ramadan fast.

Coptic Orthodox
The Copts, a large minority in Egypt, are a Christian sect which separated from the Byzantine and Latin churches in AD 451 over a disagreement in religious doctrine. Copts founded the world's first monasteries, and the continuing monastic tradition is an important part of the Coptic faith.

Religious Observances
Visitors may attend any Coptic service. Non-Muslims should not enter mosques while prayers are in progress, and may be asked, in mosques listed as antiquities, to pay entry fees at other times. Muslims may enter any mosque at any time free of charge. Listed below is a small selection of Christian services. Hours should be checked against the weekend newspapers.

Catholic Churches
Church of the Annunciation, 36 Muhammad Sabri Abu Alam, near Midan Talaat Harb. Tel: 393-8429. Armenian Rite. Holy Liturgy Sunday 8.15am (in Coptic with Arabic readings); 9.30am, 10.30am and 6.30pm.
Our Lady of Peace (Melkite, Greek Catholic), 4 Midan el Sheikh Yusef, 96 Qasr el Aini. Byzantine Rite in Arabic. Holy Liturgy Sunday at 8.30am, 10.30am, and 6pm.
Holy Family Catholic Church, 55 Road 15, Maadi. Latin Rite. Daily Mass in French 8am Friday. Family Mass 10am Saturday in English. Saturday Mass 6pm in German, 7pm in French. Sunday Mass 9.30am in French, 10.30am and 6pm in English.
St Joseph's Church (Italian and Egyptian Franciscan Friars), 2 Bank Misr at corner of Muhammad Farid. Tel: 393-6677. Latin Rite. Holy Mass Sunday 7.30am in French; 8.30am in Arabic; 10am in Italian; 12.30pm in French; 5.30pm in English; 6.30pm in French. Weekdays 7.30am and 6.30pm in French.
St Joseph's Roman Catholic Church, 4 Ahmed Sabri, Zamalek. Tel: 340-8902, 340-9348. Latin Rite. Holy Mass Sunday 8.30am in Arabic; 11am in English; 6pm in French. Weekdays 6pm in French. Saturday 6pm in Italian (sometimes Spanish).

Orthodox Churches

Armenian Orthodox, Cathedral of St Gregory the Illuminator, 179 Ramses near Coptic Hospital. Armenian Rite in Armenian. Holy Liturgy Sunday 9–11am.

Abu Serga Church, Old Cairo. Coptic Rite in Coptic and Arabic. Holy Liturgy Sunday 8am–noon.

St Mark's Cathedral, 222 Ramses, Abbassiyah. Coptic Rite in Coptic and Arabic. Holy Liturgy Sunday 6–8am.

Church of the Virgin Mary, 6 Muhammad Marashli, Zamalek. Tel: 340-5153. Coptic Rite in Coptic and Arabic. Holy Liturgy Sunday 7.30–9.30am and 9.30–11am.

Protestant Churches

All Saints' Cathedral, 5 Michel Lutfallah, Zamalek, behind the Marriott Hotel Episcopal/Anglican. Services in English: Sunday 8am.

Christian Science Society, 3 Midan Mustafa Kamil. Service and Sunday School, Sunday 7.30pm. Testimony Meeting Wednesday 7.30pm. Reading Room with Bible references and Christian Science literature open Wednesday and Sunday 6–7.20pm and Friday 11am–2pm.

Church of Christ, 14A Road 206, Apt. 4, Digla.

Church of God, 15 Emad el Din, Apt. 45. Sunday service 10.30am.

Church of God Cairo Christian Fellowship, St Andrew's Church, corner of Galaa and 26 July. Sunday service 6pm in English.

Church of Jesus Christ of Latter-Day Saints (Mormon), 44 Road 20, Maadi. Weekly sacrament service Friday at 9.30am.

Maadi Community Church (The Church of St John the Baptist). Corner of Port Said and Road 17, Maadi. Services in English Friday 8.30am and 11am, with nursery; Sunday 7pm, no nursery.

Saint Andrew's United Church, 38 26 July and Ramses. Service in English Sunday 9.30am.

Seventh Day Adventist Church, 16 Kubba, Roxi Heliopolis. Tel: 258-0292, 258-0785.

Media

Radio

European Radio Cairo: 557 AM and 95 FM, 7am–midnight, is a music station playing European classical, pop, and jazz music. News in English at 7.30am, 2.30pm, and 8pm; in French at 8am, 2pm and 9pm; in Greek at 3pm; in Armenian at 4pm; in German at 6pm.

BBC: World Service broadcasts to Egypt on 639 kHz and 1323 kHz. The higher metre band provides better reception between sunrise and sunset. There are also shortwave alternatives. News is on the hour.

The **VOA** Voice of America broadcasts on a variety of wavelengths from 3–10am daily.

Television

Channel 1: on the air from 3.30pm–midnight (local time), and found on 1 and 5 on the dial, is mainly in Arabic.

Channel 2: broadcasting from 3pm–midnight daily, and also from 10am–noon on Fridays and Sundays, has many foreign language programmes.

Channel 3: is a Cairo-only station broadcasting, in Arabic, from 5–9pm.

CNN: arrived in Egypt in 1991. It broadcasts to subscribers 24 hours a day with an uncensored programme.

See the *Egyptian Gazette* for daily television schedules. Schedules vary during Ramadan and in the summer.

Newspapers & Magazines

In Cairo all major English, French, German and Italian daily newspapers are available at larger hotels and at newsstands in Zamalek and Maadi usually a day late. The two most important local dailies are *Al-Ahram* and *Al-Akhbar*. *Al-Ahram*, "The Pyramids", was established in 1875, making it the oldest newspaper in Egypt. Published daily, it also has a UK edition, a weekly English-language edition, *Al-Ahram Weekly* and a weekly French-language edition, *Al-Ahram Hébdo*. Other English-language weeklies include the *Middle East Times* and the *Arab Times*. *Al Akhbar al Yawm*, "The News", established in 1952 offers a weekly edition in Arabic.

The *Egyptian Gazette*, established in 1880, is the oldest foreign language daily newspaper still in operation in Egypt.

In French there are *Le Progres Egyptien* and *Le Journal d'Egypte;* in Greek, *Phos;* and in Armenian, *Arev.*

Informal newsletters serve the foreign residents in Egypt: the *British Community Association News* for the British community; *Helioscope*, serving the residents of Heliopolis; the *Maadi Messenger* for foreigners in Maadi, and *Papyrus* for the German community.

English-language magazines include *Arab Press Review*, a biweekly political magazine, *Business Monthly*, featuring business news, *Cairo's*, a monthly what's on, *Egypt Today*, a monthly general interest magazine, *Places in Egypt*, designed for tourists, and *Prism*, a literary quarterly.

Postal Services

The Central Post Office at Midan al Ataba in Cairo (Tel: 912-356) is open 24 hours a day except Friday and occasional holidays. All other post offices are open from 8.30am–3pm daily, except Fridays. Mailboxes found on street corners and in front of post offices are red for regular Egyptian mail, blue for overseas airmail letters and green for Cairo and express mail within Cairo. Allow 7 days for air mail post to Europe, 14 days to America.

Express Mail Agencies

DHL, 20 Gamal el Din Abdul Mahasen, Garden City. Tel: 355-7301, 355-7118; 34 Abdel Khalek Sarwat. Tel: 392-9198, 393-8988; 35 Ismail Ramzi, Heliopolis. Tel: 246-3571, 246-0324.

Federal Express, 1079 Corniche el Nil, Garden City. Tel: 355-0427; 24 Syria Mohandeseen. Tel: 349-0986; 31 Golf, Maadi. Tel: 350-7172.

IML Air Couriers, 2 Mustafa Kamel, Maadi. Tel: 350-1160, 350-1240.

Middle East Courier Service, 1 Mahmoud Hafez, Heliopolis. Tel: 245-9281.

SOS Sky International, 45 Shehab, Mohandeseen. Tel: 346-0028, 346-2503.

TNT Skypac International Express, 33 Dokki, Dokki. Tel: 348-8204, 348-7228.

World Courier Egypt, 17 Qasr el Nil. Tel: 777-678, 741-313.

Telecoms

Most 5-star hotels offer direct dial service in your room and via the telephone operator in the hotel. The Central Telephone and Telegraph Offices (8 Adli; Midan Tahrir; 26 Ramses) are open 24 hours a day, as are many branch exchanges. Others are open from 7am–10pm daily. Telex and fax services are also available from the above, and fax facilities in particular are available at business centres dotted around the city.

If your have an AT&T calling card it is possible to charge a call from Egypt to the United States to a US account. You may place a call with a New York operator by dailing 356-0200 or 510-0200. You must supply both the American number and the number of your AT&T account.

Telephone codes in Egypt

Alexandria	03
Aswan	097
Asyut	088
Cairo	02
Fayyum	084
Hurghada	062
Ismailia	064
Luxor	095
Port Said	066
Suez	062

Internet facilities are available through both commercial offices and educational institutions.

Embassies in Egypt

Australia: Cairo Plaza, Corniche el Nil, Bulak. Tel: 777-900, 777-994.
Canada: 6 Muhammad Fahmi el Sayed, Garden City. Tel: 354-3110/9.
Great Britain: 7 Ahmed Ragheb, Garden City. Tel: 354-0850-9.
Ireland: 3 Abu el Feda Tower, Zamalek. Tel: 340-8264, 340-8547.
USA: 5 Latin America, Garden City. Tel: 355-7371, 354-8211.

Emergencies

Security & Crime

Like many other countries, such as Italy and the USA, Egypt has been troubled in recent years by right-wing extremists. Like the US in the late 1960s and more recently, Germany in the 70s, the UK and France throughout the 70s, 80s, and early 90s, it has also suffered from terrorist violence. The terrorists' campaign in Egypt, however, was amateur, half-hearted, unorganized, and short-lived; and even during a six-month period, from September 1991 to March 1992, when tourists were supposed to have been specifically targeted, a tourist was statistically much safer from violence in Cairo than in Miami, several million times less likely to be assassinated than an American President. Ironically, however, the Western myth of Egypt as a politically unstable country about to transform itself into a theocracy run by religious fanatics has been largely the creation of American media. Since 1979, for example, the *New York Times*, has regularly used "Islamic fundamentalism" as a bugbear to provide dramatic background for otherwise unsensational stories about the discovery of tombs or the opening of new discothèques.

Such being the case, visitors from abroad should nevertheless be warned that restrictions still pertain on travel into or through Middle Egypt, the zone along the Nile in Upper Egypt between Minya and Luxor. This region is Egypt's equivalent to Appalachia, Sicily, or the Balkans: beautiful, but poverty-stricken, and historically given to violence, much of it directed against officialdom or formal authority. Since it also contains many of Egypt's most interesting and least spoiled ancient sites, some of them only recently opened to visitors, one hopes the restrictions will be increasingly relaxed.

In Luxor the volatile male temperament characteristic of Upper Egypt may become overt in sexual aggressiveness. A century or so of casual adventuring by female tourists has fostered belief in the universal concupiscence and generosity of Western women. Unaccompanied women of any age or configuration should therefore not be surprised, especially on the West Bank, at sexual exhibitionism or vehement advances. Elsewhere, common prudence is advised, of the kind appropriate in a crowded country where human nature flourishes in all its variety. Serious difficulties should be reported immediately to the nearest police station.

HOSPITALS

There are good hospitals in Cairo and Alexandria. However they operate on a cash basis and patients cannot use foreign medical insurance plans. Some hospitals are:
Anglo-American Hospital Zohoreya, next to the Cairo Tower, Zamalek. Tel: 341-8630.
As Salam International Hospital, Corniche el Nil, Maadi. Tel: 363-8050, 363-4196, 363-8424, 363-8764.
Arab Contractors Hospital Autostrade, Nasr City. Tel: 828-907, 832-534, 838-642, 833-501, 833-408.
Italian Hospital, Abbassia. Tel: 821-433.
Nile Badrawi Hospital, Corniche el Nil, Maadi. Tel: 363-8688, 363-8167/8.
Al Salam Hospital, 3 Syria, Mohandeseen. Tel: 346-7062/3.

PHARMACIES

Pharmacies are usually open from 10am to 10pm and are staffed by competent professionals. Both locally made and imported medication is subsidized by the government and is inexpensive. Some medication requiring prescriptions abroad is sold over the counter in Egypt.

24-hour pharmacies in Cairo:
Attaba: **Attaba Pharmacy**, 17 Midan Attaba. Tel: 910-831.
Central Cairo: **Isaaf Pharmacy**, 3 26th July. Tel: 743-369; **Seif Pharmacy**, Qasr el Aini. Tel: 354-2678.
Maadi: **As Salam International Hospital**, Maadi Corniche. Tel: 842-188; **Esam Pharmacy**, 101 Road 9. Tel: 350-4126; **Mishriki Pharmacy**, 81 Road 153. Tel: 350-3333.
Zamalek: **Zamalek Pharmacy**, 3 Shagaret el Dorr, Zamalek. Tel: 340-2406.

Left Luggage

At the airport luggage is claimed via airline offices. In hotels consult the manager.

Photography

There's no doubt about it: Egypt is a photographer's paradise. The best film speeds for daylight outdoors are low (100 and under), but fast film (400, 1000) is necessary for interiors, high-powered lenses and night shots like the moon over the Nile or the sound and light at the pyramids or Karnak.

Photography is forbidden in security zones, often curiously defined, and a variety of rules pertains to Pharaonic monuments. Signs are usually posted in restricted areas. Heed them. In other areas you are permitted to take photographs if you pay a fee. Fees for still cameras run as high as LE50, for video cameras up to LE200. There are no restrictions on photography anywhere in the historic zone of Cairo.

Scholars and professional photographers working on projects may apply for a special permit to take pictures from the Supreme Council for Antiquities. The procedure may well take some time, and passes are not given out freely.

Photographing individual people requires a bit of common sense and consideration. The Egyptian people are constantly having cameras pushed in their faces, so be courteous and ask first. If a person does not want you to take his or her photo, do not take it. If he or she wants to be paid, pay. If you don't want to pay, don't take the picture. You will find plenty of good shots elsewhere.

Getting Around

Orientation

The Nile flows through the country from south to north. Upper Egypt is therefore the south, Lower Egypt the Delta. Upstream is south, downstream north. Many good maps are available.

From The Airport

All airports in Egypt have a taxi service to city centres, operated on a flat fee basis (ask your airline). In Cairo transport includes limousine, taxi, and bus. Curbside limousine service is offered by Misr Limousine (Tel: 259-9831).

Official Cairo taxis are predominantly black and white and Alexandria taxis are black and orange. There are also Peugeot taxis in a variety of colours and sizes, but they all have an emblem and number painted on the driver's door. Fees are the same as the limousine service.

The Airport Bus Service operates from Terminal 1. The bus leaves when full and stops at Midan Tahrir in downtown Cairo, in Mohandeseen, and along Pyramids Road in Giza.

Public Transport

By Rail

The Egyptian State Railway is a government-owned system founded in 1851 which services the entire Nile Valley down to Aswan, the Red Sea cities of Suez and Port Said, the Delta and Northern Coast cities of Alexandria (two stops) and Mersa Matruh. There are at least half a dozen through trains a day on major routes. Fares are inexpensive, but unless one is travelling with a tour, tickets must be purchased at the main railway stations (in Cairo at the Ramses Station at Midan Ramses).

There is one privately-owned train operating in Egypt, the Wagon Lits sleeper with first-, second- and third-class compartments. The train travels overnight from Cairo to Aswan and back again, leaving Cairo at around 7 in the evenings and arriving in Aswan at 9 the following morning. Bookings are one week in advance through a travel agent or from Compagnie Internationale des Wagons Lits Egypte, 9 Sh Menes, Heliopolis, Tel: 290-8802/4; 48 Sh Giza, Giza, Tel: 348-7354, 349-2365.

By Bus

Air-conditioned buses link most parts of Egypt to Cairo and Alexandria. Seats may be reserved up to two days in advance. There is also a fleet of cheaper non-air-conditioned buses. Although bus times may change without any notice, departures are so frequent that schedule changes are not a problem at all.

The principle carrier to Aswan and Luxor is the Upper Egyptian Bus Company, 4 Yussef Abbas, MN. Tel: 260-9304, 260-9297/8. Departures are from 45 al Azhar and the terminal at Midan Ahmed Helmi. Two buses a day complete the run to Aswan, departing early morning and arriving in the evening.

To Alexandria the main carriers are the West Delta Bus Company, Super Jet, and the Federal Arab Land Transport Company, which leave from behind the Hilton.

BY BUS AROUND CAIRO

The large red-and-white and blue-and-white buses are usually so overcrowded they assault one's sense of private space. They also provide ample opportunity for petty theft and sexual adventure. But here are a few interesting routes for the adventurous tourist:

- Number 400 from the airport to downtown.
- Number 66 from the Nile Hilton in Midan Tahrir to the Khan al-Khalili.
- Number 72 from the Nile Hilton in Midan Tahrir to the Citadel.
- Numbers 800 and 900 from the Mugama'a in Midan Tahrir to the pyramids.

More comfortable are the smaller orange-and-white buses which do not permit standing. Here are a few major routes (from Midan Tahrir):

- Number 24 to Ramses statue, Abbassiyah and Roxi.
- Number 27 to Ramses statue, Abbassiyah and the Airport.
- Number 82 to the pyramids.

Metro & Tram

Both Alexandria and Cairo have tram or metro systems that run through at least part of the city. Trains run every few minutes from early morning (5.30am) to midnight and fares are inexpensive, usually under a pound to the farthest destination.

BY TRAM AROUND ALEXANDRIA

Tram lines in **Alexandria** run only between Ramleh Station (called "Terminus") near the Cecil Hotel and destinations to the east of the city.

- Tram 1, (Bacos line), Ramleh Station to Sidi Bishr.
- Tram 2, (El Nasr line), Ramleh Station to Sidi Bishr.
- Tram 3, Ramleh Station to Sidi Gaber.
- Tram 4, Circular route: Sidi Gaber, Ramleh Station, Sidi Gaber.
- Tram 5, Ramleh Station to San Stefano via Bacos.
- Tram 6, Ramleh Station to Sidi Bishr via Glym.

BY METRO AROUND CAIRO

In **Cairo** the metro system is identified by circular signs with a big red M. The system runs north–south from

Heliopolis to Helwan through the heart of the city. Additional routes, east and west, are currently under construction. Useful stations:

Mubarak Station: Ramses Square with access to the main train station and bus stations to Upper Egypt and the Oases.

Urabi Station: Sh Gala'a. *Al Ahram* newspaper.

Nasser Station: Midan Tawfiqiyyah.

Sadat Station: Midan Tahrir with ten entrances and access to Egyptian Antiquities Museum, the American University in Cairo, Nile Hilton, all major airline offices, and the Mugama'a.

Mar Girgis: at Old Cairo with access to the Coptic Museum, Coptic churches, and Roman fortress.

Zaghlul Station: The National Assembly. Zaghlul monument.

BY TRAM AROUND HELIOPOLIS

Cairo also has tram systems and Heliopolis is served by six tram lines. The major three lines are:

Abd el Aziz Fahmi line (green) from Midan Abd el Monim Riad (behind the Egyptian Museum) via Ramses to Roxi, Merryland, Mahkama, Heliopolis Hospital to the Shams Club;

Nuzha line (red) runs Midan Abd el Monim Riad, Ramses, Roxi, Heliopolis Sporting Club, Salah el Din, and Midan el Higaz to Nuzha;

Mirghani line (yellow) Midan Abd el Monim Riad, Ramses, Roxi, Sharia el Merghani, Saba Emarat, Midan Triomphe, Military College.

By Taxi

For one of the experiences of your life, take an Egyptian taxi. Taxi drivers seem to need to fill every empty space on the road (and sometimes the pavement). All taxis have orange license plates and are identified by a number on the driver's door. Drivers are required to have their license and identity numbers displayed on the dashboard. Sharing a taxi is not unusual. In Cairo and Alexandria taxis ply the streets at all hours of the day or night and can be flagged down. There are also taxi ranks at all the major hotels and public squares.

Official or metered prices are unrealistic and meters are seldom used. The fare should be agreed beforehand. The majority of taxi drivers are honest, but some try to cheat unwary foreigners, especially between five-star hotels and such destinations as the pyramids or Khan al-Khalili. Do not hesitate to ask for assistance from the tourist police. At your destination, pay the fare in exact change and walk away. No tip is expected.

Taxi drivers are friendly, many speak English, some are college graduates moonlighting to supplement their incomes, and most are very eager to be hired by the day. The fee is negotiable. Such an arrangement is ideal for shopping or for seeing several scattered monuments.

Taxis in Luxor and Aswan are easier to find (they line up at all hotels), but for distance travelled they are more expensive than those in Cairo.

Private Transport
Car Rental

Driving in Egypt demands complete attention. The best alternative is to hire a driver and a car together, thus freeing yourself to enjoy the scenery.

Car rental agencies exist at most major hotels. Foreigners must have an International Driver's License and be at least 25 years of age to rent a car in Egypt. Some agencies offer 4x4s, with or without driver, for desert travel. You will need your passport, driver's license, and a prepayment. Credit cards are accepted.

RENTAL AGENCIES

Avis, 16 Maamal el Sukkar, Garden City. Tel: 354-8698.

Bita, 15 Mahmud Bassiouni. Tel: 774-330, 753-130.

Budget, 5 Sh el Maqrizi, Zamalek. Tel: 340-0070, 340-9474; 85 Road 9, Maadi. Tel: 350-2724; 1 Sh Muhammad Ebeid, Heliopolis. Tel: 291-8244.

Max Rent-a-Car, 27 Sh Lubnan, Mohandeseen. Tel: 347-4712/3. Fax: 341-7123. Also for four-wheel drive vehicles with our without experienced desert drivers. Branch office in Sharm el Shaykh.

Sunshine Tours & Services, 106 Muhammad Farid. Tel: 760-559, 393-1955.

Limousines are available for those who want to travel in style:

Bita Limousine Service, Gazirah Sheraton. Tel: 341-1333, 341-1555. Marriott Hotel. Tel: 340-8888.

Budget Limousine Service, Semiramis Intercontinental Hotel. Tel: 355-7171 x 8991.

Limousine Misr, 7 Aziz Bil-Lah, Zeitoun. Tel: 259-9813/4.

Egyptrav, Nile Hilton. Tel: 755-029, 766-548, 393-2644.

The roads that go from Cairo to Upper Egypt are the longest, most congested, and most dangerous in Egypt. Most traffic moving south from Cairo must travel a route along the western shore of the Nile.

It is not advisable to drive at night; vehicles stop dead on the road and turn out their lights; unlit donkey carts move at a snail's pace and are usually not seen until it is too late; and long distance taxis and overloaded trucks travel too fast, often without lights, and are driven by drivers who use "stimulants".

There are petrol stations throughout the country, with those operated by Mobil, Esso, and Shell offering full service with mini-markets on the premises. Fuel, inexpensive and sold by the litre, is available in 90 octane (*tisa'iin*) which is super, or 80 (*tamaniin*), regular. Super is better for most purposes.

Road signs are similar to those used throughout Europe. Driving is on the right-hand side of the road. Speed limits are posted on major highways and are enforced by radar.

Desert Travel

Use common sense. Bring a compass. Check your car. Be sure to have a good spare tyre. Drive on loose sand as you would on snow. If your wheels get stuck in soft sand, put a rug under the back tires and move out slowly. If you spin your tires, you will sink deeper into the sand. If your car breaks down along the road, don't abandon your vehicle; even in remote areas another vehicle will pass by. If you break down on a desert track (you should never leave the main road for long distances with only one vehicle), hike to the nearest road and wait. On all desert travels, have ample food, water, salt tablets, a hat and sunglasses. Cover the head and the back of the neck.

Top up your tank at every petrol station, as the next one may be hundreds of miles away. If your tank is small, carry a jerry can on long hauls like

Dakhla to Farafrah (390 km/243 miles). Dehydration can sneak up on you in desert travel. In an emergency one teaspoon of salt and two tablespoons of sugar in a cup of water will revive you.

Desert driving is very monotonous. Remember you are still on a highway. When you wish to pass, sound your horn very deliberately, in order to make it clear that you are going to do something extraordinary. Egyptian drivers need an extra signal, since nearly all of them over-use the horn even when no-one is around. Another bad habit is misusing lights at night, either leaving them off or flickering the high beams dangerously. When a car is approaching he may blind you. Blink back and he may stop. He may be checking to see if you are awake.

Distances between Cairo and other cities
City/miles/kilometres
north to Alexandria/140/225
    (Delta road)
    Alexandria/138/221
    (desert road)
    Damietta/119/191
    Barrages/15/25
south to Minya/151/236
    Asyut/224/359
    Luxor/415/664
    Esna/449/719
    Edfu/484/775
    Kom Ombo/521/835
    Aswan/550/880
east to Port Said/137/220
    Ismailia/87/140
west to Fayyum/64/103
    Baharia Oasis/197/316
    Farafra Oasis/262/420
    Dakhla Oasis/413/690
    Kharga Oasis/366/586

On Foot

Even in their few green spaces, Alexandria and Cairo are crowded cities, and walking through their business areas is too slow to be satisfactory as exercise. There are plenty of distractions, however, and no-one is ever bored by a stroll through Cairo's historic zone, which should be a highlight of an Egyptian trip. Walking in Luxor and Aswan, however, is a pleasure. These towns are not crowded and there is a pleasant country atmosphere. Hiking as a pastime is not popular in Egypt and

should not be undertaken in remote areas without a guide. Local people may be willing to act as guides in the Eastern Desert, Sinai and the Oases.

Hitchhiking

Hitchhiking is not a common practice in Egypt and is not recommended, especially for women.

Where To Stay

Hotels

Price ranges for double rooms with bath are 5-star, $60–400; 4-star, $35–60; 3-star, $20–40; 2-star, $10–30; 1-star, $6–20. In 3-, 4-, and 5-star hotels, payment for non-Egyptians and nonresident foreigners must be made in foreign currency, by credit card, or in Egyptian currency accompanied by a bank exchange receipt. Motels do not exist in Egypt.

Alexandria
☆☆☆☆☆
Muntazah Sheraton, Corniche, Muntazah. Tel: 968/969-220.
Helnan Palestine Hotel, Montazah Palace Grounds. Tel: 861-799, 958-554.
Ramada Renaissance, 544 Sh. al-Gaysh (Corniche). Tel: 866-111/112.

☆☆☆☆
Salamlik, Montazah Palace. Tel: 860-585.
Venezia, 21 Maydan Al Nasr, Manshiyyah. Tel: 802-698/322.
Windsor, 17 Al Shuhada, Ramleh Station. Tel: 808-700/123.
Pullman Cecil Hotel, 16 Maydan Saad Zaghlul. Tel: 480-7055/7758.
Landmark, 10 Sh. Abdel Salam Aref, San Stefano. Tel: 586/587-7850.

☆☆☆
Agami Palace, Agami. Tel: 433-0386, 422-0230.
Amoun Hotel, 32 Maydan an-Nasir, Manshiyyah. Tel: 807-131/126/253

Corail Hotel, 802 Sh. al-Gaysh (Corniche). Tel: 548-0996.
Delta, 14 Champollion, Azarita. Tel: 482-5542, 482-9053.
Desert Home, Umar Mukhtar, King Mariut. Tel: 484-4434/3572.
Al Haram, 162 Sh. al-Gaysh (Corniche), Cleopatra. Tel: 963-984/974.
Maamura Palace Plaza, 394 Sh. al-Gaysh (Corniche), Zizinia. Tel: 586-2723, 587-5399.
Al Mahrak, 173 Sh. al-Gaysh (Corniche) , Sporting. Tel: 960-737.
Makka, 88 Sh. al-Gaysh (Corniche), Camp César. Tel: 597-3923/3935.
Metropole, 52 Saad Zaghlul, Ramleh. Tel: 482-1467/1466.
Plaza Hotel, 394 Sh. al-Gaysh (Corniche), Zizinia. Tel: 586-2723, 587-5399.

Cairo
☆☆☆☆☆
Cairo Concorde, Cairo International Airport. Tel: 664-242. Located on the fringes of the airport, the Concorde is handy for people who need airport facilities, but far from the centre of Cairo.
Cairo Marriott, Sh. Saray al Gazirah, Zamalek. Tel: 340-8888. The Marriott Hotel has built this facility around the former palace of the Khedive Ismail. Antique furniture graces the halls and public rooms. Restaurants include: Almaz Nightclub operating in the garden during the summer months; Empress Nightclub, open year round in one of the rooms of the palace; Eugénie's Lounge, an elegant cocktail bar in the former rooms of the Empress Eugénie; Garden Promenade, open air café in the Khedive Ismail's garden; Gazirah Grill, French cuisine elegantly served in the former billiard room; Omar's Café, coffeeshop with good snacks and dining; Roy Rogers, a salad bar, with hamburgers and other fast foods; the View, an elegant lounge at the top of the hotel with a panorama of the city.
Cairo Sheraton, Midan el Galaa, Dokki. Tel: 348-8600, 348-8700. One of the first international hotels in Cairo, near the city centre. Aladin, Middle-Eastern cuisine and entertainment; Alhambra, a nightclub with excellent oriental floor show; Arousa al Nil, continental and Middle-Eastern cuisine; also check out La Mamma, one of the best Italian restaurants in Cairo.

Gazirah Sheraton, Gazirah. Tel: 341-3442, 341-1333, 341-1555. South of the Cairo Opera House, the Gazirah Sheraton has an excellent view of the Nile. Gazirah Andalus Café, 24-hour coffeeshop; Abu Kir, seafood out of doors on the Nile; outdoor summer nightclub with an oriental show; Le Gandool Bar; Paradise Island, a floating restaurant on the Nile offering barbecues and mazzahs. The Grill has a Nile view and international cuisine. Kebabgy al Gazirahh offers oriental cuisine.

Heliopolis Mövenpick, Hurriyyah, Heliopolis. Tel: 664-242, 247-0077, 679-799. Situated near the airport. In Mövenpick tradition it offers good food: Al Sarraya, French restaurant; Il Giardino, an Italian *taverna* with snacks and live entertainment; Orangerie, buffet breakfast, lunch and dinner; Gourmet Shop, a pastry shop with Swiss sweets; Karawan, Middle-Eastern cuisine and barbecues in a garden atmosphere; Mövenpick, for Swiss and Middle-Eastern meals and snacks with a special ice cream menu. Papillon disco; St Germain bar.

Helnan Shepheard Hotel, Corniche, Garden City. Tel: 355-3804/14. Planned as a replacement, it now has neither the name, the site, nor the glamour of the original and famous Shepheard's Hotel, which was burnt down in 1952. Caravan offers international and Middle-Eastern meals and snacks; Asia House offers oriental foods; Régence offers French cuisine; and Italiano has pastas and pizzas.

Mena House Oberoi, end of Sh. al-Haram (Pyramid's Road), Giza. Tel: 855-444, 857-999, 855-174. A historic landmark refurbished by the Oberoi chain, the Mena House is the only hotel in Egypt to have a golf course. Outlets include: the Greenery Coffeeshop, a buffet in the garden; Khan al Khalili, a coffeeshop featuring international and Middle-Eastern entrées; the Mogul Room offers Indian food and is one of the best restaurants in Egypt; the Rubayyat is the main dining room with continental and Middle-Eastern meals and live entertainment. Bars include the Mameluke Bar and El Sultan Lounge. Nightclubs are Oasis Summer Nightclub and Abu Nawas Nightclub. The disco is The Saddle.

Meridien, Rawdah Island, entered from the Corniche in Garden City. Tel: 362-1717. A riverfront hotel situated in the heart of the city. Fontana Coffeeshop offers international and Middle-Eastern meals and snacks. Qasr al Rashid provides a Middle-Eastern atmosphere, food and entertainment. La Belle Epoque is a nightclub and restaurant. La Palme d'Or offers French dining to live music. Nafoura is a summer restaurant with Middle-Eastern specialities.

Meridien Heliopolis, 51 Oruba, Heliopolis. Tel: 290-5055, 290-1819. Located on the busy airport road. Outlets include Le Marco Polo Restaurant for Italian food and Café St Germain for snacks. Cakes and pastries at La Boulangerie.

Nile Hilton, Corniche, Midan Tahrir. Tel: 750-666, 740-777. One of the first international hotels in Cairo, the Hilton, located on the Nile in the city centre, has an authentic ancient Egyptian statue in the lobby. Abu Ali's Café serves *sheesha*, green tea, and light snacks on the terrace; Belvedere is the winter night club while the Tropicana is the summer night club around the pool; Ibis Cafe has continental cuisine; Jackie's is the popular disco. The main dining room is the Rotisserie, which offers international cuisine. La Pizzeria offers Italian pizzas and an open buffet; Le Gateau is a pastry shop. Bars include the Safari Bar, Lobby Bar, and the Taverne du Champ de Mars, an Art Nouveau pub offering drinks, snacks, and buffet.

Pullman Maadi Towers, Corniche, Maadi. Tel: 350-6092/3. On the Nile to the south of the city centre, the Pullman offers a wonderful panorama of the desert plateau on the west bank of the Nile including the pyramids of Giza, Saqqarah, and Dahshur. Outlets include Le Clovis for international cuisine; Maadi Café, open 24 hours; and Darna for traditional Egyptian food.

Ramada Renaissance, Cairo/Alexandria Desert Road. Tel: 538-995/6. North of the pyramids in a former citrus and palm grove, this hotel has excellent grounds. Outlets include: Garden Coffeeshop featuring continental meals and snacks; Les Fontaines offers continental food; and Sultan, with Middle Eastern food. Habiba is the nightclub. Golden Club is the disco.

Ramses Hilton, 1115 Corniche, Maspero. Tel: 777-444, 758-000, 744-400. Located on the Nile in one of the busiest sections of the city, the 36-storey Ramses Hilton has no grounds, but its upper floors offer an interesting panorama of Cairo. Citadel Grill offers elegant dining with seafood and grills; Falafel offers Middle Eastern foods and snacks; La Patisserie coffeeshop has excellent cakes and ice-cream specialities. Terrace Café coffeeshop presents international and Middle-Eastern meals and snacks. Bars include Club 36 with piano entertainment and a panorama of the city.

Safir ETAP Hotel, 4 Midan Misaha, Dokki. Tel: 348-2424, 348-2828, 348-2626. In a residential square not far from the city centre, the Safir is a favourite hotel for visitors from the Gulf states. Diar El Andalos caters Lebanese and Middle-Eastern cuisine with *sheesha*; Filaka coffeeshop has an excellent daily buffet; Gazirat al Dahab offers French and Middle-Eastern food; Khan Morgan is the bar.

Semiramis Intercontinental, Corniche, Garden City. Tel: 355-3900, 355-3800. Built on the Nile-side site of the legendary Semiramis Hotel, the current hotel offers good facilities but no grounds. Restaurants include: Feluka Brasserie featuring Middle-Eastern and continental open buffets; Far East offering oriental foods; Semiramis Grill with French cuisine; Sultana's Disco offering international live shows.

Siag Pyramids, 59 Mariutia, Saqqarah Road. Tel: 856-022/623, 857-399. Near the desert with a view of the Giza pyramids, the Siag is host to the Pharaoh's Rally every October. Dining room only, but excellent food.

Sonesta, 4 Tayaran, Nasr City. Tel: 611-066, 609-444. Le Café for pastries and breads; the Garden Grill is an open-air summer restaurant featuring grills; Gondola offers Italian dining; Borobodur offers Indonesian food; Greenhouse coffeeshop has international meals and snacks; Rib Room is a steakhouse. Bars include Arabic Lounge and Speke's Bar. The disco is Sindbad.

Swissôtel El-Salam Heliopolis, 61 Abdel Hamid Badawi, Heliopolis. Tel: 245-5155, 245-2155. Although the Hyatt is far from the centre of town, it is housed in a former palace with lovely grounds. Restaurants include

Café Jardin Coffeeshop, with a buffet; Marquis for light snacks; Ezbetna, for traditional Egyptian foods; Whispers, a bar offering a happy hour. Ya Salam is the Nightclub and Vito's is the disco.

☆☆☆☆
Atlas Zamalek, 20 Gam'at al Dowal al Arabiya, Mohandeseen. Tel: 346-4175, 346-5782, 346-6569. Chez Zanouba is Middle-Eastern dining while Kahraman is French dining. Tamango is the hottest dance spot in Cairo.
Baron Hotel, Heliopolis off Oruba, Heliopolis. Tel: 291-2468/7, 291-5757. Le Baron coffeeshop features international and Middle-Eastern meals and snacks; the Terrace, caters an international buffet each evening; Baron Patisserie; Le Jardin is the daily buffet. Pasha is the bar.
Bel Air Cairo Hotel, Muqattam. Tel: 922-685, 922-816, 922-884. The only hotel on the Muqattam hills, but you must leave the grounds to have a view of the city.
Jolie Ville Mövenpick, Cairo/Alexandria Desert Road. Tel: 855-118, 855-539, 855-612. Newly reopened after a fire. Mövenpick Restaurant offers daily buffets; Orangerie, breakfast, lunch, and dinner buffets; Pavillon des Pyramides, French dining. Terrace, snacks.
Novotel, Cairo Airport, Heliopolis. Tel: 671-715, 679-080, 661-330.

☆☆☆
Cairo Inn, 26 Syria, Mohandeseen. Tel: 349-0661/2/3. Eagle Arms English pub; Taberna Espanola with Spanish entertainment in the evening. Excellent Spanish food.
Cleopatra, 2 Bustan, Midan Tahrir. Tel: 708-751.
Egyptel, 93 Merghani, Heliopolis. Tel: 661-716.
El Borg, Saray al Gazirah, Zamalek. Tel: 341-7655.
El Nil, 12 Ahmed Ragheb, Garden City. Tel: 354-2808.
Khan al Khalili, 7 Bosta, Attaba. Tel: 900-271.
President, 22 Dr. Taha Hussein, Zamalek. Tel: 341-6751, 341-3195. Cairo Cellar, excellent food. Lebanese *Mezzah* a speciality.

☆☆
El Hussein, Midan Hussein, al-Azhar. Tel: 918-664, 918-089.
El Nil Garden, 131 Abdel Aziz al Saoud, Manial. Tel: 985-767, 983-931.
Viennoise, 11 Mahmoud Bassiouni. Tel: 751-949, 743-153.
Windsor, 19 Alfy Bey. Tel: 915-277, 915-810.

Unclassified
Anglo-Swiss Pensione, 14 Champollion. Tel: 751-479.
Bodmin House, 17 Hasan Sabri, Zamalek. Tel: 340-2842.
Dokki House, 42 Madina al Munawara, Dokki. Tel: 705-611, 705-713.
Garden City House, 23 Kamal el Din, Garden City. Tel: 354-8126. Rub elbows with archaeologists and anthropologists.
Hotel of Youth & Sports, Masaken, Madinat Nasr. Tel: 260-6991/2.
Mayfair Pension, 9 Aziz Uthman, Zamalek. Tel: 340-7315.
Pensione Roma, 169 Muhammad Farid (Emad ad-Din). Tel: 342-0055, 341-8447/8.

Minya

☆☆☆☆☆
PLM Azur Nefertiti, Corniche. Tel: 326-281. Offers a view of the Nile.

☆☆
Palace, Main Square. Tel: 327-071. A surrealistic experience in a clean place.
Ibn Khasib, 5 Sharia Ragib. Tel: 24535. In a garden.
Akhenaten, Corniche. Tel: 325-918. View of the Nile. Clean and inexpensive.

Asyut

☆☆☆☆☆
Badr Hotel, Salah Salem. The only recommended hotel in Asyut.

Luxor

☆☆☆☆☆
Club Mediterranee, Sharia Khalid ibn Walid. Tel: 377-7575. Typical Club Med facilities overlooking the Nile.
Hilton International Luxor, Village of New Karnak, north of Luxor. Tel: 384-933. Hilton hospitality overlooking the Nile.
Mövenpick Jolie Ville, Crocodile Island, south of Luxor. Tel: 384-855. Excellent food and excellent accommodation in a pastoral atmosphere.

PLM Azur, Corniche. Tel: 382-166. The former ETAP in the heart of the city.
Sheraton, Awamiya. Tel: 384-544. Offering several restaurant outlets overlooking the Nile.
Winter Palace, Corniche. The granddaddies of hotels in Luxor, the Winter Palaces, both old and new, have recently been renovated by the Pullman Hotel chain.

☆☆☆☆
EGOTEL, located behind Luxor Temple.
Isis, Sharia Khalid ibn Walid. Tel: 382-750.

☆☆☆
Horus, Sharia Suk. Tel: 382-165.
Phillip, Sharia Nefertiti. Tel: 282-284.
Windsor, Sharia Nefertiti. Tel: 382-847.

☆☆ *and under*
New Karnak. Across from the train station. Tel: 382-427.
Happy Home. Off Mahatta. Cheap, friendly, and clean.

Aswan

☆☆☆☆☆
Aswan Oberoi, Elephantine Island. Tel: 762-835. An aggressive, rather ugly, modern tower which offers a fine view of the river.
New Cataract, Corniche el Nil. Tel: 333-222. Next to the Old Cataract.

☆☆☆☆
Cleopatra, Sharia Saad Zaghloul. Tel: 322-983.
Old Cataract, Corniche el Nil. Tel: 323-222. Grand, exotic and colonial, worth visiting even if you're not intending to stay there.
Amon Village, Sahara City. Tel: 24826.

☆☆☆
Hapi Hotel, Abdel el Tahrir. Tel: 322-028.

☆☆ *and under*
Abu Shelib Hotel, Abdel el Tahrir. Tel: 323-051.
Hathor Hotel, Corniche el Nil. Tel: 322-590.

Hurghada

☆☆☆☆☆
Hurghada Al Nour Hilton Resort. Tel (Cairo): 575-8000, 575-4400, 768-888.

Paradisio, Al-Guwna, 22 km north of Hurghada, with free shuttle to Hurghada and Hurghada airport. Tel: (065) 447-934/5/6/7/8/9. Cairo reservations, Tel: 348-5949, 708-919.

☆☆☆☆
Magawish Village, Safaga Highway, New Hurghada. Tel: (062) 441-759, (065) 446-759. 442-759. Fax: 065-442-255, 446-255. Cairo reservations: Misr Travel, P.O. Box 1000, 1 Sh. Talaat Harb. Tel: 393-0077, 393-0010, 393-0063. Fax: 392-4440. Telex: 20771, 22777.

Mashrabia Village Hotel, Corniche, New Hurghada. Tel: (065) 443-330/1, 443-602/603. Cairo reservations: AMCON Group, 32 Sh. Al-Misaha, Duqqi. Tel: 360-0736. 348-5381. Telex: 20021 AMCON UN.

Sheraton Hurghada, Corniche, New Hurghada. Tel: (065) 442-000, 440-779, 440-604. Fax: 065-443-333. Telex: 92750 SHRGA UN. Cairo Office P.O. Box 125 Sh. Urman, Gizah. Cairo Tel: 348-8215. Telex: 227161/ 93355 UN.

Sonesta Beach Resort. (065) 443-661. Fax: 064-443-660. Cairo reservations: Sonesta Hotel, 4 Sh. at-Tayaran, Madinat Nasr. Tel: 262-8111, 261-7100. Fax: 619-981, 263-5731.

☆☆☆
Arabiyya Village. Tel: (065) 441-790, 441-799. Cairo reservations: Victoria Hotel, 66 Sh. Gumhurriyyah. Tel: 910-771, 918-038, 918-869, 915-707. Fax: 913-008.

Giftun Village, Corniche, New Hurghada. Tel: (065) 440-665, 441-669, 442-667, 440-666. Fax: (065) 440-666. Cairo reservations: same as Arabiyya Village above.

Hur Palace, Corniche, New Hurghada. Tel: (065) 441-710, 440603, (065) 443-710, 440-710. Fax: 065-442-603. Cairo Tel: 341-9358.

Jasmine Village, Safaga Highway, New Hurghada. Tel: (065) 442-442. Fax: 065-442-441. Cairo reservations: Hamburg Hotel building, 18 Sh. Bursa, Maydan Tawfiqiyyah, Cairo. Tel: 744-447, 777-238. Fax: 760-159.

Samaka Holiday Village, Corniche, New Hurghada, Tel: (065) 440-227/8. Cairo reservations: Zoser Tours, 54 Sh. Nazih Khalifa, Heliopolis. Tel: 258-3028, 258-0678, 259-0509.

Shadwan Golden Beach Village Hotel, Corniche, Dahar. Tel: (065) 442-240, 441-044, 441-007. Fax: 443-045. Cairo reservations: Cairo Express Travel. Tel: 245-9363, 245-9594, 243-1316. Fax: 248-4038.

☆☆ and unclassified
Abu Ghazal, Dahar. Tel: (065) 441-699, 440-617, 440-618.

Abu Ramada, Dahar. Tel: (065) 440-617.

Africa, Dahar. Tel: (065) 440-629.

Al Gazirah, Dahar. Tel: (065) 441-707, 441-708.

Andalus, Dahar. Tel: (065) 440-639.

Arabia Beach Hotel, Corniche, New Hurghada. Tel: (065) 443-790, 441-610. Fax: 065-443-792.

La Bambola, Corniche, New Hurghada. Tel: (065) 442-085. Fax: 065-442-013.

Beach Albatross Resort Hotel, Tel: (065) 442-571.

El Mashrabiya, Corniche, New Hurghada. Tel: (065) 443-330. 441-190. Fax: 065-443344.

El Mirette, Cairo reservations: 13 Sh, Ahmad Sami Sa'id Duqqi. Tel: 707-798.

El Morgan, Corniche, New Hurghada. Tel: (065) 440-974.

Friendship Village, Corniche, New Hurghada. Tel: (065) 443-100, 441-717. Fax: 065-443-109.

Geisoum Village, Dahar. Tel: (065) 446-692.

Gobal Hotel, Dahar. Tel: (065) 440-623.

Grand Hotel, Corniche, New Hurghada. Tel: (065) 443-749. Fax: 065-443-750. Cairo, tel: 754-717.

Happy Land, Dahar. Tel: (065) 440-118.

Hurghada (Ghardaqa) Hotel, Dahar. Tel: (065) 440-393.

Hurghada Beach. Tel: (065) 443-710.

Hotel Intercontinental. Tel: (065) 443-911.

Luxor Palace, Dahar. Tel: (065) 441-458.

Moon Valley Hotel, Corniche, New Hurghada. (065) 440-074.

Nesmat Amal, Dahar. Tel: (065) 441-816.

New Mino Hotel, Dahar. Tel: (065) 440-105.

La Perla, Tel: (065) 443-280.

Princess Club Village, Corniche, New Hurghada. Tel: (065) 441-717, 443-100. Cairo reservations: 14 Sh. Marashli, Zamalek. Tel: 340-1239.

Ramoza, Dahar. Tel: (065) 440-608.

Reem Hotel, Dahar. Tel: (065) 441-120.

Sahara Hurghada Resort. Tel: (065) 447-556.

Al-Samak Club. Tel: (065) 443-041.

Sand Beach Hotel, Corniche. Tel: (065) 447-992. Fax: 065-447-822.

Scuba Doo Diving Centre, Moon Valley. Tel: (065) 440-074.

Seahorse Hotel, Sh. Al-Bahr. Dahar. Tel: (065) 447-016, 441-704, 441-699. Fax: 065-443-704.

Sealand Village, Sharm an-Naga, Safaga Highway, New Hurghada. 47 Sh. Al-Falaki. Tel: 354-5060, 354-5576. Telex: 94109 SEENA UN.

Seol Hotel, Dahar. Tel: (065) 441-539.

Sherry Hotel, Sigalla. Cairo Tel: (065) 850-586, 866-257.

Sindbad Beach Resort. Tel: (065) 443-261.

Three Corners Village, 2 Corniche, Dahar. Tel: (065) 447-816, 441-816, 441-515. Cairo Tel: 347-0850/347-6840.

Westin Resort. Tel: (065) 443-250.

Sinai

☆☆☆☆☆
Egoth Oberoi, Al-Arish. (068) 383-3444. Cairo Tel: 387-7444.

Fayrouz Hilton, Na'ama Bay, Sharm ash-Shaykh. Tel: (062) 769-400.

Mövenpick Hotel Jolie Ville, Na'ama Bay, Sharm ash-Shaykh. Tel: (062) 6700-100, 600-1/2/3. Fax: 600-111. Cairo reservations: Mövenpick Heliopolois. Tel: 696-799. Fax: 667-374.

Sharm Hilton Residence, Na'ama Bay, Sharm ash-Shaykh. Tel: (062) 770-424, 770-466.

Taba Hilton, Taba. Tel: (062) 768-200, 736-677, 747-616, 770-393, 771-888, 770-655. Cairo reservations: Ramses Hilton Hotel. Tel: 744-400, 777-444, extension 3146.

☆☆☆☆
Aquamarine Pullman Hotel, Na'ama Bay, Sharm ash-Shaykh. Tel: (062) 600-178/9. Cairo reservations: Cairo Pullman Hotels, 12 Al-Ubur Buildings, Madinat Nasr. Tel: 609-710, 262-1679. Fax: 262-8115.

Baraka Village, Sharm al-Maya. (062) 770-550.

Clifftop Village, Sharm ash-Shaykh. Tel: (062) 770-448.

Ghazala Hotel and Resort, Na'ama Bay, Sharm ash-Shaykh. Tel: (082) 771-284, 600-150/1/2/3/4, 770-217, 771-348. Fax: (062) 771-349. Cairo reservations: South Sinai Travel, 79 Sh. al-Mirghany, Heliopolis. Tel: 664-013, 664-510, 672-064, 672-441. Fax: 290-9189.

☆☆☆
Bawaki Beach Hotel, Bawaki Beach, 18 km north of Nuwayba. Cairo reservations: 16 26 Yulyu, 4th floor, Tel: 745-273.
Dahab Holiday Village, Dahab. Tel: (062) 772-220, 770-788, 770-301. Pullman International Cairo. Tel: 290-8802, 290-8804, 660-249, 679-577.
Bawaki Village, Bawaki Beach, 15 km. north of Nuwayba. Tel (Cairo): 745-273.
Helnan Marina Sharm, Na'ama Bay, Sharm ash-Shaykh. Tel: (062) 762-704. Cairo reservations: Helnan Shepheard Hotel. Tel: 355-3800/900, 393-0200, 393-0301.
Nuwayba Holiday Village, Nuwayba. (062) 762-701, 768-832, 770-393. Cairo Tel: 768-832, Reservations c/o Sinai Hotels and Diving Clubs, 32 Sh. Sabri Abu Alam, PO Box 2366, Cairo 11111. Tel: 393-0200, 393-0301, 3931543. Telex: 94002 OHTEG UN.
Sanafir Hotel, Na'ama Bay, Sharm ash-Shaykh. Tel: (062) 600-197/8. Fax: 600-195/6. Cairo reservations: Spring Tours, 3 Sh. Sayyid al-Bakri, Zamalek. Tel: 341-5972/3/4/5. Fax: 341-5967.
Al Sayadin Tourist Village, Nuwayba. Tel: (062) 757-398. Cairo reservations: Sharm Tours, 13 Sh. Dr. Ahmad Khalil, Maydan al-Higaz, Heliopolis. Tel: 245-4183. Fax: 247-6535.
Sallyland. Stone-built chalets, 30 kms north of Nuwayba. Tel: (062) 743-689.
Semiramis El Arish, Al-Arish. Tel: (068) 344-166/7/8. Fax: (068) 344-168.

☆☆ and unclassified
Basata. A simple, charming and scrupulously clean campsite 29 km north of Nuwayba. Communal cooking and dining facilities. Cairo Tel: 350-1929.
Clifftop Village, Sharm al-Shaykh. Tel: (062) 770-448.
Club Aquasun and Diving Center. Between Nuwayba and Taba. Cairo reservations: Dar House of Travel, 11 Sh. A'naab, Muhandisiin. Tel: 360-3293. Fax: 348-5479.

Gaffyland, Sharm ash-Shaykh. Tel: 600-210/11.
Kanbesh Village, Na'ama Bay, Sharm ash-Shaykh. Tel: (062) 600-184/5/6. Fax: (062) 770-980.
Tiran Village, Na'ama Bay, Sharm ash-Shaykh. Tel: (062) 600-220/1/2.

Eating Out
Where To Eat

In addition to their regular fare, 5-star hotels often fly in European chefs for week long extravaganzas. See the hotel section for listing of hotel restaurants. The list below tries to provide a good cross section of restaurants outside hotels. By international standards, even the most expensive restaurants in Egypt are cheap. No restaurant has a good wine list – local beer is the preferred option and some establishments do not serve alcohol.

Alexandria
Cosmopolitan in its attitudes towards food, as in other respects, Alexandria is most famous for seafood and coffeehouses. Many people also claim that its pizzerias and their products are the best in the Mediterranean. All Alexandrian hotels have restaurants, which are generally as undistinguished as they are easy to find. All but two have been omitted from the list below.

SEAFOOD
Aflatun. Sh. al-Gaysh (Corniche), Miami. Tel 548-7024.
Athineios (coffeehouse). 21 Sh. Saad Zaghlul (Iskandir al-Akbar) near the Ramleh tram terminus. Tel: 482-0421.
Bella Vista. 43 Sh. al-Gaysh (Corniche). Tel: 560-0628.
Calithea. 180 26 Yulyu (Corniche), Ramleh Station. Tel: 489-7754.
Délices (coffeehouse). 46 Sh. Saad Zaghlul. Tel: 482-5657.
Denis (take-away orders a speciality). 1 Sh. Ibn Bassam, between Maydan Saad Zaghlul and the Corniche. Tel: 483-0457.
Farag Fish Restaurant. 7 Sh. Suq Tabakhayn. Tel: 811-047.

Fish Abu Ashraf International. 28 Sh. Safar Bash al-Gumruk. Tel: 816-597 . No alcohol.
Fish Market. Marine Scout Club Building, 26 26 Yulyu (Corniche), Ramleh Station, near Maydan Muhammad Ali. Tel: 805-114/119, 809-842.
International Seafood. 606 Sh. al-Gaysh (Corniche). Tel: 873-951, 873-154.
Kaddoura (Qaddura). 74 Yulyu (Corniche), Ramleh Station. Tel: 800-967 .
Le Roi. 716 Sh. Al-Gaysh (Corniche), Asafra. Tel: 871-187.
Lorantus. 44 Sh. Safiya Zaghlul. Tel: 482-2200.
Nassar. 145 Sh. al-Gaysh (Corniche), Ramleh. Tel: 809-724, 805-370.
Pastroudis (the city's most famous coffeehouse) 39 Tariq Gamal ᶜAbd an-Nasir (al-Hurriyyah) overlooking the Kom ad-Dikka excavations. Tel: 492-9609.
Samakmak. 42 Sh. Qasr Ras At-Tin, Anfushi. Tel: 811-560.
Sea Gull. Al-Maks. On the road to Agami. Tel: 445-5575. Next to Al-Mina al-Faransawi. Tel: 445-8777.
Sea Horse. Helnan Palestine Hotel, Muntazah Palace Grounds. Tel: 547-3500.
Trianon (Le Salon – classic Alexandrian coffeehouse and restaurant, with superb period décor, indifferent coffee and excellent chocolate). 52 Maydan Saad Zaghlul at Sh. Safiya Zaghlul. Tel: 482-0986, 482-0973, 482-7053.
Zephyrion. 41 Sh. Khalid ibn Walid, Abu Qir. Tel: 546-2016, 560-1319.

GREEK
Taverna al-Raml. 1 Maydan Saad Zaghlul, Ramleh Station. Tel: 482-8189.
Taverna Iqbal. 31 Sh. Iqbal. Tel: 586-4802.
Taverna Manshiyya. 6 Sh. Tahrir, Manshiyya. Tel: 810-391, 804-907.
International
Alexander's Terrace. Ramada Renaissance Hotel, 544 Sh. al-Gaysh (Corniche), Sidi Bishr. Tel: 548-3977, 549-0935.
Le Clovis. Pullman Romance Hotel, 303 Sh. al-Gaysh (Corniche). Tel: 587-6429, 587-6508.
Coach House. Agami Beach. No telephone.
Sayyid Darwish. 202 Sh. al-Gaysh (Corniche), Ramleh Station. Tel: 482-8938 .

Mustafa Darwish. 202 Sh. al-Gaysh (Corniche), Ramleh Station. Tel: 482-9021/9680. No alcohol.

Delta Hotel. (French) 14 Sh. Champollion. Tel: 482-9053.

El Foutah. San Stefano Hotel, Maydan San Stefano. Tel: 526-3580, 586-3587.

Lord's Inn (German). San Stefano Hotel, 12 Sh. Muhammad Ahmad al-Afifi, San Stefano. Tel: 586-5664.

Lord's Inn Center (Café Fleur, Pianola, Victor's). 17 Sh. Suria, Rushdi. Tel: 546-2016. Coat and tie required.

McDonald's. 66 Sh. Safiya Zaghlul, Ramlah Station, Alexandria. Tel: 483-2466, 483-2802, 483-2639. 68 Sh. Bitash, Al-Bitash, Agami. Tel: 433-2198/92/95. 253 Sh. al-Gaysh (Corniche), Stanley. Tel: 541-0249, 545-6885, 545-6899.

Ras al Tin. Landmark Hotel, Maydan San Stefano. Tel: 586-7850, 587-7850/1.

Refeara. Muntazah Palace, Muntazah. Tel: 457-4228.

Regency. Regency Hotel, 696 Corniche, Miami. Tel: 871-547, 870-592. Nightclub with band, belly-dancer.

San Claude. Regency Hotel, 696 Corniche, Miami. Tel: 871-547, 870-592.

San Giovanni Restaurant (French) San Giovanni Hotel, Sh. al Gaysh (Corniche). Tel: 546-773/4/5.

Santa Lucia (Alexandria's most famous restaurant, a favourite of many celebrities. Its beef and veal are more highly regarded than its seafood). 40 Sh. Safiya Zaghlul. Tel: 482-0332, 482-4240.

Pastroudis Love Boat. Glymenopoulo. Tel: 586-4470.

Sophia Napoulo. (The thriving coffee shop at the front selling only roasted beans and ground coffee hides the excellent modestly priced restaurant in the rear). 21 Sh. Saad Zaghlul. Tel: 483-1517.

Stereo Belvedere (bar, disco). 164 Sh. 26 July (Corniche). Tel: 807-350.

Weedo's. Agami. Tel: 530-1649.

ITALIAN

Chez Gaby au Ritrovo (pizzeria). On the left side of an alley running southward from 22 Tariq al-Gamal ᶜAbd an-Nasir (al-Hurriyyah) at the Misrland Travel office, east of La Pizzeria. Tel: 483-4306, 483-4404, 483-8377, 683-4300.

Italian Restaurant. Ramada Renaissance Hotel, 544 Sh. al-Gaysh (Corniche), Sidi Bishr. Tel: 548-3977, 549-0935.

Manouche. Ma'amura Beach. No telephone.

Petro. Sh. al-'Assal, 'Agami. No telephone.

La Pizzeria (pizza). 14 Tariq Gamal ᶜAbd an-Nasir (al-Hurriyyah). Tel: 483-8082.

ORIENTAL

Dynasty. Ramada Renaissance Hotel, 544 Sh. al-Gaysh (Corniche), Sidi Bishr. Tel: 548-3977, 549-0935.

New China. Corail Hotel 802 Sh. al-Gaysh (Corniche). Tel: 548-0996 .

Paxy's (Korean and Chinese). Amoun Hotel, 32 Maydan an-Nasir, Manshiyyah. Tel: 807-131/126/253.

MIDDLE EASTERN

Agami Palace Hotel Restaurant. Agami Palace (Qasr al-'Agami), Agami. Tel: 433-0386, 422-0230.

Andrea. Sh. al-'Assal, Agami. 433-327. Summertime only

Au Privé (Lebanese). 14 Tariq Al-Gamal cAbd an-Nasir (Hurriyyah) (between Pastroudis and Sh. Nabi Danyal). Tel: 483-8082.

Chicken Tikka Grill Restaurants (speciality: grilled chicken). Muntazah Palace Park. Tel: 547-4338. No alcohol.

Eino. 66 Sh. Safiya Zaghlul, Ramleh Station. Tel: 482-8212.

El Mashrabia. Ma'amura Beach. Tel: 567-2603.

Omar al Khayam. 200 26 Yulyu (Corniche), Ramleh Station. Tel: 483-3665, 482-5444, 483-3169.

Oriental Restaurant. Corail Hotel 802 Sh. al-Gaysh (Corniche). Tel: 548-0996.

Restaurant Husni. 30 Safar Basha, Ras at-Tin. Tel: 812-350. No alcohol.

Muntazah Grill. Muntazah Palace Park. Tel: 547-5438.

Sindband. 21 Maydan al-Nasir, Mandshiyyah. Tel: 802-399, 802-376.

SPECIALITIES

Gelati ᶜAzza. (The only place in Egypt still regularly serving *dondurma*, the gorgeously white and sticky Turkish ice-cream that evokes instant nostalgia in older Egyptians). 11 Sh, 26 July (Corniche). Tel: 801-943.

Cairo

Four- and five-star hotels have small coffee shops and restaurants from ethnic eateries to smart supper clubs with live music. Outstanding are:

Aladin (Lebanese). Cairo Sheraton Hotel, Duqqi. Tel: 348-8600.

Le Bistro (French). El Gezirah Sheraton Hotel, Gazirah. Tel: 341-1333, 341-1555.

Cairo Cellar. President Hotel, 22 Sh. Taha Husayn, Zamalek. Tel: 341-3195/341-6751.

Le Champollion (French). Forte Méridien Hotel, Rawdah opposite Garden City. Tel: 362-1717.

Darna (Egyptian). Sofitel Maᶜadi Towers Hotel, Maᶜadi. Tel: 350-6092.

Florencia. Flamenco Hotel, tenth floor, 2 Gazirat al-Wusta, Zamalek. Tel: 340-0815.

La Gondola (Italian/Turkish). Sonesta Hotel, 4 Sh. at-Tayaran (Airport Road), Madinat Nasr. Tel: 609-444.

Ibis Café (Egyptian/International). Nile Hilton Hotel. Tel: 765-666, 767-444. Lunch or light supper: central, fast, efficient, and reliable.

Lebanon Corner (Lebanese *mazzah*). El Gezirah Sheraton Hotel, Gazirah. Tel: 341-1333, 341-1555.

Marco Polo. Forte Mériden Heliopolis Hotel, Sh. at-Tayaran (Airport Road), Heliopolis (Misr al-Gadidah). Tel: 290-5055, 290-1819.

Moghul Room (Indian). Mena House Oberoi Hotel, Pyramids Road (Sh. al-Haram), Gizah. Tel: 85-5444/7999 Ext. 661.

Rôtisserie. Nile Hilton Hotel, Cairo. Tel: 765-666, 767-444.

Spaghetteria. Semiramis Intercontinental Hotel, Garden City. Tel: 355-7171. Do-it-yourself pasta dishes with a wide choice of sauces.

The Grill. Semiramis International Hotel, Garden City. Tel: 355-7171.

Yamato (Japanese). Ramses Hilton Hotel Annexe, Maspero. Tel: 752-3999.

Establishments outside major hotels offer even more variety. The following is a list of some of the better-known.

FISH AND SEAFOOD

Flying Fish (seafood). 166 Sh. an-Nil, Aguza. Tel: 349-3234.

Kaddura (fish, home delivery). 66 Sh. Gam^ciat ad-Dawal al-^cArabiyyah, Maydan al-Hur, Muhandisiin. Tel: 360-8660, 360-8665.

Rossini's (Italian seafood). 55 Sh. ^cUmar ibn al-Kattab, Heliopolis (Misr al-Gadidah). Tel: 291-8282, 417-1401.

Seahorse. 5 Corniche an-Nil, en route to Ma^cadi. Tel 363-8830.

Silver Fish. 39 Sh. Muhiy ad-Din Abu'l-^cIzz, Duqqi. Tel: 349-2272/ 73.

Vue des Pyramides/Christo (fish). 10 Sh. al-Haram, Gizah. Tel: 383-3582.

FRENCH

La Charmerie. 110B Sh. 26 Yulyu (July), Zamalek. Tel: 340-2645, 340-9640.

La Cloche d'Or. 3 Sh. Abu'l-Fida, Zamalek. 340-2314, 340-2268.

Creeks (French/International, home delivery) 15 Maydan Ahmad Sami al-Sa^cid, off Sh. ath-Thawra, Muhandisiin. Tel: 360-7326.

Don Quichotte (French/International). 9A Sh. Ahmad Hishmat, Zamalek. Tel: 340-6415.

Piano, Piano (French/Chinese). World Trade Center, 1191 Corniche an-Nil, Bulaq. Reservations only.

INTERNATIONAL

Angus Brasserie. 34 Sh. Yehya Ibrahim, Zamalek. Tel: 341-1321.

Cairo Cellar. President Hotel, 22 Sh. Taha Husayn, Zamalek Tel: 341-3195/ 341-6751.

Caroll. 12 Sh. Qasr an-Nil, Cairo. Tel: 746-739.

Le Chalet (International/Swiss). Sh. al-Nil (Gizah Corniche, Sh. Gamal ^cAbd an-Nasir), Gizah Tel: 348-5321. Fax: 672-191.

Le Chantilly (International/Swiss). 11 Sh. Baghdad, Heliopolis (Misr al-Gadidah). Tel: 669-026, 665-620. Fax: 672-191.

Le Château (International/Swiss). Sh. al-Nil (Gizah Corniche, Sh. Gamal ^cAbd an-Nasir), Gizah Tel: 348-5321. Fax: 672-191.

La Chesa (International/Swiss). 2 Sh. ^cAdli. Cairo. Tel: 393-9360. Fax: 672-191.

Estoril. 114 Sh. Tal^cat Harb (may also be entered from passage behind Air France between Sh Tal^cat Harb and Qasr an-Nil). Tel: 5780-3102. A Cairo institution.

Katcho's 417 (Middle Eastern/International). World Trade Center, ground level. 1191 Corniche an-Nil, Bulaq. Tel: 578-6324.

Pub 28. 28 Sh. Shagar ad-Durr, Zamalek. Tel: 340-0927.

Swiss Air Restaurants. See **Le Chalet. Le Chantilly, Le Château, and La Chesa**.

ITALIAN

Al Dente (pasta, take-away). 26 Sh. Bahgat ^cAli, Zamalek. Tel: 340-9117.

Il Camino (Italian). Burg Riyadh, 5 Sh. Wissa Wasif (off Gizah Corniche, Sh. Gamal ^cAbd an-Nasir) 6th Floor, Gizah. Tel: 737-592/595. No alcohol.

Il Capo (Italian). 22 Shari^c Taha Husayn, next to the President Hotel. 341-3870. Catering, party and delivery service.

La Casetta (Italian). 32 Sh. Kambiz, Muhandisiin. Tel: 348-7970. 139 Sh. al-Mirghani, Heliopolis (Misr al-Gadidah). Tel: 291-0219. Residence Hotel, 11 Sh. 18, Ma^cadi. Tel: 350-7276. 28 Sh. 9. Muqattam. Tel: 505-039.

Cortigiano (Italian). 44 Sh. Michel Bakhum, Duqqi. Tel: 710-647.

El Patio Italian Restaurant and **Surprise Piano Bar**. 5 Sh. Sayyid al-Bakri, Zamalek. Tel: 340-2702.

Snaps. Siag Pyramids Hotel, Saqqarah Road, Gizah. Tel: 385-6022, 385-3005, 385-6623.

Tia Maria (home-made pasta, savories, take-away). 32 Sh. Jiddah, Muhandisiin. Tel: 713-273.

MEXICAN

Chili's (American, Tex-Mex). 13 Sh. ath-Thawra, Heliopolis (Misr al-Gadidah). Tel: 417-5299. 2 Sh. al-Fawakih, at the corner of Sh. ath-Thimar, behind the Mustafa Mahmud Mosque, Muhandisiin.

Mermaid Columbus. 54 Sh. 9, Ma^cadi. Tel: 351-2778.

MIDDLE-EASTERN

Andrea's (Speciality: spit-grilled chicken). 14 Maryutiyyah Canal (Kirdassah Road), Gizah. Tel: 383-1133. 47 Sh. 7, Ma^cadi. Tel: 351-1369. Al-Hadaba al-Alia, Muqattam. Tel: 902-017.

Arabesque. 6 Sh. Qasr an-Nil, Cairo Tel: 574-7898, 575-9896.

Al Dar (Egyptian). Saqqarah Road, Gizah. Tel: 852-289.

Felfela (Egyptian) 15 Sh. Hoda Sha^carawi with an entrance at 15 Sh. Tal^cat Harb, Cairo. Tel: 392-2833. Corniche at Sh. al-Nahda, Ma^cadi. Tel: 350-3327. Maryutiyyah Canal Road, Gizah. Tel: 854-209. 27 Cairo-Alexandria Desert Road, Gizah. Tel: 850-234.

Al Mashrabiyyah (Egyptian). 4 Sh. Ahmad Nissim, Duqqi. Tel: 348-2801.

Naguib Mahfouz Café. 5 Sikkat al-Badistan, Khan al-Khalili, Cairo. Tel: 590-3788, 932-262. No alcohol.

Papillon (Lebanese). Sh. 26 Yulyu (July), Tirsana Shopping Centre (Suq Nadi at-Tirsana), Muhandisiin. Tel: 347-1672.

Paprika (Lebanese). 1129 Corniche, near the Radio and Television Building, Maspero. Tel: 749-447.

Al Ruwsha (Lebanese). 3 Sh. Gam^ciat ad-Dawal al-^cArabiyyah, Maydan al-Hor, Muhandisiin, Tel: 344-5773, 345-5100. Fax: 345-8866.

Il Yotti (Lebanese/international). 44 39 Muhiy ad-Din Abu'l-^cIzz St. Duqqi Tel: 349-4944. Ring the bell.

Zahle (Lebanese). Siag Pyramids Hotel, Saqqarah Road, Gizah. Tel: 385-6022, 385-3005, 385-6623.

ORIENTAL

Balmoral (Chinese: take-away and delivery service). 157 Sh, 26 Yulyu (July), Zamalek. Tel: 340-6761, 340-5473.

Bua Khao (Thai). 9 Sh. 151, Ma^cadi. Tel: 350-0126.

Bukhara (Indian). 43 Sh. Misr-Helwan (Agricultural Road), Ma^cadi. Tel: 375-5999.

Fu Ching (Chinese). 28 Sh. Sh. Tal^cat Harb. Tel: 575-6184.

Kandahar (Indian: tandoori). 3 Sh. Gam^ciat ad-Dawal al-^cArabiyyah, Maydan al-Hur, Muhandisiin. Tel: 344-5773, 345-5100. Fax: 345-8866.

Kowloon (Chinese). Cleopatra Hotel, 2 Sh. ^cAbd as-Salam Araf (Sh. Bustan), Maydan at-Tahrir. Tel: 759-831.

Maxie's Long Feng (Chinese). Ghadet el Maadi Towers (Burg Ghadat al-Ma^cadi), Corniche an-Nil, Ma^cadi. Tel: 375-9966.

Okamoto (Japanese). 7 Sh. Ahmad ^cUrabi, Aguza. Tel: 349-5774.

Pei-Ching (Chinese). 9 Sh. 151 Ma^cadi. Tel: 351-8328.

Peking (Chinese). 14 Sh. Saray al-Azbakiyyah (behind Cinema Diana), Cairo. Tel: 591-2381. 26 Sh. al-^cAtabah, Muhandisiin. Tel: 349-9086. 9 Sh. 151 Ma^cadi. Tel: 351-8328.

Taj Mahal (Indian). 5 Sh. Lubnan, Muhandisiin. Tel: 302-5669.
Tandoori (Indian). 11 Sh. Shihab, Muhandisiin Tel: 348-6301.
Tokyo (Japanese). 2 Sayyid al-Bakri, Zamalek. Tel: 351-0502.
Yamato (Japanese). Ramses Hilton Hotel Annexe, Maspero. Tel: 752-3999.

SPANISH

España (Spanish). Cairo Inn Hotel, 26 Sh. Suria, Muhandisiin. Tel: 346-0661.
La Paella (Spanish). 20 Sh. Riyadh, Muhandisiin. Tel: 347-5135.
Restaurant Complexes
Four Corners. Four restaurants in one building: **Justine** (French), **Matchpoint** (International), **La Piazza** (Italian), **Chin Chin** (Chinese). 4 Sh. Hasan Sabri, Zamalek. Tel: 341-2961, 340-1647.
Omam Restaurants. Four restaurants in one building: **Al-Fanuws** (Moroccan), **Chandani** (Indian), **Il Camino** (Italian), and **Sakura** (Japanese). Burg Riyadh, 5 Sh. Wissa Wasif (off Gizah Corniche, Sh. Gamal ᶜAbd an-Nasir) 6th Floor, Gizah. Tel: 737-595/592. No alcohol.
Le Pacha 1901. Restaurants and bars in a boat moored opposite the Gazirah Sporting Club main entrance, Sh. Saray al-Gazirah: **Johnny's Pub, Le Pacha, Le Palais, Piano Forte, Piccolo Mondo, L'Oasis, River Boat, Le Steak, Le Tarbouche.** Tel: 340-6730/1/2.

FAST FOOD

Kentucky Fried Chicken (Take-away and delivery service). 93 Sh. 9 (opposite Maᶜadi Metro station), Maᶜadi. Tel: 351-7604, 351-9714. Sh. Muhammad Mahmud (opposite American University), Cairo, and other locations.
Pizza Hut (fast food, home delivery). 64 Sh. Musaddeq, Duqqi. Tel: 360-8048, 349-7609; 85 Sh. 9, Maᶜadi. Tel: 375-9362; Maydan Messaha, Duqqi. Tel:706-899, 361-1347; Sh. Ahram, Misr al-Gadidah (Heliopolis). Tel: 258-0518, 259-113.

Middle Eastern Food

Major influences on Egyptian food during the past ten centuries have wafted from the classic cooking pots of Persia, Syria and especially Ottoman Turkey, as well as from Italy, France, and even England. Truly native dishes are based upon an ancient indigenous tradition of stewing vegetables, but even they make extensive use of the to-mato, the New World's irreplaceable contribution to Old World cookery. Menus in all hotels are international.

Mazzah, which Egypt owes to the Levant, are hors d'oeuvres, salads, or garnishes, but may be served as a meal. They are eaten with the fingers, scooped up in pieces of flatbread. The most common is *tahinah*, sesame paste mixed with water and lemon juice to form a dip or dressing. It is eaten with flatbread either by itself or mixed with other things, such as white cheese, parsley, or chopped tomatoes. *Babaghanoug*, *tahinah* mixed with roasted eggplant and crushed garlic, is a Lebanese speciality, as is *hommos bi tahinah*, tahinah mixed with crushed chickpeas and garlic. Often found among *mazzah*, however, are stewed brown beans, *ful medames*, Egypt's national dish, which may be offered with *tahinah*, yoghurt, white cheese, cottonseed or olive oil, fried or boiled eggs. Dried white broad beans are the basis for the deep-fried beancakes called *ta'amiya*, known elsewhere as *felafel*. Other vegetables served as *mazzah* are likely to be stuffed with a rice mixture, in which case they are called *mahshi*, and range from vine leaves, tomatoes and small eggplant to zucchini or green peppers. Meat served as *mazzah* usually appears in the form of meatballs or meat fingers (*kofta, kibbih*, or *kubaybah*) made of ground beef, veal, or lamb.

Street foods, delicious, but almost certain to distress an unacclimatized stomach, include: ta'amiya, flatbread sandwiches of *ful medames* or *shawirma* (the Turkish *çevirme* – slices of lamb stacked and broiled vertically – better known internationally by its other Turkish name, *döner kebab*), *kusheri* (pasta, rice, and lentils with a hot sauce), *fattah* (hot broth poured over crumbled bread), roast corn or sweet potatoes, and various kinds of bread. Every major hotel now serves refined and hygienic versions of these dishes from elegant counters or carts.

FAST FOOD & ICE CREAM

Al Mastaba, 65 Mohi el Din Abu el Ezz, Dokki. Tel: 249-1157. Kebab, kufta and other Middle Eastern dishes. (Inexpensive).
Egyptian Pancakes, 7 Khan el Khalili. Tel: 908-623. Made to order *fitir*. (Inexpensive).

Farghaly Fruits, 45 Midan Dokki. Tel: 348-2341. Fresh fruit juices. (Inexpensive).
Free Time, 75 Mosaddaq, Dokki. Tel: 348-0006. North American food: subs and burgers. (Inexpensive).
La Dolce Vita, 21 Misr Helwan Road, Maadi. Excellent homemade ice cream and cones. (Inexpensive).
McBurger, 16 Gamat el Dowal el Arabiya, Mohandeseen. Tel: 344-24109. Burgers, pies, onion rings, the works. (Inexpensive).
Wienerwald Batal, Ahmed Abdel Aziz, Mohandeseen. Tel: 346-6940. Bavarian chain with German and Austrian dishes. (Inexpensive).

FLOATING RESTAURANTS

Nile Pharaoh, docks at 31 Nil, Giza. Tel: 726-713. Lunch cruise 2.30–4pm. Summer early dinner cruise 7.15–9pm. Dinner cruise 9.30–noon. Pharaonic boat complete with lotus decor.
Scarabée, docks across from Shepheard's Hotel. Tel: 984-967. Lunch at 2.30pm and dinner at 9.30pm.

In Luxor and Aswan travellers usually dine in the hotels. However, there are several places to eat scattered throughout.

Luxor

Marhaba, Corniche. Middle Eastern. Try the *sharkasayyia*.
Hatey, Sharia el Mahatta. Tel: 382-210. Middle Eastern. Try the *shish kebab*. (Inexpensive).
New Karnak Restaurant. Variety.
Amun, Karnak Street. Middle Eastern. (Inexpensive).

Aswan

Mona Lisa, Corniche. Middle Eastern. Try the baked fish. (Inexpensive).
Moon, Corniche. Middle Eastern. Grilled chicken and ice cream. (Inexpensive).
Madina, Sharia el Suq. Middle Eastern. Grilled chicken and meat. (Inexpensive).

Drinking Notes

The traditional **hot and cold drinks** served in coffeehouses are delicious and thought to be health-giving. The usual idea of American coffee is instant Nescafé. If you want decaffeinated coffee then you will have to bring your own.

Fresh juices such as orange, mango, strawberry, pomegranate, lime or whatever, depending on the season, are available everywhere *except* in major hotels.

Internationally formulated drinks made and bottled locally under license include a range of Schweppes and Canada Dry mixes, Coca-Cola, Seven-Up, Sport, and Pepsi-Cola.

The local **beer** is Stella, a lager that comes in four varieties: Stella Export or ordinary Stella, which is less sweet and therefore usually preferred to Export; the increasingly rare Stella Aswali, a dark beer from Aswan; and seasonal Stella Marzen, a bock or Märzenbier. The adventurous may encounter a mild home-brew called *buza*, which is recorded to have been made as long ago as the Third Dynasty.

Egyptians were making **wine** even earlier. Reds include Omar Khayyam, Pharaohs, and Château Gianaclis; there is one rosé, called Rubi d'Egypte. Among the whites – Gianaclis Village, Cru des Ptolemées, Castel Nestor, Nefertiti, and Reine Cléopatre – Gianaclis Village (ask for *Qaryah*) is the driest and is preferred with fish or seafood. Reine Cléopatre (ask for *Kliobatra*), sweeter and fruitier, is a suitable accompaniment to turkey or veal. Caution is advised when dining out, however, since Egyptian wine has only recently recovered from several years of faulty manufacture and quality is still apt to vary from bottle to bottle. If there is a risk of spoiling an evening, the worst should be sent back immediately. Mediocre French or Italian wine is available in the major hotels, of course, at prices roughly ten times their maximum value on the western market.

Imported spirits are also available. Local spirits are quite popular among Egyptians. They include several kinds of brandy and various versions of **zibeeb** or **araq**, the Arab World's heady equivalent to *ouzo, raki, anisetta,* or *pastis.*

It is extremely important to know that there is one brand of locally-bottled **mineral water**, called *Baraka* (accent on the first syllable), produced in association with Vittel. Tap-water in most places in Egypt is either risky or so heavily treated with chemicals as to be unpalatable.

Attractions

Tourist Attractions

Egypt is the greatest outdoor museum in the world. The tourist with limited time will have a problem deciding what not to see.

Alexandria

ROMAN SITES

Pompey's Pillar. Dedicated in 297 AD to Emperor Diocletian, the pillar is made of Aswan rose granite. It rises to a height of 84 feet (25 metres) and stands on the site of the ruins of the **Serapeum**, one of the greatest temple complexes of the ancient world.

Roman and Byzantine Remains. Council-chambers, lecture halls, baths and the foundations of houses are visible dating mostly from the 4th century AD.

Catacombs of Kom esh-Shawqafa. Discovered in 1900, the catacombs are dug 100 feet into the rock bed and date back to the 2nd century AD. The reliefs blend Greek and Egyptian symbolism.

MEDIEVAL

The Fort of Qaitbay. Located at the northern end of the harbour entrance, the fort stands on the site of the Pharos lighthouse. Built in the 15th century, it is now a naval museum.

MODERN

Muntazah Palace. Set in a seaside park, the Muntazah Palace complex was a summer residence of Abbas II Hilmi (1874–1944, Khedive 1892–1914). At the outbreak of World War I, the British deposed Abbas and seized his estate, which they used as a military hospital until 1919. It later belonged to King Fu'ad. The park is open to the public.

DAY TRIPS

Al Alamayn. Sixty-two miles (104 km) west of Alexandria lies the site of a major World War II battle between the Afrika Corps led by Rommel and the Allied forces led by Montgomery.

Cairo

ISLAMIC SITES

Mosque of Amr ibn al-As. A mosque, the first in Egypt, was built on this site by Amr ibn al-As, the Muslim general who conquered the country in the name of Islam in AD 641.

Mosque of Ibn Tulun. Graceful and serene, this mosque, built between 876 and 879, is the oldest intact mosque in Cairo and one of the most impressive buildings in the world.

SOUTHERN CEMETERY

The **Mausoleum of Imam al Shafi'i** built in 1211, is a shrine, a pilgrimage site and a functioning mosque. Note the dome, made of wood covered with lead, the boat on top of the dome, the latticework, screen and teak cenotaph in the interior.

Hawsh al Basha or **Tomb of the Family of Muhammad Ali**. Near Imam al Shafi'i is the multiple-domed tomb of many members of the dynasty founded by Muhammad Ali, who is himself buried at the Citadel. Some family members originally buried in Alexandria were moved here.

THE CITADEL

The Citadel overlooks the **Madrasah of Sultan Hasan**, the greatest of the Bahri Mamluk monuments, and the **Rifa'i Mosque** finished in 1912, an impressive dynastic shrine containing the tombs of Khedive Ismail, Sultan Husayn, King Fuad, and Muhammad Reza Shah Pahlevi, the late Shah of Iran. The most obvious feature of the Citadel itself is the **Muhammad Ali Mosque**, built between 1830 and 1848, but not really completed until 1857, an Ottoman-style congregational mosque in which the great Muhammad Ali himself is entombed. Other attractions at the Citadel include the **Police Museum**, the **Military Museum**, the **Gawharah Palace**, the **Mosque of Sultan An-Nasir Muhammad**, the **Well**, the **Mosque of Sidi Sarya**, and a small museum of wheeled vehicles.

DARB AL AHMAR

This colourful street is studded with monuments, including the **Mosque of Maridani**, one of the most exquisite monuments of the 14th century. It runs to **Bab Zuwayla** and **The Khiyamiyyah** or Tentmakers' Bazaar which is the last existing example of a covered bazaar.

AL QAHIRAH

Al Qahirah, the Fatimid enclosure that gave its name to the city as a whole, is described in detail in the Cairo chapter of this book.

NORTHERN CEMETERY.

Complex of Farrag ibn Barquq. This was the first massive monument built in the Northern Cemetery. Everything is in duplicate: two minarets, two domes, and, on either end of the *qibla* wall, two delicate wooden screens.
Complex of Qaitbey. Built near the end of the Mamluk era, it epitomises the power and exquisite taste of Egypt's slave dynasty.

CHRISTIAN

The section of the city that contains most ancient Christian structures is called **Old Cairo**. The **Fortress of Babylon**, not to be confused with the remains of the Babylon on the Euphrates, houses the following churches:
Convent of St George. A reception hall in the convent should be seen.
The Hanging Church. The most impressive features of this church are the screens from the 13th and 14th centuries.
The Church of Abu Serga. Dating from the 5th century AD, this church was built above the cave where the Holy Family allegedly took refuge in their flight from Herod.
The Church of Saint Barbara. The wooden portal of this church is a masterpiece in woodwork.

MODERN

Camel Market. It begins at dawn on Fridays and Sundays. Men from the Sudan trek their camels over lonely caravan routes through the Western Desert to sell them here.
Cairo Zoo. Established in 1890, it is one of the oldest in the world with a comprehensive collection of animals. It is a favourite outing place for Cairenes especially on Friday.

Saqqarah Plateau

Near Saqqarah, 16 miles (27 km) southwest of Cairo, is a major part of the Memphite Necropolis (cemetery) that runs from above Giza in the north, to below Maydum in the south. Begun before the advent of the Old Kingdom, its monuments span some 5,000 years. The important sites to see are:
The Funerary Complex of Zoser. Built by the architect Imhotep in the Third Dynasty, the funerary complex of Zoser contains the **Step Pyramid** is the first attempt at pyramid building and was a precursor of the famous **Giza pyramids**.
The Pyramid of Unas. The exterior of this pyramid looks like a heap of rubble, but the interior walls are covered with Pyramid Texts, the mortuary literature of the ancient Egyptians.
Tombs of Ptah-Hotep, Ti and **Mereruka**. These tombs contain the finest tomb reliefs of the Old Kingdom. They give us an interesting and comprehensive insight into the daily lives of the ancient Egyptians.
Serapeum. This temple of Serapis stood over the underground burial gallery of the sacred Apis Bulls. Discovered by French Egyptologist Auguste Mariette in 1851.
Memphis. The capital of the Old Kingdoms never lost its importance to the ancient Eygptians. In the museum compound are the **Alabaster Sphinx** and the **Colossus of Ramses II**.
The Pyramids of Abu Sir. A few miles north of Saqqarah and visible from the Saqqarah plateau are three pyramids of the pharaohs of the Fifth Dynasty.
The Pyramids of Dahshur. South of Saqqarah, this site is part of the Necropolis with four pyramids. The two Old Kingdom pyramids, both belonging to the Pharaoh Snefru, are in much better condition than the two Middle Kingdom pyramids.

Giza Plateau

The monuments of the Giza plateau are the most famous in Egypt.
The Pyramid of Khufu. This is the greatest pyramid ever constructed by the ancient Egyptians.
The Pyramid of Khafre. The second pyramid on the Giza plateau gives the best picture of a mortuary temple complex of the Old Kingdom. Near the Sphinx is the valley temple where the pharaoh's body was brought after

mummification. Leading up the hill is the causeway by which the priests would carry the body of the pharaoh to the mortuary temple. Here prayers for release of the pharaoh's soul took place. Then the body was placed in the tomb chamber.
The Sphinx. This is the largest of many sphinx statues to be found in the Nile valley, but the only one in the Giza necropolis.
The Pyramid of Menkaure. The smallest pyramid of the Giza trio, it is the last great pyramid of the age. All later pyramids were of inferior quality.

The sound-and-light shows at Giza are presented in the area in front of the Sphinx in various languages – Saturday: English and French; Sunday: French and German; Monday: English and French; Tuesday: French and German; Wednesday: English and French; Thursday: Arabic and English; Friday: English and French.

The Delta Barrage

The barrage and its gardens are some 15 miles (24 km) north of Cairo, where the Nile branches into the Rashid (Rosetta) and Dumyat (Pamietta) streams. Very crowded on Friday, but a pleasant place to end a ride on the Nile. A public water-taxi leaves from the **Maspero** stop next to the television building on Fridays and Sundays. Do not ride on it during hot weather.

Bani Suef

The Pyramid of Mayidum. The first true pyramid in Egypt, south of Cairo off the main highway to Upper Egypt. It can be seen from the distance. The turn off is posted and appears to be beyond the pyramid. Built after the Step Pyramid, it represents the second stage in pyramid building. Today only the core remains, but it is still an impressive sight. Bring a picnic lunch.

Fayyum

Travelling to the historic sites in the Fayyum – a fertile, well-irrigated bowl to the west of the Nile – is not always easy as many sites are along unpaved, unmarked desert tracks; but the drive is pleasant, the air is clean and the green fields and the lakes are worth seeing.
Kom Aushin in the Fayyum is the best preserved Roman city in Egypt. Called Karanis in Roman times, it contains

the ruins of domestic architecture, two temples and a nearby museum of antiquities. The museum has an excellent Fayyum (mummy case) portrait.

Qasr es-Sagha. Far into the desert to the north of Lake Qarun is the Middle Kingdom temple of Qasr-el Sagha. It stands on a rocky hill commanding an exquisite view of the Fayyum. One should take this trip in at least two four-wheel-drive vehicles. Bring a compass. Guides can be found at the museum in Kom Aushim.

Dimayh. Twenty minutes from Qasr el-Sagha is Dimayh. It was once a caravan town and port for traders from the Nile valley and the Western Desert. Today the treasure hunters visit its ruins with metal detectors. The same travel precautions apply.

Pyramids of Hawarah and **el-Lahun**. The Pyramid of Hawarah was built by Amenemhat III. The Pyramid of el-Lahun was built in the 12th Dynasty by Pharaoh Sesostris II.

Middle Egypt

Travel and tourism in the zone between Minya and Luxor is currently restricted though it includes some of the most interesting and least spoiled sights in Egypt. Among them are:

Al-Minya: Most of the sites here are an hour's drive south of Al-Minya. You can hire a taxi for the day at reasonable rates. Do bring your candle or flashlight since the tombs are dark.

Beni Hassan: On the east bank of the Nile are the 39 noblemen's tombs of the 11th and 12th Dynasty (Middle Kingdom). The interior decoration is painted on plaster and depicts scenes of sports, crafts and farming. The most interesting tomb is that of **Kheti**, a governor during the 11th Dynasty, with scenes of fishing, hunting, wrestling and weaving.

Ashmunayn and Tunah Al-Gebel: Ashmunayn is the site of the important ancient city of Hermopolis Magna, marked by columned ruins in the Hellenic style. In the desert near Tunah al-Gabal, 4 miles (6 km) west, was the city's necropolis, which offers the **Tomb of Petosiris**, a **Temple of Thoth** built by Ptolemy IV, and the **Boundary Stone of Akhet-Aten**.

Abydos, which existed "at the dawn of history" was the cult centre of Osiris. As Osiris' importance grew, so did

Abydos. By the Middle Kingdom it had become a place of pilgrimage. By the New Kingdom all Egyptians tried to visit Abydos before they died. Those who did not, often had their mummies transported to Abydos before burial. The earliest monuments of this site are in total ruin and the New Kingdom Temple of Ramses II has little left of what must have been a magnificent temple, but the New Kingdom Temple of Seti I is among the finest in Egypt.

Temple of Seti I. Built of limestone, the temple is dedicated to no fewer than seven deities and holds seven sanctuaries. The reliefs of the second **Hypostyle Hall** break with the rigid style found in Egyptian art before the Amarna period. The **Seven Shrines** are from right to left: Horus, Isis, Osiris, Amon-Ra, Ra-Harakhte, Ptah and Seti I. **The Corridor of Kings** lists 76 cartouches of the pharaohs of Ancient Egypt. This list was the beginning of a chronology of Ancient Egypt.

The current temple at **Dendera**, dedicated to Hathor the Goddess of Love and Joy, dates from the Ptolemaic and Roman periods. The zodiac on the ceiling of the great hypostyle hall is the best preserved in the whole of Egypt. The crypts below the temple have excellent reliefs dating from the reign of Ptolemy XIII. The relief of Cleopatra VI and Caesarion, her son by Julius Caesar, is found on the south outer wall. It is the only place in Egypt where Cleopatra VI is depicted.

Basilica at Dendera. One of the earliest structures of the Christian era, this basilica, built of sandstone, is now in ruins. It is beside the birth house of the Temple of Dendera. A beautifully carved niche from the Christian period can be seen by looking just inside.

Luxor

Luxor is ancient Thebes, the heart of the New Kingdom and of rural Egypt, where the pace is slow in harmony with nature. The winter sunsets are breathtaking. Awaiting the tourist are some of the most impressive monuments of ancient Egypt, including **Karnak** and the **Valley of the Kings**.

GREAT TEMPLE OF AMON AT KARNAK. This sacred area saw 1,300 years of pageantry. Pharaohs from the Middle Kingdom to the 30th Dynasty built temples, obelisks, pylons and shrines at

Karnak, primarily in honour of the God Amon-Ra, his consort Mut and their son Khonsu.

The First Pylon. The largest at Karnak, not added until the 25th Dynasty. In front of it, forming an impressive entrance, is the Avenue of the Sphinxes.

The Temple of Ramses III. A typical New Kingdom temple in a good state of repair.

Great Hypostyle Hall. Erected by Seti I and Ramses the II, the hypostyle hall is the largest and most magnificent in Egypt. Inside there are 134 massive columns decorated with reliefs. On the outer southern walls are records of Ramses II's **Battle of Kadesh** and on the outer northern walls are Seti I's battles in Lebanon and Syria.

Obelisks of Hatshepsut. Of the two obelisks erected by Hatshepsut at Karnak, one remains standing. The second was toppled centuries ago. The top of the second obelisk has been placed near the **Sacred Lake**. The relief shows Hatshepsut being crowned Pharaoh by the God Amon.

One of the best sight-and-sound shows is held here. Two performances each night, at 6pm and 8pm. It lasts for 90 minutes and requires some walking. The show are in various languages – Sunday: French and German; Monday: English; Tuesday: French and German; Wednesday: English and French; Thursday: Arabic; Friday and Saturday: English and French. Bring something warm.

Luxor Temple. Located in the heart of modern Luxor. Built by Amenhotep III and Ramses II, it is the southern sanctuary of god Amon. The Avenue of the Sphinxes once connected Luxor Temple to Karnak. Spectacular statuary found here is on display in the nearby **Luxor Museum**.

West Bank opposite Luxor

You can cross to the West Bank on a tourist ferry or take the local ferry with the farmers. There is also a car ferry. Tickets available at all the landings. You can rent bicycles in Luxor to ride on the West Bank. Taxis and donkeys are available.

Colossi of Memnon. These statues once graced the entrance to the mortuary temple of Amenhotep III, the largest temple on the West Bank.

VALLEY OF THE KINGS

There are 62 known tombs in this desert valley; several have electricity and are open to the public on a continuous basis. Among the most famous tombs is the **Tomb of Tutankhamun**. Discovered by Howard Carter in 1922, this is the smallest tomb in the Valley of the Kings.

Tomb of Ramses VI. The vaulted ceiling in the tomb chamber is the most outstanding feature of this tomb. Painted primarily in blue and gold, it represents the heavens. The goddess Nut circles the sky enclosing the representations of the day, the year and the entire zodiac.

Tomb of Seti I. This is the largest and finest tomb in the valley. Features of special note are the unfinished room used as a decoy to fool tomb robbers and the burial chamber with a black and gold astronomical ceiling.

VALLEY OF THE QUEENS

Over 70 tombs of the queens and royal children of the 18th–20th Dynasties are found in this valley. Only a few are open to the public, but not the best: the **Tomb of Nefertari**, the wife of Ramses II. This tomb has become a victim of the ravages of salt erosion and is currently under restoration.

Tomb of Amon-her-Khopshef. In the small tomb are reliefs depicting the son of Ramses III being escorted by his father into the underworld. The colours are spectacular and the light is very good.

Over 400 **noblemen's tombs** cut into the Theban hills provide an intimate portrait of the men who served the pharaoh. Many are closed to the public, but those not to be missed are:

Tomb of Nakht. Nakht was a scribe of the 18th Dynasty. His tomb, although small, is the finest nobleman's tomb, and some say, the best on the West Bank. The scenes of harvesting, banqueting, hunting and fishing are all known for their detail and brilliant colours. The three female musicians so often reproduced on postcards are found here.

Tomb of Menna. Menna was the Scribe of the Fields. His tomb has reliefs of agricultural scenes and also includes the pilgrimage to Abydos that every Ancient Egyptian tried to make. The most famous fishing and fowling scene often printed on postcards is in Menna's tomb.

Tomb of Ramose. The reliefs in this tomb, one of the largest in Qurnah, are wonderful. The details are realistic and worth close attention. Outstanding is the mourning scene on the left wall.

Mortuary Temple of Seti I. On the northern end of the Theban plateau, this temple is often missed by the traveller. Built during the same period as the Temple of Abydos, it contains fine reliefs depicting the life and times of Egyptian royalty.

Mortuary Temple of Ramses II. The Ramesseum was built in honour of the great propagandist of ancient Egypt and the walls depict his wars and conquests. In the courtyard is the fallen colossus that Shelley used as a subject in his poem *Ozymandias*.

Mortuary Temple of Ramses III. Located at Medinet Habu, in the southern part of the Theban Plateau, this mortuary temple is the best preserved on the West Bank. These temples shouldn't be visited as a single unit of the tour.

Dayr el Bahri. Below the cliffs that form the barrier between the desert and the Nile stands the graceful **Mortuary Temple of Hatshepsut**. This elegant building, so different from any other building in the Nile valley, forms a graceful symmetry with its surrounding environment. Be sure to view the Punt Colonnades.

Esna To Kom Ombo

The Temple of Esna. Built during the Ptolemaic period in honour of Khnum, the God of the Cataract region, this is the least impressive of the later temples built along the Nile. The last Roman name to appear in a cartouche is found here.

The Temple of Edfu. Dedicated to Horus the elder and taking two centuries to complete, this temple is the best preserved in Egypt.

The Temple of Kom Ombo. This temple stands on a picturesque knoll at a bend in the Nile and is particularly striking when approached from the river. The temple is dedicated to two gods, Horus and Sobek.

Aswan

Dry and warm with a splendid location on the first cataract of the Nile, Aswan forms the barrier between Egypt and Africa. It has played a major role in the history of the region for over 5,000 years. It also offers a glimpse into Nubian culture.

Abu Simbel. Abu Simbel is south of Aswan on Lake Nasser. You can fly from Cairo, Luxor or Aswan, take a hydrofoil, or go overland on a newly paved road. Flights usually allow a two-hour stay at the temples. The methods used to dismantle the temples and move them to a new location above the former site are depicted in the interior of the man-made mountain that now houses the **Temple of Ramses II**. The **Temple of Nefertari** is the second temple at Abu Simbel. It is dedicated to Nefertari, the favourite wife of Ramses II, as well as to the Goddess Hathor.

Elephantine Island. You reach the island by *felucca*, which docks at the quay of one of the few remaining villages in Nubia. At the southern end of the island are the Nilometer, the ancient gauge for measuring the height of the flood each year; the temple dedicated to the god Khnum and also a museum.

Tombs of the Nobles. The tombs are situated across the river from Aswan, high on a hill. The two rows of tombs belonged to local rulers of the Old and Middle Kingdom. The journey up is difficult and the tombs themselves are not all that impressive, but the view is magnificent.

Granite Quarries. Just about every temple in Egypt has some granite taken from the great quarries at Aswan. There is a half-hewn obelisk at one of these quarries.

Philae. The original island of Philae became susceptible to flooding by the Nile after the first heightening of the dam at Aswan, so it was decided to relocate the temples.

The final drama was played out in the 1960s as coffer dams surrounded the island while salvage work was in progress. Piece by piece the temple was dismantled, moved to the nearby island of Agilka which had in the meantime been contoured to resemble Philae, and there the temple was reconstructed as we see it today.

In Greco-Roman times Philae was to become the cult centre of Isis and the most important shrine in the whole of Egypt. Apart from the **Temple of Isis** there are several other features.

The Gateway of Hadrian. With reliefs about the source of the Nile as it was understood in Pharaonic times. The God Hapi is shown pouring the waters of the Nile from a pot.

The Temple of Hathor. Depicts scenes of the God Bes dancing, laughing as well as playing musical instruments.

The Kiosk of Trajan. The most famous monument of Philae. It was the only thing visible above the water's surface when the island was flooded during the first part of this century. There is an audio-visual show in the evening.

The Temple of Kalabsha. This temple is another salvage miracle. Dismantled block by block, it was saved from a watery grave in Nubia and re-erected above the High Dam.

Mausoleum of the Aga Khan. The Aga Khan III, the head of the Ismailia sect of Islam, is buried in this tomb on a hill above Aswan which has a spectacular view over the city and the river.

Kitchener's Island. Given to Lord Kitchener by the Egyptian people when he was Consul General of Egypt, the island is a botanical paradise begun by Kitchener. Today there are plants and trees from all over the world.

The High Dam and the Lake. Two miles wide and 364 feet (110 metres) high, Aswan's High Dam was completed in 1971 as a co-operative effort between the Soviet Union and Egypt. Built to solve Egypt's electric and agricultural problems, the dam has, in the past few years, proven its value: drought in Ethiopia and Sudan has not affected Egypt.

Market at Daraw. Open daily, but Sundays and Tuesdays find this native market on the Nile north of Aswan in full swing. It is best known as a camel market where Sudanese and Rashida herdsmen trek in from the desert to trade. This is not a place for the squeamish and you should be properly attired and should ask permission before taking photographs.

The Western Desert

Wadi Natrun. At one time there were many monasteries in this remote desert region. Today only a few remain. Open for visitors are St Makarious, Deir al-Baramus, Deir Anba Bishoi and Deir as-Suryam. They are closed during fasts and festivities. Bring your own lunch and a gift for the monks (soap, tea, sugar, etc.).

For scenic beauty, take the loop road that links the four oases of Kharga, Dakhla, Farafrah and Bahriyyah. The oases are best visited in the winter when it is possible to walk in the sand dunes.

Kharga Oasis. The **Temple of Hibis**, begun by Darius I and the Christian **Cemetery of Al-Bagawat**, dating from the 7th century, greet the traveller at the outskirts of Kharga City. There are hundreds of interesting sites scattered throughout the depression; but the biggest thrill is getting there. On the way one finds the **Valley of the Melons**, where huge circular boulders, seemingly flung from some mighty hand, are scattered on the ground. At the Kharga escarpment, the road descends downward like a serpent into the depression below, leaving an impressive image of natural beauty. There is a hotel and government resthouse at Kharga City.

Between Kharga and Dakhla. The quietness begins to impress itself upon you as you head toward Dakhla. The most arresting sight of the entire journey is a line of hills that resemble great pyramids on the Giza plateau. The early settlers of the Nile valley passed this way and these hills could have inspired them to construct the pyramids.

Dakhla Oasis. This oasis is the largest in the Western Desert and has several towns. Set amid a palm grove is **Qasr**, the largest. It has wonderful gardens, a fortified fortress and a mosque dating from the Ayyubid era. A climb to the top of the minaret, though a bit precarious, gives an excellent view of the countryside, including the pink and white escarpment. There is a government resthouse.

Between Dakhla and Farafrah. The longest and loneliest stretch of road links Dakhla, in the south, to Farafrah in the north. The dunes beg to be climbed. Near the end of the journey, at **Bir Abu Mungar**, there is a checkpoint and the road appears to double back before it ascends the escarpment. Pause at the top. The view in either direction is spectacular. The long valley beyond has a variety of desert features including a wonderful chain of sand dunes. Try to arrive in the late afternoon.

Farafrah Oasis. This is the largest depression and the smallest oasis. No one really knows its importance during

pharaonic times, but it is mentioned in papyri and there are a few burial sites. Wonderful features lure the traveller: **Qasr**, the fortress, built in the Middle Ages, is still inhabited and a walk through the covered streets brings intimate contact with the people. Women have the greatest chance of being invited in for a cup of tea. **The Gardens** of Farafrah are cool and pleasant, under trees that are laden with fruit in season. Visit the *Umda*, and as part of desert hospitality, you will be offered a cup of tea in his garden. (With the oasis becoming a tourist spot, this hospitality has become quite a burden: bring tea or sugar as a gift.) **The Springs** are a delightful place to swim. Bring something modest for bathing. There is a government resthouse here.

Bahriyyah. There are five pharaonic tombs at **al-Bawiti**, the capital of Bahriyyah oasis. They are located beneath the houses on the ridge called **Qarat al-Subi**. The settlement of **Manddisha** offers a true picture of oasis life, including the harsh reality of destruction caused by a sand dune. Part of the village is being swallowed up as year by year the ridge of dunes continue their march. There is a government resthouse at al-Bawiti.

Siwah Oasis. Permission to visit Siwah is obtained at **Mersa Metruh**. You will need your passport and an up-to-date visa. The intelligence office is closed on Friday. Getting permission takes 2–3 hours. When you arrive at Siwah you must register with the police, or let the new hotel register for you.

The Temple of the Oracle. Located at Aghurmi, this was the destination of travellers who wished to consult the oracle. Perhaps the most famous visitor was Alexander the Great who came here in the fourth Century BC. The temple is located atop a huge rock (as are most things in this oasis) and is accessible via the northwestern corner. There are still things to see in the temple complex, but the rock is in danger of collapsing.

The Temple of Umm Ubaydah. This temple lies on the plain below the rock of Aghurmi, amidst a grove of palm trees. Hundreds of **rock-cut tombs** dot the escarpment at Siwah. The most important are the **Tombs of Jabal al Mawta**, but none are as spectacular as the tombs in the Nile valley.

Fortress of Siwah. The people of Siwah built a fortified village atop one of the hills of the oasis to protect themselves against desert invaders. For centuries all the inhabitants of the oasis lived within its gate. Today such defences are no longer necessary and the fortress is falling into ruin.

The Eastern Desert

Hurghada (Gharda'a). Once a fishing village, Hurghada is the main resort town on the Red Sea Coast. Several hotels offer all beach facilities including sailing, windsurfing, snorkelling and scuba diving. Fishing boats are available for hire and there is good camping on the many islands in the area.

The Sinai

In modern times when the British built a railroad linking Egypt to Palestine, El Arish served as a major station. Today you can still travel over the Via Maris and see portions of the **Allenby Railroad**. The city itself is disappointing. The inhabitants exist on tourism, fishing, date farming and trade. Unfortunately, the once beautiful beaches have been ruined by concrete block houses, but there is a local *suq* every Friday for good Bedouin finds. All facilities are available.

Rafah. A border town 5 miles (4 km) east of El Arish. The most interesting thing about it is the Bedouin *suq*, where amid produce and camels, Bedouin jewellery and dresses can be found. The *suq* day is Thursday. It begins at dawn and dwindles by noon. Bring your own food and water unless you are willing to eat and drink from the stalls at the site.

Hammam Fara'un (Pharaoh's Baths). Situated below Suez, on the western shore of Sinai (signs mark the way). Seven in number, they are rich in minerals and the Bedouin have been trekking to them for centuries. Their hot water flows into the Gulf of Suez creating steam when it hits the cool water of the gulf.

Turquoise Mines of Maraghab. Following a desert track 15 miles (25 km) into the Sinai hills from Abu Zunaymah one reaches the main turquoise mines of the ancient Egyptians. Worked as early as the First Dynasty, there were many reliefs and stelae on the site. In an attempt to re-open the mines in 1901, the British unfortunately caused a substantial amount of damage. However, a few inscriptions remain and the mine shafts are still visible. There are no facilities here.

Request a Bedouin guide at **Abu Zunaymah** before you try to explore the area.

Sarabit al-Khadim. The temple area, dedicated to Hathor and accompanied by many commemorative stelae of the Middle and New Kingdoms, covers approximately an acre. In it was found the bust of Queen Tiy of the Old Kingdom (now in the Egyptian Antiquities Museum in Cairo). Over 400 inscriptions were found in this area, praising Hathor or giving instructions about the turquoise mines on the site. More important, however, are the graffiti of the workers. Among them are unknown scripts called **protosinaitic**. They form the link between hieroglyphics and the Phoenician alphabet from which our own alphabet is derived. No facilities. Ask for a Bedouin guide at Abu Zunaymah.

St Catherine's Monastery. Started in the 6th century, the monastery lies in the valley between the Mount of Moses (Mt Sinai), where Moses allegedly received the Ten Commandments from God, and **Mount Saint Catherine's**. Still a functioning monastery of the Greek Orthodox Church, its main features are: the **Basilica Church** built by Justinian in 527 AD, the **Crusader's Church** and the **library** with thousands of rare manuscripts (special permission required to look at them). Treks up the mountain are arranged by the monks each day before dawn. It is possible to ride a camel part of the way. Near the summit hundreds of steps await, but the view from the top is astounding. Although the monks provide sleeping accommodation, you must bring your own food and water. There is a hotel nearby.

Wadi Feran. At the foot of **Gebel Serbal** is the largest wadi in Sinai, which may have been the site of the battle between the Amalakites and Israelites. Within the mountain are the remains of monasteries, chapels and hermit cells of the early Christian monks who believed this to be the Elim of the Bible. The oasis is the most fertile in Sinai, with many tamarish trees that some scholars argue are the source of the manna spoken of in Judaeo-Christian tradition. Tranquil and serene, it is difficult to imagine that Feran was a cathedral city in the Middle Ages. You can stock up on supplies in the village shops.

Sharm el Shaykh. At the tip of Sinai, this is the most developed resort area in Sinai. There are both hotel and camping facilities. A good base for day trips elsewhere.

Ras Mohammad. Thirty-one miles (50 km) south-west of Sharm el Shaykh, Ras Mohammad is a coral peninsula thrusting its head into the Red Sea. It is a nature reserve and one of the most outstanding snorkelling and diving areas in the world. At the Shark's Observatory a coral ridge falls over 262 feet (80 metres) into the open sea and the wary diver can float along its edge (under a metre/3 feet deep at high tide) and look out into an underwater paradise. Although a haven for large fish, especially sharks, there has been no reported shark attack in the Red Sea for 25 years.

Ras Mohammad can be visited for a day, but a permit is required for overnight camping. Permits are obtainable at El Tur, on the west coast of Sinai. Bring your passport.

Gazirat Tiran. The island stands as a guardian over the entrance to the Gulf of Aqaba. There are dangerous reefs and currents in the sea. Shipwrecks dot the shoreline testifying to the degree of navigational difficulty between the reefs.

Dahab. Dahab, which means "gold", is a resort village on the east coast of Sinai with a hotel, snorkelling and diving facilities.

Nuwayba. The ferry to Aqaba leaves daily from the port. Camel treks lasting four to five days into the Sinai mountains led by a local Bedouin are available. Ask at the fuel station or the Bedouin village nearby. Hotel and camping facilities available.

Gazirat Fara'un. The island is crowned with a castle built by Saladin to protect the overland route of the Haj, the annual pilgrimage to Mecca. There is excellent swimming, snorkelling and diving in the bay.

Nile Cruises

Scores of Nile cruise-companies offer packages to suit every pocket and taste. Most offer 4-, 5- and 7-day tours between Luxor and Aswan. Trips are as comfortable and often cheaper if they are arranged outside Egypt. Here are some of the boats and operators:

☆☆☆☆☆
Alexander the Great, Jolley Travel and Tour Company, 23 Qasr el Nil. Tel: 393-9390. This cruise ship was featured in the American series *The Love Boat.*
Anni, Aton, Hotp, and *Tut,* Sheraton Management Corporation, 48B Sharia Giza, Dokki. Tel: 348-8215.
Golden Boat, International Nile Cruise, 87 Sharia Ramses. Tel: 760-198.
Isis and *Osiris,* Hilton International Company, Nile Hilton Hotel. Tel: 740-880. The first modern day cruise boats on the Nile, these sister ships offer 5-day cruises.
Neptune, Trans Egypt Travel Company, 37 Qasr el Nil. Tel: 392-4313. Seven-, 10-, and 11-day cruises.
Nile Admiral, Nile Emperor, Nile Legend, Nile President, Nile Princess, Nile Ritz, Nile Symphony, Presidential Nile Cruises, 13 Marashli, Zamalek. Tel: 340-0517; 4-, 7-, and 10-day cruises.
Nile Majesty I, Nile Majesty II, Mo Hotels Travel and Nile Cruises, 41 Sherif. Tel: 392-5674.
Nile Queen, Nile Sphinx, Sphinx Tours, 2 Behler Passage, Qasr el Nil. Tel: 392-0704.
Oberoi Shehrayar and *Oberoi Shehrazad,* Oberoi Corporation Ltd. Mena House Hotel. Tel: 387-1225.
Ra, Eastmar Travel, 13 Qasr el Nil. Tel: 753-216.
Seti II, Seti III, Magdy G. Henein, 16 Ismail Muhammad, Zamalek. Tel: 341-9820.

☆☆☆☆
Atlas and *Nile Star,* Eastmar Travel, 13 Qasr el Nil. Tel: 753-216.
Fleur, International Nile Cruises Company, 3 Monshat el Katab. Tel: 392-4656.
Horus, International Company for Hotels and Nile Cruises, 23B Ismail Muhammad, Zamalek. Tel: 340-0675/6.
Seti I and *Seti IV,* Magdy G. Henein, 16 Ismail Muhammad. Tel: 341-9820/2. Part of a fleet of six ships ranging from 5-star to unclassified.

☆☆☆
Abu Simbel, Aswan, Nile Delta, Hapi Travel and Tourism Company, 17 Qasr el Nil. Tel: 393-3611/93, 393-3562. Seven- and 14-day cruises.

Karnak, Pyramids, Queen Nefertiti, and *Akhenaten,* Pyramids Nile Cruise Company, 56 Gamet el Dowal el Arabia, Mohandeseen. Tel: 360-0146/7.
Nefertari, Eastmar Travel, 13 Qasr el Nil. Tel: 753-305; 13-day cruises.

Unclassified
Unclassified cruise ships may be 3–5 star and above. This is a selected list.
Aida I and *Aida II,* Nile Valley Tours, 80 Gamel el Dowal el Arabia, Mohandeseen. Tel: 349-5482, 349-3768.
Ambassador I and *Ambassador II,* Ambassador Nile Cruises Company, 33 Hosny Saleh, Mohandeseen. Tel: 347-1015.
Excelsior and *Seti the Great,* Magdy G. Henein, 16 Ismail Muhammad, Zamalek. Tel: 341-9820/2.
Nile Pullman Fleurette and *Nile Pullman L'Egyptien,* Pullman International Hotels, 9 Menes St, Heliopolis. Tel: 290-8802/3.

Felucca Trips

Feluccas can be hired to sail between Luxor or Aswan, taking 2–4 days and visiting temples on the way. Ask along the Corniche in either Luxor or Aswan.

Tour Operators

There are hundreds of tour operators in Egypt offering a variety of packages. This list services travellers on the Nile.
Amarco Tours, 5 Talaat Harb. Tel: 759-146.
American Express, 15 Qasr el Nil. Tel: 75044.
Bestours, 37 Qasr el Nil. Tel: 392-4741.
Eastmar, 13 Qasr el Nil. Tel: 753-147.
Egypt Panorama Tours, 11 Tourist Center, **Mohandeseen**. Tel: 344-9590.
Misr Travel, 1 Talaat Harb. Tel: 392-4737.
Thomas Cook, 4 Champollion. Tel: 743-955.

Culture

Museums

ALEXANDRIA

Cavafy Museum, Sh. Sharm ash-Shaykh. Housed in this flat for 25 years, this small museum pays tribute to Constantine Cavafy (1863–1933), one of Alexandria's major contributions to the world of poetry. Monday–Friday, 10am–1pm.

Greco-Roman Museum, Shari Musée. The only museum in Egypt to honour the Hellenistic and Roman-period heritage of the country is justly placed in Alexandria, the intellectual centre of Hellenistic civilisation. The collection includes mosaic pavements, glass, coins, sculpture, sarcophagi, and the wonderful Tanagra figures. 9am–4pm daily, closed Friday from 11.30am–1.30pm.
Marine Life Institute and Aquarium, near the Fort of Qaitbay. There are two buildings here, the Museum of Hydro-Biology with a collection of boats and the Aquarium with fish and other marine species found in Egyptian waters. 9am–2pm daily.
Royal Jewellery Museum, 27 Shari Ahmed Yehya Pasha, Zizinia. Jewellery and other luxury items of the Muhammad Ali family. 9am–4pm daily, closed Friday from 11am–1.30pm.

CAIRO

The most famous of the city's museums is the Egyptian Antiquities Museum, but many others are well worth visiting. The usual hours are from 9am to 4pm daily except Friday, when all museums are closed between approximately 11.30am and 1pm.
Agricultural Museum, Ministry of Agriculture, Dokki. Tel: 702-366, 700-063, 702-879, 702-933. The oldest in the world (founded 1938), with 27 acres (11 hectares) of garden, contains a **Museum of Ancient Egyptian Agriculture**, a **Natural History Museum**, a **Museum of the Social Life of the Arab Nations**, and a **Cotton Museum**.
Amr Ibrahim Palace (Qasr Ali Ibrahim), corner of Sh. Gazirah and Sh. Shaykh al-Marsafi (next to the Marriott Hotel), Zamalek. Tel: 987-495. An exquisite neo-Islamic house confiscated during the Revolution from Amr Ibrahim, a great-great-grandson of Ibrahim Pasha.
Bayt Gamal ad-Din, east of the Qasabah between the Fakahani Mosque and the Ghuriyyah. Residence of a 17th-century gold merchant.
Bayt al-Kiridliyyah. (*See Gayer-Anderson House,* below.)
Bayt Ibrahim Katkhuda as-Sinnari, 17 Harat Monge, off Shari an-Nasiriyya, Sayyidah Zaynab. Tel: 938-565. An 18th-century townhouse, one of three requisitioned for Bonaparte's *savants* in 1798.

Bayt as-Sihaymi, Darb al-Asfar, Gamaliyyah. An Ottoman-period townhouse, largely intact, with Chinese porcelain made for the Arab market.

Coptic Museum, Mar Girgis, Old Cairo (Misr al-Qadimah). Tel: 841-766. Arts of Egypt's Christian era: textiles, metalwork, woodwork, ceramics, glass.

Egyptian Antiquities Museum, Midan Tahrir. Tel: 754-319. The world's greatest collection of Pharaonic antiquities, including the Menkauré triads, the finds from the tomb of Hetepheres, and the treasures of Tutankhamun.

Entomological Society Museum, 14 Sh. Ramsis, near Main Railway Station. Tel: 354-5350.

Ethnological Museum, 100 Sh. Qasr al-Ayni (ground floor of the Geographical Society building). Tel: 354-5450.

Higher Institute of Folklore Museum, Sh. Borsa al-Khediwiyyah (Rue de la Bourse Khédiviale). Tel: 752-460.

Gayer-Anderson House, adjoining Ibn Tulun Mosque. Tel: 354-6950. Two houses, 16th and 17th century, joined together and furnished with his collections by Major Robert Gayer-Anderson Pasha, who lived here 1935–42.

Gawharah Palace Museum (Qasr al-Gawharah), Citadel. Tel: 926-187. Muhammad Ali's Citadel *salamlik* (reception palace), restored since 1971 and fitted with furniture formerly owned by the Muhammad Ali family. The name of the palace means *bijou* or jewel, but there has never been a "jewel collection" in it.

Gazirah Museum, Planetarium building, Gazirah Exhibition Grounds, next to the National Cultural Centre. Tel: 806-982. Paintings, bibelots, and objets d'art, some inherited from the defunct Museum of Modern Art and some confiscated from the Muhammad Ali family.

Geological Museum, Corniche, Old Cairo (Misr al-Qadimah), entrance from Sh. Asar an-Nabi. Tel: 354-6950, 982-608, 982-580.

Helwan Palace Museum, Helwan. Tel: 340-5198. Closed to the public.

Islamic Art Museum, corner of Sh. Port Said, Sh. Qala'a (Sh. Muhammad Ali), and Sh. Sami al-Barudi, Abdiin. Tel: 341-8672. Important collections of arms and armour, ceramics, coins, carpets and textiles, manuscripts and printed papers, metalwork, stonework and woodwork from the period of the city's greatest glory.

Manastirli Palace and the Nilometer, southern end of Rawdah. Restored in 1990, this early 19th-century *salamlik* is the public portion of a palace complex that belonged to a distinguished Cairene Turkish family. The Nilometer is the oldest intact Islamic monument in Cairo.

Manyal Palace Museum, Rawdah Island. Tel: 936-124. A complex of gardens and buildings constructed between 1901 and 1929 and bequeathed to the nation in 1955 by Prince Muhammad Ali, younger brother of Khedive Abbas II Hilmi and first cousin of King Faruq. Apart from the prince's residence with all its furnishings, there are buildings housing splendid collections of family memorabilia, costumes, calligraphy, glass, porcelain, silver, and trophies of the hunt.

Military Museum, Citadel. Tel: 920-955. Housed in the Harim Palace, chief residence of rulers belonging to Muhammad Ali's family from 1827–74, itself worth seeing. Collections include uniforms, weapons and models.

Muhammad Ali Museum, Qasr ash-Shubra, Shubra. Closed to the public at time of press.

Muhammad Mahmud and Emilienne Luce Khalil Collection. Installed between 1971 and 1991 in the Amr Ibrahim Palace (*see above*), but now returned to the **Muhammad Mahmud and Emilienne Luce Khalil Museum** on the Giza Corniche (Sh. Gamal Abd an-Nasir) in Giza. Paintings, chiefly 19th and 20th-century French, including works by Ingres (2), Delacroix (8), Corot (12), Daumier (4), Courbet (4), Millet (6), Renoir (6), Degas (2), Fantin-Latour (2), Manet, Monet (5), Pissarro (6), Sisley (5), Toulouse-Lautrec, Gauguin (3), van Gogh and others, sculpture (Houdon, Barye, Carpeaux, and Rodin), chinoiserie, japonaiserie, and turquoiserie. Bequeathed with their house to the nation by Muhammad Mahmud Khalil (died 1955), landowner, industrialist, and politician, and his French wife, Emilienne Luce Khalil (died 1962).

Mukhtar Museum, Gazirah near Galaa Bridge. Tel: 805-198. Designed by Ramses Wissa Wasif, founder of the Harraniyyah weaving project, and dedicated to Mahmud Mukhtar, sculptor of *Awakening Egypt*, the monument at the Giza end of the Kubri Gaamah (University Bridge), as well as the monumental statues of Saad Zaghlul in Cairo and Alexandria.

Musafir-khana, Darb at-Tablawi, Gamaliyyah, behind the mosque of Sayyidna Husayn. Tel: 920-472. Townhouse built in 1779, birthplace of Khedive Ismail.

Museum of Hygiene and Medicine, Midan Sakakini, Abbasiyyah. Housed in the extraordinary Sakakini Palace, built in 1898 by the Syrian financier Henri Sakakini Pasha, head of the firm of Sakakini Frères, Cairo agent for the Dervieux (Paris) and Oppenheim (London) banks.

Museum of Modern Egyptian Art, Gazirah Exhibition Grounds. Moved in 1991 to new quarters opposite the Opera House – an old Exhibition Ground display pavilion lavishly rebuilt for the purpose – the Museum houses a collection of representative works by 20th-century Egyptian artists. Outstanding are the paintings of Mahmud Said (1897–1964), who was for three decades one of Egypt's best known painters. Not to be confused with the defunct Museum of Modern Art.

Museum of the People's Assembly, in the People's Assembly (Meglis ash-Shaab) Building, Shari Meglis ash-Shaab. Photographs, documents, including Khedive Ismail's charter for the first parliamentary assembly and copies of the 1923 Constitution and its republican successors; and the State Coach used for the opening of sessions by Ismail, Fu'ad, and Faruq.

Mustafa Kamil Museum, May Salah ad-Din, below the Citadel. Tel: 919-943. Houses the tomb and memorabilia of the founder (1874–1908) of the Nationalist Party.

Nagi Museum, below the Giza Pyramids. Dedicated to the life and work of Muhammad Nagi (1888–1956), Alexandrian neo-Impressionist painter.

National Museum for Civilisation (Museum of Egyptian Civilisation), Planetarium building, Gazirah Exhibition Grounds, next to the National Cultural Centre. Tel: 340-5198.

National Police Museum, The Citadel. Uniforms, weapons and various criminological exhibits.

Ornithological Museum, Giza Zoo, Sh. Giza (Sh. Murad). Tel: 726-313, 726-233.

Post Office Museum, Midan al-Atabah. P.O. Bldg, 2nd floor. Tel: 917-575.

Royal Carriage Museum, 82 Sh. 6 July, Bulaq. Tel: 774-437. Entry from behind the Ministry of Foreign Affairs on the Corniche or from next to the Abu'l-Ila mosque on Sh. 26 July. A world-class collection of 78 viceregal, khedivial, and royal horse-drawn vehicles representing 22 types, with displays of harness, livery and trappings.

Saad Zaghlul Museum, Bayt al-Umma, 2 Sh. Saad Zaghlul, Munira. Tel: 534-5399. Residence of the nationalist leader (1854–1927) who inspired the 1919 Revolution, founder of the Wafd (opposition party), Prime Minister 1924–25.

Shawqi Museum, 6 Sh. Ahmad Shawqi, between Sh. Giza (Sh. Murad) and the Giza Corniche (Sh. Gamal Abd an-Nasir). Tel: 729-947. Elegant residence of Ahmad Shawqi (1868–1932), court poet to Khedive Abbas II Hilmi, exiled by the British between 1915 and 1919.

Boat Museum, beside Cheops Pyramid, Giza. Tel: 857-928. Houses the Old Kingdom boat found on the site and painstakingly reassembled.

State Railway Museum, Sh. Bab al-Hadid (Main Railway Station). Tel: 977-393. Splendid collection of viceregal rolling stock and British-made models.

LUXOR

Luxor Museum, on the Corniche. A small but excellently laid out museum which features a collection of Amarna art and royal statues of the 18th Dynasty. 4–9pm in winter and 5–10pm in summer.

Art Galleries & Studios

El Patio, 6 Road 77c, Maadi. Tel: 351-6654. Occasional exhibits in the upstairs gallery. 10am–6pm, closed Sunday.

Mashrabia, 8 Champollion, near Thomas Cook. Tel: 778-623. Group and individual shows. 11am–2pm and 5.30–8pm.

Music

Arabic Music Troupe, (Shirket al Musiqa al Arabia) al Galaa Building, Sh Galaa. Tel: 742-864. Also known as the Classical Orchestra and Choir of Arabic Music, this all male choir performs songs for mixed voices, solo and group, and classical pieces.

Cairo Conservatoire, City of Art, Pyramids Road. Tel: 851-475, 851-561.

Egypt's leading music school has instruction in composition, musicology, percussion, piano, singing, string, and wind, and offers concerts at the Sayed Darwish Concert Hall.

Cairo Symphony Orchestra. They perform at the Cairo Opera House every Friday at 8.30pm from September to mid-June.

Om Kalthum Classical Arabic Music Troupe. Performs classical Arabic music September–May, Thursdays 8.30 pm at the Sayed Darwish Concert Hall.

Ballet & Dance

Ballet. Egyptian ballet dancers are trained at the National Ballet Institute in the City of Art complex on the Pyramids Road. The Institute was founded with Russian help in 1960 and staffed with Russian experts. In 1966 the Institute's first graduating class premiered with performances of *The Fountain of Bakhchiserai* in the old Cairo Opera House. The Cairo Ballet currently includes Russian and Italian dancers and performs in the new Opera House.

Folk Dance Troupes. Folk dancing is very popular in Egypt and there are over 150 troupes in the country. The most prominent are the National Troupe and Reda Troupe which perform regularly in Cairo and Alexandria.

Opera

Cairo Opera Company. From 1869 to 1971 Cairo was regularly visited by foreign opera troupes, which performed in the old Opera House. A local company has performed in Arabic since 1961, and features fine individual singers. Performances are at the Cairo Opera House.

Venues

Balloon Theatre (Om Kalthum Theatre), 26th July and Sharia Nil, Agouza. Tel: 347-1718. Various performances, mostly in Arabic, fill this vast theatre from October to May. A favourite venue for folklore troupes.

Cairo Opera House (The Egyptian Education and Culture Centre). In 1971 the Cairo Opera House, an elegant wooden structure with perfect acoustics built to celebrate the opening of the Suez Canal in 1869. It burned to the ground with the scenery, costumes, and props of one hundred years. Included in the loss were the

original costumes for the first performance of Aida. In 1988 a new facility opened at the Gazirah Exhibition Grounds on Gazirah Island and the performing arts of Egypt are enjoying season after season of first class entertainment. Built with the cooperation of the Japanese, the new facility includes three theatres (the largest containing about 1,000 seats), an art gallery, conference rooms, and a library.

Gumhuria Theatre, 12 Gumhuria. Tel: 852-137. Used as temporary quarters for the performing arts in Egypt until the Cairo Opera House was built, the Gumhuria Theatre is still a venue for performing arts.

Sayed Darwish Concert Hall, Gamal al Din al Afghani, Giza. Tel: 852-473. There are two Sayed Darwish Concert Halls, one in Cairo and another in Alexandria in the old Alexandria Opera House. This one is used by the ballet, opera company, student performers of the conservatory and the Academy of Arts. It is a showcase for performers of traditional Arabic music and composers working to develop new music with classical themes. There are Classical Arabic Music concerts every Thursday at 9.30pm.

Cairo International Conference Centre (CICC) is on Sh. an-Nasr, next to the Monument of the Unknown Soldier and the Sadat Memorial in the northeastern suburb of Madinat Nasr. Magnificently set in an unusually large tract of land, it was presented to Egypt in 1991 as a gift from the Chinese people, who also gave the surrounding park, with a landscape and buildings in the style of the Emperor K'ang-Hsi. Its auditorium seats 2,500 and was inaugurated for performances in February 1992 by the Grigorovich Ballet of the Bolshoi Theatre, the young troupe created in 1990 by Yuri Grigorovich, Artistic Director of the Bolshoi. Unlike the Opera House, operated by the Ministry of Culture, the CICC is operated by the Ministry of Tourism. Tel: 263-4632/4631/4637. Fax: 263-4640.

Theatres

Theatre season in Cairo is September–May. There is a summer season in Alexandria. Curtain is at 9.30pm, 10.30pm during Ramadan. Theatres are dark on Tuesday or Wednesday. Except at the American University, all performances are in Arabic.

Al Warsha (The Workshop), 10a Abdel Hamid Sayed. Tel: 779-261. The repertory of this exploratory troupe includes translated and new Egyptian plays.

The American University in Cairo Theatre Company. Tel: 354-2964. Performs in the Wallace Theatre and Howard Theatre on the AUC campus.

Avant Garde Theatre, Talia Theatre, Midan Attaba. Tel: 937-948, 763-466. This large company performs modern Arabic plays and western plays in translation in two halls, the Zaki Tolaimat and the Salah Abdel Sabour (Pocket Theatre).

Cairo Puppet Theatre, Azbakkiyah Gardens. Tel: 910-954. Dialogue is in Arabic, but the gestures and meanings of the local and visiting performers are not too difficult to follow. Thursday–Saturday at 6.30pm, Friday and Sunday at 11am.

Children's Theatre, Metropole Theatre, Sh Alfi. Tel: 933-334. Founded in the 1980s.

Comedy Theatre. Star-studded casts perform at the Muhammad Farid Theatre, Sh Muhammad Farid, Tel: 770-603, and the Floating Theatre, next to University Bridge, Manyal, Tel: 849-516.

Modern Theatre, Al Salam Theatre, 101 Qasr al Aini. Tel: 355-2484, 354-3016. The hardworking cast performs contemporary Arabic plays in three nightly shows beginning at 5.30pm.

National Theatre (Qawmi), Midan Attaba. Tel: 917-783, 911-267. Arabic plays and western plays in translation at the George Abiad Theatre.

Samir Ghanem Troupe. Named after the famous Egyptian comedian who is often the star of the show, this troupe performs comedies at the Bab al Luq Theatre, Midan Falaki. Tel: 355-3195.

United Artists Theatre, 30 Ramses. Tel: 775-393. Two companies of stars perform regularly in two venues.

Youth Theatre, Abdel Wahab, Ramses. Tel: 763-466. Venue for young artists. 8.30pm or 9.30pm Closed Tuesday, Wednesday.

Cinemas

Most of Cairo's film houses are old with poor acoustics and sound systems. A few new venues have opened in recent years, most featuring western films. Films are shown at around 10am and 3, 6 and 9pm. Some of the better houses are:

Hyatt Al Salam Hotel, Abdel Hamid Badawi, Heliopolis. Tel: 245-5155, foreign films at 6 and 9pm Thursday–Saturday, Ramadan at 9pm and midnight.

Karim I, Karim II, Emad al Din. Tel: 924-830. Two new theatres offering current international films.

Bookshops

Cairo is the publishing capital of the Middle East and there are hundreds of bookshops. English language books can be found in all major hotels. For rare books try The Orientalist on Qasr el Nil Street, Cairo. Second-hand books, in Arabic and English, can be found at the stalls in Opera Square, Cairo. Some bookstores that offer foreign language publications are:

Al Ahram. Outlets: 165 Muhammad Farid; Cairo Sheraton; Cairo International Airport; Meridien Hotel; Semiramis Inter Continental Hotel; Nile Hilton Hotel; Ramses Hilton Hotel Annex; Maadi Club.

American University in Cairo Bookshop, 113 Qasr al Aini. Excellent collection of English language books on Egypt.

International Publications Ltd, 95 Road 9, Maadi. Tel: 351-6244. Imported Christian, children, travel.

Lehnert and Landrock Bookshop, 44 Sherif. Tel: 392-7606. German and English books, maps, and old postcards.

Madbouli, 6 Talaat Harb. Tel: 756-421. Arabic, English, French and German.

Reader's Corner, 33 Abdul Khalek Sarwat. Tel: 392-8801; and Nile Hilton. General English.

Zamalek Bookshop, 19 Shagaret el Dorr, Zamalek. Tel: 341-9197.

Coffeehouses Of Distinction

Pastroudis, 374 Sh al Gaysh, Alexandria. Tel: 586-4470.

Atelier, 2 Karim al Daoula, off Talaat Harb. Tel: 746-730. Continental. Frequented by literary personalities.

Cafe Saint Germain, 41 Babel, Dokki. Tel: 704-519. European bakery and coffeeshop. Branches also at 97 Higaz, Heliopolis, and 59 Zahraa, Mohandeseen.

Fishawi, Khan al Khalili. Tel: 906-755. 24-hour. Traditional. Founded in 1773. Much changed but never closed.

Groppi, Midan Talaat Harb (Sulayman Pasha). Tel: 743-244. Once glittery, now rather down-market.

Groppi Garden, 2 Abdel Khalek Sarwat. Tel: 391-6619.

Phoenix, Emad el Din. Traditional. Coffee and backgammon.

Simonds, 112 26 July, Zamalek. Tel: 340-9436. Small coffeeshop with pastries, expresso and cappuccino.

Gambling

Gambling is available in Egypt, but only for foreigners and only in 5-star hotels. Casinos are mainly located in Cairo, but there is a casino at the Hilton International in Luxor. The hotel casinos offer the traditional games (roulette, black jack, chemin de fer, slot machines) and are open until the early hours. (Note: the word casino otherwise in Cairo traditionally and normally means "teahouse").

Shopping

What To Buy

If your items cannot be easily carried it is best to let the merchant handle the export. Items over LE200 require export licences.

Amber

Pale yellow, honey, brown, red, white, and almost-black amber can be found in shops in the Khan al Khalili in the form of beads, necklaces, pipe parts and cane handles. The most famous shop is Mohammed R. El Kady.

Antiquities and Antiques

Pharaonic and Islamic antiquities can only be exported though a few shops. Each sale should be accompanied by a letter of authenticity and permission to export the item. Street vendors selling antiquities are selling fakes, worth purchasing for their own merit, but not as authentic articles. In fact, the best buys in Cairo are European antiques. There are many little antique shops in Cairo around Sh. Huda Shaarawi in Zamalek, and in Maadi. In Alexandria the Attarin district around the street of the same name is popular with antique-hunters.

Appliqué
The Tentmakers' Bazaar (Suq al Khiyamiyyah), the only covered bazaar left in Cairo, is the place to buy appliqué tenting. This wonderful craft, probably traceable to ancient Egypt, when appliqué banners billowed from the tops of temple gates, comes in Pharaonic and Islamic designs in the form of pillow cases, tablecloths, and wall hangings.

Baskets
Every region has its own distinct type of basket. The best places to buy them are in the village *suqs*. In Aswan, the flat Nubian baskets are still available. The oases crafts shops have an abundance of extraordinary baskets.

Brass & Copper
The Suq au-Nahhasiin in the Qasabah near Khan al Khalili is the best place in Egypt to buy brass and copper, both antique and modern. But a good alternative is Sh. q in Maadi.

Clothing
Ready to wear clothing is beautifully designed and well-made. The world's finest cotton is Egypt's major export. For sleeping, lounging, or informal wear there is nothing like an Egyptian *gallabiyyas*. They come in all sizes and designs or can be made to order in a day. Bedouin dresses are handmade and most have a great deal of embroidery on them. Those from Northern Sinai are cross-stitched in reds, oranges and yellows, or blues and pinks. They can be bargained for in the villages on the way to Al Arish, or in Khan al Khalili, or at Kirdassah.

Furniture and Woodwork
Mashrabiyyati, traditional screens of turned wood, covered the windows of old-fashioned Cairene houses and shielded the sanctuaries of mosques. Expensive, but top quality work is available at NADIM, the National Art Development Institute of Mashrabia, 47 Suliman Gohar, Dokki. Tel: 715-927.

Jewellery
From modern pharaonic cartouches to antique Turkish, Art Deco, and Art Nouveau, jewellery is one of the best buys in Egypt. Gold is sold up to 21 carat for traditional jewellery, and 18 carat for modern jewellery of chains and charms. One of the best places to shop is the Suq el Sagha in the Khan al Khalili. Here you will find traditional designs coveted by the farmers' wives in the form of necklaces, earrings and bracelets. Special shops sell 21 carat handtooled or stamped Nubian designs. Shops that sell gold plate are identified by a large gilded camel in the window. Modern designs are found in jewellery stores throughout the city. Many are found on Abdel Khalek Sarwat west of Opera Square in Cairo. In Luxor the jewellery bazaar is just behind Luxor Temple to the north of the Luxor Hotel. In Aswan look for jewellery shops in the *suq*.

Although gold is the preferred metal today, silver traditionally dominated the market. Designs tend to be large and heavy, and are therefore too costly to be made in gold. If you are interested in Bedouin ware, ask, for these wonderful items are often hidden away in giant sacks under the counter. Silver items are sold in all shopping areas and suqs in Egypt but predominate in the Khan al Khalili in Cairo.

Leather
Everything from large and small pieces of luggage to clothing is found in an abundance of designs. Leathers include buffalo, gazelle, crocodile, serpent, lizard, cow, moose and goat.

Musical Instruments
Middle Eastern musical instruments of all qualities are made in Cairo. The people who make them and those who sell them are all found along Shari Muhammad Ali near the Citadel.

Muski Glass
Recycled glass products come in six main colours: navy blue; brown; turquoise; green; aqua; and purple. The glass is hand-blown into pitchers, beakers, cups, tumblers, vases, dishes, Christmas ornaments, and amulets. The imperfections, cracks, and bubbles make this inexpensive glass extremely fragile.

Papyrus
A few decades ago the particular reed from which papyrus is made was virtually extinct in Egypt, but its cultivation was revived by the Dr Raghab Papyrus Institute. There are now shops all over Egypt selling hand-painted papyrus sheets. Designs are quite stunning and many duplicate famous ancient Egyptian wall paintings.

Perfume
Perfume shops with their beautifully decorated bottles are easy to spot and exist in all shopping areas of the country, especially the suqs in Alexandria, Cairo, Luxor, and Aswan. Egypt grows and exports jasmine, geranium, rose, violet, camomile, and orange for the major perfumiers in France, from whom essence is then re-imported. Shelf life is a problem.

Weaving
Kirdassah, on the western fringes of greater Cairo, has a large market where weaving is sold. Harraniyyah, on the Saqqarah road, is world-famous for its tapestries, woven by villagers using naturally-dyed wools. Bedouin rugs, made on small looms in the desert, vary in design between tribes. The most popular are red and white striped from the northern coast; the most difficult to find are green and orange diamond patterns from the Sinai.

Sports

Participant

Fishing
The Nile, Lake Nasser and the lakes along the northern coast support commercial fishing. Fishing is forbidden off Sinai, but a thriving sport elsewhere in the Red Sea and in the Mediterranean. Boats and guides can be hired at Hurghada. For information about international tournaments contact the Shooting Club, Shari an Nadi as Sayd, Dokki. Tel: 704-333.

Gliding

For a spectacular view of the pyramids and portions of the city of Cairo, gliding excursions are available on a hit and miss basis on Thursday and Friday at the Imbaba Airfield to the west of Cairo. The Egyptian Gliding Institute and the Egyptian Aviation Society offer motorgliders and lessons.

Golf

There are two nine-hole courses in Cairo, at the Gazirah Club in Zamalek and at the Mena House Oberoi in Giza (with the pyramids as a backdrop). Equipment can be rented, but the courses are extremely busy.

Pharaoh's Rally

The Pharaoh's Rally has earned a niche in the rally world and is second in endurance and difficulty only to the Paris-Dakkar Rally. It is a 12 day, 2,790 mile (4,500 km) endurance race through the deserts of Egypt for dirt bikes, cars, and trucks. For information contact Rami Siag, tel: 856-022, or Fenouil SA des Pharaons, 47 Rue Emile, Roux 94120, Fontenay-DousBois, France.

Riding

There is little to compare with a dawn or dusk gallop through the desert. The Bedouin at the Giza pyramids have been catering for eager riders for generations and there are several good stables in the area. Horses and camels are on offer. Lessons are available. Overnight trips to Saqqarah can be arranged. Stables include MG, KM, SA, AA (850531), and FF.

Rowing

There are ten rowing clubs in Cairo, and almost all are located on the west bank of the Nile from Giza to Imbaba. Competitions start in November and run through April. They are held every Friday on the Nile. Schedules can be obtained from any rowing club and lessons are available at some clubs. For information see the Egyptian Rowing Club, 11 Sharia al Nil, Giza, near the Cairo Sheraton. Tel: 731-639.

On and under Water

Diving and snorkelling in the Red Sea are among the best sports offered in Egypt. On good days, the sea is calm, the visibility near perfect, and the currents mild. However, swells do develop and it is easy to lose sight of the boat after swimming below the surface. All diving should be done in the company of experts after suitable instruction, which is available at many hotels (*see "Scuba Diving and Water Sports", p.265*). Dive shops exits at Hurghada and Safaga on the mainland and at Sharm el Shaykh, Nuwayba, and Dahab in Sinai. Most of the resorts on the Red Sea provide lessons for windsurfing. Equipment can be rented.

Shooting

Large mammals are increasingly rare, but the migration of wild-foal attracts legal and illegal sportsmen. Would-be hunters must have a local hunting licence and respect protected areas. It is extremely difficult for the authorities to control the sport and illicit hunting trips are sometimes offered to travellers. Illegal hunters face severe penalties and unwanted publicity. For trap-shooting, target-shooting and advice on hunting contact the Shooting Club, Sharia an Nadi as Sayd. Tel: 704-333.

Yachting

Docking facilities exist at major ports in Egypt and along the Nile at major cities. Yachts may enter the country through the various ports if they have the proper documents. The Egyptian Tourist Information Centres throughout the world have a booklet for yacht enthusiasts entitled *Egypt for Yachtsmen* giving entry information and maps. See *Useful Addresses* for listing.

Spectator

Horses

There are several spectator equine sports. Horse racing takes place on Saturday and Sunday, mid-November through May, at the Heliopolis Hippodrome Course in Heliopolis, in Cairo, and at the Smouha Race course in Alexandria. Races begin at 1.30pm.

Arab horses are known throughout the world for their beauty, stamina, and intelligence. Originally bred on the Arabian Peninsula, stud farms for Arab horses now exist worldwide. Characteristics include a compact body with a straight back, a small head, wide eyes, wide nostrils, a wide forehead, small ears and a wide jawbone.

There are many stud farms in Egypt, but only four major ones. The biggest, with 300 horses, is the government-owned Egyptian Agricultural Organisation (EAO), El Zahraa Station, Sharia Ahmad Esmat. Tel: 243-1733. This farm has only pure-bred bloodlines and is the home of the most famous Arabian stallion of this century, Nazeer. Every important stud farm in the world has some of his offspring.

Soccer

Every vacant lot in Cairo is a soccer field and young enthusiasts have been known to use just about anything for a ball, including an unlucky hedgehog. Professional soccer has been known to cause traffic jams, slow down service in restaurants, and empty the streets. It is the national pastime of Egypt. Three leagues compete at 3pm each Friday and Sunday afternoon from September to May at various stadiums throughout Egypt. Among the top teams in Egypt are Ahly, Zamalek, and the Arab Contractors.

Language

Sounds

Many sounds in spoken Arabic do not get represented by transliteration. A particularly characteristic Arabic sound, however, is represented in the following list: ᶜ*ayn*, represented as ᶜ. All Arabic-speakers, native and otherwise, delight in producing the appropriate noise, described as a guttural hum or a voiced emphatic "h", which occurs in such common names as ᶜAbbas, ᶜAbdallah, Ismaᶜil, and ᶜAli (which is not, incidentally, accented on the last syllable). Non-Arabic-speakers generally find pronouncing ᶜ impossible without instruction and practice; and if it seems too difficult, it may be ignored. One will merely be marked as a non-Arabic-speaking foreigner or as having a speech impediment.

Most Cairenes know a few words of English, though real ability to use languages other than Arabic is confined to the educated. A few words of colloquial Egyptian Arabic are therefore useful. The words and phrases listed below are not transliterated, but spelled more or less phonetically, according to the following rules:

VOWELS

c = cayn, as explained above
' = glottal stop
a = a as in *father*
aa = a as in standard English *bad, mad, glad*
e = e as in *very*
i = i as in *if, stiff*
ii = ee as in *between*
o = o as in *boss*
u = u as in *put*
uu = o as in *fool*

CONSONANTS (all emphatic consonants have been omitted):

All consonants are pronounced individually and as in English with these exceptions:

kh = ch as in Scottish *loch*.
sh = sh as in *shut*.
gh = Arabic *ghayn*, usually described as resembling a (guttural) Parisian *r*.
q = Arabic *qaf*, frequently pronounced in Cairo as a *k* or a glottal stop.

Vocabulary

airport/*matár*
boat/*mérkeb*
bridge/*kubri*
car/*carabiyya, sayára*
embassy/*sefára*
hospital/*mustáshfa*
hotel/*fúnduq*
post office/*bosta*
restaurant/*matáam*
square, maydan/*midáan*
street/*shaaric*
right/*yemiin*
left/*shemáal*
and/or/*wa/walla*
yes/no/*aywa/laa'*
please/thank you/*minfadlak/shukran*
big/little/*kibiir/sughayyar*
good/bad/*kwáyyis/mish kwáyyis*
possible/*mumkin*
impossible/*mish mumkin*
here/there/*hena/henáak*
hot/cold/*sukn/baarid*
many/few/*kitiir/olayyel*
up/down/*fo' (foq)/taht*
more/enough/*kamáan/kefáya*

breakfast/*íftar*
dinner/*asha*
today/*innahárda*
tomorrow/*bokra*
yesterday/*embáareh*
morning/*is-sobh*
noon/*id-dohr*
afternoon/*bcad id-dohr*
at night/*belayl*
next week/*il esbuul-iggáy*
next time/*il mara-iggáya*
last time/*il-mara illi fáatit*
after a while/*bcad shwayya*
I/you/*ana/enta/*
he/she/*huwwa/hiyya*
they/we/*humma/ehna*

Common Expressions

Hello, welcome/*ahlan wa sahlan*
Good morning/*sabáh-il-kheyr*
Good evening/*masáal-kheyr*
Goodbye/*mcas-saláama*
What is your name? (to a male)/*íssmak ey?*
What is your name? (to a female)/*íssmik ey?*
How are you? (to a male)/*izzáyak*
How are you? (to a female)/*izzáyik*
I am fine/*kwayiss* (M), *kwayíssa* (F)
Thank God/*il-hamdo li-lah* (standard reply)

Often heard is "insha'Allah", which means "God willing" and is a reminder that all things are ultimately in the hands of Providence. The standard reply to a casual "see you tomorrow", for instance, is "Insha'Allah".

Numerals

1/*wáhid*
2/*itnéyn*
3/*taláatah*
4/*arbcá*
5/*khamsa*
6/*sitta*
7/*sébca*
8/*tamánya*
9/*tíssah*
10/*áshara*
11/*hedásher*
12/*itnásher*
13/*talatásher*
14/*arbatasher*
15/*khamastásher*
16/*sitásher*
17/*sabatásher*
18/*tamantásher*
19/*tisscatásher*

20/*ashríin*
30/*talatíin*
40/*arbacíin*
50/*khamsíin*
60/*sittíin*
70/*sabacíin*
80/*tamaníin*
90/*tissacíin*
100/*miiya, miit*

Money

money/*filúus*
50 piastres/*khamsíin 'ersh (qersh)*
75 piastres/*khamsa wa sabacíin 'ersh (qersh)*
change/no change/*fakka/mafiish fakka*
the bill/*al hesáb*
this/that/*di/da*
how much?/*bekáam?*
how much do you want? (to a male)/*cayiz kaam?*
how much do you want? (to a female)/*cayza kaam?*
all/half/*kull/nus*

Days/Months

Sunday/*yowm al had*
Monday/*yowm al-itnéyn*
Tuesday/*yowm it-taláat*
Wednesday/*yowm al-árba*
Thursday/*yowm al-khamíis*
Friday/*yowm ig-gómca*
Saturday/*yowm is-sabt*
January/*yanáyer*
February/*febráyer*
March/*máris*
April/*abreel*
May/*mayuu*
June/*yuunyuu*
July/*yiilyuu*
August/*aghustus*
September/*sibtímbir*
October/*októbir*
November/*nofímbir*
December/*disímbir*

Further Reading

Cairo

Abu-Lughod, Janet. *Cairo: 1001 Years of the City Victorious*. Princeton: Princeton University Press, 1971.
Aldridge, James. *Cairo*. London: Macmillan, 1970.

Butler, Alfred J. *Babylon of Egypt: A Study in the History of Old Cairo*. Oxford: Clarendon Press, 1914.

Early, Evelyn. *Women of Cairo: Playing with an Egg and a Spoon*. Boulder: Lynne Rienner, 1993.

Lane, Edward William. *The Thousand and One Nights*, commonly called in England, The Arabian Nights' Entertainments: A New Translation from the Arabic with Copious Notes. Reprint of the edition of 1838. London and Cairo: East-West Publications and Livres de France, 1979-1981. Three volumes.

Lane-Poole, Stanley. *The Story of Cairo*. London: J.M. Dent and Sons, 1902.

Macleod, Arlene Eloise. *Accommodating Protest: Working Women, the New Veiling, and Change in Cairo*. New York: Columbia University Press, 1991.

Raafat, Samir W. *Maadi 1904-1962: Society and History in a Cairo Suburb*. Cairo: Palm Press, 1994.

Ruthven, Malise and the Editors of Time-Life Books. *Cairo*. Amsterdam: Life Books, 1980.

Staffa, Susan. *Conquest and Fusion: The Social Evolution of Cairo A.D.642-1850*. Leiden: Brill, 1977.

Stewart, Desmond. *Great Cairo, Mother of the World.* Second Edition. Cairo: The American University in Cairo Press, 1981.

Wahba, Magdi. "Cairo Memories," *Encounter*, LXII (May 1984), 74-79. Reprinted in *Studies in Arab History: The Antonius Lectures, 1978–1987.* Edited by Derek Hopwood. London: Macmillan/The World of Islam Festival Trust in association with St. Antony's College, Oxford, 1988, pp. 103-116.

Wiet, Gaston. *Cairo: City of Art and Commerce.* Trans. Seymour Feiler. Norman, Oklahoma: University of Oklahoma Press, 1964.

Wikan, Unni. *Life Among the Poor in Cairo.* Translated by Ann Henning. London: Tavistock, 1980.

Alexandria

Bell, H.I. *Egypt from Alexander to the Arab Conquest: A study in the diffusion and decay of Hellenism*. Oxford: Oxford University Press, 1956

Bowman, Alan K. *Egypt After the Pharaohs: 332 BC-AD 642 from Alexander to the Arab Conquest*. London: British Museum Publications, 1986.

El-Abbadi, Mostafa. *The life and fate of the ancient Library of Alexandria*. Paris: UNESCO, 1990.

Ellis, Walter M. *Ptolemy of Egypt* . Routledge: London, 1993.

Fraser, P.M. *Ptolemaic Alexandria*. Oxford: Oxford University Press, 1972. Three volumes.

Grant, Michael. *Cleopatra: A Biography*. London: Weidenfeld and Nicolson, 1972. Second edition. New York: Dorset Press, 1992.

Heckel, Waldemar. *The Marshals of Alexander's Empire*. London: Routledge, 1993.

Keeley, Edmund. *Cavafy's Alexandria: Study of a Myth in Progress*. Cambridge, Mass. Harvard University Press, 1976.

Kitroeff, Alexander. *The Greeks in Egypt 1919–1937: Ethnicity and Class*. London: Ithaca Press, for St. Antony's College, Oxford, 1989.

Liddell, Robert. *Cavafy: A Critical Biography.* London: Duckworth, 1974.

Manzalaoui, Mahmud. "Mouths of the Sevenfold Nile: English Fiction and Modern Egypt." *Studies in Arab History: The Antonius Lectures, 1978-1987.* Edited by Derek Hopwood. London: Macmillan/The World of Islam Festival Trust with St. Antony's College, Oxford, 1988, pp. 131–147.

Marlowe, John. *The Golden Age of Alexandria*. London: Victor Gollancz, 1971.

Parsons, Edward Alexander. *The Alexandrian Library of the Hellenic World: Its Rise, Antiquities and Destruction*. New York: American Elzevier, 1967.

Pinchin, Jane Lagudis. *Alexandria Still: Forster, Durrell, and Cavafy*. Princeton: Princeton University Press, 1977. Reprint Cairo: The American University in Cairo, 1989.

Pomeroy, Sarah B. *Women in Hellenistic Egypt from Alexander to Cleopatra*. New York: Schocken Books, 1984.

Saad El-Din, Mursi, Mokhtar, Gamal, El-Abbadi, Mostafa and Ramadan, Abdel-Azim. *Alexandria: The Site and the History*. New York and London: New York University Press, 1993.

Whitehorne, John. *Cleopatras*. Routledge: London, 1994.

The Oases

Belgrave, C. Dalrymple. *Siwa: The Oasis of Ammon*. London: John Lane, The Bodley Head, 1923.

Fakhry, Ahmed. *The Oases of Egypt*. Volume I. *Siwa Oasis*. Volume II. *Bahriyah and Farafra Oases*. Cairo: American University in Cairo Press, 1973, 1974.

Maugham, Robin. *Journey to Siwa*. With photographs by Dimitri Papadimou. London: Chapman and Hall, 1950.

Sinai

Forsyte, George and Weitzman, Kurt. *The Monastery of St. Catherine: The Church and Fortress of Justinian*. Princeton: Princeton University Press, 1973.

Galey, John. *Sinai and the Monastery of St Catherine*. Foreword by George Forsyte and Kurt Weitzman. Stuttgart and Zurich: Belser AG für Verlsgeschäfte and Co., 1979.

Jarvis, Major C.S. *Desert and Delta*. London: John Murray, 1938.

Jarvis, Major C.S. *The Back Garden of Allah.* London: John Murray, 1939.

Jarvis, Major C.S. *Three Deserts*. London: John Murray, 1936.

Jarvis, Major C.S. *Yesterday and Today in Sinai*. Edinburgh and London: William Blackwood and Sons, Ltd, 1931.

Ancient Egypt

Baines, John and Malek, Jaromir. *Atlas of Ancient Egypt*. Oxford: Phaidon, 1980.

Edwards, I.E.S. *The Pyramids of Egypt*. London: Ebury Press and Michaal Joseph, 1972.

Kamil, Jill. *Aswan and Abu Simbel*. Cairo: American University in Cairo Press, 1993.

Kamil, Jill. *Luxor*. New, revised edition. Cairo: Egypt International Publishing-Longman, 1996.

Kamil, Jill. *Upper Egypt and Nubia: The Antiquities from Amarns to Abu Simbel.* New, revised edition. Cairo: Egypt International Publishing-Longman, 1996.

Lichtheim, Miriam. *Ancient Egyptian Literature*. Berkeley: University of California Press, 1975, 1976, 1980. Three volumes.

Lewis, N. *Life in Egypt Under Roman Rule*. Oxford: Oxford University Press, 1985.

Lindsay, Jack. *Daily Life in Roman Egypt*. London: Frederick Muller, 1963.

Lindsay, Jack. *Leisure and Pleasure in Roman Egypt*. London: Frederick Muller, 1965

Lindsay, Jack. *Men and Gods on the Roman Nile*. London: Frederick Muller, 1968.

Murnane, William. *The Penguin Guide to Ancient Egyptian Monuments*. Hammersmith: Penguin, 1983.

Murnane, William. *United with Eternity: A Concise Guide to the Monuments of Medinet Habu*. Cairo: The Oriental Institute, University of Chicago/American University in Cairo Press, 1980.

Portman, Ian. *Luxor: A Guide to the Temples and Tombs of Ancient Thebes*. Cairo: Palm Press, 1989.

Redford, Donald B. *Akhenaten: The Heretic King*. Princeton: Princeton University Press, 1984.

Medieval Egypt

Glubb, Sir John Bagot. *Soldiers of Fortune: The Story of the Mamlukes*. London: Hodder and Stoughton, 1973.

Holt, P.M. *The Age of the Crusades: The Near East from the Eleventh Century to 1517*. London: Longman, 1986.

Irwin, Robert. *The Middle East in the Middle Ages: The Early Mamluk Sultanate (1250-1382)*. London: Croom Helm, 1986.

Lane, Edward William. *Arabian Society in the Middle Ages: Studies from the Arabian Nights*. London: Curson Press, 1987.

Lane-Poole, Stanley. *A History of Egypt in the Middle Ages*. London: Methuen, 1901.

Lyons, Malcolm Cameron and Jackson, D.E.P. *Saladin and the Politics of the Holy War*. Cambridge: Cambridge University Press, 1982.

Egypt, 16th–19th Centuries

Herrold, J. Christopher. *Bonaparte in Egypt*. New York: Harper and Row, 1962.

Holt, P.M. *Egypt and the Fertile Crescent (1516–1922)*. Ithaca: Cornell University Press, 1966.

Hunter, F. Robert. *Egypt Under the Khedives (1805–1879)*. Pittsburgh: University of Pittsburgh Press, 1984.

Lane, Edward William. *An Account of the Manners and Customs of the Modern Egyptians*. London: Charles Knight, 1836. Reprint of eighth (1895) edition: London and Cairo: East-West Publications and Livres de France, 1978, 1981.

Lutfi al-Sayyid [Marsot], Afaf. *Egypt and Cromer: A Study in Anglo-Egyptian Relations*. London: John Murray, 1968.

Lutfi al-Sayyid Marsot, Afaf. *Egypt in the Reign of Muhammad Ali*. Cambridge: Cambridge University Press, 1984.

Mansel, Philip. *Sultans in Splendor: Monarchs of the Middle East 1869–1945*. London: André Deutsch, 1988.

Marlowe, John. *The Making of the Suez Canal*. London, 1964.

Mostyn, Trevor. *Egypt's Belle Epoque (1869–1952)*. London: Quartett Books, 1989.

Richmond, J.C.B. *Egypt (1798–1952)*. London: Methuen, 1977.

Schölch, Alexander. *Egypt for the Egyptians! The Socio-Political Crisis in Egypt 1878–1882*. St. Antony's Middle East Monographs, no. 14. London: Ithaca Press, 1981.

Tugay, Emine Foat. *Three Centuries: Family Chronicles of Turkey and Egypt*. Westport, Conn.: Greenwood Press, 1963. Reprinted 1973.

Zevi, Filippo, ed. *Photographers and Egypt in the XIXth century*. Rome: Alinari for Monte dei Paschi Banking Group, 1984.

Egypt, 20th Century

Berque, Jacques. *Egypt: Imperialism and Revolution*. London: Faber and Faber, 1972.

Little, Tom. *Modern Egypt*. New York: Praeger, 1967.

Palmer, Monte, Ali, Leila, and Yassin, El Sayed. *The Egyptian Bureaucracy*. Syracuse: Syracuse University Press, 1988.

Tripp, Charles, ed. *Contemporary Egypt through Egyptian Eyes: Essays in Honour of P.J. Vatikiotis*. London and New York: Routledge, 1993.

Vatikiotis, P.J. *The History of Egypt from Muhammad ᶜAli to Sadat*. Second Edition. London: Weidenfeld and Nicholson, 1980.

Waterbury, John. *The Egypt of Nasser and Sadat: The Political Economy of Two Regimes.* Princeton: Princeton University Press, 1983.

Arts and Crafts

Ammoun, Denise. *Crafts of Egypt*. With photographs by Jean-Louis Bersuder. Cairo: The American University in Cairo Press, 1991.

Brown, Luanne, and Rachid, Sidna. *Egyptian Carpets: A Practical Guide*. Cairo: The American University in Cairo Press, 1985.

Flora and Fauna, Geology

Bruun, Bertel. *Common Birds of Egypt*. Ilustrations by Sherif Baha el Din. Cairo: American University in Cairo Press, 1985.

Hoath, Richard. *Natural Selections: A Year of Egypt's Wildlife*. Cairo: American University in Cairo Press, 1992.

Osborne, Dale and Hilmy, Ibrahim. *The Contemporary Land Mammals of Egypt Including Sinai.* Chicago: The Field Museum, 1980.

Randall, John E. *Red Sea Reef Fishes*. London: Immel Publishing Ltd, 1986.

Randall, John E. *Sharks of Arabia*. London: Immel Publishing Ltd, 1986.

Said, Rushdy. *The River Nile: Geology, Hydrology and Utilization*. Oxford: Pergamon Press, 1993.

Täckholm, Vivi. *Students' Flora of Egypt*. Second edition Beirut: Cairo University, 1974.

Vine, Peter. *Red Sea Invertebrates.* London: Immel Publishing Ltd, 1986.

Other Insight Guides

Among the 190 *Insight Guides*, the following titles highlight destinations in this region: *Cairo, The Nile, Jordan, Israel* and *Jerusalem*.

Apa Publications has two other series of guidebooks: *Insight Pocket Guides*, which give detailed tours and daytrips, and *Insight Compact Guides*, which are mini travel encyclopedias designed for convenient on-the-spot reference. *Insight Compact Guide: Egypt* is a companion to this volume.

Index

A
B
C
D
E
F
G
H
I
J
a
b
c
d
e
f
g
h
i
j
k
l